THE RELATIVE NATIVE

HAU
BOOKS

www.haubooks.com

THE RELATIVE NATIVE
ESSAYS ON INDIGENOUS CONCEPTUAL WORLDS

Eduardo Viveiros de Castro

Hau Books
Chicago

Chapter Two is a reprint of Viveiros de Castro, Eduardo. "(Anthropology) AND (science)," an after-dinner speech at "Anthropology and Science," the 5th Decennial Conference of the Association of Social Anthropologists of Great Britain and Commonwealth, 14 July 2003. Published in Manchester Papers in Social Anthropology, 7, 2003. © 2003 University of Manchester Department of Social Anthropology. All rights reserved. Republished by permission of the copyright holder.

Chapter Three is a reprint of Viveiros de Castro, Eduardo. 2004. "Perspectival anthropology and the method of controlled equivocation." *Tipití: Journal of the Society for the Anthropology of Lowland South America* 2 (1): 3–22. © 2003 Society for the Anthropology of Lowland South America. All rights reserved. Republished by permission of the copyright holder.

Chapter Four is a reprint of Viveiros de Castro, Eduardo. 2011. "Zeno and the art of anthropology: Of lies, beliefs, paradoxes, and other truths." *Common Knowledge* 17 (1): 128–45. © 2011 Duke University Press. All rights reserved. Republished by permission of the copyright holder, Duke University Press. www.dukeupress.edu

Chapter Five is a new translation of Viveiros de Castro, Eduardo. 2002. "Atualização e contra-efetuação do virtual: O processo do parentesco." In *A inconstância da alma selvagem (e outros ensaios de antropologia)*, 401–56. São Paulo: Cosac & Naify. © 2002 Cosac & Naify. All rights reserved. Published and translated by permission of the copyright holder, Editora Cosac & Naify. http://editora.cosacnaify.com.br

Chapter Six is a reprint of Viveiros de Castro, Eduardo. 2009. "The gift and the given: Three nano-essays on kinship and magic." In *Kinship and beyond: The genealogical model reconsidered*, edited by Sandra Bamford and James Leach, 237–68. Oxford: Berghahn. © 2009 Berghahn Books. All rights reserved. Republished by permission of the copyright holder, Berghahn Books. www.berghahnbooks.com

Cover and layout design: Sheehan Moore
Typesetting: Prepress Plus (www.prepressplus.in)

ISBN: 978-0-9905050-3-7
LCCN: 2014953508

Hau Books
Chicago Distribution Center
11030 S. Langley
Chicago, IL 60628
www.haubooks.com

Hau Books is marketed and distributed by The University of Chicago Press.
www.press.uchicago.edu

Contents

PART I

Methods

CHAPTER ONE

The Relative Native

TRANSLATED FROM THE PORTUGUESE BY JULIA SAUMA AND MARTIN HOLBRAAD

> *The human being, such as we imagine him, does not exist.*
> —Nelson Rodrigues

GROUND RULES

The "anthropologist" is a person whose discourse concerns the discourse of a "native."[1] The native need not be overly savage, traditionalist nor, indeed, native to the place where the anthropologist finds him. The anthropologist, on his part, need not be excessively civilized, modernist, or even foreign to the people his discourse concerns.[2] The discourses in question (and particularly that of the native) are not necessarily texts, but rather may include all types of meaning

---

1. The original article was prefaced by the author with the following preamble: "The pages that follow have been adapted from the introductory remarks of a book, currently in preparation, in which I develop ethnographic analyses that have been sketched out in earlier work. The main one is an article published in *Mana*, 'Cosmological deixis and Amerindian perspectivism' (Viveiros de Castro 1996 [this appeared in English in *JRAI* in 1998]), whose metatheoretical premises, as it were, are rendered explicit in the present work. While the text presented here requires no previous familiarity with that earlier work, the reader may bear in mind that such notions as 'perspective' and 'point of view,' as well as the idea of 'indigenous thought,' are elaborated there also." —Trans.

2. The use of the masculine is arbitrary.

practice.[3] What is essential, however, is that the discourse of the anthropologist (or the "observer") establishes a certain relation with that of the native (or the "observed"). This relation is one of meaning or, when the anthropologist's discourse aspires to be Scientific, a relation of knowledge. By this token, anthropological knowledge is also a social relation, since it is the effect of the relationships that reciprocally constitute the knowing subject, on the one hand, and the subject he comes to know, on the other. As with all relations, this form of knowledge brings about a transformation in the relational constitution of anthropologist and native alike.[4]

The (meta)relation between anthropologist and native is not one of identity: the anthropologist always says and, therefore, does something different than what the native says or does, even when he intends to do nothing more than repeat the native's discourse in a "textual" form, or when he tries to establish a dialogue—a dubious notion—with the native. This difference is nothing other than the knowledge effect created by the anthropologist's discourse, which is produced by the relation between the meaning of this discourse and the meaning of that of the native.[5]

Clearly, this kind of discursive alterity is grounded in an assumption of similarity. The anthropologist and the native are of the same species and share in its

---

3. The fact that, canonically as well as literally speaking, anthropological discourse takes the form of texts has a host of implications, which cannot be explored here, though the topic has received exhaustive attention in recent currents of auto-anthropological reflection. The same can be said of the fact that native discourse is, generally, not a text, as well as of the fact that it is often treated as if it were.

4. "Knowledge is not a connection between a subject-substance and an object-substance, but rather a relation between two relations, one located in the domain of the object and the other in the domain of the subject; . . . the relation between two relations is a relation itself" (Simondon [1964] 1995: 81; translation, emphases removed). I translated the word *rapport*, which Gilbert Simondon distinguishes from *relation*, as "connection": "we can call a relation the disposition of the elements in a system, which is beyond the spirit's simple and arbitrary target, and reserve the term connection for an arbitrary and fortuitous relation . . . the relation would be a connection that is as real and important as the terms themselves; consequently, we could say that the true relation between two terms is actually equivalent to the connection between three terms" (Simondon [1964] 1995: 66; translation).

5. For an analysis of the relational assumptions of this knowledge effect, see Strathern (1987). The author argues that the native's relation with his discourse is not, in principle, the same as the anthropologist's relation with his own discourse, and that this difference at once conditions the relation between the two discourses and imposes limits to the whole auto-anthropological enterprise.

condition: they are both human, and each of them is positioned in their respective culture, which could (even) be the same. But this is where the game starts to get interesting or, better, strange. For even when the anthropologist and the native share the same culture, the relationship of meaning between their respective discourses serves to differentiate them: the anthropologist's and the native's relationship with their respective cultures are not exactly the same. What makes the native a native is the presumption, on the part of the anthropologist, that the native's relationship with his culture is natural, which is to say, intrinsic, spontaneous, and, if possible, nonreflexive or, even better, unconscious. Thus, the native gives expression to her culture in his discourse. The anthropologist does so too, but if he hopes to be something other than a native, he must also be able to express his culture culturally, which is to say, reflexively, conditionally, and consciously. The anthropologist's culture is contained (in both senses of the word) in the relationship of meaning that his discourse establishes with that of the native. The native's discourse, by contrast, is merely penned in by his own culture. The anthropologist's deployment of his own culture is a necessary condition of his humanity, one might say, while for the native *being deployed by his* is a sufficient one.

Obviously, these differences are not in the so-called nature of things. They are a feature of the language game that we are describing here, and serve to define the very characters we have been designating as "the anthropologist" and "the native." So let us turn to some other ground rules.

The anthropological idea of culture places the anthropologist and the native on an equal footing, inasmuch as it implies that the anthropologist's knowledge of other cultures is itself culturally mediated. In the first instance, this sense of equality is simply empirical or de facto, since it refers to the common (or generic) cultural condition of the anthropologist and the native. However, their differently constituted relationships with their respective cultures, and therefore also with each other's, are such that this de facto sense of equality does not imply an equality *de jure*—that is, an equality with regard to their respective claims to knowledge. The anthropologist tends to have an epistemological advantage over the native. Their respective discourses are situated on different planes. While the anthropologist's capacity to produce meaning does depend on the meanings produced by the native, the prerogative to determine what those native meanings mean remains with the anthropologist—explaining and interpreting, translating and introducing, textualizing and contextualizing, justifying and signifying native meanings are all jobs of the anthropologist. The anthropological discourse's relational matrix is hylomorphic: the anthropologist's meaning is form; the native's is matter. The native's discourse is not the master of its own meaning. *De facto*, as Geertz might say, we are all natives; but *de jure*, some are always more native than others.

This article proposes the following questions: What if we refuse to give this kind of strategic advantage to the anthropologist's discourse over that of the native? What would happen if the native's discourse were to operate within the discourse of the anthropologist in a way that produced reciprocal knowledge effects upon it? What might occur if the form intrinsic to the matter of native discourse were to be allowed to modify the matter implicit in the form of anthropological knowledge? It is said that to translate is to betray. But what happens when the translator decides to betray his own tongue? What happens if, unsatisfied with a mere passive or de facto equality between discursive subjects, we claim an active or de jure equality between their respective discourses? What if, rather than being neutralized by this equivalence, the disparity between the meanings produced on either side, by anthropologists and natives, is introduced into both discourses, thus releasing its full potential? What if instead of complacently admitting that we are all native, we take the opposite wager as far as it can go, namely, that we are all "anthropologists" (Wagner [1975] 1981: 36)—and, to boot, not some a little more than others, but just each in their own way, which is to say, very differently? In short, what changes when anthropology is taken to be a meaning practice that is epistemically continuous with the practices that it discusses, and equivalent to them? What changes, in other words, when we apply the notion of "symmetrical anthropology" (Latour 1991) to anthropology itself, not to condemn it as colonialist, exorcise its exoticism, or landmine its intellectual field, but rather to turn it into something else? Something different not only to the native's discourse (for that is a difference that is constitutive of anthropology), but different also to the discourse that anthropologists habitually enunciate about themselves, often in hushed tones, when commenting on native discourses.[6]

---

6.   We are all natives, but *no one is native all the time*. As Lambek (1998: 113) remarks in a comment about the notion of *habitus* and its analogs, "[e]mbodied practices are carried out by agents who can still think contemplatively; nothing 'goes without saying' forever." Thinking contemplatively, one should say, does not mean thinking as anthropologists think: reflexive techniques crucially vary. The native's reverse anthropology (the Melanesian *cargo cult*, for example; Wagner [1975] 1981: 31–34) is not the anthropologist's auto-anthropology (Strathern 1987: 30–31): symmetrical

If we do all of this, I would say that we would be doing what has always been called "anthropology," properly speaking, rather than (for example) "sociology" or "psychology." My hesitation here is due to the fact that much of what goes, or has gone, by the name of anthropology turns on the contrary assumption that the anthropologist has a privileged grasp of the reasons for the native's reasons—reasons to which the native's reasonings are oblivious. The anthropologist, according to this view, is able to provide a full account of how universal or how particular any given native might be, as well as of the illusions that the latter may have about himself—at times providing an example of his native culture while imagining that he manifests human nature in general (the native as unselfconscious ideologue), while at other times manifesting his human nature while thinking that he is displaying his own particular culture (the native as unwitting general cognizer).[7] Here, the knowledge relation is conceived as unilateral, such that the alterity between the anthropologist's and native's respective discourses dissipates as the former encompasses the latter. The anthropologist knows the native de jure, even as he may not know him de facto. Or we could go the other way around: even though the native may know the anthropologist de facto (often better than the anthropologist knows him in turn), he does not know him de jure, precisely because the native is not an anthropologist, which is what the anthropologist, well, is. Needs must, the anthropologist's science/knowledge is of a different order to the native's: the condition of possibility for the former includes the denial of the latter's claim to legitimacy—an act of "epistemocide," to use Bob Scholte's acute expression (1984: 964). The subject's knowledge requires the object's ignorance.

---

anthropology carried out from the tradition that generated anthropology is not symmetrical to symmetrical anthropology conducted from beyond that tradition's boundaries. Symmetry does not cancel difference, because the virtual reciprocity of perspectives that is at issue here is not a "fusion of horizons." In short, we are all anthropologists, but *no one is an anthropologist in the same way*: "it's fine when Giddens affirms that 'all social actors . . . are social theoreticians,' but the phrase is empty when the theoretical techniques have little in common" (Strathern 1987: 30–31).

7.   As a rule, it is assumed that the native does both things—natural ratiocination and cultural rationalization—without knowing what he does, at different phases, registers, or situations during his life. The native's illusions are, one might say, taken as necessary, in the double sense of being inevitable as well as useful (or as others would say, they are evolutionarily adaptive). Such a necessity defines the "native," and distinguishes him from the "anthropologist": the latter may err, but the former deludes himself.

But we need not be overly dramatic about all this. As the discipline's history attests, this discursive game and its biased rules provided lots of instructive information about the natives. The experiment proposed in the present article, however, consists precisely in refusing to play it. This is not because this game results in objectively false results, say in representing the native's nature erroneously; the concept of objective truth (along with the notions of representation and nature) is part of the rules of *that* game, not of the one proposed here. In any case, once the aims of that classic game are set, its results are frequently convincing, or at least, "plausible" as adepts of the game like to say.[8] To refuse to play the game amounts simply to giving oneself a different set of goals, appropriate to different rules, as outlined above.

What I am suggesting, in short, is that there are two incompatible ways of conceiving anthropology, and that one needs to choose between them. On one side, anthropological knowledge is presented as the result of applying concepts that are extrinsic to their object: we know what social relations, cognition, kinship, religion, politics, etc. are in advance and the task is to see how these play out in this or that ethnographic context—how they play out, of course, without the knowledge of the people involved. On the other side (and this is the game proposed here), we have an idea of anthropological knowledge that is founded on the basic premise that the procedures involved in anthropological investigation[9] are of the same *conceptual order* as the procedures being investigated. It should be emphasized that this particular equivalence of procedure at once presupposes and produces the radical *non*equivalence of everything else. For, if the first conception of anthropo-logy imagines each culture or society as embodying a specific solution to a generic problem—or as filling a universal form (the anthropological concept) with specific contents—the second, in contrast, raises the prospect of the problems themselves being radically diverse. Above all, such an approach takes off from the principle that the anthropologist may not know in advance what these problems might be. In such a case, anthropology poses relationships between different problems, rather than placing a single

---

8.   "Implausibility" is an accusation that is frequently raised by practitioners of the classic game, against those who might prefer other rules. But this notion belongs in police interrogation rooms, where one must indeed be careful to ensure the "plausibility" of one's stories.

9.   This is how I interpret Wagner's ([1975] 1981: 35) declaration: "We study culture through culture, and so whatever operations characterize our investigation must also be general properties of culture."

("natural") problem in relation to its different ("cultural") solutions. The "art of anthropology" (Gell 1999), I suggest, is the art of determining the problems posed by each culture, not of finding solutions for the problems posed by our own. It is just for this reason that positing a continuity between the procedures of the anthropologist and the native is such an epistemological imperative.[10]

It bears repeating that this pertains to the procedures, not to those that carry them out. After all, none of this is about condemning the classic game for producing faulty results that fail to recognize the native's own condition as Subject—observing him with a distant gaze, devoid of empathy, which constructs him as an exotic object, diminishes him as primitive rather than the observer's coeval, denying him the human right of interlocution—we are familiar with the litany. The problem is rather the opposite. It is precisely because the anthropologist very easily takes the native to be an other *subject* that he cannot see him as an *other* subject, as an Other figure that, more than subject or object, is the expression of a possible world. It is by failing to accept the native's condition of "nonsubject" (i.e., his being other than a subject) that the anthropologist introduces his sneaky advantage *de jure*, under the guise of a proclamation of *de facto* equality. Before the game even starts, he knows too much about the native: he predefines and circumscribes the possible worlds expressed by this other, radically separating the other's alterity from his capacity to induce difference. The authentic animist is the anthropologist, and participant observation is the true (meaning, false) primitive participation.

It is therefore neither a matter of advocating a kind of intersubjective idealism, nor of standing up for some form of "communicative reason" or "dialogic consensus." My touchstone here is the concept evoked above, namely the Other as an *a priori* structure. This concept is proposed in Gilles Deleuze's well-known commentary of Michel Tournier's *Vendredi*.[11] Reading Tournier's book as a fictional description of a metaphysical experiment— what is a world without Others?—Deleuze proceeds to gauge the effects

10. See Jullien (1989b: 312) on this. Other cultures' real problems are only possible problems for our own culture; the role of the anthropologist is to give this (logical) possibility the status of an (ontological) virtuality, determining—or rather, constructing—its latent operation in our own culture.

11. Published as an appendix to *The logic of sense* (Deleuze 1969a: 350–72; see also Deleuze 1969b: 333–35, 360). It is reconsidered in practically identical terms in *What is philosophy?* (Deleuze and Guattari 1991: 21–24, 49), (almost) his final work.

of the Other's presence through the effects of its absence. The Other thus
appears as a condition of the field of perception: the existential possibility
of those parts of the world that lie beyond actual perception is guaranteed
by the virtual presence of an Other that perceives them; what is invisible
to me subsists as real by being visible to an other.[12] Without an Other the
category of possibility disappears; the world collapses, reduced to the pure
surface of the immediate, and the subject dissolves, turning into a thing-in-
itself (while things-in-themselves, in turn, unravel into phantom doubles).
An Other is thus *no one* (neither subject nor object) but rather a structure
or rela-tion—the absolute relation that provides concrete actants with their
rela-tive positions as subjects or objects, as well as their alternation between
the two positions: the Other refers (to) me to the other I and the other I
to me. The Other is not an element within the field of perception; it is the
principle that constitutes such a field, along with its content. The Other is
thus not a specific point of view to be defined in relation to the subject (the
"point of view of the other" in relation to my point of view or vice-versa),
but rather it is the possibility that there may be a point of view at all—that
is, it constitutes the *concept* of a point of view. It is *the* point of view that
allows the I and the Other to adopt *a* point of view.[13]

On this point, Deleuze is critically extending Sartre's famous analysis
of the "gaze," by providing a prior structure for the reciprocity of perspectives associated with the Sartrian *regard*. What is this structure? It is
the structure of the possible: *the Other is the expression of a possible world.*
A possible world that exists, really but not actually—or not beyond its
expression in the form of an Other. This express possibility is implicated
in, and constitutive of, the perspective from which it is expressed (which
nevertheless remains heterogeneous), and is effectuated in language, or the
sign, which provides the reality of the possible as such—meaning. Thus, the
I renders explicit this implication, actualizing its possibility by taking its

12. " . . . Others, from my point of view, introduce the sign of the unseen in what I do
    see, making me grasp what I do not perceive as perceptible to an Other" (Deleuze
    1969a: 355, English translation 2003: 306).

13. This "he," as Other, is neither a person—a third person to I and you, awaiting his
    turn in a dialogue—nor a thing—a "this" to speak about. The Other would be the
    "fourth-person singular"—situated along the river's third bank, one might say,—
    and is therefore logically anterior to the perspectival game of personal pronouns
    (Deleuze [1979] 1995: 79).

> rightful place in the language game. The subject is therefore an effect, not a
> cause, inasmuch as it interiorizes a relation that is initially exterior to it—
> or rather, a relation to which it is initially interior: relations are originally
> exterior to the terms, because the terms are interior to the relations. "There
> are many subjects because there are others, and not the contrary." (Deleuze
> and Guattari 1991: 22)

The problem is thus not that of seeing the native as an object, and the solution is
not to render him a subject. There is no question that the native is a subject; but
what the native forces the anthropologist to do is, precisely, to put into question
what a subject *can be*. This is the cogitation peculiar to anthropology: one that
allows anthropology to take on the virtual presence of an Other who is also its
condition—the condition for passage from one possible world to another—and
that is only as a consequence able to determine the derivative and vicarious
positions of subject and object.

The physicist questions the neutrino, and cannot disagree with it; the anthropologist answers for the native, who can thus only (*de jure* and, frequently, de facto)
agree with him. The physicist must associate himself with the neutrino—he must
think with his recalcitrant object; the anthropologist associates the native with
himself, thinking that his object makes the same associations as he does—that is,
that the native thinks like him. The problem is that, like the anthropologist, the
native certainly *thinks,* but, most probably, he does not think *like* the anthropologist. The native is certainly a special object: a thinking object, or, a subject. But if
he is objectively a subject, then his thinking also takes objective form—just as the
anthropologist's thinking does—as the expression of a possible world. Thus, the
Malinowskian distinction between what the native thinks (or does) and what he
thinks that he thinks (or does), is spurious. It is precisely this cleavage, this *bifurcation of the nature* of the other, that the anthropologist (who would have himself
do exactly as he thinks)[14] hopes to exploit. However, a better distinction—the

---

14. The anthropologist does exactly what he thinks because the bifurcation of his *own*
    nature, while admitted perhaps in principle, is ruled out of court when it comes
    to his own role as anthropologist. After all, for the anthropologist it is just such
    a bifurcation that distinguishes the "native" from the "anthropologist" in the first
    place. The expression "bifurcation of nature" is coined by Whitehead ([1920]
    1964: chap. II) as part of his argument against the division of reality into primary
    qualities, that are inherent to the object, and secondary qualities, that are attributed

difference that really makes a difference—is between what the native thinks (or does) and what the anthropologist thinks the native thinks (and acts accordingly). The true confrontation is between these two manners of thinking (and acting). Such a confrontation, note, need not be reduced to similar forms of equivocation in each case—the misunderstandings are never the same on either side, just as the sides are not the same in the first place. In any case, who could venture to define what may count as mutual understanding here? But nor is it necessary to content ourselves by imagining this manner of confrontation as some kind of edifying dialogue. The confrontation should implicate the two sides mutually, altering the discourses it brings into play in equal measure, since the aim of the procedure is not to arrive at a consensual optimum, but a conceptual maximum.

I evoked earlier the critical distinction between *quid facti* and *quid juris*. This seemed a useful distinction since the first problem consists in evaluating the claim to knowledge that is implicit in the anthropologist's discourse. The problem is not a cognitive or a psychological one, since it is not about whether knowing another culture is empirically possible.[15] The problem is rather epistemological, which is to say, political. It speaks to the properly transcendental question of how to decide on the legitimacy of discourses that enter into a relationship of knowledge. In particular, it speaks to the manner in which relations of order are established between these discourses—these relations are in no way innate, after all, and nor are their enunciative poles. No one is born an anthropologist and, as curious as it may seem, even less a native.

---

to it by the subject. Primary qualities are the proper object of science, although, in an ultimate sense, they remain inaccessible to it; secondary qualities are subjective and, ultimately, illusory. "Thus there would be two natures, one is the conjecture and the other is the dream" (Whitehead [1920] 1964: 30; see the quote and its commentary in Latour 1999: 62–76, 315 n49 and n58). Such a bifurcation is identical to the anthropological opposition between nature and culture. And when the object is also a subject, as in the native's case, the bifurcation of *his* nature transforms itself through the distinction between the anthropologist's conjecture and the native's dream: cognition vs. ideology (Bloch), primary vs. secondary theory (Horton), unconscious vs. conscious model (Lévi-Strauss), propositional vs. semi-propositional representations (Sperber), and so on.

15. See Strathern et al (1999: 172), on the terms of the possible knowledge relation between, for example, Western anthropologists and Melanesians: "This has nothing to do with understanding, or with cognitive structures; it is not a matter of knowing if I can understand a Melanesian, if I can interact with him, behave appropriately, etc. These things are not problematic. The problem begins when we begin to produce descriptions of the world."

AT THE LIMIT

In recent years, we anthropologists have worried greatly about the identity, as well as the destiny, of our discipline: what it is, if it continues at all, what it should be, if it has the right to exist, what its proper object might be, its method, its mission, and so on (see, for example, Moore 1999). Let us focus on the question of our discipline's object, since the rest of these questions turn on it. Is it culture, as in the North American tradition of anthropology? Or is it social organization, as it was for the British? Or maybe human nature, as per the French approach? I think that the appropriate response is: all and none of the above. Culture, society, and nature—much of a muchness: such notions do not so much designate anthropology's object or topic, but rather point to its basic *problem*, namely that it cannot adopt (Latour 1991: 109–10, 130) any such themes as its own, if in doing so it neglects to take into account the one "anthropological tradition" that counts most, namely, that of the native.

If we must start somewhere, let us be British and acknowledge from the outset that the anthropologist's privileged domain of concern is human sociality, that is, what we are happy to call "social relations." We could then also suggest that "culture," for example, cannot exist beyond its actualization in such relations.[16] And we could add, importantly, that these relations vary in time and space. So, if culture does not exist beyond its relational expression, then relational variation is also cultural variation. Or, to put it another way, "culture" is the word anthropologists use to talk about relational variation.

Thinking, then, about relational variation: would such a notion not willy-nilly imply some kind of subject—an invariable substrate to which relational variations would stand as predicates? This seems to be the ever-latent question, insistent always on some sort of immediate evidence. But this question is, above all, badly formed. For what varies, most crucially, is not the content of relations, but rather the very idea of a relation, i.e., what counts as a relation in this or that culture. *It is not the relations that vary, but rather the variations that are related.* And if this is so, then what is imagined as the substrate of variation, namely "human nature"—to turn to the darling concept of the third great anthropological tradition—would completely change its function, or better, it would stop being a substance and would become a true function. Nature would stop being

---

16. This is Alfred Gell's (1998: 4) suggestion. Of course, it could be applied just as well to "human nature."

a type of highest common *denominator* of cultures (the minimum high, so to speak, of a *humanitas minima*), or a sort of backdrop of similarity generated by cancelling differences so as to arrive at a constant subject—a stable referent capable of emitting variable cultural meanings (as if differences were not just as natural!). Instead, human nature could be conceived as something like a minimum common *multiple* of difference—bigger than cultures, rather than smaller—or something like the partial integer of the different relational configurations we call "cultures."[17] The "minimum," in this case, is the multiplicity that is common to humans—*humanitas multiplex*. Thus conceived, nature would no longer be a self-same substance situated *within* some naturally privileged place (such as the brain, for example). Instead, nature itself would be accorded the status of a differential relation, best placed *between* the terms that it "naturalizes." It would consist in the set of transformations that are necessary in order to describe variations between different known relational configurations. Or, to use yet another image, nature would become a pure *limit*—but not in the geometric sense of limitation, understood as a perimeter or a term that constrains and defines some substantive form (recalling the idea of "mental enclosures" [*enceintes mentales*], which is ever present in the anthropological vocabulary), but rather in the mathematical sense, as the point to which a series or relation converges: a *tension-limit*, as opposed to a *contour-limit*.[18] In such a case, human nature would be the theoretical operation of a "passage to the limit," indicating what human beings are capable of virtually, rather than a limitation that consigns them actually to being nothing other than themselves.[19] If culture is a system of differences, as the structuralists liked to say, then so is nature: differences of differences.

---

17. This argument is only apparently similar to the one Sperber (1982: chap. 2) levels at relativism. For the author does not believe that cultural diversity is an *irreducible* politico-epistemological problem. For him, cultures are contingent examples of the same substantive human nature. The maximum for Sperber is a common denominator, never a multiple—see Ingold's criticism (2000: 164) of Sperber, advanced from a different perspective, but compatible with the one adopted here.

18. On these two ideas of limit, one Platonic and Euclidian, the other Archimedean and Stoic (reappearing in the infinitesimal calculus of the seventeenth century), see Deleuze (1981).

19. In the same sense, see Jadran Mimica's (1991: 34–38) dense phenomenological argumentation.

The theme of the contour-limit (so characteristically Kantian, and ever-present in the discipline's imaginary) is at its most conspicuous when it provides a limiting horizon in the guise of so-called *human nature*, as is the case with naturalist-universalist approaches such as sociobiology, evolutionary psychology and, to a large degree, in structuralism itself. But it is also present in discourses about *human cultures*, where it renders clear the limitations—if I may call them thus—of the classic cultural-relativist position. This recalls the notion enshrined in Evans-Pritchard's phrase about Zande witchcraft—a Zande man "cannot think that his thought is wrong" ([1937] 1976: 109)—or the current anthropological image of culture as a prosthesis of the eye (or classificatory sieve) that only permits one to "see things" in a certain way (or which hides certain aspects of reality); or even, to cite a more recent example, the fishbowl metaphor, which encloses each historical period (Veyne 1983).[20] Whether in regard to nature or cultures, the theme appears equally "limited." If we were to be perverse, we could say that its strategic neutrality, its copresence in the otherwise opposed camps of universalism and relativism, is a good indi-cation that the notion of a "mental enclosure" is one of the mental enclosures that most characterize our common historical "fishbowl." In any case, it demonstrates that the supposed opposition between naturalist universalism and culturalist relativism is, at least, very relative (and perfectly cultural), for it can be summed up as a matter of choosing the dimensions of the bowl, or of the size of the cell where we are imprisoned: should it include all of human kind ecumenically, or should it be made to order for each culture? Or perhaps we might have one great "natural" prison with different cultural cell-blocks, some of them with slightly more spacious cells than others?[21]

---

20. Veyne inadvertently paraphrases Evans-Pritchard, when, in characterizing this (universal) condition of being a prisoner in a (particular) historical fishbowl, he writes that "when one does not see *what* one does not see, one does not even see *that* one is blind" (Veyne 1983: 127, my emphasis, for greater clarity).

21. I am obviously interpreting Veyne's essay here with some malice. His work is much richer (because it is so much more ambiguous) than this, taking the fishbowl beyond the "fishbowl's" sorry image.

Thus understood, anthropology's object would be the variation of social relations. Not of social relations as a distinct ontological province, but of all possible phenomena taken as social relations, or as implying social relations: of all relations, in short, as social. This, however, would require adopting a perspective that is not completely dominated by the Western doctrine of social relations—a perspective that would be ready to accept that handling all relations as social could lead to a radical reconceptualization of what "the social" might be. Let us say, then, that anthropology distinguishes itself from other discourses on human sociality, not by holding any firm doctrine about the nature of social relations, but, on the contrary, by maintaining only a *vague initial idea* of what a relation might be. For its charac-teristic problem consists less in determining which social relations constitute its object, and more in asking itself what its object constitutes as a social relation—what a social relation is in that object's terms, or better, in terms that can be formulated through the (social, naturally, and constitutive) relationship between the "anthropologist" and the "native."

FROM CONCEPTION TO CONCEPT

Would all of this not simply suggest that the point of view defended here, and exemplified in my work on Amerindian perspectivism (Viveiros de Castro 1998a), is "the native's point of view," which anthropologists have professed to be grasping for some time now? To be sure, there is certainly nothing particularly original in the point of view that I am adopting here. The only rightful claim to originality belongs to the indigenous point of view itself, and not to my commentary on it. Still, when it comes to the question of whether the object of anthropology ought to be the native's point of view, the response must be both "yes" and "no." "Yes" (certainly!), because my problem in the above-cited article was to discover what a "point of view" is *for* the native. In other words, what concept of a point of view do Amazonian cultures enunciate—what is the native point of view on the point of view? The answer is "no," on the other hand, because the native concept of a point of view does not coincide with the concept of "the native's of point of view." After all, my point of view cannot be the native's own, but only that of my relation with it. This involves an essentially *fictional* dimension, since it implies making two entirely heterogeneous points of view resonate with each other.

My article on perspectivism, then, was at once a thought experiment and an exercise in anthropological fiction. Here, however, the expression "thought experiment" should not be understood in the usual way, as an attempt to think oneself into another form of experience but rather as a manner of experiencing for oneself an other's form of thought. It is not a matter of imagining a form of experience, if you like, but of experiencing a form of imagination.[22] The experience, in this case, is my own—as ethnographer, as well as reader of the ethnological literature about indigenous Amazonia—and the experiment is a fiction that is controlled by that experience. In other words, the fiction that is involved is anthropological, but the anthropology that it produces is not fictional!

What does such a fiction consist in? It consists in taking indigenous ideas as concepts, and following through on the consequences of such a decision: to determine the preconceptual ground or plane of immanence that such concepts presuppose, the conceptual personae that they deploy, and the material realities that they create. And note that treating these ideas *as* concepts does not mean that, objectively or actually speaking, they are something else. Individual cognitions, collective representations, propositional attitudes, cosmological beliefs, unconscious schemata, embodied dispositions and so forth: these are the kinds of theoretical fictions I choose *not* to heed here.

Thus, the type of work for which I am advocating is neither a study of "primitive mentality" (supposing such a notion might still make sense at all), nor an analysis of the natives' "cognitive processes" (supposing these were accessible, given the current state of psychological and ethnographic knowledge). My object is less the indigenous manner of thinking than its objects, the possible world that its concepts project. Nor is it a matter of reducing anthropology to a series of ethnosociological essays about *worldviews*. This is because, in the first place, no world that is ready to be viewed exists—no world that would precede one's view of it, or precede even the distinction between the visible (or thinkable) and the invisible (or presumed), which provides the coordinates for this manner of thinking. Second, because treating ideas as concepts involves refusing attempts to explain them in terms of some transcendent notion of *context* (ecological, economic, political, etc.), opting rather to treat them immanently as problems, i.e., placing them in the field of problems in which ideas are implicated. And

---

22. This reading of the notion of *Gedankenexperiment* is applied by Thierry Merchaisse to the work of François Jullien on Chinese thought (Jullien and Marchaisse 2000: 71). See also Jullien (1989b: 311–12), about comparative "fictions."

nor is it, finally, a matter of proposing an *interpretation* of Amerindian thought, but rather one of carrying out an experiment with it, and thus also with our own. In Roy Wagner's words: "every understanding of another culture is an experiment with one's own" ([1975] 1981: 12).

To treat indigenous ideas as concepts is to take an antipsychologizing stance, since what is at stake here is a *de jure* image of thought, irreducible to empirical cognition, or at least to the empirical analysis of cognition psychologists provide. The domain of concepts does not coincide with subjects' cognitive faculties or internal states: concepts are intellectual objects or events, not mental states or attributes. They certainly "cross the mind," as the English expression has it, but they do not stay there and, above all, they are not to be found there readymade. They are invented. To be clear: I am not suggesting that Amerindians "cognize" differently to us, or that their "mental" categories are different to those of any other human being. Certainly, it is not a matter of imagining them as instantiating some peculiar form of neurophysiology that processes difference in a different way. For my own part, I am inclined to think that Amerindians think exactly "like us." But I also think that *what* they think, that is, the concepts that they deploy, the "descriptions" that they produce, are very different to our own—and thus that the world described by these concepts is very different to ours.[23] And as far as the Amerindians are concerned (if my analyses concerning perspectivism are correct), I think that *they* think that all humans, and aside from them many other nonhuman subjects, think exactly "like them"—this being precisely the *reason* for subjects' divergences of perspective; that is, the very opposite of a universal convergence of reference.

-----

23. Responding to critics of her analysis of Melanesian sociality, who accuse her of negating the existence of a "human nature" that includes the peoples of that region, Marilyn Strathern et al (1999: 172) clarifies: "[The] difference lies in the fact that the modes through which Melanesians describe, cope with human nature, are radically different to our own—and the point is that we only have access to descriptions and explanations, we can only work with them. There is no means to elude this difference. So we cannot say: very well then, now I understand, it is just a matter of different descriptions, so we can turn to the commonalities between us and them . . . from the moment we enter into communication, we do so through these auto-descriptions. It is essential that we can account for this." In effect, the point is essential. See also what Jullien says about the difference between the affirmation of the existence of different "modes of orientation in thought" and the affirmation of the operation of "other logics" (Jullien and Marchaisse 2000: 205–7).

The notion of a concept implies an image of thought as something other than cognition or a system of representations. What interests me in Amerindian thought, then, is neither local knowledge and its more or less accurate representations of reality—the so-called "indigenous knowledge" that is currently the focus of so much attention in the global market of representations—nor indigenous cognition, its mental categories, and how representative they are of the species' capacities—this being the main concern of human psychology as a "natural science." Neither *representations*, whether individual or collective, rational or ("apparently") irrational, which might partially express states of affairs prior and exterior to themselves; nor *categories* and cognitive processes, whether universal or particular, innate or acquired, which manifest the properties of some thing of the world, whether it be the mind or society. My objects are indigenous *concepts*, the worlds they constitute (worlds that thus express *them*), the virtual background from which they emerge and which they presuppose. In short, my objects are the concepts, which is to say the ideas and problems of indigenous "reason," rather than indigenous categories of "understanding."

It should be clear by now that the notion of concept has a very specific meaning here. Treating indigenous ideas as concepts means taking them as containing a properly philosophical significance, or as being potentially capable of philosophical use.

It might be said that this is an irresponsible decision, since neither the Amerindians nor even (and this must be stressed) the present author are philosophers. One might wonder, for example, how to apply the notion of a concept to a form of thought that has, apparently, never found it necessary to dwell on itself, and which would rather evoke the fluent and variegated schematism of symbols, images, and collective representations than the rigorous architecture of conceptual reason. Is there not, after all, any sign of the well-known historical and psychological abyss, or "decisive rupture," between a panhuman mythical imagination and the universe of Hellenic-occidental rationalism (Vernant [1966] 1996: 229); between the sign's bricolage and the concept's engineering (Lévi-Strauss 1962a); between the paradigmatic transcendence of the Figure and the syntagmatic immanence of the Concept (Deleuze and Guattari 1991); between an imagistic intellectual economy and a doctrinal one (Whitehouse 2000)? On all of this, which is more or less a direct legacy from Hegel, I have my doubts. I insist instead on talking about concepts, and this for a number of reasons. And the first among them, on which I shall comment here, stems from the decision to place native ideas on the same footing as anthropological ones.

As stated above, the experiment I am proposing posits an equivalence *de jure* between the anthropologist's and the native's discourses, taking them as mutually constitutive of each other, since they emerge *as such* when they enter into a knowledge relation with one another. Anthropological concepts actualize this relation and therefore can only be construed as being completely relational, both in the manner of their expression and in their content. They are to be construed neither as truthful reflections of the native's culture (the positivist dream), nor as illusory projections of the anthropologist's culture (the constructionist nightmare). They reflect, rather, a certain relation of intelligibility *between* two cultures; a relation that produces the two cultures in question by back projection, so to speak, as the "motivation" of the anthropological concepts. As such, anthropological concepts perform a double dislocation: they are vectors that always point in the other direction, transcontextual interfaces that function to represent, in the diplomatic sense of the term, the other in one's own terms (that is, in the other's other's own terms)—both ways.

In short, anthropological concepts are relative because they are relational, and they are relational because their role is to relate. Indeed, their relational origin and function is marked by the habit of designating them with alien-sounding words: mana, totem, kula, potlatch, tabu, gumsa/gumlao. . . . Other concepts, no less authentic, carry an etymological signature that evokes analogies between the cultural tradition from which they emerged and the traditions that are their object: gift, sacrifice, kinship, person. . . . Yet other (and just as legitimate) ones constitute terminological inventions the role of which is to generalize the conceptual mechanisms of the people being studied—animism, segmentary opposition, restricted exchange, schismogenesis . . . —or, inversely, and more problematically, terms that are deployed in order to inject notions that are already diffuse in our own tradition into the interior of a specific theoretical economy—incest taboo, gender, symbol, culture—so as to universalize them.[24]

We can thus see that numerous concepts, problems, entities, and agents that are to be found in anthropological theories emerge through the imaginative efforts of societies on which the discipline hopes to shed light. Might one not say, then, that anthropology's originality lies in just this synergy, between conceptions and practices pertaining to two worlds—the "subject's" and the "object's" respectively? Recognizing this might help, among other things, to mitigate

---

24. On the "signature" of philosophical and scientific ideas, and the "baptism" of concepts, see Deleuze and Guattari (1991: 13, 28–29).

our complex of inferiority in relation to the "natural sciences." As observed by Latour:

> The description of kula is on a par with that of black holes. The complex systems of alliances are as imaginative as the complex scenarios conceived for selfish genes. Understanding the theology of Australian Aborigines is as important as charting the great undersea rifts. The Trobriand land tenure system is as interesting a scientific objective as polar icecap drilling. If we talk about what matters in a definition of science—innovation in the agencies that furnish our world—anthropology might well be close to the top of the disciplinary pecking order. (1996a: 5)[25]

In this passage an analogy is made between indigenous *concepts* and the *objects* of the so-called natural sciences. This is one possible, and even necessary, perspective: it should be possible to produce a scientific description of indigenous ideas and practices, as if they were things of the world, or better, so that they can become things of the world. (One must not forget that for Latour the objects of science are anything but "objective" and indifferent entities, patiently awaiting description.) Another strategy would be to compare indigenous *conceptions* with scientific *theories*, as suggested by Horton in his "similarity thesis" (1993: 348–54), which anticipates some aspects of Latour's symmetrical anthropology. And yet another is the strategy advocated here. In this connection it is worth noting that anthropology has always been overly obsessed with "Science," not only in relation to itself (is it a science? can it be? should it be?), but above all—and this is the real problem—in relation to the conceptions of the peoples it studies. The question then becomes whether to disqualify such conceptions as errors, dreams, or illusions, in order then scientifically to explain how and why the "others" cannot explain them(selves) scientifically; or to promote native conceptions as more or less continuous with science, fruits of the same desire to know, which unites all humans. Horton's similarity thesis and Lévi-Strauss' science of the concrete are two examples (Latour 1991: 133–34). And indeed, the image of science may well be considered a kind of gold standard of thought, at least as far as our own intellectual tradition is concerned. It is not, however, the *only* or necessarily the *best* terrain on which to establish fruitful epistemo-political

25. The quote, and the paragraph that precedes it, have been cannibalized from Viveiros de Castro (1999: 153).

relations with the intellectual activity of peoples who have no truck with our much-cherished cult(ure) of Reason.

So, we might imagine a form of analogy different to the one suggested by Latour, or a manner of similarity other than Horton's. A form of analogy in which, instead of taking indigenous conceptions as entities similar to black holes or tectonic faults, we took them as being of a kind with the *cogito* or the monad. We could thus say, to paraphrase the previous citation, that the Melanesian concept of the "dividual" person (Strathern 1988) is as imaginative as Locke's possessive individualism; that understanding the "Amerindian philosophy of chieftainship" (Clastres [1962] 1974a) is as important as commenting on Hegel's doctrine of the State; that Māori cosmology is equivalent to the Eleatic paradoxes and Kantian antinomies (Schrempp 1992); that Amazonian perspectivism presents a philosophical challenge of the same order as Leibniz's system. . . . And when it comes to what matters most in a given philosophical elaboration, namely its capacity to create new concepts, then without any desire to take the place of philosophy, anthropology can be recognized as a formidable philosophical *instrument* in its own right, capable of broadening a little the otherwise rather ethnocentric horizons of our philosophy—and, in passing, ridding us of so-called "philosophical" anthropology too. In Tim Ingold's (1992: 696) pithy phrase: "anthropology is philosophy with the people in." By "people," Ingold means "ordinary people" (ibid.), to be sure. He is also playing, however, with the term's connotation of "the people" or, more likely yet, "peoples." A philosophy, then, with other peoples in it: the possibility of a philosophical endeavor that places itself in relation to the nonphilosophy—simply, the life—of other peoples on the planet, beyond our own.[26] Not only the common people, but above all with *un*common people, those that are beyond our sphere of "communication." If in "real" philosophy imaginary savages are altogether abundant, the geophilosophy proposed by anthropology conducts an "imaginary" philosophy with real "savages." "Real toads in imaginary gardens," as the poet Marianne Moore has it.

Note the significant displacement involved in the above paraphrase. It is no longer (only) a question of the kula's anthropological description (as a form of Melanesian sociality), but (also) of the kula as a peculiarly *Melanesian* description (of "sociality" as a form of anthropology). Similarly, it would still be necessary to understand "Australian theology," but now as constituting a form of

---

26. On "non-philosophy"—the plane of immanence or life—see Deleuze and Guattari (1991: 43–44, 89, 105, 205–206), as well as Prado Jr.'s brilliant commentary (1998).

understanding in its own right, just as, to give another example, complex alliance or land tenure systems can be seen as exercises of an indigenous sociological imagination. Clearly, it will always be necessary to describe the kula as a description, to understand Aboriginal religion as an understanding, and to form images of the indigenous imagination. Doing so is a matter of transforming *conceptions* into *concepts*, extracting the latter and returning them to the former. And a concept is to be understood here as a complex relation between conceptions—a manner of activating preconceptual intuitions. In the case of anthropology, the conceptions that enter into this kind of relation include, before all else, the anthropologist's and the native's—a relation of relations. Native concepts are the anthropologist's concepts. Or so we may suppose.

NEITHER EXPLAIN, NOR INTERPRET: MULTIPLY AND EXPERIMENT!

In *The invention of culture*, Roy Wagner was one of the first anthropologists to draw out the radical consequences of the idea that anthropologist and native can be treated on an equal footing due to their common cultural condition. From the fact that the anthropologist's attempt to approach another culture can only be conducted through terms taken from his own, Wagner concludes that anthropological knowledge is defined by its *"relative objectivity"* ([1975] 1981: 2). At issue here is not a deficient objectivity, that is, subjective or partial, but an intrinsically *relational* objectivity, as can be gathered from what follows:

> The idea of culture . . . places the researcher in a position of equality with his subjects: each "belongs to a culture." Because every culture can be understood as a specific manifestation . . . of the phenomenon of man, and because no infallible method has ever been discovered for "grading" different cultures and sorting them into their natural types, we assume that every culture, as such, is equivalent to every other one. This assumption is called "cultural relativity." . . . The combination of these two implications of the idea of culture, the fact that we ourselves belong to a culture (relative objectivity) and that we must assume all cultures to be equivalent (cultural relativity), leads to a general proposition concerning the study of culture. As the repetition of the stem "relative" suggests, the understanding of another culture involves the relationship between two varieties of the human phenomenon; it aims at the creation of an intellectual relation between

them, as understanding that includes both of them. The idea of "relationship" is important here because it is more appropriate to the bringing together of two equivalent entities, or viewpoints, than notions like "analysis" or "examination," with their pretensions of absolute objectivity. (Wagner 1981: 2–3)

Or as Deleuze might say, it is not a matter of affirming the relativity of the true, but rather of affirming the truth of the relative. It is worth observing that Wagner associates the notion of a relation to that of a point of view (the terms that are related are points of view), and that the idea of the truth of the relative defines what Deleuze calls "perspectivism." Whether it be Leibniz's or Nietzsche's, or, equally, Tukanoan or Jurunoan, perspectivism is not relativism, that is, the affirmation of the relativity of truth, but relationalism, through which one can affirm that *the truth of the relative is the relation*.

I asked what would happen if we refuse the epistemological advantage of the anthropologist's discourse over that of the native: what if we took knowledge relations as modifying, reciprocally, the terms they relate or, rather, actualize? This is the same as asking: what happens when native thought is taken seriously? What happens when the anthropologist's objective ceases to be that of explaining, interpreting, contextualizing, or rationalizing native thought, but instead begins to deploy it, drawing out its consequences, and verifying the effects that it can produce on our own thinking? What is it to think native thought? I say "think," here, without worrying whether what we think (namely, others' thoughts) is "apparently irrational,"[27] or, even worse, rational by nature.[28] At issue is a manner of thinking that does not think itself from within the coordinates provided by these alternatives—a form of thinking entirely alien to this kind of game.

For a start, taking native thought seriously is to refuse to neutralize it. For example, one ought to put in parentheses all questions of whether and how native thinking illustrates universal processes of human cognition; whether it can be explained as a result of particular modes of the social transmission of knowledge; or as the expression of a particular cultural world; or whether its functional role is to validate a particular distribution of political power. All such forms of

27. The expression "apparently irrational" is a secular cliché in anthropology, from Andrew Lang in 1883 (cf. Detienne 1981: 28) to Dan Sperber in 1982.

28. As the "common-sense school of anthropology" professes, as penned by authors such as Obeyesekere (1992) or LiPuma (1998), for instance.

neutralizing foreign thought should be resisted. Suspending such questions or, at least, refusing to enclose anthropology within them, one might opt rather, say, to think other thought simply (so to speak) as an actualization of as yet unsuspected virtualities of thinking.

Would taking the Amerindians seriously mean "believing" in what they say, taking their thought as an expression of certain truths about the world? Absolutely not; here is yet another of those questions that are famously "badly put." Believing or not believing in native thought implies first imagining it as a system of beliefs. But problems that are properly anthropological should never be put either in the psychologistic terms of belief, or in the logicist terms of truth-value. It is not a matter of taking native thought as an expression of opinion (the only possible object for belief and disbelief) or as a set of propositions (the only possible objects for truth judgments). We know the mess anthropology made when it decided to define natives' relationship to their own discourse in terms of belief: culture instantly becomes a kind of dogmatic theology. And it is just as bad to shift from "propositional attitudes" to their objects, treating native discourse as a repository of opinions or a set of propositions: culture turns into an epistemic teratology—error, illusion, madness, ideology.[29] As Latour observes (1996b: 15), "belief is not a mental state, but an effect of the relation between peoples"—and it is precisely that effect that I *do not* mean to produce.

Take animism, for example—about which I have written previously (Viveiros de Castro 1998a). Lalande's *Vocabulary*, which is hardly incompatible with more recent psycho-anthropological studies on this topic, defines "animism" in just these terms: as a "mental state." But Amerindian animism is anything but: it is an *image of thought* that separates *de facto* from *de jure*, that which pertains to thought by right from what contingently refers to a state of affairs; it is, more specifically, an *interpretive convention* (Strathern 1999: 239) that, formally speaking, involves

---

29. Wittgenstein's observations on the *Golden bough* remain pertinent in this regard. Among others: "A religious symbol does not rest on any *opinion*. An error belongs only with opinion"; "I believe that what characterizes primitive man is that he does not act according to his *opinions* (contrary to Frazer)"; "The absurd here consists in the fact that Frazer presents these ideas [about rain rituals, etc.] as if these peoples had a completely false (and even foolish) representation of nature's course, when all they actually have is a strange interpretation about the phenomena. That is, if they could put their knowledge of nature into writing it wouldn't be so *fundamentally* different from our own. It is only that their *magic* is different from ours" (Wittgenstein [1930–48] 1982: 15, 24, 27). Their magic or, we could say, their concepts.

personifying objects of knowledge, thus turning thought into an activity—an effect of the ("social") relation between the thinker and what she or he thinks. After all, would it be appropriate to imagine, say, legal positivism and jus-naturalism as mental states? The same is (not) the case for Amazonian animism: it is not a mental state of individual subjects, but rather a transindividual intellectual disposition that, if anything, deploys the "mental states" of different beings in the world as one of its objects. It is not the *native's* mental condition, but a "theory of the mind" applied *by* the native. Indeed, it is a manner of resolving—or better, dissolving—the eminently philosophical problem of "other minds."

If it is not a matter of describing American indigenous thought as a set of beliefs, then nor is it a question of relating to it via some prior notion of belief that might lend it its credibility—either by benevolently pointing to its allegorical "grain of truth" (a social allegory, for the Durkheimians, or a natural one, for the cultural materialists) or, even worse, by imagining that it provides access to the intimate and final essence of things, acting as a portal into some kind of immanent esoteric science. "An anthropology that . . . reduces meaning to belief, dogma and certainty, is forced into the trap of having to believe either the native meanings or our own" (Wagner [1975] 1981: 30). But the plane of meaning is not populated by psychological beliefs or logical propositions, and the "truth" of Amerindian thought is not, well, granular! Neither a form of *doxa*, nor of logic—neither opinion, nor proposition—native thought is taken here as an activity of symbolization or meaning practice: a self-referential or tautegorical mechanism for the production of concepts, that is, "symbols that stand for themselves" (Wagner 1986).

The refusal to pose the question in terms of belief seems to me a critical anthropological decision. To emphasize this, we might reinvoke the Deleuzian Other: the Other is an expression of a possible world; but in the course of social interaction, this world must always be actualized by a Self: the implication of the possible in an Other is explicated by me. This means that the possible goes through a process of *verification* that entropically dissipates its structure. When I develop the world expressed by an Other, it is so as to validate it as real and enter into it, or to falsify it as unreal: the "explication" thus introduces the element of belief. To describe this process, Deleuze indicated the limiting condition that allowed him to determine the concept of the Other:

> These relations of development, which form our commonalities as well as our
> disagreements with the other, dissolve their structure and reduce it either to the

status of an object or to the status of a subject. That is why, in order to grasp the other as such, we felt right to insist upon special conditions of experience, however artificial: the moment at which the expressed still has no existence (for us) beyond that which expresses it—the Other as the expression of a possible world. (1969b: 335) [Emphasis removed in author's translation. —Trans.]

And he concludes by recalling a maxim that is fundamental to his thinking: "The rule invoked earlier—not to explain too much—meant, above all, not to explain oneself too much with the other, not to explain the other too much, but to maintain one's implicit values and multiply one's world by populating it with all those things expressed that do not exist outside of their expressions" (ibid.). Anthropology can make good use of this: maintaining an Other's values implicit does not mean celebrating some numinous mystery that they might hide but rather amounts to refusing to actualize the possibilities expressed by indigenous thought—opting to sustain them as possible *indefinitely*, neither dismissing them as the fantasies of others, nor by fantasizing ourselves that they may gain their reality for us. The anthropological experiment, then, involves formally interiorizing the "special and artificial conditions" that Deleuze discusses: the moment in which the world of the Other does not exist beyond its expression transforms itself into an abiding condition, that is, a condition internal to the anthropological relation, which renders this possibility *virtual*.[30] Anthropology's constitutive role (its task *de jure*), then, is not that of *explaining the world of the other*, but rather of *multiplying our world*, "populating it with all those things expressed that do not exist outside of their expressions."

OF PIGS AND BODIES

Rendering native possibilities as virtualities is the same as treating native ideas as concepts. Two examples.

---

30. Rendering exterior this special and artificial condition—that is, generalizing and naturalizing it—gives rise to the classic anthropological mistake: the formal eternity of the possible is transmuted onto a historical scale, rendering anthropologist and native noncontemporaneous with one another. We then get the Other as primitive, freeze-framed as an object (of the) absolute past.

Amerindians' pigs

In American ethnography one often comes across the idea that, for Amerindians, animals are human. This formulation condenses a nebula of subtly varied
conceptions, which we shall not elaborate here: that not all animals are humans,
and they're not the only ones (plants, etc. may also be human); that animals
are not humans at all times; that they were human but no longer are; that they
become human when they're out of view; that they only think that they're human; that they see themselves as human; that they have a human soul beneath
an animal body; that they are people like humans are, but are not exactly human like people are; and so on. Aside from all that, "animal" and "human" are
equivocal translations of certain indigenous words—lest it be forgotten, we are
faced with *hundreds* of different languages, and in most of them the copula
is not commonly marked by a verb. But no matter, for present purposes. Let
us suppose that statements such as "animals are humans" or "certain animals
are people" make sense for a certain indigenous group, and that their meaning
is not merely "metaphorical"—as much sense, let us say (though not exactly
the same kind of sense), as the apparently inverse (and no longer scandalous)
affirmation—"humans are animals"—makes to us. Let us suppose, then, that
the first statement makes sense to, for example, the Ese Eja of the Bolivian
Amazon: "The affirmation, that I frequently heard, that 'all the animals are Ese
Eja'" (Alexiades 1999: 179).[31]

Right then. Isabella Lepri, an anthropology student who, coincidentally, at
the time was working with the same Ese Eja, asked me whether I believed that
the peccaries are humans, like the Amerindians say they are. I answered that I
did not—doing so because I suspected (without any particular reason) that she
believed that, if the Amerindians say such a thing, then it must be true. I added,
perversely and rather untruthfully, that I only "believed" in atoms and genes, the
theory of relativity and the evolution of the species, class war, and the logic of
capital, in short, in that type of thing; but that, as an anthropologist, I took the
idea that peccaries are humans perfectly seriously. She challenged me: "How can
you maintain that you take what the Amerindians say seriously? Isn't that just a

---

31. Alexiades cites his interlocutor in Spanish—"Todos los animales son Ese Eja." We
     should note that there is a further twist here: "all" the animals (the ethnographer
     shows numerous exceptions) are not "humans," but they are "Ese Eja," an ethnonym
     that can be translated as "human people," and understood in opposition to "spirits"
     and "strangers."

way of being polite with your informants? How can you take them seriously if you only pretend to believe in what they say?"

To be sure, this intimation of hypocrisy obliged me to reflect. I am convinced that Isabella's question is absolutely crucial; that all anthropology deserving of the name must answer it; and that it is not at all easy to do so very well.

Naturally, one possible response is that contained in Lévi-Strauss' cutting remark on Ricoeur's mythical (and mystical) hermeneutics: "It is necessary to choose which side you are on. Myths do not say anything capable of instructing us on the order of things, on the nature of reality, the origin of man or his destiny" (1971: 571). Instead, the author continues, myths do teach us much about the *societies* from which they originate and, above all, about certain fundamental (and universal) operative modes belonging to the *human mind* (Lévi-Strauss 1971: 571). One can thus oppose the referential vacuity of myths to their diagnostic richness: to say that peccaries are human does not "say" anything to *us* about the peccaries, but is highly telling about the humans who say it.

The solution is not specific to Lévi-Strauss—ever since Durkheim or the Victorian intellectualists, it has been a standard anthropological posture. In our days, for example, much of so-called cognitive anthropology can be seen as a systematic elaboration of this attitude, which consists in reducing indigenous discourse to a set of propositions, selecting those that are false (or alternatively, "empty") and producing an *explanation* of why humans believe in them, *given that* they are false or empty. One such explanation, to continue with the examples, would be to conclude that such propositions are really forms of citation—statements to be placed between implicit quotation marks (Sperber 1974, 1982)—and therefore do not refer to the world, but rather to the relation between the natives and their discourse. This relation is, once again, the core theme for so-called "symbolic" anthropologies, of the semantic or pragmatic type: statements such as the one about peccaries, "in reality," say something about society (or do something to it), not about what they are about. They teach us nothing about the order of things and the nature of reality, however, neither for us *nor for the Amerindians*. To take an affirmation such as "peccaries are humans" seriously, in this case, would consist in showing how certain humans can take it seriously and even believe in it, without showing themselves to be irrational—and, naturally, without the peccaries showing themselves to be human. The world is saved: the peccaries are saved, the natives are saved and, above all, so is the anthropologist.

This solution does not satisfy me. In fact, it profoundly bothers me. It seems to imply that to take Amerindians seriously, when they affirm things such as "peccaries are humans," is precisely *not* to believe in what they say, since if we did we would not be taking *ourselves* seriously. Another way out is needed. As I do not have either the space or, above all (and evidently), the ability to go over the vast philosophical literature that exists on the grammar of belief, certainty, propositional attitudes, et cetera, in what follows I will simply present certain considerations that have emerged intuitively, more than reflexively, through my experience as an ethnographer.

I am an anthropologist, not a swinologist. Peccaries (or, as another anthropologist once said about the Nuer, cows) are of no special interest to me, humans are. But peccaries are of enormous interest to those humans who say that peccaries are human. As a result, the idea that the peccaries are human interests me also, because it "says" something about the humans that say this. But *not* because it says something that these humans are not capable of saying by themselves, and rather because in it the humans in question are saying not only something about the peccaries, but also about what it is to be "human." (Why should the Nuer, for example, not say in their turn that cattle are human?) If the statement on the peccaries' humanity definitely *reveals* something about the human mind (to the anthropologist), it also does more than that (for the Amerindians): it affirms something about the concept of humanity. It affirms, among other things, that the notion of "human mind" and the indigenous concept of sociality include the peccaries in their extensions—and this radically modifies these concepts' intension in relation to our own.

The native's belief or the anthropologist's disbelief has nothing to do with this. To ask (oneself) whether the anthropologist ought to believe the native is a category mistake equivalent to wondering whether the number two is tall or green. These are the first elements of my response to Isabella. When an anthropologist hears from his indigenous interlocutor (or reads in an ethnography) such things as "peccaries are human," the affirmation interests him, no doubt, because he "knows" that peccaries are not human. But this knowledge (which is essentially arbitrary, not to say smugly tautological) ought to stop there: it is only interesting in having awoken the interest of the anthropologist. No more should be asked of it. Above all, it should not be incorporated implicitly in the economy of anthropological commentary, as if it were necessary (or essential) to explain why the Indians *believe* that peccaries are human whereas *in fact* they are not. What is the point of asking oneself whether the Indians are right in this respect—do we not already "know" this? What is indeed worth knowing is that to which we *do not* know the answer, namely what the Indians are saying when they say that peccaries are human.

Such an idea is far from evident. The problem that it creates does not reside in the proposition's copula, as if "peccary" and "human" were common notions, shared by anthropologist and native, the only difference residing in the bizarre equation between the two terms. We should say in passing that it is perfectly possible for the lexical meaning or semantic interpretation of "peccary" and "human" to be more or less the same for both interlocutors; it is not a translational problem, or a matter of deciding whether we and the Amerindians share the same "natural kinds" (perhaps we do . . .). The problem is that the idea that peccaries are human is part of the meaning of the "concepts" of peccary and human in that culture, or better, it is just *this* idea that constitutes the conceptual potency of the statement, providing the concept that determines the manner in which the ideas of peccary and human are to be related. For it is not "first" the peccaries and the humans each in their own place, and "then" the idea that the peccaries are humans: on the contrary, peccaries, humans and their relation are all given *together*.[32]

The intellectual narrowness that afflicts anthropology, in such cases, consists in reducing the notions of peccary and human merely to a proposition's independent variables, when they should be seen—if we want to take Amerindians seriously—as inseparable variations of a single concept. To say that peccaries are humans, as I have already observed, is not simply to say something about peccaries, as if "human" were a passive and inert predicate (for example, the genus that includes the species of peccaries). Nor is it simply a matter of giving a verbal definition of "peccary," much as a statement of the type "'bass' is (the name of) a fish." To say that peccaries are human is to say something about peccaries

---

32. I am not referring to the problem of ontogenetic acquisition of "concepts" or "categories," in the sense given to these terms by cognitive psychology. The simultaneity of the ideas of peccary, human and their identity (conditional and contextual) is, from an empirical point of view, characteristic of the thought of adults in that culture. Even if we admit that children begin by acquiring or manifesting the "concepts" of peccary and human before being taught that "the peccary are human," it remains for the adults, when they act or argue this idea, not to re-enact this supposed chronological sequence in their heads, first thinking about humans and then peccaries, and then their association. Aside from that and above all, this simultaneity is not empirical, but transcendental: it means that the peccaries' humanity is an *a priori* component of the idea of peccary (and the idea of human).

and about humans, something about what the human can be: if peccaries have humanity as a potential, then might humans not have a peccary-potential? In effect, if peccaries can be conceived as humans, then it should be possible to conceive of humans as peccaries: what is it to be human if one is also "peccary," and what is it to be peccary if one is "human"? *What are the consequences of this?* What concept can be extracted from a statement like "peccaries are human"? How can we transform the conception expressed in a proposition like this into a concept? That is the true question.

Hence, when told by his indigenous interlocutors (under conditions that must always be specified) that peccaries are human, the anthropologist should ask herself or himself, not whether or not "he believes" that they are, but rather what such an idea could show him about indigenous notions of humanity and "peccarity." What an idea such as this, note, teaches him about these notions and about other things: about relations between him and his interlocutor, the situations in which this statement is produced "spontaneously," the speech genres and language games in which it fits, et cetera. These *other things*, however—and I would like to insist on this point—hardly exhaust the statement's meaning. To reduce the statement into a discourse that only "speaks" of its enunciator is to negate the latter's intentionality, obliging him to exchange *his* peccary for *our* human—a bad deal for a peccary hunter.

Thus understood, it is obvious that the ethnographer has to believe (in the sense of trusting) his interlocutor: the native is not giving the ethnographer an opinion, he is effectively teaching him what peccaries and humans are, explaining how the human is implied in the peccary. Once more, the question should be: what does this idea do? What assemblages can it help constitute? What are its consequences? For example: what is eaten when one eats a peccary, if peccaries are human?

Furthermore: we still need to see if the concept that can be built by way of such statements can be expressed adequately in the "X is Y" form. For it is not so much a matter of predication or attribution but of defining a virtual set of events and series into which the wild pigs of our example can enter: peccaries travel in a pack . . . they have a leader . . . they are noisy and aggressive . . . they appear suddenly and unpredictably . . . they are bad brothers-in-law . . . they eat palm fruit . . . there are myths that say they live in huge underground villages . . . they are incarnations of the dead . . . and so forth. It is not a matter of establishing correspondences between peccaries' and human's respective attributes—far from it. The peccaries are peccaries *and* humans, they are humans inasmuch as humans *are not* peccaries; peccaries imply humans, as an idea, in their very *distance* from them. Thus, to state that peccaries are human is not to identify them with humans, but rather to differentiate them from themselves—and therefore us from ourselves also.

Previously I stated that the idea of peccaries being human is far from evident: to be sure, no interesting idea is ever evident. This particular idea is not nonevident because it is false or unverifiable (Amerindians have many different ways to *verify* it), but because it says something nonevident about the world. Peccaries are not evidently humans, they are so nonevidently. Could this mean that the idea is "symbolic," in the sense given to this adjective by Sperber? I think not. Sperber conceives of indigenous concepts as propositions, and worse, as second-class propositions, "semi-propositional representations" that extend "encyclopedic knowledge" in a nonreferential manner: he seems to identify the self-positive with the referentially void, the virtual with the fictional, immanence with closure. . . . But one can see "symbolism" differently from Sperber, who takes it as something logical and chronologically posterior to the mind's encyclopedia or to the semantic capacities it informs: something that marks the limits of true or verifiable knowledge, as well as the point at which this knowledge becomes transformed into an illusion. Indigenous concepts can be called symbolic, but in a very different sense; they are not *sub*propositional, but *super*propositional, as they suppose encyclopedic propositions but define their most vital *significance*, their meaning or value. It is the encyclopedic propositions that are semiconceptual or subsymbolic, not the other way round. The symbolic is not semi-true, but pre-true, that is, important or relevant: it speaks not to what "is the case," but to what matters in what is the case, to what is interesting in its being the case. What is a peccary worth? This, literally, is the *interesting* question.[33]

Sperber (1982: 173) once wrote, ironically, "profound: another semi-propositional word." But then it is worth replicating—banal: another word for propositional. In effect, indigenous concepts certainly are profound, as they project a background, a plane of immanence filled with intensities, or, if the reader prefers a Wittgensteinian vocabulary, a *Weltbild* composed of foundational

---

33. "The notions of relevance, necessity, the point of something, are a thousand times more significant than the notion of truth. *Not as substitutes for truth, but as the measure of the truth of what I am saying*" (Deleuze 1990: 177, my emphasis, English translation 1997: 130).

"pseudo-propositions" that ignore and precede the distinction between true and false, "weaving a net that, once thrown over chaos, can provide it with some type of consistence" (Prado Jr. 1998: 317). This background is a "foundationless base" that is neither rational/reasonable nor irrational/unreasonable, but which "simply is there—much like our own lives" (Prado Jr. 1998: 319).[34]

Amerindian bodies

My colleague Peter Gow once narrated the following scene to me, which he witnessed during one of his stays among the Piro of the Peruvian Amazon:

A mission teacher in [the village of] Santa Clara was trying to convince a Piro woman to prepare food for her infant child with boiled water. The woman replied: "If we drink boiled water, we catch diarrhea." The teacher, laughing in mockery at this response, explained that common infant diarrhea is caused precisely by the ingestion of unboiled water. Without being flustered the Piro woman answered: "Perhaps that is true for the people from Lima. But for us, people native to this place, boiled water gives diarrhea. Our bodies are different from your bodies" (Gow, personal comm., October 12, 2000).

What can the anthropologist do with the Amerindian woman's response? Many things. Gow, for example, wove a shrewd commentary on this anecdote:

This simple statement ["our bodies are different"] elegantly captures what Viveiros de Castro (1996a) called cosmological perspectivism, or multinaturalism: what distinguishes the different types of people are their bodies, not their cultures. However, it should be noted that this example of cosmological perspectivism was not obtained in the course of an esoteric discussion about the occult world of spirits, but during a conversation about eminently practical concerns: what causes diarrhea in children? It would be tempting to see the positions of the teacher and of the Piro woman as representing two distinct cosmologies, multiculturalism and multinaturalism, and imagining the conversation as a clash of cosmologies or cultures. I believe that this would be a mistake. Both cosmologies/cultures have been in contact for some time, and their imbrication precedes the ontogenetic processes through which the teacher and the Piro woman came to formulate them as being self-evident. But above all such an interpretation

---

34. The quotations from Bento Prado Jr. are translations by this article's translators. — Ed.

would translate the dialogue in the general terms of one of the parts involved, namely, multiculturalism. The coordinates for the Piro woman's position would be systematically violated by the analysis. Of course, this does not mean that I believe that children should drink unboiled water. But it *does* mean that the ethnographic analysis cannot go forward if the general meaning of such a meeting has been decided from the word go.[35]

I concur with much of this. The anecdote told by Gow is certainly a splendid illustration of the irreducible divergence between what I have called "multiculturalism" and "multinaturalism," particularly as it stems from a banal everyday incident. But Gow's analysis does not seem to be the only possible one. Thus, on the question of the conversation's translation into the general terms of one party—in this case, the teacher's—would it not be equally possible, and above all necessary, to translate it into the general terms of the *other*? For there is no third position, no *absolute* vantage point, from which to show the others' *relative* character. It is necessary to take sides.

It may be possible to say, for instance, that each of the two women is "culturalizing" the other in this conversation—that is, attributing the other's idiocy to her "culture," while "interpreting" her own position as "natural." In such a case, one might also say that the Piro woman's argument about the "body" amounts to a kind concession to the teacher's assumptions. Still, if this were to be so, then note that the concession was not reciprocated. The Piro woman may have agreed to disagree, but the teacher in no way did the same. The former did not contest the fact that people in the city of Lima should ("maybe") drink boiled water, while the latter peremptorily refuted the idea that people from the Santa Clara village should not.

The Piro woman's relativism—a "natural" rather than a "cultural" relativism, it should be noted—could be interpreted with reference to certain hypotheses on the cognitive economy of nonmodern societies, or those without writing, or traditional, et cetera. Take Robin Horton's (1993: 379ff.) theory, for example. Horton posits what he called "worldview parochialism" as a prime characteristic of these societies: contrary to Western modernity's rationalized cosmologies' implicit demand for universality, traditional peoples' cosmologies seem to be marked by a spirit of great tolerance, although it would be fairer to say that

---

35. This is a translation of the author's translation of an email conversation with Peter Gow. —Trans.

they are altogether *indifferent* to competing worldviews. The Piro's apparent relativism would thus not be manifesting the breadth of their views, but much to the contrary their myopia: they remain unconcerned with how things are elsewhere.[36]

There are a number of good grounds to resist readings such as Horton's. Among others, one reason is that so-called primitive relativism is not only intercultural, but also intracultural and even "autocultural," and, to boot, expresses neither tolerance nor indifference, but rather an absolute departure from the cryptotheological idea of "culture" as a set of beliefs (Tooker 1992; Viveiros de Castro 1993b). The main reason to resist such readings, however, is perfectly prefigured in Gow's own comments, namely, that the idea of "parochialism" translates the Santa Clara debate into the terms of the teacher's position, with her natural universalism and (more or less tolerant) cultural particularism. There are many worldviews, but there is only one *world*—a world in which all children should drink boiled water (if, of course, they find themselves in a place where infant diarrhea is a threat).

Let me propose a different reading. The anecdote on different bodies raises questions as to the possible world that the Piro woman's judgment might express. A *possible* world in which human bodies can be different in Lima and in Santa Clara—a world in which it is necessary for white and Amerindian bodies to be different. Now, to define this world we need not invent an imaginary world, a world endowed with a different physics or biology, let us say, where the universe is not isotropic and bodies can behave according to different laws in different places. That would be (bad) science fiction. It is rather a matter of finding the real problem that renders possible the world implied in the Piro woman's reply. The argument that "our bodies are different" does not express an alternative, and naturally erroneous, biological theory, or an imaginarily nonstandard[37] objective

---

36. In effect, the Piro woman's response is identical to a Zande observation, which can be found in the bible for those anthropologists of a Hortonian persuasion: "I once heard a Zande say of us: 'Maybe in their country people are not murdered by witches, but here they are'" (Evans-Pritchard 1976: 274). I must thank Ingrid Weber for reminding me of this.

37. As Gell (1998: 101) forewarned in a similar context, magic is not a mistaken physics, but a "meta-physics": "Frazer's mistake was, so to speak, to imagine that practitioners of magic afforded a nonstandard theory of physics, when, in fact, 'magic' is what one has when one goes without a theory of physics due to its superfluousness, and when one seeks support in the perfectly practicable idea that the explanation for any given event . . . is that it is caused intentionally."

biology. What the Piro argument manifests is *a nonbiological idea of the body*, an idea in which the question of infant diarrhea cannot be treated as the object of a biological theory. The argument affirms that our respective "bodies" are different, by which we should understand that Piro and Western *concepts* (rather than "biologies") of the body are divergent. The Piro water anecdote does not refer to an *other* vision of the *same* body, but another concept of the body—the problem being, precisely, its discrepancy from our own concept, notwithstanding their apparent "homonimy." Thus, for example, the Piro concept of the body cannot be, as ours is, in the soul or "in the mind," as a representation of a body that lies beyond it. On the contrary, such a concept could be inscribed *in the body itself* as a perspective (Viveiros de Castro 1996a, 1998). So, this would not be the concept taken as a representation of an extra-conceptual body, but the body taken as a perspective internal to the concept: the body as an implication of the very concept of perspective. And if, as Spinoza said, we do not know what a body can do, how much less do we know of what *such* a body could do. Not to speak of its soul.

CHAPTER TWO

And

Professor Fardon, distinguished colleagues,

I've spent half my time over the last few months asking myself why the conference organizers decided to bestow the overwhelming honor of inviting me to address you all on this occasion. And the other half I've spent asking myself how I had the gall to accept such an invitation. Eventually I came to the conclusion that the answer to both questions is probably one and the same: both our hosts and I like to live dangerously. Indeed I have a sneaking suspicion Penny Harvey, Peter Wade, and Jeanette Edwards were looking for the most unlikely person to speak at an ASA Conference dedicated to the theme of "anthropology and science": someone, let's say, resembling an obscure foreign scholar who doesn't practice an especially scientific anthropology, who has never undertaken any kind of anthropological study of science, and who, on top of all this, speaks English rather quirkily. I just hope they haven't gone too far in their eagerness to surprise you. As for myself, suffice to say that the responsibility of succeeding the great Sahlins in marshalling your postprandial entertainment could only have been taken on by someone blessed with the most complete sense of irresponsibility. Even more so since Sahlins left you, ten years ago, waiting for none other than Foucault. . . . Look what you've got instead—I'm not even bald.

* * *

Still, I accepted the challenge of attempting to amuse you with some trifles on the theme "anthropology and science" because of this little magic word "and"— a connective which is to the universe of relations as the notion of *mana* (I mean Lévi-Straussian *mana*) is to the universe of substances. *And* is a kind of zero-relator, a relational *mana* of sort—the floating signifier of the class of connectives—whose function is to oppose the absence of relation, but without specifying any relation in particular. "And" covers all thinkable connections, and therefore allows one to say all sayable things about the terms it connects— which naturally enough doesn't demand the work of a specialist. Indeed this explains how I plucked up the courage to come here. But maybe not. Maybe there is a relation which "and" excludes, perhaps because it is not a true relation—the relation of identity. Who would dream of giving a physics conference the title "Physics and Science"? Physics is Science! We have to be able to imagine that anthropology isn't constitutively a science, at least not all the time, in all respects and in all relations, in order for us to imagine this contingent connection expressed in the formula "anthropology and science." A relation can be contrived, then, between "and," the minimal relator, and "is," the maximal substantializer, poles between which all our discourses and sciences are distributed. Now, if anthropology "is" a science of something, it is undoubtedly the comparative science of the relations that make us human. But since comparing is relating, and vice-versa, our discipline is twice over the science of the "and," that is, of universal relational immanence. Not of the "is," therefore, and still less of the "ought"—but simply of the "and."

* * *

Everyone here will recall the famous last words of *Primitive culture*: ours is announced as a reformer's science, a Ghostbusters-like enterprise committed to tracking down and wiping out all superstition. Later on we learnt how to functionalize and rationalize superstition, arguing that it was merely an unselfconscious metaphoric sociology or an evolutionary spandrel precipitated by the cognitive make-up of the human species. Be that as it may, the fact that we have always defined anthropology, officially or officiously, as the science of non-science imbues the recent interest in an "anthropology of science" with a reflexive piquancy all its own. The discomfort provoked by the idea of an anthropological description of scientific activity—a queasiness felt not just by practitioners of the hard sciences, but also by many anthropologists—suggests we are seen, and maybe we even see ourselves, as an accursed race of anti-Midases capable of transforming everything we touch into error, ideology, myth, and illusion. So danger looms when the reformer's science turns its gaze to science at large: the latter seems set to be denounced as just one more kind of superstition. This was how the so-called Science Wars, or Culture Wars, exploded, in which anthropologists featured among the prime suspects—based as usual on somewhat fabricated evidence—accused of possessing weapons of mass destruction. Or should I say, mass deconstruction.

Of course it should be the complete opposite of all this. What the anthropology of science should be teaching us—and this, for myself at least, is its primary lesson—is the impossibility of continuing to practice our discipline within an economy of knowledge where the anthropological concept functions as a kind of surplus value extracted by the "observer" from the existential labor—the life—of the "observed."

What follows is an attempt to make this clearer.

* * *

Obviously I cannot speak here for all my generation, those of us who turned adults around 1968, but for many of us anthropology was and still is the absolute opposite of a reformer's science or a Reason police. It was an insurrectionary, subversive science; more specifically, the instrument of a certain revolutionary utopia which fought for the conceptual self-determination of all the planet's minorities, a fight we saw as an indispensable accompaniment to their political self-determination. In the case of Brazilian anthropologists, this possessed an especially urgent relevance. The start of the 1970s saw the indigenous minorities in my country begin to establish themselves as political agents. Our aim as anthropologists was to assist this process by providing it with a radical intellectual dimension, enabling the thought of American peoples to escape the ghetto in which it had been enclosed since the sixteenth century. As part of this politico-cultural struggle, which may be imagined as a process of multiplicity-building (that is, of anti-empire building), the work of Lévi-Strauss—some of you may be surprised to hear, others not so—was of enormous importance, since it was through Lévi-Strauss' mediation that the intellectual style of Amerindian societies was for the first time in a position to modify the terms of the anthropological debate as a whole. In sum, for us the expression "la pensée sauvage" did not signify "the savage mind." To us it meant untamed thought, unsubdued thought, wild thought. Thought against the State, if you will. (In remembrance of Pierre Clastres.)

Sure enough, all of us were hippies of a kind. We were primitivists, anarchists, and essentialists; perhaps we had a slightly inflated sense of anthropology's importance; we were all highly prone to exoticism, too. But we weren't quite so hopelessly naïve: our primitivism was a desire for self-transformation; our anarchism needs no excuse; our essentialism was strategic (but of course); and as for our exoticism, well, those were strange times indeed when the concept of the Other designated a radically positive value, while the concept of Self was a position to be detested. In other words, our world had yet to wake up to the now pervasive sentiment against difference and alterity which sees them as harbingers of violence and oppression. All difference seems nowadays to be read as an opposition, while alterity is conceived as the absence of a relation: "to oppose" is taken to be synonymous with "to exclude"—a weird idea, which I can only put down to the guilty supposition that others conceive otherness as we do. Well, they don't: others are "other" precisely because they have other "others"—Captain Cook, for example, as Sahlins has memorably argued. Anyway, I guess there's no need to remind you that "othering" is not the same kind of politico-metaphysical swindle everywhere. And come to think of it, why should "saming" be such a better thing to do to others? Who wants to be samed? All those double-bind claims to "tolerance" rush to mind; as the philosopher Isabelle Stengers asks—would you like to be tolerated?

In my view, anthropology is consistently guided by this one cardinal value: working to create the conditions for the conceptual, I mean ontological, self-determination of people. Or peoples to be more exact. Its success or failure as a science hinges on this, and not, as some of our more nihilistic colleagues wishfully think, on its willingness to proclaim its own self-extinction and divide its legacy between a neo-evolutionist psychology and a neo-diffusionist history; yuppifying itself out of existence, in effect, not with a big bang but a spluttering whimper. In fact maybe it's time for us to reinvent a neo-functionalist social anthropology . . . ? Since we're living through a moment in our discipline's history when it seems increasingly urgent for us to reclaim and proclaim the very dimension of reality with which anthropology concerns itself: a collective reality—a relational reality, in other words—, one possessing a disposition towards the transcontextual stability of form. I believe anthropology must escape self-imposed doom and keep firmly focused on its proper object: social relations in all their variations. Not social relations taken as a distinct ontological domain (there is no such thing), but all phenomena as potentially comprising or imply-ing social relations. This means taking all relations as social. Not though from a viewpoint completely dominated by the western doctrine of social relations, but from one ready and willing to admit that treating all relations as social may entail a radical reconceptualization of what "the social" may be. Indeed anthropology distinguishes itself from other discourses on human sociality by not possessing a particularly solid doctrine on the nature of social relations. On the contrary, it tends from the outset to have only a vague idea of what a rela-tion may be, since its problem typically consists not so much in determining what social relations constitute its object, but in asking itself what its object constitutes as a social relation. In other words, what a social relation is in its object's terms, or better still, in the terms formulated by the relation between the "anthropologist" and the "native."

This of course leads us to our crunch question: what is an anthropologist, and who's the native?

* * *

The "anthropologist" is someone who discourses on the discourse of a "native." The native need not be particularly savage, nor traditionalist, nor even natural to the place where the anthropologist finds him; the anthropologist need not be excessively civilized, nor modernist, nor even a stranger to the people about whom she discourses. The discourses of the anthropologist and above all the native are not necessarily texts: they are any kind of meaningful practice. The essential factor is that the discourse of the anthropologist (the "observer") es-tablishes a certain relationship with the discourse of the native (the "observed"). This relationship is a relation of meaning, or, as one says when the former dis-course aspires to the status of a Science, a relation of knowledge.

Such a relation is not one of identity: the anthropologist always says, and thus does, something different from the native, even if her intention is to do no more than "textually" reiterate the native's discourse, or contrive a "dialogue" with him.

Discursive alterity is of course premised on similarity. Anthropologist and native are entities of the same kind and condition: equally human and equally embedded within their respective cultures, which may even be one and the same. But it's here that things start to become interesting, or should I say, strange. Even when the anthropologist and native share the same culture, the relation between the two discourses acts to differentiate this community: the anthropologist's relation to her culture and that of the native to his are not exactly the same. What makes the native a native is the presupposition, on the part of the anthropologist, that the former's relation to his culture is natural, that is, intrinsic and spontaneous, and, if possible, non-reflexive—or better still, unconscious. The native expresses his culture in his discourse; likewise the anthropologist, but if she intends to be something other than a native, she must express her culture culturally, that is, reflexively, conditionally, and consciously. The anthropologist necessarily uses her culture; the native is sufficiently used by his.

Needless to say, this difference isn't to be found in the so-called nature of things. It's an intrinsic element of the language game I'm describing and defines the figures labelled "the anthropologist" and "the native." Let's consider a few more rules of this game.

The anthropological idea of culture places the anthropologist on equal terms with the native by implying that all anthropological knowledge of another culture is culturally mediated. However this equality is in the first instance purely empirical or *de facto*: it corresponds to the equally cultural condition of anthropologist and native. It doesn't imply an equality *de jure*—an equality on the plane of knowledge. The anthropologist typically enjoys an epistemological advantage over the native. The two discourses are situated on different planes: the meaning established by the anthropologist depends on the native meaning, but it is she who determines this meaning's meaning—she who explains and interprets, translates and relates, textualizes and contextualizes, justifies and signifies this meaning. The relational matrix of anthropological discourse is hylomorphic: the anthropologist's meaning is form to the native's matter. The native's discourse can't determine the meaning of its own meaning. As Geertz said somewhere, we are all (*de facto*) natives; sure; but some of us are (*de jure*) always more native than others.

This prompts the following questions. What happens if we deny the anthropologist's discourse its strategic advantage over the native's discourse? What happens when the native's discourse functions within the anthropologist's discourse in such a way it produces a reciprocal "knowledge-effect" on the latter? When the form intrinsic to the content of the first modifies the content implicit in the form of the second? Translator, traitor, as the Italian saying goes; but what happens if the translator decides to betray her own language? What would ensue if, dissatisfied with the mere passive or *de facto* equality between the subjects involved, we were to claim an active or *de jure* equality between the discourses themselves? In sum, what changes when anthropology is taken as a meaning-producing practice in epistemological continuity with the practices on which it discourses—as their equivalent? In other words, when we apply the Latourian notion of "symmetrical anthropology" to anthropology itself, not to lambaste it as colonialist, exorcize its exoticism, or mine its intellectual field, but to induce it to say something completely different? Not only different from the native's discourse, since this must remain one of anthropology's functions, but different to the discourse which anthropology pronounces about itself, usually subvocally, when discoursing on the discourse of the native?

Were we to pursue all this in active fashion, I would say that we would be doing what was always properly called "anthropology," instead of, say, "sociology" or "psychology." I say I would say, because much of what was or is done in this name supposes, on the contrary, that the anthropologist holds total sway over those reasons of which the native's reason knows nothing. She knows the exact doses of universality and particularity contained in the native, and the illusions which the latter entertains about himself—whether manifesting his native culture all the while believing he's manifesting human nature (the native ideologizes without knowing), or manifesting human nature all the while believing he's manifesting his native culture (he cognizes unawares). (Generally it's supposed the native does both things without being aware of either—natural reasoning and cultural rationalizing—in different phases, registers, or situations of his life. Moreover, the native's illusions are taken as necessary in the double sense of inevitable and useful; they are, to hijack a phrase, evolutionarily adaptive. It is this necessity which defines the "native" and distinguishes him from the "anthropologist": the latter may be wrong about the former, but the former must be deluded about himself.)

Thus the anthropologist knows the native *de jure*, even though she may not know him *de facto*. The complete opposite occurs when moving from the native to the anthropologist: although he knows the anthropologist *de facto* (frequently better than she knows him), he doesn't know her *de jure*, since the native is precisely not an anthropologist like the anthropologist. The anthropologist's knowledge is a wholly different animal from the native's knowledge. Indeed it has to be: the condition of possibility of the former entails the delegitimation of the claims of the latter, its "epistemocide," in Bob Scholte's forceful expression. Knowledge on the part of the subject requires a sort of transcendental nescience on the part of the object.

It's all very well—or rather, quite ill. But there is no reason for us to be excessively squeamish about all this. As the discipline's history attests, this discursive game with its unequal rules has told us many an insightful thing about natives. Nevertheless, the experiment I propose here precisely involves refusing to play this game. Not because it produces objectively false results, or misrepresents the native's nature, so to speak. Given the objects which the classic game takes as given, its results are very often convincing, or at least "plausible," as adepts of this game like to say. Refusing to play this game simply implies positing different objects compatible with different rules.

What I'm suggesting, in a nutshell, is the need to choose between two conceptions of anthropology. On one side, we have an image of anthropological knowledge as the outcome of applying concepts extrinsic to its object: we know beforehand what social relations are, or cognition, kinship, religion, politics, and so on, and our aim is to see how these entities take shape in this or that ethnographic context—how they take shape unbeknown to the interested parties, needless to say. On the other side (and this is the game I'm proposing), is an idea of anthropological knowledge which starts out from the premise that the procedures characterizing the investigation are conceptually of the same kind as those to be investigated. This equivalence at the level of procedures, we should note, supposes and produces a radical non-equivalence at all other levels. For while the first conception of anthropology imagines each culture or society as the embodiment of a specific solution to a generic problem—as the specification of a universal form (the anthropological concept) with a particular content (the indigenous representation)—, the second by contrast imagines that the problems themselves are radically distinct. More than this: it starts out from the principle that the anthropologist cannot know beforehand what these problems may be. Anthropology in this case places in relationship different problems, not a single ("natural") problem and its different ("cultural") solutions. Thus the "art of anthropology" is to my mind the art of determining the problems posed by each culture, not the art of finding solutions to those problems posed by our own. This has been one of the most important lessons I've learnt from Marilyn Strathern. And it is for this very reason that the postulate of the continuity of procedures is an epistemological imperative.

Of procedures, I repeat, not of those who carry them out. Since neither is it a question of condemning the classic game for producing subjectively falsified results by a failure to recognize the native's condition as a Subject: by fixing him with a distant and cold gaze, constructing him as an exotic object, diminishing him as a primitive on another time-band to the observer, denying him the human right of interlocution—the litany is well known. Nothing of the sort, I believe. In fact very much the opposite: it is precisely because the anthropologist takes the native so readily as another subject that she fails to see him as an other subject, as a figure of Another who, prior to being a subject or object, is the expression of a possible world. It is by refusing to accept the native's condition as a "non-subject" (in the sense of being other than the subject) that the anthropologist introduces, under the guise of a proclaimed *de facto* equality with the former, her wily *de jure* advantage. She knows much too much about the native before the game even starts; she predefines and circumscribes the possible worlds expressed by this other; the alterity of the other is already radically separated from his capacity for alteration. The authentic animist is the anthropologist, and participant observation is the true (meaning false) primitive participation.

Consequently the problem doesn't reside in seeing the native as an object, nor does the solution reside in casting him as a subject. That the native is a subject is beyond doubt; but what the native forces the anthropologist to cast into doubt is precisely what a subject could be—such is the properly anthropological "cogitation." It alone allows anthropology to assume the virtual presence of Another as its condition, indeed precondition, and which determines the derivative and vicarious positions of subject and object.

I evoked the Kantian distinction between *quid facti* and *quid juris* questions. It struck me as useful because the first problem to be solved involves evaluating the claim to knowledge implied in the anthropologist's discourse. This problem is not cognitive or psychological; it doesn't concern the empirical possibility of knowing another culture. It is epistemological—and thus political. It relates to the properly transcendental question of the legitimacy attributed to the discourses entering into a relation of knowledge, and, in particular, the relations of order one decides to stipulate between these discourses, since such relations are clearly not innate. Nobody is born an anthropologist, and, curious though this may seem, still less is anyone born a native.

* * *

As I stated earlier, anthropology as I understand it begins by asserting the *de jure* equivalence between the discourses of anthropologist and native, as well as the mutually constitutive condition of these discourses, which only come into existence as such on entering into a relation of knowledge. Anthropological concepts actualize this relation, though this makes them neither true reflections of the native's culture (the positivist dream), nor illusory projections of the anthropologist's culture (the constructionist nightmare). What they reflect is a certain relation of intelligibility between the two cultures, while what they project are the two cultures themselves as their imagined presuppositions (as Roy Wagner amply demonstrated). As a result, they perform a double deterritorialization: they amount to transcontextual interfaces whose function is to represent, in the diplomatic sense of the term, the other in the midst of the same, here, there, and everywhere. The interminable debate on the universality or otherwise of certain concepts and oppositions therefore seems to me of scant interest. Worse than interminable, this debate is indeterminable: all said and done, everything is relatively universal. The real problem lies in knowing which are the possible relations between our descriptive practices and those employed by other peoples (this is something else Marilyn Strathern taught me). There are undoubtedly many possible relations; but only one impossible relation: the absence of a relation. We cannot learn these other practices—other cultures—in absolute terms; we can only try to make explicit some of our implicit relations with them, that is, apprehend them in relation to our own descriptive practices. Universalizing the Christian metaphysics of body and soul, the modern theory of the social contract or the contemporary biopolitics of kinship is one of the ways of doing just this—of relating. A very unimaginative way, to be sure. But the alternative cannot be the fantasy of an intellectual intuition of other forms of life "in their own terms," for there is no such thing. "Their terms" are only determined as such in relation to "our terms," and vice-versa. Every determination is a relation. Nothing is absolutely universal, not because something is relatively particular, but because "everything" is relational. All perfectly obvious, you'll say. For sure. Admitting the obvious is one thing, though: it's a very different kettle of fish drawing from it all the possible consequences.

In sum, anthropological concepts are relative because they are relational—and they are relational because they are relators. This origin and function is usually marked in the characteristic "signature" of these conceits by a foreign word: mana, totem, kula, potlatch, taboo, gumsa/gumlao. . . . Other no less authentic concepts carry an etymological signature which evokes instead the analogies between the cultural tradition where the discipline emerged and the traditions making up its object: gift, sacrifice, kinship, personhood. . . . Finally, other concepts—equally legitimate—are lexical inventions which seek to generalize conceptual devices of the peoples studied—animism, segmentary opposition, restricted exchange, schismogenesis . . . — or, inversely, and far more problematically, suck certain more widespread notions from our tradition—the incest prohibition, gender, symbol, culture—into a specific theoretical economy with the aim of universalizing them.

It's clear then that numerous concepts, problems, entities, and agents proposed by anthropological theories originate in the imaginative work of the very societies these theories seek to explain. Doesn't anthropology's irreducible originality reside in this synergy between the conceptions and practices deriving from the worlds of the "subject" and the "object"? Among other plus points, recognizing this would help mitigate our inferiority complex vis-à-vis the "natural sciences." As Latour (1996a: 5) observes:

> The description of kula is on a par with that of the black holes. The complex systems of social alliances are as imaginative as the complex scenarios conceived for the selfish genes. Understanding the theology of Australian Aborigines is as important as charting the great undersea rifts. The Trobriand land tenure system is as interesting a scientific objective as the polar icecap drilling. If we talk about what matters in a definition of science—innovation in the agencies that furnish our world—anthropology might well be close to the top of the disciplinary pecking order.

This observation was made, we may recall, in the context of an 1996 AAA-sponsored debate on "Science and Anthropology." Now, the analogy made in this passage is between indigenous conceptions and the objects of so-called natural sciences. This is a possible, and indeed necessary, perspective: anthropology should be able to produce a scientific description of indigenous ideas and practices as if they were objects in the world, or better, in order for them to be objects in the world. (Lest we forget, Latour's scientific objects are anything but than "objective" and indifferent entities lying patiently in wait of a description.) Another possible strategy involves comparing indigenous conceptions with scientific theories, an approach adopted by Robin Horton, for example, in his "similarity thesis." Nonetheless, the strategy I advocate here is different again. In my opinion, anthropology has always been somewhat over-obsessed with "Science," not only in relation to itself—whether it is or isn't, can or can't, must or mustn't be a science—but above all, and this is the real issue, in relation to the conceptions of the peoples it studies: whether to disqualify them as errors, dreams, and illusions, and subsequently explain scientifically how and why the "others" fail to produce scientific explanations (of themselves, among other things); or to promote such conceptions as more or less homologous to science,

fruits of the same will-to-knowledge driving all humankind: then we end up
with Horton's similarity, or Lévi-Strauss' science of the concrete. However, the
image of science, this gold-standard of thinking, is not the only terrain, nor
necessarily the most fertile, for us to relate with the intellectual activity of peoples foreign to the western tradition. If you will allow me a financial metaphor,
I'd suggest it's more interesting for us to float the world conceptual exchange
rates, dispensing with the 'relic of barbarism' which is mononaturalism, that is,
the essentializing reserve currency of a single ontology (to which science enjoys
privileged access) capable of guaranteeing the inter-conversion of the various
epistemologies.

So a different analogy to Latour's can be imagined. Instead of taking indigenous conceptions as entities akin to black holes or tectonic faults, we can take
them as something similar to the cogito or the monad. Paraphrasing our Latour
quote, we might say that the Melanesian concept of the person as a "dividual"
(M. Strathern) is just as imaginative as the possessive individualism of Locke;
that understanding the "philosophy of the Indian chieftainship" (P. Clastres) is
just as important as commenting on the Hegelian doctrine of the State; that
Maori cosmogony is on an equal par with Eleatic paradoxes or Kantian antinomies (G. Schrempp); that Amazonian perspectivism is just as interesting a
philosophical challenge as comprehending the system of Leibniz. . . . Indeed,
if it is a question of knowing what matters in evaluating a philosophy—its capacity to create new concepts—, then anthropology, without looking to substitute for philosophy, remains a powerful philosophical tool, capable of airing
the stuffy ethnocentric corridors of our philosophy, while freeing us in passing
from so-called "philosophical anthropology." In Tim Ingold's punchy definition:
"anthropology is philosophy with the people in." By "people" Ingold intends "ordinary people"; but he's also playing with the meaning of "people" as "a people"
or further still as "peoples." So, a philosophy with other peoples in: the possibility of a philosophical activity which maintains a meaningful relationship with
the non-philosophy—the life—of other peoples of the planet, as well as with
our own. Not just "ordinary people," therefore, but above all "extraordinary" or
"uncommon" peoples, those who live beyond our sphere of "communication."
If real philosophy abounds in imaginary savages, the geophilosophy implied by
anthropology strives to articulate an imaginary philosophy with the help of real
savages. (In remembrance of Marianne Moore.)

I've looked at what would happen were we to deny anthropological discourse
any epistemological advantage over the native's discourse. This is the same as

asking: what happens when we take native thought seriously? When the anthropologist's aim ceases to be to explain, interpret, contextualize, and rationalize this thought, and becomes one of using it, drawing out its consequences, and
ascertaining the effects it may produce on our own? What does it mean to think
native thought? Think, I say, without thinking that what we think (the other's
thought) is "apparently irrational," or, God forbid, essentially rational, but think
of it as something remaining unthought within the terms of this alternative—
something totally alien to this game? Taking seriously means above all not neutralizing. It means, for instance, bracketing the question of knowing whether
and how this thought illustrates cognitive universals of the human species, is a
sequel of certain technologies of knowledge transmission, expresses a culturally
specific worldview, functionally validates the distribution of political power, and
many other forms of neutralizing alien thought. It means suspending this question, or at the very least avoiding enclosing anthropology within it, and taking
another tack: deciding, for instance, to think of the other thinking as only (if you
will) an actualization of unsuspected virtualities of thought.

* * *

Everything I've just said boils down to the idea that we need to make the notion
of symmetrical anthropology reflexive; make it "supersymmetrical," as M. Fukushima once phrased it. But to achieve this aim, it is highly desirable we produce
an anthropological concept of the concept, i.e., an anthropological theory of the
imagination. As I've already spoken way too much, I'll limit myself here to a few
"sketchy observations," a euphemism, naturally, for "peremptory declarations":

1) I think it's about time we rethought the notion of practice. Especially
since the radical contrast between theory and practice is, in the end, purely
theoretical: pure practice exists only in theory; in practice, it always comes heav-
ily mixed with theory. What I'm trying to say is that the theory of practice, as
classically formulated by Bourdieu, supposes a theoretically obsolete concept of
theory, which sees the latter as a transcendent meta-practice of a contemplative
or reflexive type, existing above and after practice, as its moment of "purification" (in Latour's sense). In other words, we need a new theory of theory: a
generalized theory of theory, one enabling us to think of theoretical activity
in radical continuity with practice, that is, as an immanent or constitutive (as
opposed to purely regulative) dimension of the intellect embodied in action.
This continuity is exactly the same—and this is an important point—as the

continuity I identified as obtaining (*de jure*) in the relation between the discourses of "anthropologist" and "native." The anthropology of science obviously has a vital contribution to make here, given that one of its core objects is "theory in practice": the practice of production and circulation of theories.

2) But as a first step we have to resolve our highly ambivalent attitude concerning the propositional model of knowledge. Contemporary anthropology, both in its phenomenological-constructionist and in its cognitive-instructionist guises, has proven notable for insisting on the severe limitations of this model when it comes to dealing with intellectual economies of "non-western"type (I mean non-modern, non-written, non-theoretical, non-doctrinal, or non-whatever intellectual economies). Indeed, anthropological discourse has embroiled itself in the paradoxical pastime of heaping propositions on top of propositions arguing for the fundamentally non-propositional nature of other peoples' discourses—chattering away endlessly about what goes without saying, so to speak. We count ourselves lucky when our natives display a blissful disdain for the practice of self-interpretation, and even less interest in cosmology and system. We're probably right, since the lack of native interpretation has the great advantage of allowing the proliferation of anthropological interpretations of this lack. Simultaneously, the native's disinterest in cosmological order fosters the production of neat anthropological cosmologies in which societies are ordered according to their greater or lesser inclination towards systematicity (or doctrinality, or whatever). In sum, the more practical the native, the more theoretical the anthropologist. Let us also not forget that the non-propositional mode is held to be characterized by a constitutive dependency on its "context" of transmission and circulation. This makes it the exact opposite (supposedly, it goes without saying) of scientific discourse—a discourse whose aim is precisely universalization. To repeat a refrain: all of us are context-bound, but some are so much more context-bound than others.

My issue here isn't with the thesis of the quintessential non-propositionality of untamed thought, but with the underlying idea that the proposition is in any sense a good model of conceptuality in general. The proposition continues to serve as the prototype of rational statements and the atom of theoretical discourse. The non-propositional is seen as essentially primitive, as non-conceptual or even anti-conceptual. Naturally, such a state of affairs can be used both "for" and "against" this non-conceptual Other: the absence of rational-propositional concepts may be held to correspond to a super-presence of sensibility, emotion, sociability, intimacy, relational-cum-meaningful engagement in/with the world and what not. For or against, though, all this concedes way too much to the proposition, and reflects a totally archaic concept of the concept, one which continues to define it as the subsumption of the particular by the universal, that is, as essentially a movement towards classification and abstraction. Now, rather than simply divorcing, for better or worse, the concept from "cognition in practice" (to pay homage to Jean Lave's great book), I believe we need to discover the infra-philosophical, i.e., the vital, within the concept, and likewise (perhaps more importantly) the virtual conceptuality within the infra-philosophical. What kind (or "form") of life, in other words, is virtually projected by ideas such as the Cartesian Cogito or the Kantian synthetic a priori? (Recall Wittgenstein's indignation against the petty spiritual life presumed by Frazer's interpretations of primitive rites.) And in like manner, what sort of virtual conceptuality pulsates within Amazonian shamanic narratives, Melanesian initiation rituals, African hunting traps, or Euro-American kinship usages? (Think of the ludicrously stunted conceptual imagination presumed by many an anthropological expatiation upon wild thought.)

We need less by way of context and more by way of concept. In other words, we need an anthropological concept of the concept, which assumes the fundamental extra-propositionality of all thought in its integral positivity, and develops in a completely different direction to our traditional notions of "innate category," "collective representation," and "belief." In brief, we need an anthropological theory of conceptual imagination: the faculty of creating those intellectual objects and relations which furnish the indefinitely many possible worlds of which humans are capable. This theory must be anthropological, that is, based on the relational matrix of human thinking-and-acting. In *Art and agency*, Alfred Gell remarks that anthropological theories must conjoin a theory of social efficacy with cognitive considerations, "because cognition and sociality are one." Indeed, but the equivalence cuts both ways: a theory of human cognition is relational—i.e., anthropological—or it is nothing.

3) Finally, in order to achieve this we need to draw all the necessary implications from the fact that the native's discourse speaks about something else besides just the native, that is, his society or mind: it speaks about the world. This means accepting that "anthropology's true problems are not epistemological, but ontological," as Vassos Argyrou pithily put it some time ago. And I would like to add: anthropology's true objects are not epistemologies, but ontologies. I call your attention to the increasingly frequent use of this word, "ontology," in the contemporary anthropological literature. It strikes me as symptomatic of

our growing dissatisfaction with the uncompromisingly Kantian inspiration of our discipline. The image of Being is obviously dangerous analogic ground when it comes to anthropological re-imaginings of non-western conceptual imaginations, and the notion of ontology is not without its own risks. Perhaps Gabriel Tarde's bold suggestion that we should abandon the irremediably solipsist concept of Being and relaunch metaphysics on the basis of Having (Avoir)—with the latter's implication of intrinsic transitivity and an originary opening towards an exteriority—is a more enticing prospect in many cases. Nonetheless, I think the language of ontology is important for one specific and, let's say, tactical reason. It acts as a counter-measure to a derealizing trick frequently played against the native's thinking, which turns this thought into a kind of sustained phantasy, by reducing it to the dimensions of a form of knowledge or representation, that is, to an "epistemology" or a "worldview." As if whatever there is to know or view was already decided beforehand—and decided, of course, in favor of our ontology. So the notion of ontology isn't evoked here to suggest that all thought, be it Greek, Melanesian, African, or Amazonian, expresses a metaphysics of Being, but to underline the fact that all thought is inseparable from a reality which corresponds to its exterior. This signifies that the epistemological democracy usually professed by anthropology in propounding the cultural diversity of meanings reveals itself to be, like so many other democracies with which we are familiar, highly relative, since it is based "in the final instance" on an absolute ontological monarchy, where the referential unity of nature is imposed. It is against this pious relativist hypocrisy that I shall conclude by once more claiming that anthropology is the science of the ontological self-determination of the world's peoples, and that it is thus a political science in the fullest sense, since its motto is—or should be—that which was written on the walls of Paris in May 1968: *l'imagination au pouvoir*. The rest is business as usual. Thank you.

CHAPTER THREE

Perspectival Anthropology and the Method of Controlled Equivocation

Tropical Americanism has proven to be one of the most dynamic and creative areas of contemporary anthropology, exerting a growing influence on the wider conceptual agenda.[1] Yet despite this flourishing, and although the fundamental work of Lévi-Strauss—within which Amerindian thought is given pride of place—has already been in circulation for more than half a century, the radical originality of the contribution of the continent's peoples to humanity's intellectual heritage has yet to be fully absorbed by anthropology. More particularly, some of the implications of this contribution for anthropological theory itself are still waiting to be drawn. This is what I intend to begin to do here by suggesting some further thoughts on Amerindian perspectivism, a theme with which I have been occupied (or perhaps obsessed) over the last few years.[2]

---

1. This essay was first presented as the keynote address at the meetings of the Society for the Anthropology of Lowland South America (SALSA), held at Florida International University, Miami, January 17–18, 2004.

2. See Viveiros de Castro 1998; 2002a.

TRANSLATION

The title of this paper is an allusion to a famous article by Fred Eggan (1954) entitled "Social anthropology and the method of controlled comparison," which made up part of the toolbox of the well-known Harvard-Central Brazil Project, of which I am one of the academic descendants. The double difference between the tides registers the general direction of my argument, which, truth be known, has little to do with Eggan's. The substitution of "perspectival" for "social" indicates first of all that the "anthropology" I am referring to is a hybrid formation, the result of a certain recursive imbrication among Western anthropological discourses (our very own ethno-anthropology), which are rooted in our modern multiculturalist and uninaturalist ontology, and the anthropological image conveyed by Amerindian cosmopraxis in the form of a perspectivist theory of transpecific personhood, which is by contrast unicultural and multinatural.

Second, and more generally, this substitution expresses my conviction that contemporary anthropology is social (or, for that matter, cultural) only in so far as the first question faced by the anthropologist is to work out what constitutes, both by extension and comprehension, the concept of the social (the cultural) for the people studied. Said differently, the question is how to configure the people as theoretical agent rather than as passive "subject." As I argued in a recent paper (Viveiros de Castro 2002b: 122; see Chapter 1, this volume), anthropology's defining problem consists less in determining which social relations constitute its object, and much more in asking what its object constitutes as a social relation—what a social relation is in the terms of its object, or better still, in the terms that emerge from the relation (a social relation, naturally) between the "anthropologist" and the "native."

Put concisely, doing anthropology means comparing anthropologies, nothing more—but nothing less. Comparison is not just our primary analytic tool. It is also our raw material and our ultimate grounding, because what we compare are always and necessarily, in one form or other, comparisons. If culture, as Marilyn Strathern wrote, "consists in the way people draw analogies between different domains of their worlds" (1992c: 47), then every culture is a gigantic, multidimensional process of comparison. Following Roy Wagner, if anthropology "stud[ies] culture through culture," then "whatever operations characterize our investigations must also be general properties of culture" ([1975] 1981: 35). In brief, the anthropologist and native are engaged in "directly comparable intellectual operations" (Herzfeld 2001: 7), and such operations are above all else comparative. Intracultural relations, or internal comparisons (the Strathernian "analogies between domains"), and intercultural relations, or external comparisons (the Wagnerian "invention of culture"), are in strict ontological continuity.

But direct comparability does not necessarily signify immediate translatability, just as ontological continuity does not imply epistemological transparency. How can we restore the analogies traced by Amazonian peoples within the terms of our own analogies? What happens to our comparisons when we compare them with indigenous comparisons?

I propose the notion of "equivocation" as a means of reconceptualizing, with the help of Amerindian perspectivist anthropology, this emblematic procedure of our academic anthropology—comparison. I have in mind something distinct from Eggan's comparison, which was comparison between different spatial or temporal instantiations of a given sociocultural form. Seen from the viewpoint of the "rules of anthropological method," this type of comparison is just a regulative rule—and other forms of anthropological investigation exist. Rather, the comparison of which I am thinking is a constitutive rule of the discipline. It concerns the process involved in the translation of the "native's" practical and discursive concepts into the terms of anthropology's conceptual apparatus. I am talking about the kind of comparison, more often than not implicit or automatic (and hence uncontrolled), which necessarily includes the anthropologist's discourse as one of its terms, and which starts to be processed from the very first moment of fieldwork, if not well before. Controlling *this* translative comparison between anthropologies is precisely what comprises the art of anthropology.

Today it is undoubtedly commonplace to say that cultural translation is our discipline's distinctive task. But the problem is knowing what precisely is, can, or should be a translation, and how to carry such an operation out. It is here that things start to become tricky, as Talal Asad demonstrated in a noteworthy article (1986). I adopt the radical position, which is I believe the same as Asad's, and that can be summarized as follows: in anthropology, comparison is in the service of translation and not the opposite. Anthropology compares *so as to translate*, and not to explain, justify, generalize, interpret, contextualize, reveal the unconscious, say what goes without saying, and so forth. I would add that to translate is always to betray, as the Italian saying goes. However, a good translation—and here I am paraphrasing Walter Benjamin (or rather Rudolf Pannwitz via Benjamin)[3]—is one that betrays the destination language, not the source

---

3.   Pannwitz in Benjamin in Asad (1986: 157).

language. A good translation is one that allows the alien concepts to deform and subvert the translator's conceptual toolbox so that the *intentio* of the original language can be expressed within the new one.

I shall present a brief account (a translation) of the theory of translation present in Amerindian perspectivism in order to see whether we can succeed in modifying our own ideas about translation—and thus about anthropology—in such a way as to reconstitute the *intentio* of Amerindian anthropology in the language of our own. In doing so I shall make the claim that perspectivism projects an image of translation as a process of controlled equivocation—"controlled" in the sense that walking may be said to be a controlled way of falling. Indigenous perspectivism is a theory of the equivocation, that is, of the referential alterity between homonymie concepts. Equivocation appears here as the mode of communication par excellence between different perspectival positions—and therefore as both condition of possibility and limit of the anthropological enterprise.

PERSPECTIVISM

I use "perspectivism" as a label for a set of ideas and practices found throughout indigenous America and to which I shall refer, for simplicity's sake, as though it were a cosmology. This cosmology imagines a universe peopled by different types of subjective agencies, human as well as nonhuman, each endowed with the same generic type of soul, that is, the same set of cognitive and volitional capacities. The possession of a similar soul implies the possession of similar concepts, which determine that all subjects see things in the same way. In particular, individuals of the same species see each other (and each other only) as humans see themselves, that is, as beings endowed with human figure and habits, seeing their bodily and behavioral aspects in the form of human culture. What changes when passing from one species of subject to another is the "objective correlative," the referent of these concepts: what jaguars see as "manioc beer" (the proper drink of people, jaguar-type or otherwise), humans see as "blood." Where we see a muddy salt-lick on a river bank, tapirs see their big ceremonial house, and so on. Such difference of perspective—not a plurality of views of a single world, but a single view of different worlds—cannot derive from the soul, since the latter is the common original ground of being. Rather, such difference is located in the bodily differences between species, for the body and its affections (in Spinoza's sense, the body's capacities to affect and be affected by other bodies) is the site and instrument of ontological differentiation and referential disjunction.[4]

Hence, where our modern, anthropological multiculturalist ontology is founded on the mutual implication of the unity of nature and the plurality of cultures, the Amerindian conception would suppose a spiritual unity and a corporeal diversity—or, in other words, one "culture," multiple "natures." In this sense, perspectivism is not relativism as we know it—a subjective or cultural relativism—but an objective or natural relativism—a multinaturalism. Cultural relativism imagines a diversity of subjective and partial representations (cultures) referring to an objective and universal nature, exterior to representation. Amerindians, on the other hand, propose a representative or phenomenological unity that is purely pronominal in kind applied to a real radical diversity. (Any species of subject perceives itself and its world in the same way we perceive ourselves and our world. "Culture" is what one sees of oneself when one says "I.")

The problem for indigenous perspectivism is not therefore one of discovering the common referent (say, the planet Venus) to two different representations (say, "Morning Star" and "Evening Star"). On the contrary, it is one of making explicit the equivocation implied in imagining that when the jaguar says "manioc beer" he is referring to the same thing as us (i.e., a tasty, nutritious and heady brew). In other words, perspectivism supposes a constant epistemology and variable ontologies, the same representations and other objects, a single meaning and multiple referents.

Therefore, the aim of perspectivist translation—translation being one of shamanism's principal tasks, as we know (Carneiro da Cunha 1998)—is not that of finding a "synonym" (a co-referential representation) in our human conceptual language for the representations that other species of subject use to speak about one and the same thing. Rather, the aim is to avoid losing sight of the difference concealed within equivocal "homonyms" between our language and that of other species, since we and they are never talking about the same things.

---

4. Accordingly, Amazonian myths deal mostly with the causes and consequences of the species-specific embodiment of different precosmological subjects, all of them conceived as originally similar to "spirits," purely intensive beings in which human and nonhuman aspects are indiscernibly mixed.

This idea may at first sound slightly counterintuitive, for when we start thinking about it, it seems to collapse into its opposite. Here is how Gerald Weiss (1972: 170), for instance, described the Campa world:

> It is a world of relative semblances, where different kinds of beings see the same things differently; thus human eyes can normally see good spirits only in the form of lightning flashes or birds whereas they see themselves in their true human form, and similarly in the eyes of jaguars human beings look like peccaries to be hunted.

Now, the manner in which Weiss "sees things" is not an error but is more precisely an equivocation. The fact that different kinds of beings see the same things differently is but a *consequence* of the fact that different kinds of beings see different things in the same way. The phantasm of the thing-in-itself haunts Weiss's formulation, which actually expresses an inversion of the problem posed by perspectivism—a typically anthropological inversion.

Perspectivism includes a theory of its own description by anthropology—since it is an anthropology. Amerindian ontologies are inherently comparative: they presuppose a comparison between the ways different kinds of bodies "naturally" experience the world as an affectual multiplicity. They are, thus, a kind of inverted anthropology, for the latter proceeds byway of an explicit comparison between the ways different types of mentality "culturally" represent the world, seen as the unitary origin or virtual focus of its different conceptual versions. Hence, a culturalist (anthropological) account of perspectivism necessarily implies the negation or delegitimization of its object, its "retroprojection" (Latour 1996b) as a primitive and fetishized kind of anthropological reasoning.

What I propose as an experimental program is the inversion of this inversion, which starts out from the following question: what would a perspectivist account of anthropological comparison look like? As I lack the space in this essay to reply in full with detailed examples of "controlled equivocation," I will discuss just its general principles.

BODIES AND SOULS

One of the starting points for my first analysis of perspectivism, published in 1996, was an anecdote told by Lévi-Strauss in *Race et histoire*. It illustrates the pessimistic thesis that one of the intrinsic aspects of human nature is the denial of its own universality. A congenital and narcissistic avarice, preventing the attribution of the predicates of human nature to the species as a whole, appears to be part of these predicates. In sum, ethnocentrism, just like good sense (which is perhaps the sociological translation of ethnocentrism) is the best shared thing in the world. Lévi-Strauss ([1952] 1973: 384) illustrates the universality of this antiuniversalist attitude with an anecdote based on Oviedo's History, and which took place in Puerto Rico:

> In the Greater Antilles, some years after the discovery of America, whilst the Spanish were dispatching inquisitional commissions to investigate whether the natives had a soul or not, these very natives were busy drowning the white people they had captured in order to find out, after lengthy observation, whether or not the corpses were subject to putrefaction.

The parable's lesson obeys a familiar ironic format, but is none the less striking. The favoring of one's own humanity at the cost of the humanity of another manifests a similarity with this scorned other. And since the Other of the Same (of the European) is revealed to be the same as the Other of the Other (of the Indian), the Same ends up revealing itself—unknowingly—to be exactly the same as the Other.

The anecdote was recounted by the author in *Tristes tropiques*. There it illustrates the cosmological shock produced in sixteenth-century Europe by the discovery of America. The moral of the tale continues to be that of the previous book, namely the mutual incomprehension between Indians and Spaniards, equally deaf to the humanity of their unheard-of others. But Lévi-Strauss introduces an asymmetry, observing tongue-in-cheek that, in their investigations into the humanity of the other, the Whites invoked the social sciences, while the Indians placed more trust in the natural sciences. The former came to the conclusion that the Indians were animals, while the latter were content to suspect that the Whites were gods. "In equal ignorance," concludes the author, the latter was an attitude more befitting of human beings (Lévi-Strauss 1955: 81–83).

Therefore, despite sharing an equal ignorance about the Other, the Other of the Other was *not* exactly the same as the Other of the Same. — It was in pondering this difference that I began to formulate the hypothesis that indigenous perspectivism situated the crucial differences between the diversity of subjects on the plane of the body and not the spirit. For the Europeans, the ontological diacritic is the soul (are Indians humans or animals?). For the Indians, it is the body (are Europeans humans or spirits?). The Europeans never doubted that the Indians had bodies. After all, animals have them too. In turn, the Indians never doubted that the Europeans had souls. Animals and spirits have them too. In sum, European ethnocentrism consisted in doubting whether other bodies have the same souls as they themselves (today we would call the soul "the mind," and the sixteenth-century theological problem would now be the philosophical "problem of other minds"). Amerindian ethnocentrism, on the contrary, consisted in doubting whether other souls had the same bodies.

MISTAKING ANTHROPOLOGY

This anecdote from the Antilles casts some light on one of the core elements of the perspectivist "message"—the idea of difference being inscribed in bodies, and the idea of the body as a dispositional system of affectability (do Europeans putrefy?) rather than as a material morphology. It was only very recently, though, that it dawned on me that the anecdote was not simply "about" perspectivism, it was *itself* perspectivist, instantiating the same framework or structure manifest in the innumerable Amerindian myths thematizing interspecific perspectivism. Here I have in mind the type of myth where, for example, the human protagonist becomes lost deep in the forest and arrives at a strange village. There the inhabitants invite him to drink a refreshing gourd of "manioc beer," which he accepts enthusiastically and, to his horrified surprise, his hosts place in front of him a gourd brimming with human blood. Both the anecdote and the myth turn on a type of communicative disjuncture where the interlocutors are not talking about the same thing, and know this. (In the case of the anecdote, the "dialogue" takes place on the plane of Lévi-Strauss comparative reasoning on reciprocal ethnocentrism.) Just as jaguars and humans apply the same name to two very different things, both Europeans and Indians "were talking" about humanity, that is, they were questioning the applicability of this self-descriptive concept to the Other. However, what Europeans and Indians understood to be the concept's defining criterion (its intension and consequently its extension) was radically different. In sum, both Lévi-Strauss's anecdote and the myth turn on an equivocation.

If we think about it carefully, the Antilles anecdote is similar to countless others we can come across in the ethnographic literature, or in our own recollections from fieldwork. In actual fact, I think this anecdote encapsulates the anthropological situation or event par excellence, expressing the quintessence of what our discipline is all about. It is possible to discern, for example, in the archi-famous episode of the death of Captain Cook, as analyzed by Marshall Sahlins (1985), a structural transformation of the cross experiments of Puerto Rico. We are presented with two versions of the archetypical anthropological motive, that is, an intercultural equivocality. Life, as always, imitates art—events mime myth, history rehearses structure.

I shall propose one or two more examples of equivocation below. But what I wish to make clear is that equivocation is not just one among other possible pathologies that threaten communication between the anthropologist and the "native"—such as linguistic incompetence, ignorance of context, lack of personal empathy, indiscretion, literalist ingenuity, commercialization of information, lies, manipulation, bad faith, forgetfulness, and sundry other deformations or shortcomings that may afflict anthropological discursivity at an empirical level. In contrast to these contingent pathologies, the equivocation is a properly transcendental category of anthropology, a constitutive dimension of the discipline's project of cultural translation. It expresses a *de jure* structure, a figure immanent to anthropology.[5] It is not merely a negative facticity, but a condition of possibility of anthropological discourse—that which justifies the existence of anthropology (*quid juris?* as in the Kantian question). To translate is to situate oneself in the space of the equivocation and to dwell there. It is not to unmake the equivocation (since this would be to suppose it never existed in the first place) but precisely the opposite is true. To translate is to emphasize or potentialize the equivocation, that is, to open and widen the space imagined not to exist between the conceptual languages in contact, a space that the equivocation precisely concealed. The equivocation is not that which impedes the relation, but that which founds and impels it: a difference in perspective. To translate is to presume that an equivocation always exists; it is to communicate by differences, instead of silencing the Other by presuming a univocality—the essential similarity—between what the Other and We are saying.

Michael Herzfeld recently observed that "anthropology is about misunderstandings, including anthropologists' own misunderstandings, because these are usually the outcome of the mutual incommensurability of different notions of

---

5. This idea is inspired by a beautiful page of Deleuze and Guattari's *Quest-ce que la philosophie?* (1991: 53–54).

common sense—our object of study" (2001: 2). I agree, but I would simply insist on the point that, if anthropology exists (*de jure*), it is precisely (and only) because that which Herzfeld calls "common sense" is not common. I would also add that the incommensurability of the clashing "notions," far from being an impediment to their comparability, is precisely what enables and justifies it (as Michael Lambek argued [1998]).

Since it is only worth comparing the incommensurable, comparing the commensurable is a task for accountants, not anthropologists. Finally I should add that I conceive the idea of "misunderstanding" in the specific sense of equivocality found in Amerindian perspectivist cosmology. An equivocation is not just a "failure to understand" (*Oxford English Dictionary*, 1989), but a failure to understand that understandings are necessarily not the same, and that they are not related to imaginary ways of "seeing the world" but to the real worlds that are being seen. In Amerindian cosmology, the real world of the different species depends on their points of view, since the "world in general" consists of the different species themselves. The real world is the abstract space of divergence between species as points of view. Because there are no points of view onto things, things and beings are the points of view themselves (as Deleuze would say, 1988: 203). The question for Indians, therefore, is not one of knowing "how monkeys see the world" (Cheney and Seyfarth 1990), but what world is expressed through monkeys, of what world they are the point of view. I believe this is a lesson from which our own anthropology can learn.

Anthropology, then, is about misunderstandings. But as Roy Wagner insightfully said about his early relations with the Daribi: "their misunderstanding of me was not the same as my misunderstanding of them" ([1975] 1981: 20). The crucial point here is not the empirical fact that misunderstandings exist, but the transcendental fact that it was not the *same* misunderstanding.

The question is not discovering who is wrong, and still less who is deceiving whom. An equivocation is not an error, a mistake, or a deception. Instead, it is the very foundation of the relation that it implicates, and that is always a relation with an exteriority. An error or deception can only be determined as such from within a given language game, while an equivocation is what unfolds in the *interval* between different language games. Deceptions and errors suppose premises that are already constituted—and constituted as homogenous—while an equivocation not only supposes the heterogeneity of the premises at stake, it poses them as heterogenic and presupposes them as premises. An equivocation determines the premises rather than being determined by them. Consequently, equivocations do not belong to the world of dialectical contradiction, since their synthesis is disjunctive and infinite. An equivocation is indissoluble, or rather, recursive: taking it as an object determines another equivocation "higher up," and so on ad infinitum.

The equivocation, in sum, is not a subjective failure, but a tool of objectification. It is not an error nor an illusion—we need not to imagine objectification in the post-Enlightenment and moralizing language of reification or fetishization (today better known as "essentialization"). Instead, the equivocation is the limiting condition of every social relation, a condition that itself becomes superobjectified in the extreme case of so-called interethnic or intercultural relations, where the language games diverge maximally. It goes without saying, this divergence includes the relation between anthropological discourse and native discourse. Thus, the anthropological concept of culture, for example, as Wagner argued, is the equivocation that emerges as an attempt to solve intercultural equivocality, and it is equivocal in so far as it follows, among other things, from the "paradox created by imagining a culture for people who do not imagine it for themselves" ([1975] 1981: 27). Accordingly, even when misunderstandings are transformed into understandings—like when the anthropologist transforms his initial bewilderment at the natives' ways into "their culture," or when the natives understand that what the Whites called, say, "gifts" were in reality "commodities"—even here such understandings persist in being not the same. The Other of the Others is always other. If the equivocation is not an error, an illusion or a lie, but the very form of the relational positivity of difference, its opposite is not the truth, but the *univocal*, as the claim to the existence of a unique and transcendent meaning. The error or illusion par excellence consists, precisely, in imagining that the univocal exists beneath the equivocal, and that the anthropologist is its ventriloquist.

BEING OUT THERE

An equivocation is not an error—the Spanish theologians, the Indians of Puerto Rico, the Hawaiian warriors, and the British sailors could not have been all (and entirely) wrong. I now wish to present another example of an equivocation, this time taken from an anthropological analysis. This example has been extracted from a recent Americanist monograph of the highest quality—I wish strongly to emphasize this—written by a colleague whom I admire greatly. Consider, then, this metacommentary by Greg Urban in his fine book *Metaphysical community*, on Shokleng community-making discourse. Explaining discourse's sociogenetic powers, Urban (1996: 65) observes that:

> Unlike the Serra Geral mountain range or jaguars or araucaria pines, the organization of society is not a thing that is out there, waiting to be understood. The organization must be created, and it is something elusive, intangible that does the creating. It is culture—here understood as circulating discourse.

The author is defending a moderate constructionist position. Society, qua Shokleng social organization with its groups and emblems, is not something *given*, as traditional anthropologists used to think. Rather, it is something *created* through discourse. But discourse's power has limits: geographical features and biological essences are out there. They are, so to speak, bought ready-made, not made at home through circulating discourse. It must be admitted that there is nothing in the least bit shocking about Urban's commentary. Indeed, it seems eminently reasonable, and canonically anthropological. Moreover, it also accords neatly with what some equally reasonable philosophers look to teach us about the structure of reality. Take the doctrine of John Searle (1995), for example, which argues that two and only two types of facts exist: "brute facts," such as hills, rain and animals, and "institutional facts," such as money, iceboxes or marriage. The latter are made or constructed (performed) facts, since their sufficient reason coincides entirely with their meaning. The former, however, are given facts, since their existence is independent of the values attributed to them. This may be understood in a couple of words: nature and culture.

However, what do the Shokleng have to say about the matter? At the end of reading *Metaphysical community*, the reader cannot but feel a certain unease in noting that Urban's splitting of the world—into a given realm of jaguars and pine trees, and a constructed world of groups and emblems—is not the split made by the Shokleng. Actually, it is almost exactly the inverse. The indigenous myths magnificently analyzed by Urban tell, among other things, that the original Shokleng, after sculpting the future jaguars and tapirs in araucaria wood, gave these animals their characteristic pelts by covering them with the diacritical marks pertaining to the clanic-ceremonial groups: spots for the jaguar, stripes for the tapir (1996: 156-58). In other words, it is social organization that was "out there," and the jaguars and tapirs that were created or performed by it. The institutional fact created the brute fact. Unless, of course, the brute fact is the clanic division of society, and the institutional fact is the jaguars of the forest. For the Shokleng, in fact, culture is the given and nature is the constructed. For them, if the cat is on the mat, or rather, if the jaguar is in the jungle, it is because someone put it there.

In sum, we are faced with an equivocation. The discordant distribution of the given and the constructed, which inexorably separates Shokleng discourse on the real from anthropological discourse on Shokleng discourse, is never explicitly recognized as such by Urban. The solution that he implicitly offers for this chiasma is anthropology's classical solution. It consists of a highly characteristic operation of translation, which involves the metaphysical demotion of the indigenous distribution of the world to the condition of metaphor: "Creation of the animal world is a metaphor for the creation of community" (ibid.: 158). Where would we be without this statutory distinction between the literal and the metaphoric, which strategically blocks any direct confrontation between the discourses of anthropologist and native, thereby avoiding any major unpleasantness? Urban deems that the creation of community is literal, and that of jaguars, metaphoric. Or rather, that the first is literally metaphoric and the second metaphorically literal. The creation of community is literal, but the community thereby created is metaphoric (not "something out there"). Jaguars, they will be pleased to know, are literal, but their creation by the community is of course metaphoric.

We do not know whether the Shokleng concur with the anthropologist in considering the creation of jaguars and tapirs as a metaphor for the creation of the community. We could hazard a guess that probably they do not. On the other hand, Urban deems that the Shokleng do concur with him about the metaphorical nature of the community created by themselves, or better (and literally), by their discourse. Unlike other anthropologists or (other) peoples encumbered by a more essentialist mentality, the Shokleng are aware, thinks Urban, that their division into (nominally but not really) exogamie groups is not a brute fact. Rather, it is a metadiscursive representation of the community, which merely deploys the idiom of affinity and interfamily alliance in a "playful" way (ibid.: 168). Thus, the anthropologist agrees with the Shokleng construction of the community as constructed, but disagrees with their positing of jaguars as constructed.

Later in his work, Urban interprets indigenous ceremonies as a way of representing the community in terms of relations within the family. The family is described in its turn (though we do not know whether by the anthropologist

or by the natives) as an elementary unit founded on the "psychologically primitive" relations between the sexes and generations (ibid.: 188–93). Society, meta-
phorized into its emblematic divisions and its collective rituals, is therefore
imagined either as the result of an alliance between families, or, at a deeper
("primitive") level, as a nuclear family. But the family does not seem to be,
in Urban's eyes at least, a metaphor *of* anything else—it is literal. It is a given
that usefully serves as a metaphor *for* less literal things. The family is a naturally appropriate image, due to its cognitive salience and affective pregnancy
(ibid.: 171, 192–93). It is thus more real than the community. Society is naturally metaphoric, the family is socially literal. The nuclear family, the concrete
bonds of conjugality and filiation, are a fact, not a fabrication. Kinship—not
the metaphoric and intergroup kind of the community, but the literal and in-
terindividual kind of the family—is something just as out there as the animals
and plants. Kinship is something without whose help, furthermore, discourse
would be unable to construct the community. Indeed, it may even be out there
for the same reasons as the animals and plants—by being, that is, a "natural"
phenomenon.

Urban claims that anthropologists, in general, "have been the dupes" of peoples who may have taken their own metadiscourse on social organization "too
seriously," and who thus proved to be overliteralists, that is, *horresco referens*, essentialists (1996: 137, 168–69). It may be that anthropology really has adopted
a literalist attitude vis-à-vis the essence of "society." But in counterpart, in terms
of indigenous discourse on "nature" at least, anthropology has never been duped
by the native or, above all, about the native. The so-called symbolist interpretation (Skorupski 1976) of primitive metaphysics has been in discursive circulation ever since Durkheim. It is this same interpretation that Urban applies to
Shokleng discourse on jaguars—the literality of which he rejects—but rejects
in favour of a completely literalist interpretation of the Western discourse on
"things out there." In other words, if the Shokleng concur (for the sake of hypothesis) with Urbans anti-Durkheimian ontology of society, Urban concurs
with Durkheim about the ontology of nature. What he is advocating is simply
the extension of the symbolist attitude to the case of discourses about society, which thereby ceases to be the referential substrate of crypto-metaphoric
propositions about nature (as it was in Durkheim). Now society too is metaphoric. The impression left behind is that discursive constructionism has to reify
discourse—and, to all appearances, the family— in order to be able to de-reify
society.

Was Urban wrong—was he making a false claim—in declaring that mountains and natural species are out there, while society is a cultural product? I do not believe so. But I do not think he was right either. As far as any anthropological point is at stake here, the interest of his declaration lies in the fact that it counterinvents the equivocation it enables, and that counterinvention gives it its objectifying power. Urban's professed faith in the ontological self-subsistence of mountains and animals and on the institutional demiurgy of discourse is, in the final analysis, indispensable *for us* to be able properly to evaluate the enormity of the gap separating indigenous and anthropological ontologies.

I believe that I can indeed speak of an error or mistake on Urban's part, since I am situated within the same language game as him—anthropology. I can therefore legitimately say (though I certainly may be wrong) that Urban was perpetrating an *anthropological* error by failing to take into account the equivocation within which he was implicated. The discordant distribution of the given and constructed parts between Urban and the Shokleng is not an anodyne choice, a mere swapping of signals leaving the terms of the problem untouched. There is "all the difference in the world" (Wagner [1975] 1981: 51) between a world where the primordial is experienced as naked transcendence, pure antianthropic alterity (the *non*-constructed, the *non*-instituted, that which is exterior to custom and discourse) and a world of immanent humanity, where the primordial takes on human form (which does not make it necessarily tranquilizing; for there where everything is human, the human is something else entirely). Describing this world as though it were an illusory version of our own, unifying the two via a reduction of one to the conventions of the other, is to imagine an overly simple form of relation between them. This explanatory ease ends up producing all sorts of uneasy complications, since this desire for ontological monism usually pays with an inflationary emission of epistemological dualisms—emic and eric, metaphoric and literal, conscious and unconscious, representation and reality, illusion and truth, et cetera.

"Perspective is the wrong metaphor," fulminates Stephen Tyler in his normative manifesto for postmodern ethnography (1986: 137). The equivocation that articulates Shokleng discourse with the discourse of their anthropologist leads me to conclude, to the contrary, that metaphor is perhaps the wrong perspective. This is certainly the case when anthropology finds itself face-to-face with a cosmology that is itself literally perspectivist.

NOT ALL MEN

I conclude by narrating a small translational equivoque in which I became involved a few years back. Milton Nascimento, the celebrated Brazilian musician,
had made a journey to Amazonia, guided by some friends of mine who work
for an environmentalist NGO (Non Governmental Organization). One of the
high points of the trip had been a two-week stay among the Cashinahua of the
Jordão river. Milton was overwhelmed by the warm welcome received from the
Indians. Back on the Brazilian coast, he decided to use an indigenous word as
a tide for the album he was recording. The word chosen was *txai*, which the
Cashinahua had used abundantly in addressing Milton and the other members
of the expedition.

When the album *Txai* was due to be released, one of my friends from the
NGO asked me to write a sleeve note. He wanted me to explain to Milton's fans
what the title meant, and to say something about the sense of fraternal solidarity
expressed by the term *txai* and its meaning "brother," and so on.

I replied that it was impossible to write the note in these terms, since *txai* may
mean just about everything except, precisely, "brother." I explained that *txai* is a
term used by a man to address certain kinsfolk, for example, his cross-cousins, his
mother's father, his daughter's children, and, in general, following the Cashinahua system of "prescriptive alliance," any man whose sister ego treats as an equivalent to his wife, and vice versa (Kensinger 1995: 157–74). In sum, *txai* means
something akin to "brother-in-law." It refers to a man's real or possible brothers-
in-law, and, when used as a friendly vocative to speak to non-Cashinahua outsid-
ers, the implication is that the latter are kinds of affines. Moreover, I explained
that one does not need to be a friend to be *txai*. It suffices to be an outsider, or
even—and even better—an enemy. Thus, the Inca in Cashinahua mythology are
at once monstrous cannibals and archetypical *txai* with whom, we should note in
passing, one should not or indeed cannot marry (McCallum 1991).

But none of this would work, complained my friend. Milton thinks that *txai*
means "brother," and besides it would be fairly ridiculous to give the record a
title whose translation is "*Brother-in-law*," would it not? Perhaps, I conceded.
But do not expect me to skip over the fact that *txai* signifies "other" or affine.
The end result of the conversation was that the album continued to be called
Txai, and the sleeve note ended up being written by someone else.

Note that the problem with this misunderstanding about *txai* does not
lie in the fact that Milton Nascimento and my friend were wrong concerning

the sense of the Cashinahua word. On the contrary, the problem is they were *right*—in a certain sense. In other words, they were "equivocated." The Cashinahua, like so many other indigenous peoples of Amazonia, use terms whose most direct translations are "brother-in-law" or "cross cousin" in various contexts in which Brazilians, and other peoples from the Euro-Christian tradition, would really expect something like "brother." In this sense, Milton was right. Had I remembered, I would have reminded my interlocutor that the equivocation had already been anticipated by an ethnologist of the Cashinahua. Talking about the difference between the social philosophy of this people and that held by the surrounding Whites, Barbara Keifenheim concludes: "The message 'all men are brothers' encountered a world where the most noble expression of human relations is the relation between brothers-in-law . . ." (1992: 91). Precisely, but it is for this very reason that "brother" is not an adequate translation for *txai*. If there exists anyone with whom a Cashinahua man would be reluctant to call "*txai*," it is his own brother. *Txai* means "affine," not "consanguine," even when used for purposes similar to our own, when we address a stranger as "brother." While the purposes maybe similar, the premises are decidedly not so.

My translational mishap will undoubtedly sound completely banal to the ears of Americanists who have been interested for a long time in the innumerable symbolic resonances of the idiom of affinity in Amazonia. The interest of this anecdote in the present context, however, is that it seems to me to express, in the actual difference between the idioms of "brother" and "brother-in-law," two inverse modes of conceiving the principle of translative comparison: the multiculturalist mode of anthropology and the multinaturalist mode of perspectivism.

The powerful Western metaphors of brotherhood privilege certain (not all) logical properties of this relation. What are siblings, in our culture? They are individuals identically related to a third term, their genitors or their functional analogs. The relation between two siblings derives from their equivalent relation to an origin that encompasses them, and whose identity identifies them. This common identity means that siblings occupy the same point of view onto an exterior world. Deriving their similitude from a similar relation to a same origin, siblings will have "parallel" relations (to use an anthropological image) to everything else. Thus, people who are unrelated, when conceived to be related in a generic sense, are so in terms of a common humanity that makes all of us kin, that is, siblings, or at least, to continue to use the previous image, parallel cousins, classificatory brothers: children of Adam, of the Church, of the Nation, of the Genome, or of any other figure of transcendence. All men are brothers to some extent, since brotherhood is in itself the general form of the relation. Two partners in any relation are defined as connected in so far as they can be conceived to *have something in common*, that is, as being in the *same* relation to a third term. To relate is to assimilate, to unify, and to identify.

The Amazonian model of the relation could not be more different to this. "Different" is the apposite word, since Amazonian ontologies postulate difference rather than identity as the principle of relationality. It is precisely the difference between the two models that grounds the relation I am attempting to establish between them (and here we are already using the Amerindian mode of comparing and translating).

The common word for the relation, in Amazonian worlds, is the term translated by "brother-in-law" or "cross cousin." This is the term we call people we do not know what to call, those with whom we wish to establish a generic relation. In sum, "cousin/brother-in-law" is the term that creates a relation where none existed. It is the form through which the unknown is made known.

What are the logical properties of the connection of affinity highlighted in these indigenous usages? As a general model of relationship, the brother-in-law connection appears as a cross connection with a mediating term, which is seen in diametrically opposite ways by the two poles of the relation: my sister is your wife and/or vice versa. Here, the parties involved find themselves united by that which divides them, linked by that which separates them (Strathern 1992c: 99–100). My relation with my brother-in-law is based on my being in *another* kind of relation to his relation with my sister or my wife. The Amerindian relation is a difference of perspective. While we tend to conceive the action of relating as a discarding of differences in favor of similarities, indigenous thought sees the process from another angle: the opposite of difference is not identity but *indifference*. Hence, establishing a relation—like that of the Cashinahua with Milton Nascimento—is to differentiate indifference, to insert a difference where indifference was presumed. No wonder, then, that animals are so often conceived as affinally related to humans in Amazonia. Blood is to humans as manioc beer is to jaguars, in exactly the same way as a sister to me is a wife to my brother-in-law. The many Amerindian myths featuring interspecific marriages and discussing the difficult relationships between the in-marrying affine and his/her allospecific parents-in-law, simply compound the two analogies into a single one.

The implications of these two models of social relationship for an anthropological theory of translation are evident. Such implications are not metaphorical.

If anything, the opposite happens to be the case, since relations of meaning are social relations. If the anthropologist starts out from the metaprinciple that "all men are brothers," he (or she) is presupposing that his (or her) discourse and that of the native manifest a relation of an ultimately brotherly nature. What founds the relation of meaning between the two discourses—and therefore justifies the operation of translation—is their *common referent*, of which both present parallel visions. Here, the idea of an external nature that is logically and chronologically prior to the cultures that partially represent it acts out the role of the parent who founds the relation between two siblings. We could imagine here a hierarchical interpretation of this brotherly parallelism, with the anthropologist assuming the role of literal and rational elder brother and the native his metaphoric and symbolic younger brother Or, on the contrary, we could adopt a radically egalitarian interpretation, with the two protagonists seen as twins, and so forth. Whatever the case, in this model translation is only possible because the discourses are composed of synonyms. They express the same parental reference to some (indeed any) kind of transcendence with the status of nature (physis, socius, gene, cognition, discourse, et cetera). Here, to translate is to isolate what the discourses share in common, something that is only "in them" because it is (and was already before them) "out there." The differences between the discourses amount to no more than the *residue* that precludes a perfect translation, that is, an absolute identification overlap between them. To translate is to presume redundancy.

However, if all men are brothers-in-law rather than brothers—that is, if the image of the social connection is not that of sharing something in common (a "something in common" acting as foundation), but, on the contrary, is that of the difference between the terms of the relation, or better, of the difference between the differences that constitute the terms of the relation—then a relation can only exist between what differs and in so far as it differs. In this case, translation becomes an operation of differentiation—a production of difference—that connects the two discourses to the precise extent to which they are *not* saying the same thing, in so far as they point to discordant exteriorities beyond the equivocal homonyms between them. Contrary to Derrida, I believe the *hors-texte* perfectly well exists, *de facto* and *de jure*—but contrary to the positivists, I think each text has its own *hors-texte*. In this case, cultural translation is not a process of induction (finding the common points in detriment to the differences), much less a process of *deduction* (applying a priori a principle of natural unification to cultural diversity in order to determine or decree its meaning). Rather, it is a process of the type that the philosopher Gilbert Simondon ([1964] 1995: 32) called *transduction*:

> Transduction functions as the inversion of the negative into a positive: it is precisely that which determines the non-identity between the terms, that which makes them disparate (in the sense held by this term in the theory of vision) which is integrated with the system of resolution and becomes the condition of signification; transduction is characterized by the fact that the outcome of this operation is a concrete fabric including all the initial terms . . .

In this model of translation, which I believe converges with that present in Amerindian perspectivism, difference is therefore a condition of signification and not a hindrance. The identity between the "beer" of the jaguar and the "beer" of humans is posed only the better to see the difference between jaguars and humans. As in stereoscopic vision, it is necessary that the two eyes not see the *same* given thing in order for another thing (the real thing in the field of vision) to be able to be *seen*, that is, constructed or counterinvented. In this case, to translate is to presume a difference. The difference, for example, between the two modes of translation I have presented to you here. But perhaps this is an equivocation.

CHAPTER FOUR

Zeno and the Art of Anthropology
Of Lies, Beliefs, Paradoxes, and Other Truths

TRANSLATED BY ANTONIA WALFORD

It's always night, or we wouldn't need light.
– Thelonious Monk, from Thomas Pynchon, *Against the Day*

The deliberately paradoxical nature of this symposium's title ["Comparative relativism"] encapsulates a distinctive concern of some of today's most vitally important intellectual endeavors. There is only one of these that I can or should consider as my own untransferable matter of concern—the endeavor seeking performatively to redefine anthropology as consisting essentially of (a) a theory of peoples' ontological autodetermination and (b) a practice of the permanent decolonization of thought. I am aware that the very word *anthropology* may be jeopardized by this redefinition, given that it belongs firmly among the conditions of our current civilizational deadlock (or should I say, impending downfall), which bears a more than fortuitous relation to our unrelenting determination that the world continues to revolve around the human in its various historico-conceptual guises. We could perhaps, in this case, rename the discipline "field geophilosophy" or (in reference to our armchair moments) "speculative ontography." In any case, the relevant onomastics would continue to be Greek—a detail that, there is little need to add, is neither accidental nor inconsequential from an anthropological point of view.

The question for me is how to give the expression *comparative relativism* a meaning specific to social anthropology. Much of my work—at least since I swapped field geophilosophy for ontographical speculation—has consisted in analyzing relativism not as an epistemological puzzle but as an anthropological topic, amenable to translative comparison (or controlled equivocation) rather than to critical adjudication.[1] The Amerindian-derived conceit of "perspectival multinaturalism" emerged as the result of an attempt to contrast anthropological and indigenous modes of perceiving analogies between domains; in other words, to *compare comparisons* (Viveiros de Castro 1998a). The purpose was to trace a line of flight past those infernal dichotomies—unity/multiplicity, universalism/relativism, representation/reality, and nature/culture (to name but a few)—that are like the bars of our metaphysical cage, so as to be able to have a look at that cage (as it were) from the outside.

In the present context, I want to consider the idea of anthropology *as* comparative relativism and approach the theme by means of four "formulas"—four quotations—that illustrate what I intend in various ways. My inspiration for this approach is an article by Gilles Deleuze (1986), "On four poetic formulas that might summarize the Kantian philosophy." I will keep to four formulas for reasons of paraphrastic symmetry. That anthropology is perhaps the most Kantian of all the humanities is merely a coincidence as well. However, the decision to approach the theme by means of quotations is not contingent.[2] Recourse to examples as a definitional tactic makes evident the "whatever being" (*qualunque, quodlibet)* nature of the passages chosen (Agamben 1993: 8–10).[3] They are neither individual nor generic, but exemplary or singular. They are also somewhat indirect, in the sense that they "exemplify" anthropology in terms that are, at least in part, restrictive: some quotations amount to extrinsic negations of anthropology that would paralyze it; others suggest intrinsic negativities (virtual or actual) that would propel it. All of the passages chosen evoke the idea of

---

1. For "controlled equivocation," see Viveiros de Castro 2004b (Chapter 3, this volume).

2. For another recent instance of such recourse to quotations, see Bruno Latour and Emilie Hache (2010).

3. For an encapsulated discussion of the terms, see Max Statkiewicz and Valerie Reed (2005). It is "the lack of any characteristic," they explain, that "Agamben ascribes to what he calls *qua- lunque essere* or 'whatever being.' It is in fact its original Latin designation that reveals best the 'nature' of 'whatever being': *quodlibet ens . . . quodlibet* is what is *loved* irrespective of any generic property." (ibid.: 801)

belief, which of course is profoundly implicated, in all possible senses (and especially the worse ones), in the majority of arguments that connect the themes of anthropology, comparison, and relativism.

The use of quotations here does not reflect merely a penchant for the fragment, which I do admit to. Like a postmodern intellectual or an Amazonian Indian, I think that everything has already been spoken—which does not mean, however, that everything has already been *said*. But I do not regard this effort as just one more *collage*, it is rather a *bricolage* (no etymological connection), rearranging things that have been spoken so that they say something relatively—which is to say, comparatively—new.

I

> *We Western liberal intellectuals should accept the fact that we*
> *have to start from where we are, and that this means that*
> *there are lots of visions which we simply cannot take seriously.*
> – Richard Rorty, *Solidarity or objectivity?* (1985)

If at any point it was possible to feel solidarity with the antifoundationalist pragmatism of Richard Rorty (1991b, 21–34), the sentence quoted above seems to indicate that he and we anthropologists are not on the same "side."[4] Clifford Geertz's (1986) arguments against what Rorty was proud to call his own "ethnocentrism" are well known; there is no need to rehearse them here.[5] My intention in highlighting this passage is principally heuristic. Can we learn something about anthropology from it?

---

4.   Rorty's "solidarity" means "culture," his "objectivity" means "nature"; and he is all for solidarity, just as we anthropologists have been known to be very partial to culture.

5.   Geertz likens Rorty's ethnocentrism to certain positions assumed by Lévi-Strauss in "Race and culture" (1992). It seems to me that Geertz misses a crucial difference. Rorty is extolling the virtues of ethnocentrism from the vantage point of a civilization that imagines itself as increasingly dominant: "... the gradual expansion of the imagination of those in power, and their gradual willingness to use the term 'we' to include more and more different sorts of people" (Rorty 1991a: 207). Lévi-Strauss, on the other hand, sees in a certain amount of ethnocentrism a society's protective reflex against its absorption by hegemonic projects like those for which Rorty elected himself spokesperson.

I do not know of anything obviously equivalent to this passage in the anthropological literature, with which I am more familiar; perhaps Ernest Gellner or Adam Kuper has said similar things. Rorty's sentence does bring to mind, however, that marvelous observation at the beginning of chapter four of *Witchcraft, oracles, and magic among the Azande* ([1937] 1976): "Witches, as the Azande conceive them, cannot exist." E. E. Evans-Pritchard's painstakingly detailed monograph was written exactly to resolve this problem: given that witches (as the Azande conceive them) "cannot" exist (as we conceive of possibility and existence), how then can the anthropologist take seriously the conceptions of the Azande concerning the existence of witches? How can the anthropologist reconceive—in other words, reconceptualize—witches so that they can assume a possible mode of existence—in other words, an interest—for us? (We will leave the question of who "we" are for the next paragraph.) If Evans-Pritchard's solution no longer satisfies us today, he retains the merit of having at least tried to steer us away from "where we are" and toward the Azande. Rorty could be seen as perhaps confronting the same general type of problem; only his reply is purely negative (and dismissive). Each word of his admonition converges to a perfect antidefinition of anthropology.

It is not necessary for the anthropologist to imagine him- or herself as a postcolonialist critic to feel excluded from Rorty's "we." In any case, it sounds more like an imposition than an acknowledgment. Geertz, it is true, would recognize himself willingly as a "Western liberal intellectual" (which is why, apart from their long-standing friendship, his critical dialogues with Rorty have a somewhat chummy tone). But I do not see any relation of consequence between the anthropological point of view and a self-description of this sort by a Western intellectual. The awkwardness, however, resides not in the subject of the phrase but in its self-regarding metapragmatic structure. Rorty speaks here for his internal public, his "tribespeople"—there exist only liberal intellectuals in the United States, apparently—who already are where he is and who are, by implication, *very* different from "them." This "them" are those others who do not regard themselves as liberals, perhaps not as "intellectuals" either, nor even (as Rorty is an author who is read far and wide) as "Western." The problem is that "we anthropologists" are in general known for our inability to say "we" with any self-satisfaction. That incapacity derives from our subject matter and addressee: anthropologists speak principally *about* "them"—those who are more than ready to say "we are not you"—and increasingly we speak *to* "them." And in both cases our business is to ask: *Who* are "we"? Who *says* "we" (and when, or how)?

Our problem, in sum, is to determine the multiple conditions (not necessarily convergent) under which a "we" is possible. Rorty's relativism of the rich and pragmatism of the powerful could not even begin to help us here, unless as a privative contrast: we are not t/his kind of "we."

Now, what is the meaning of this idea we are enjoined to accept—that "we have to start from where we are"? Without question that is where we have to *start* from, but saying so does not in any way inform us of where we could, should, or want to *arrive*. Neither does it tell us where *exactly* we are. Regarding this point, I see many more similarities between the "ethnographic effect" so beautifully described by Marilyn Strathern (1999) and the problem—as pragmatic as one could ask for—formulated by J. M. Coetzee just before he transforms himself into Elizabeth Costello:

> There is first of all the problem of the opening, namely, how to get us from where we are, which is, as yet, nowhere, to the far bank . . . People solve such problems every day. They solve them, and, having solved them push on. . . . Let us assume that, however it may have been done, it is done. . . . We have left behind the territory in which we were. We are in the far territory, where we want to be. (Coetzee 2004: 1)

In other words, we have to start from where we are, because here (on the Western Bank, as it were) is *not* where we want to be. On the contrary, we want anthropology to reach and remain in the far territory, out in the open, away from the ironical recesses of the liberal intellect and thus faithful to the project of exteriorizing reason—the project that, *nolens volens*, insistently takes our discipline out of the suffocation of the self. The viability of an authentic endo-anthropology, a desideratum that today finds itself at the top of the disciplinary agenda, for multiple reasons—some of them even reasonable—seems to me, therefore, to depend crucially on the theoretical airing that exo-anthropology has always enabled, it being an outdoor or "field" science in the sense that really matters.

But back to Rorty's antidefinition: calling that which "we" cannot take seriously "lots of visions" is a less than subtle manner of begging the question. "Lots of visions" can only be a Pandora's box, full to the brim with fantasies, delusions, and hallucinations—worlds worthy of "the Nazis or the Amazonians" (1991b: 31). As we all know, lies are multiple (and the devil is their father), but the truth is One (as God). It is true that pragmatism does uphold an intersubjective, consensual, and ethnocentric conception of truth; but the pragmatist's truth is still One—which leads us to conclude that what lies outside the "conversational" sphere of the pragmatic community of similars is the essence of nontruth in all its proteic monstrosity. Rorty's quantifier, "lots of," is in this respect more crucial than its complement, "visions." If there are lots of visions, it follows that we *simply* cannot take them seriously. There is nothing less simple or more dismissive than this adverb, which can (or must) be taken here in its two main senses: that of facility (it is easy not to take seriously this motley bunch of visions) and of peremptoriness (it is imperative not to take them seriously).

It is here that we arrive at the nucleus of Rorty's antidefinition. It is the very subject matter of anthropology that Rorty declares impossible to take seriously—and the discipline indeed defines itself by not accepting any liberal prohibition such as Rorty's. Anthropology is that Western intellectual endeavor dedicated to taking seriously what Western intellectuals cannot, so Rorty tells us, take seriously. Anthropology takes very seriously as well the question of *how* to take seriously what Rorty refers to as "visions." The constitutive problem of the discipline is how to acquire the tools that allow us to do so. Anthropology faces a double task. First, it must construct a concept of seriousness (a way of taking things seriously) that is not tied to the notion of belief or of any other "propositional attitudes" that have representations as their object. The anthropologist's idea of seriousness must not be tied to the hermeneutics of allegorical meanings or to the immediative illusion of discursive echolalia. Anthropologists must allow that "visions" are not beliefs, not consensual views, but rather worlds seen objectively: not *worldviews,* but *worlds of vision* (and not vision only—these are worlds perceivable by senses other than vision and are objects of extrasensory conception as well). Second, and reciprocally, anthropology must find a way *not* to take seriously certain *other* "visions." The reciprocity here is fundamental, for while we strive to take seriously things that are far from or outside of us, almost all of the things that we must *not* take seriously are near to or inside of us. "Ethnocentrism . . . is essential to serious, non-fantastical thought," Rorty declares (1991b: 30); there is always a moment in which the ironist begins to talk of seriousness—the moment when he starts to refer to himself. The famous Deleuzian distinction between humor and irony, so important to Isabelle Stengers's ecology of practices, is germane here. To take seriously what we "cannot" take seriously demands as much sense of humor as its converse, namely not to take seriously what we "simply" cannot *not* take seriously. Relativism is seriously (and serenely) humorous, not self-indulgently ironical.

A final point on this citation: "the Nazis or the Amazonians" appear in Rorty's text as twin *topoi* of alienness, as people who do not share any relevant "premise" with us. The author gives the impression that he sees the Nazis and the Amazonians (also called "primitive tribespeople") as poles indifferently and, therefore, coincidentally antipodal to a pole of lucidity and civility represented by a liberal Western consensus. Speaking as an Amazonianist, I beg to differ: from the point of view of an Amazonian "tribespeople," there are infinitely more things in common—pragmatically speaking—between the Nazis and Western liberal intellectuals than between the former and the Amazonian peoples.

II

> One of the fundamental fantasies of anthropology is that somewhere there must be a life worth living.
> – David Schneider; foreword to Roy Wagner,
> *The curse of the souw* (1967)

After the somewhat haughty tone of the previous citation, this one sounds almost tacky. The flip side of clearheaded American pragmatism, one is tempted to say, is this quality of dreamy sentimentality, a simpleminded readiness to believe in impossible worlds *somewhere,* as in "over the rainbow." As we know, *that* somewhere was, in the end, exactly where we started from—where we were. "There's no place like home"—indeed. And what a dire conclusion that is.

However, I think that David Schneider's observation could be read very differently. It seems to me to contain a very serious, utterly "nonfantastical" thought relative to the project of anthropology. His use of the idea of "fantasy" is the key to the seriousness of the matter, of course.

The respective formulas of Rorty and Schneider could be opposed point for point. First, instead of a "fact" that we "should accept," we have a "fundamental fantasy." A fantasy is not something we are *forced* to accept or reject but something that we *assess* from a pragmatic point of view, in terms of its greater or lesser power to make us think differently, to take us elsewhere so that we might have a more precise idea, by comparison, of our current location. Second, instead of an exhortation to "start from where we are," Schneider's formula points to where we are heading. The unspecified character of his "somewhere" is necessary, not accidental, as far as anthropology is concerned—a determined indetermination, as it were. Third, the object of the fundamental fantasy, its "aboutness," is not "lots of visions" but "a life": a vital difference, it seems to me. And the question raised is that of the real value of this life; instead of lots of visions that we *simply* cannot take seriously, we have a life *really* worth living. Perhaps there are lives not really worth living; but how could one simply *not* take seriously a life, *any* life?

Among those matters that could rightfully be called fundamental to the "fundamental fantasy" of anthropology is that it must remain a fantasy. Anthropology is over once the anthropologist believes that the fantasy has been realized and that he or she has "really" found a life worth living.[6] Such a belief would paralyze all conceptual creation—which is not to say that *nowhere* is there a life really worth living. Aside from being depressively nihilistic, that claim would be unaccountably definitive (in both senses) and therefore equally immobilizing.

In other words, Schneider is describing one purely regulative use, in the classic Kantian sense, of a motive fundamental to anthropology. For the question as to the existence of a life really worth living is not something we can ever objectively or satisfactorily determine, while at the same time being something we cannot refrain from contemplating. Hence the construction "there must exist" becomes the form of the epistemo-political imperative peculiar to anthropology.

In short, Schneider's formula elucidates the extent to which anthropology is moved by a quest for authenticity. Rorty opposes his own pragmatic quest for consensus to a "quest for authenticity" that he implies is always ready to veer off toward "fantasy" (as opposed to "conversation").[7] But the notion of authenticity has full rights of citizenship within anthropology—we do not need to go to Heidegger for it—and there is no reason to revoke them. Edward Sapir's article "Culture, genuine and spurious" (1985) is among the more profound reflections produced on the notion of culture, and it is perfectly clear on the subject of the difference between what the author calls the "maxima" and "minima" of culture—authentic and inauthentic collective forms of life. The maxima and

---

6.   There is nothing more hollow-sounding than those ethnographic reconstructions that confront us with Western ethical ideals impersonated by non-Western actors. I am thinking, for example, of those descriptions of Amazonian sociality in terms of a sharing-and-caring convivial "community of similar." These descriptions entirely miss the "boldeness and invention," that Roy Wagner ([1975] 1981: 88–89) sees in places like Melanesia or Amazonia.

7.   Interestingly, it is in connection with this point that we find the only mention (critical) of Deleuze in Rorty's book.

minima have nothing to do with levels of civilization but everything to do with "life," in the sense to which Roy Wagner refers in the phrase "life as an inventive sequence." Wagner writes of "a certain quality of brilliance" exhibited by cultures that he classifies as inventive (or differentiating) and that exist everywhere. Note the purposeful vagueness with which he describes the bearers of these cultures: "tribal, religious, peasant peoples, lower classes . . . " (ibid.: 89). It thus appears that these cultures are to be found *everywhere* except precisely where *we* are—for methodological reasons, precisely, if no other. "Somewhere" is the name of this methodological negativity. Anthropology must therefore find—or rather, (re)invent conceptually—a life really worth living, which can be done only by deciding to theorize with seriousness the "lots of visions" imparted by these other lives.

But what does it mean to take seriously the lives of others? Would it mean believing in what Amazonian peoples, for example, think and say—taking what they think literally, as expressive of a truth about the world? The idea that "to take seriously" is synonymous with "to take literally" and, further, that to take literally means "to believe in" strikes me as singularly naïve (or else the opposite—a case of bad faith). Only by being too literal-minded could one fail to understand that to take anything literally is heavy work, requiring good provision of symbolic competence rather than infinite credulity. In order to believe or disbelieve in a thought, it is first necessary to imagine it as part of a belief system; but problems that are authentically anthropological are never posed in terms of psychological accounts of belief or in the logistic language of truth-values. Alien thoughts cannot be taken as opinions (the only possible object of belief and disbelief) or as collections of propositions (the only possible object of truth judgments). Anthropology has already caused a great deal of damage (in the bad old days) by casting the relation between natives and their discourse in terms of belief—thus making culture look like dogmatic theology—or by treating this discourse as an opinion or a collection of propositions—thus making the study of culture into an epistemic teratology: error, illusion, madness, ideology. Bruno Latour has observed that "belief is not a mental state, but an effect of the relation between peoples." (1996b: 15). In which case, if Rorty is right—that "to be ethnocentric is to divide the human race into the people to whom one must justify one's belief and the others" (Rorty 1991b: 30)—then to be an anthropologist is to divide the human race into people whose beliefs one can legitimately challenge and the others. The problem is that each person is a people unto him- or herself (just as, in the Amazonian context, each species is human unto itself).[8] Not much room is left for a *legitimate* challenge to any beliefs but one's own.[9]

As Wagner writes: "An anthropology . . . that reduces meaning to belief, dogma and certainty, is forced into the trap of having to believe either the native meanings or our own." ([1975] 1981: 30). And as I have said, our refusing to pose the questions of anthropology in terms of belief is a decision that seems consubstantial with the concept of "seriousness" that we want to define. Anthropology wishes neither *to describe* Amazonian (or any other people's) thought in terms of belief, nor *to relate* to their thought in terms of belief, whether by suggesting that it has an anagogical or allegorical "truth" (either a social truth, as for the Durkheimians, or a natural one, as for the cultural materialists or evolutionary psychologists) or by imagining that it does provide access to the intimate and ultimate essence of things, Amazonian thought being a vessel of infused esoteric wisdom. There is a Deleuzean argument that may help us here, taken from his well-known conception of *Autrui*. For Deleuze, *Autrui*—the other, another—is an expression of a possible world, but this world has always to be actualized by the self, in the normal course of social interaction. The implication of the possible in the other is explicated by me, which means that the possible undergoes a process of verification that entropically dissipates its structure. When I develop the world expressed by the other, it is either to validate it as real and enter into it or to disavow it as unreal. Explication in this way introduces the element of belief.

Describing this process, Deleuze recalls the boundary conditions that allowed his definition of the concept. "However," he writes,

> these relations of development, which form our commonalities as well as our disagreements with each other, also dissolve its structure and reduce it either to the status of an object or to the status of a subject. That is why, in order to grasp the other as such, we were right to insist upon special conditions of experience, however artificial—namely the moment at which the expressed has (for us) no existence apart from that which expresses it; the Other as *the expression of a possible world*. (Deleuze 1994: 261)

---

8.   See Viveiros de Castro (2004a, 464–68).

9.   Though of course "legitimacy" is never the only consideration in deciding what to do (or believe!); neither is "beliefs" ever the true object of any serious confrontation with the other.

Deleuze concludes by reiterating a maxim fundamental to his reflections:

> The rule invoked earlier—not to be explicated too much—meant, above all, not to explicate oneself too much with the other, not to explicate the other too much, but to maintain one's implicit values and multiply one's own world by populating it with all those expresseds that do not exist apart from their expressions. (ibid.: 324)

Anthropology would do well to take this lesson to heart. To maintain the values of the other as implicit does not mean celebrating some numinous mystery that they enclose. It means refraining from actualizing the possible expressions of alien thought and deciding to sustain them as possibilities—neither relinquishing them as the fantasies of others, nor fantasizing about them as leading to the true reality.

The anthropological experience depends on the formal interiorization of the "artificial and special conditions" to which Deleuze refers. The moment at which the world of the other does not exist outside its expression is transformed into an "eternal" condition—that is, a condition *internal* to the anthropological relation, which realizes this possibility *as virtual*. If there is one thing that it falls to anthropology to accomplish, it is not to *explicate the worlds of others* but rather to *multiply our world*, peopling it with "all those expresseds, which do not exist apart from their expressions."

III

> *The arrow that some do not see leaving, others see arriving.*
> – Marcel Mauss and Henri Hubert, *Outline of a general theory of magic* (1904)

"La flèche que les uns ne voient pas partir, les autres la voient arriver" (1983: 88) is how Mauss and Hubert summarize their reflections concerning the "grave question" of deception and simulation in magic. It is "impossible to imagine," the authors insist in the section of the *Outline* entitled "Belief," that magicians or sorcerers believe that they do what they say they do. They cannot believe that they artfully remove the liver of their victims without killing them in the act (rather than killing them slowly) or that they can cause lancinating pain in someone's body by manipulating an effigy. Still, even if magicians cannot believe in their own magic, they may believe in magic per se: "The minimum of sincerity that can be attributed to the magician is that he believes, at least, in the magic of others." (ibid.: 88). When a sorcerer falls sick and seeks the services of another "medicine man," he will see the arrows being drawn from his body that he cannot see when he pretends to draw them from the bodies of his patients. And it is thus that the arrow that some do not see leaving, others see arriving.

Mauss and Hubert's problem here is an enigmatic entanglement of credulity and skepticism, desire and perception, first-person and third-person perspectives, that is characteristic of magic. The solution they light upon makes reference to the definition of magical beliefs as being the original (social) form of synthetic a priori judgment, where collective forces provide the pure and invariable form of truth before experience can stock it historically with empirical contents. In archaic worlds, which are under the complete jurisdiction of such collective forces, form predominates overwhelmingly over content.

But the Maussian formula seems to me strategic, insofar as—by tracing the outline of the "pure form" of anthropology, which we might call the magic of difference and vice versa—it allows us to see that anthropology's method is a particular case of its object, or rather, that the object and method of anthropology are versions of each other. In this sense, the formula could be taken as a definition of anthropology and, further, could be defined as a "definition that defines itself."[10] For the French school of sociology, magic is the epitome of *doxa* (common sense as belief), but Mauss and Hubert's phrase confronts us with a different object—*paradox*—with which anthropology (and magic) have a far more intimate relation.

As with the previous two formulas, our argument will continue to turn on the question of location. Where are we here, now? *Somewhere* along the trajectory of that mysterious arrow. As for the arrow that some do not see leaving but others see arriving, note that it is the same person doubling up in the positions of "some" *(les uns)* and "others" *(les autres)*. In his capacity as an agent, the sorcerer does not see the arrow leave; in his predicament as a patient, he sees it arrive. But the magical decoupling can affect different persons, of course, who usually express their (political) differences by way of this perspectival disjunction—as a rule, there are far more arrows seen in the moment of arrival than in

---

10. On "inventive definitions," see Martin Holbraad (2005, 2007).

the moment of departure. It is not necessary to see an arrow leave from somewhere to see it arrive where we are, and that is how sorcery usually works.

This disjunction also mutually implies in a special way the points of view of the anthropologist and of the native. The witches that Evans-Pritchard could not see *causing*, the Azande saw *effecting*, but does that mean the anthropologist's relation with the phenomena he studies (native "beliefs") is analogous to the sorcerer's relation with his sorcery? And if so, to *which side* of this double relation of magician and magic—the side of the agent, or of the patient? More than one anthropologist has gone the way of Quesalid, to be sure (Lévi-Strauss 1958); but his trajectory is not what I have in mind. The sorcerer and the anthropologist share (in different ways) the same necessity, to make belief depend on seriousness rather than the other way around. The "minimum of sincerity" is a maximum of seriousness—because magic is always somebody else's.

Taken unprejudiciously (that is, slightly out of context), the Maussian formula does not allow one to say a priori who is right, not even if it must be the case that someone—either those who did not see the arrow leave or those who saw it arrive—is *not* right. The only sure thing, however, is that the two sides cannot in principle be correct *at the same time,* which does not deny that each has good reason to see or not to see the magic arrow from where they are. Mauss' problem is a problem of observation, or of measurement: who sees what, from where, and what happens when, being unable to see it, one does not know how to establish what exactly it is that one is or is not seeing. As Wagner memorably observes of his initial relations with the Daribi, "their misunderstanding of me was not the same as my misunderstanding of them." ([1975] 1981: 20). It is as if we are dealing here with one more version of Niels Bohr's principle of complementarity; that is, the existence of simultaneously necessary but mutually exclusive descriptions of the same phenomenon. The magic arrow could be seen as a quantum particle, for which only either position or momentum can be established. Analogously, that "some" do not see the arrow leaving reciprocally presupposes that "others" do see it arrive. It appears that the arrow can only arrive for some if others do not see it leave, and vice versa.[11]

---

11. Lévi-Strauss was fond of quoting a remark of Bohr's in which he compares the differences between human cultures to the mutually exclusive ways in which a physical experiment can be described. I also remember that "perspectival

It is here that object and method meet, as this is the anthropological situation par excellence: how to connect the two arrows, that of the anthropologist and that of the native, so that they become one? Just as it was the same
individual who did not see the arrow leave and yet saw it arrive, so also is it *in
principle* the same arrow that leaves and arrives. The arrow of the anthropologist
must be the arrow of the native and not any other (not a metaphorical arrow
instead of a magical one, for example). Or, at the very least, it is necessary to
make the two arrows coincide—to build a ladder of arrows starting with these
two arrows, as exemplified by the heroes of Amerindian myths who, fastening a
succession of arrows to each other, make a continuous stairway from the earth
to the sky (starting at the end!), in so doing traversing the discrete interval—the
abyss—that separates the two extremes of the cosmos. How to make ends meet?
That is always the question.

A conjecture follows. It is possible to speculate that the perplexing mixture
of spontaneity and obligation, gratuity and interest, generosity and aggressivity,
that according to Mauss characterizes the "archaic" complex of the gift has a
more than accidental relation to the ambiguity of magic with regard to skepticism and belief, charlatanism and sincerity, "voluntary illusion" and "perfect
hallucination," that Mauss had observed in the *Outline,* some thirty years earlier in his career. I am not thinking of the notorious incapacity of primitives to
distinguish between persons and things, which shapes the gift as well as magic
in a causally negative manner.[12] Rather I am referring to an epistemological
effect on the observer, derived from a complex, overdetermined ontology common to the gift and to magic. The effect manifests itself as these two heterogeneous mixes of sentiments, both presenting an ambivalent dispositional nature
(skepticism and belief, generosity and greediness) and also jointly involving a
type of meta calculation that includes the other's point of view in defining the

---

multinaturalism" (the "spin" I was able to give to the theme of relativism with the
help of Amazonians) presupposes the same relation of complementarity or duality.
Nonhumans see themselves as we see ourselves, as humans, but we cannot both see
ourselves as humans at the same time: the apperception of one pole as human makes
the other appear (makes the other be perceived) automatically as nonhuman. Much
the same thing occurs as well, it seems to me, between the literal and figurative
modes in the semiotics of Wagner (1977b), in the Saussurian theory of the sign, and
in the anthropology of Lévi-Strauss (Maniglier 2006).

12. With the gift, people are treated like things (J. G. Frazer's barter of women); with
     magic, things are treated like people (E. B. Tylor's animism)

meaning of one's own actions for oneself. Gift and magic are intentional multiplicities, disjunctive syntheses *in vivo* (Viveiros de Castro 2009; see Chapter 6, this volume). The theory of value condensed in this arrow, which links the gift to magic, seems to me closer to the mark than the famous "false coin of our own dreams."

It was only after contemplating for some time the Maussian formula concerning the two faces of magical intentionality that I noticed the nature of the object in question: an arrow. The archetypal mediator of action at a distance and one of the most ubiquitous images of effective intentionality in folklore the world over, the arrow is a universal symbol of the index (look where the arrow is pointing and you will get somewhere) as well as the elemental vector of the "distributed person" (look to where the arrow came from and you will find someone). Every arrow is magical: while it paradoxically transforms the far into the near and vice versa—as skepticism transforms itself into belief, aggressivity into generosity, and reciprocally so on—no arrow that we see arriving is exactly the one we saw leaving. But there is *one* magical arrow whose effect makes itself felt over very long distances. It was fired two and a half millennia ago; it has not stopped flying, to this day; and it crosses, in its trajectory, the Maussian arrow. I mean, of course, the arrow in one of Zeno's four paradoxes of movement, the arrow in flight that is always at rest, in eternal freeze-frame, never reaching its target. At each instant (indivisible, by definition), Zeno's arrow occupies a portion of space equal to itself; if it were to move during the instant, it would have to occupy a space larger than itself, for otherwise it would have no room to move. As Bertrand Russell says, "it is never moving, but in some miraculous [magical!] way the change in position has to occur *between* the instants, that is to say, not at any time whatever." And Russell concludes: "The more the difficulty is meditated, the more real it becomes." The scandal of the paradox is that the real difficulty is resolved in reality, for the arrow—against all odds, as it were—rapidly arrives at its destination.

The Maussian arrow is just like Zeno's: it "never moves," given that a straight line between its point of departure and its point of arrival cannot be traced, as if these two points belonged to heterogeneous dimensions or distinct series. Such an impossible quality assimilates both of these projectiles to another object of the same illustrious family. I mean *mana*, Lévi-Strauss' "floating signifier": the concept of a perpetual disequilibrium between two series that make up the two unequal halves of the symbol—the series that contains an empty case (the arrow that some did not see leaving) and the series that contains the supranumerary element (the arrow that others see arriving). As this mismatch lies at the radical origin of semiosis, it is probable that here we have arrived at the proper place for anthropology to erect its watchtower: the crossroads of sense and nonsense. Perhaps it is unnecessary to recall here another celebrated phrase of Evans-Pritchard's (as recalled by Joseph Needham): "There is only one method in social anthropology, the comparative method—and that is impossible." (Peacock 2007: 44).

I cannot conclude my remarks on the Mauss-Hubert formula without mentioning Gregory Schrempp's splendid work *Magical arrows: The Maori, the Greeks, and the folklore of the universe* (1992). The author explores the analogical (in the strong sense) relation between Maori mythology and the antinomies of the "Transcendental Dialectic" in Kant's first *Critique*, as well as the Lévi-Straussian doctrine concerning the "passage" of the continuous to the discrete in the origin myths of clans or natural species. (Schrempp interprets the doctrine, quite correctly, as a mythical version, in the Lévi-Straussian sense of the term, of the Eleatic paradoxes.) Finally, Schrempp connects the most famous of these paradoxes, the "Achilles" one, with Amerindian narratives about the race between two animal characters, which to him suggests that the theme has an archaic, conceivably paleolithic, origin. As he comments at the beginning of the book, "such familiar little images" (for instance, the race between ill-matched competitors that culminates in the victory of the weakest) "are, in philosophy and mythology, and within and without Western knowledge, precisely the stuff out of which some of the most grand mental creations have been brought to life" (ibid.: 10). This assessment we know to be true; and we do so, in large part, thanks to anthropology and especially to Lévi-Strauss. We know also that Zeno's paradoxes are a constitutive philosopheme of Western metaphysics; if there is one place, therefore, at which "we Western intellectuals" have to start—because we never manage to leave it—it is at this "vision" of Zeno's immobile arrow, floating in a supranumerary dimension equidistant between the two poles of meaning and nonsense, subject and object, language and being, self and other, the near and the far side of experience. And we do get to the far side, with a little help from anthropology.

A quick aside, *in fine*. Schrempp calls our attention to the universality of the magical arrow theme; yet, curiously, he does not mention the frequency and centrality of the motive in *Mythologiques*, despite his taking *The raw and the cooked* as one of its principal axes of comparison among Zeno, Kant, and Lévi-Strauss (ibid.: 188–91) It should be noted, if only in passing, that

Amerindian myths mobilize an astonishing diversity of quite unusual arrows, archers, and firing techniques, bestowed with logically complex and evocative properties. There are the arrows that become deadly accurate only after being broken into segments and reconstituted by a supernatural animal; the arrows so powerful that they need to be weakened with a magic ointment, lest they return to kill those who fired them; and the arrows that reach their target only if the archer looks in the other direction—that is, that only arrive where one desires if they are not seen leaving (as in the Maussian formula). Respectively, these three sets of arrows, one might say, teach integral and differential calculus, the dangers of hyperreflexivity, and the art of indirection.[13] The anthropologist must have arrows possessing of all these qualities in her quiver; but most importantly, she must have those that connect disjunct worlds like the earth and the sky, or the two banks of a wide river of meaning. She must have arrows that serve to make ladders or bridges between where we are now and wherever we must be.

IV

> *Even if it is true, it is false.*
> – Henri Michaux, *Face aux verrous* (1954)

This fourth and final quotation—"Même si c'est vrai, c'est faux"—is my favorite one, of course. Science, as classically conceived, is based in the principle—to call it a "belief" would be a cheap shot—that it is possible and necessary to distinguish between true and false propositions, separating everything that is affirmed about being into truths and falsities. Or rather, science can only exist where it is possible (*de jure*) to separate the true from the false and where the law of the excluded middle (*"If it is true, then it is not false,"* and vice versa) is maintained. The most that one can admit—and it is a fundamental maxim of scientific good sense or "best practice"—is that *ceteris paribus* conditions always apply and that a frame of reference should always be specified as well. I would call this attitude

---

13. They also call to mind another famous philosophical arrow: "Nature propels the philosopher into mankind like an arrow; it takes no aim but hopes the arrow will stick somewhere. But countless times it misses and is depressed at the fact . . ." (Nietzsche 1983: 177–78)

"sensible relativism." Anthropology's mission, as a social *science,* is to describe the forms by which, and the conditions under which, truth and falsity are articulated according to the different ontologies that are presupposed by each culture (a culture here being taken as analogous to a scientific theory, which requires its own ontology—that is, its own field of objects and processes—in order for the theory to generate relevant truths).

Religious belief, on the other hand—dogma as the propositional form of belief—is based in the principle that the distinction between truth and falsity is subordinated to what we could call "suprasensible absolutism." *Credo quia absurdum est,* I believe because it is absurd: in the terms of Michaux's formula, this dictum of Tertullian's is equivalent to affirming, *"Even if it is false, it is true."* The dictum, which, as is well known, is a misquotation, does not accurately reflect the historical or theological truth of Christian dogma; but it does express rather well the French sociological theory of truth, which I briefly invoked when commenting on Hubert and Mauss' phrase about magic. Magical and religious beliefs are synthetic a priori judgments (coming before individual experience), and such is the original form of all truth. It is society that separates the true from the false, in a way homologous to the self-separation of the social from the individual, the supersensible from the sensual. Truth is social because society is the source and the reference of truth; what is false could only originate in the individual. Therefore, whatever it is that society *authorizes* is true, even if it be false from the subordinate, a posteriori perspective of the individual. Per Durkheim's notorious equation, God = Society, theological suprasensible absolutism becomes the cultural relativism of the social sciences. Anthropology's mission, as a *social* science, is to determine which nontruths are taken as "God's truth" in any given society.

Between science and religion there is, naturally, opinion or *doxa*—that vast ocean of statements that one cannot pronounce true or false, neither, or both. The caricatural, (auto)deconstructive form of *doxa* is, precisely, paradox, which exposes the impossibility of univocal meanings and the precariousness of every identification, a predicament (or a power) that is immanent to language. Epimenides' paradox—the liar's paradox—is a particularly apt example: *"If it is true, then it is false, and vice versa."* Here, we are, in a sense, beyond cultural relativism, down among the paradoxical roots of human semiosis. Anthropology, conceived as a branch of semiology, shows in this case a predilection for studying the processes by which language and being, the signifier and the signified, the literal and the figurative, the sensible and the intelligible, are reciprocally determined.

The anagrammatic foundation of all signification, the arbitrary differentiation between a "nature" and a "culture" that, as it predates them, does not belong to either of the two, becomes the prototypical anthropological object. *Doxa*—the culturally "different notions of common sense" that are "the object of study" of our discipline—should be taken in this case to be the result of a decay (as we speak of "radioactive decay") of paradox, which is the true genetic element of meaning (Herzfeld 2001: 2).

There is, however, a fourth possibility, the most disturbing of all, summed up in Michaux's dictum, which introduces us directly into the world of simulacra and the powers of the false, a world that is not only beyond relativism but also beyond paradox. Insofar as it is the inversion of Tertullian's pseudoformula (just as the formula of the paradox would be the inverse of the scientific principle of the univocality of truth), Michaux's aphorism shows that the true opposite of "religious belief" is not "scientific truth." Nor is it the indiscernibility of true and false as presupposed by formal anthropological semiotics. Michaux's formula is, literally, a magical formula: *pace* Mauss, it permits one to evaluate the width of the gap that distances magic from religion and, reciprocally, to appreciate the proximity of religion and science, which fight ferociously just as they unite in a common cause, both seeking possession of eminent causality. Magic, on the other hand, is a doctrine of *effects,* and all effect, from a point of view haunted by the cause (the concern) of the cause, is always an artifact, a "special effect," a lie. He who says, "even if it is true, it is false," is someone who is preoccupied with the effects produced by what is said—by its *effectiveness,* which has nothing to do with its truth. Even the truth—especially the truth, it is tempting to say—is capable of prodigious effects of falsity and falsehood. (As we all know, the best way to lie is to tell the truth.) The only possible pragmatics of truth depends on the axiom "even if it is true, it is false." The pragmatics of truth has nothing in common with the hermeneutics of suspicion, so typical of critical sociology, which seeks the (always nasty) truth behind the lies that are told within and by society. The truth is not a "particular case" of the lie but a "whatever" (again, in Agamben's usage) case of the lie. This "even-handed intolerance," to borrow Barbara Herrnstein Smith's vigorous expression, projects a possible image of anthropology as a type of enlightened, humorous demonology rather than as a dismal, laicized theology (in the spirit of the French sociological school and its innumerable descendants) and moreover suggests a path toward freeing our discipline definitively of the problematics of both belief and unbelief.

Ezra Pound defined literature as "news that stays news," as a discourse able to change, to *not* stay put, to exist as a perpetual, extrahistorical becoming—always new, always news. In the same spirit, we might say that anthropology is alterity that stays alterity or, better, that *becomes* alterity, since anthropology is a conceptual practice whose aim is to make alterity reveal its powers of alteration—of making a life worth living. Cosmology is gossip; politics is sorcery; and *anthropology is alterity that becomes alterity* (and I mean "becomes" also in the sense of "that hat becomes you"). This fifth formula is mine and suggests the proper way of taking life—our own as much as any other—seriously.

PART II

Virtual Kinship

CHAPTER FIVE

Along the spider thread
Virtuality, Actualization, and the Kinship Process in Amazonia

TRANSLATED BY DAVID RODGERS

In general, a state of affairs does not actualize a chaotic virtual without taking from it a potential that is distributed in the system of coordinates. . . . The most closed system still has a thread that rises toward the virtual, and down which the spider descends.
– Gilles Deleuze & Felix Guattari, *What is Philosophy?*

Every man is two men, and the real one is the other
– Jorge Luis Borges, *Los Teólogos*

THE GIVEN OVER THERE

The gift is not given—the author of the *Essay* forewarns us.[1] At least not given to the anthropologist, who must begin by observing what is given, and "the

---

1. The main arguments of this article were originally presented at a meeting of Americanists held in honour of Peter Rivière at Linacre College, Oxford, in December 1998. A number of the papers from the meeting (including a modified version of the present text) were subsequently published in a *Festschrift* (Rival and Whitehead 2001). My thanks to Peter Gow, Aparecida Vilaça, Claude Lévi-Strauss,

given is Rome or Athens, the average Frenchman, the Melanesian from this island or another, and not prayer or law by itself" (Mauss [1950] 1990: 103). We appear to have learned the lesson well: too well, perhaps, seeing that prayer, law, the gift, and similar objects (a complete list would merge with anthropology's conceptual inventory) are today considered to be not just ideal constructs, but imaginary—if not malevolent—essences. Even the "given-ness" of that disciplinary icon, the Melanesian, is met with suspicion. The given as a whole has beaten a retreat.

But whether the Melanesian is the given of the anthropologist, as Mauss averred (who was careful to add: from this island or another), or non-existent, as we now appear to believe, one question remains open: what would be the given *of the Melanesian?* This question is, of course, far from irrelevant. If we accept that "anthropology seeks to elaborate the social science of the observed" (Lévi-Strauss 1963: 363), then one of our primary tasks must be to elucidate what, for the peoples we study, is taken as given—as the sphere of the innate circumscribing and conditioning human agency—and what, correlatively, is perceived to be constructible or made, or in other words pertaining to the sphere of action and responsibility of these agents. By chance we owe a specialist in Melanesia for an especially rich formulation of this problem (Wagner [1975] 1981).

The present article transplants the "problem of the given" to indigenous Amazonia. Drawing its argument from the contrast developed by Roy Wagner in *The invention of culture* between the very distinct ways in which different traditions presuppose the contrast between the "given" and the "constructed," here I outline what might be taken as a general theory of Amazonian sociality, based on the indigenous concept of kinship.

What follows is taken from a manuscript in preparation where I discuss, among other things, contemporary anthropology's tendency to insist on the socially constructed—in the practical-processual rather than theoretical-discursive sense of the term—character of this kinship nexus.[2] Although I appreciate the fecundity of this idea, I would add that no dimension of human experience

Marcela Coelho de Souza, Michael Houseman, Bruce Albert, Cristiane Lasmar, and Anne-Christine Taylor for their comments and criticisms.

2.   See Hacking (1999) for a carefully equilibrated (or perhaps equilibrist) exploration of the theme of "social construction"; his discussion concentrates on the discursive-conceptual sense of the expression, closely related to the practical-processual sense yet with distinct connotations.

is (given as) entirely constructed; something must always be (constructed as) given.

Indigenous and western constructions of the given differ radically, though. I have already explored some of these differences in the context of the transformations that an Amazonian perspective imposes on our nature/culture dualism (Viveiros de Castro 1996b); the discussion is extended here to kinship and, more generally, to the basic categories of indigenous sociality. I say extended, but I should say restricted, since we shall be observing—and dislocating—a specific manifestation of the cosmological dualism analyzed in the earlier work, the way in which it invests and polarizes the field of social relations. Hence the terms of the problem remain the same, likewise the proposed solution.

> The relation between the approach adopted in my 1998 article on indigenous perspectivism and Wagner's ideas passed me by completely at the time. The present text recognizes this relation and expands on it. Deferring an exposition of my points of divergence from Wagnerian semiotics for another occasion, here I wish, on the contrary, to underline my proximity to it. Indeed the critique of the constructionist argument outlined by myself below should not be confused with certain recent attacks to which it has been subjected in relation to kinship, gender, emotions, the person, etc. These reactions boil down to an assertion of the transcultural stability of categories and experiences characteristic of western modernity, an assertion that, as a rule, ends up restoring the classic division of ontological work between nature and culture. In other words, the given of the Melanesian is imagined to be precisely the same as our own, "given" certain universals—whether physico-material (nature), psycho-cognitive (human nature), or socio-phenomenological (the human condition). Contrary to these reactions, I agree with Wagner—if I have understood him clearly—that what is prehistoric and generic is that a given is always presumed, but not its specification; what is given is that something will always be constructed *as* given.

The focal point of this analysis is a dichotomy central to Western kinship theory and practice: the distinction between consanguinity and affinity made famous by Morgan. My argument, in a nutshell, is that Amazonian kinship distributes the values that we associate with this distinction very differently, assigning affinity the function of the given within the cosmic relational matrix, while consanguinity constitutes the realm of the constructed, which human intention and action is responsible for actualizing.

Anthropology's theoretical treatment of the notions of consanguinity and affinity oscillates between two well-known extremes. Many anthropologists take them as a given, a formal universal of kinship, seeing their own task, therefore, to be simply one of determining the variable contexts of their distinction: what types of kin are defined (constructed) as consanguines or affines "on such-and-such island." Other anthropologists, by contrast, consider the distinction itself to be a Western construct, and thus inapplicable to other relational worlds. The discipline, they assert, must rid itself of this dichotomy and the culturally specific notion of "kinship" associated with it.

I reject these alternatives. I am too much of a structuralist to believe that the distinction that we name as "consanguinity/affinity" is not one of the constitutive dimensions of human kinship. At the same time, though, I think that it is the form (or comprehension) rather than just the content (or extension) of these notions that varies crucially. It is not so much *who* is a consanguine or an affine that differs from one relational world to another, but, first and foremost, *what* is a consanguine or an affine. The Amazonian concepts of affinity and consanguinity not only determine other referents than our own, they also involve other components.

But if so, the reader may wonder, why apply the terms "consanguinity" and "affinity," and even "kinship," to the Amazonian world? Precisely, I think, so that we may discern the difference connecting this world to our own. I presume that a relation exists, for example, between our concept of kinship and what I shall call kinship in the Amazonian context. However this relation is not one of identity, or equivalence, nor does it express a common ground—and still less a "family resemblance," a Wittgensteinian notion whose application here would be a form of begging the question, since it already fully implies our own conception of kinship. Following the indigenous lesson on this point, we are compelled to imagine a concept of relation that does not take identity as a prototype. In other words, we have no need to appeal to some sort of thing-in-itself, an Essence out there as an ultimate referent of the relation between Amazonian and Western concepts. The analogical inter-expression of these concepts expresses nothing other than their differential relations to the other concepts from their respective planes of immanence (Deleuze and Guattari [1991] 1994); their dissonances are just as or even more significant that their resonances. The decision to bestow the same name to two different concepts or multiplicities is not justified, then, by their similarities, despite their differences, but the contrary: the homonymy looks to emphasize the differences, despite the similarities. The intention is precisely to make *kinship* mean something else.

POTENTIAL AFFINITY

Anthropologists have long paid attention to the deep symbolic resonances of the notion of affinity in indigenous South America, extending back, at least, to an early text by Lévi-Strauss where he compares aspects of Nambikwara social life with that of the Tupinambá, leading to his observation that: "a certain kinship tie, the brother-in-law relationship, once possessed a meaning among many South American tribes far transcending a simple expression of relationship [of matrimonial affinity]" (1943: 398).

True enough, these symbolic resonances do not exclude theoretical dissonances. Lévi-Strauss' affirmation clearly contrasts, for example, with Peter Rivière's doubts as to "whether the notion of affinity, as the term is generally understood, is applicable within the Guiana region" (1984: 69). Lévi-Strauss is saying that indigenous affinity signifies *more* than our notion; Rivière suggests that it signifies *less*, given that, in the Guianese context, it only applies when someone marries a foreigner (a member of another local group). In the strongly endogamic societies of this region, an ideal marriage does not produce affinity, he argues, since it merely reaffirms pre-existing cognatic connections and does not entail any change in the kinship attitudes of those involved. Hence affinity not only signifies less, it may signify nothing, at least for "some tribes" of South America.

How are we to reconcile these two opinions? Their apparent disagreement is not due, I believe, to ethnographic differences between the indigenous groups in question (which certainly exist and are far from negligible). In truth I think that both authors express the same situation. This similarity becomes visible if we extend Rivière's observation about affinity only applying to marriages between strangers. Amazonian affinity may apply to relations with strangers *even* if no marriage occurs: in fact, it applies *especially* to those strangers with whom marriage is not a real possibility. This takes us back to Lévi-Strauss' point about the extra-kinship usages of the brother-in-law idiom. We may recall that *tovajar*, the Tupinambá word signifying "brother-in-law" and "enemy," expressed both friendly alliance within and deadly enmity without, and very probably vice-versa. It approximated and opposed in one fell swoop.

In my previous works on Amazonian kinship I observed that the Dravid-
ianate terminologies so common in this region diverge in important aspects
from the eponymous schema described by Louis Dumont for South India.[3] The
main difference is that the categories of consanguinity and affinity in Amazonia
do not form the kind of "distinctive" or "equistatutory" opposition found in the
Tamil model proposed by the author. The concentric pattern of Amazonian
sociopolitical classifications, and the cognatic language in which they are usually expressed, inflect the diametric configuration of the terminology, creating a
pragmatic, ideological, and sometimes even terminological imbalance between
the two categories. As we move from the proximal to distal regions of the relational field, affinity gradually prevails over consanguinity, becoming the generic
mode of social relatedness. Rather than the Dravidian box diagram with its
symmetrically deployed categories, the Amazonian structure evokes Chinese
boxes (or Russian dolls) with consanguinity nested within affinity. Put succinctly, affinity hierarchically encompasses its opposite, consanguinity.

This twist to the Dravidian model was produced by applying Dumont's theory back onto itself, as it were, allowing the concepts of hierarchy and encompassment of the contrary to infiltrate the equipollent structure of the Dravidian
system. Dumont, though, was perfectly aware that the two kinship categories
could be interconnected in this way. Indeed, he observed that the main difference between the South Indian (Dravidian) and North Indian (Indo-Aryan)
kinship configurations resides in the fact that the former are not organized
through hierarchical oppositions, while the latter are. In North India, he wrote,
the notion of *bhai* ("brother") effectively connects kinship and caste "by taking
increasingly wide meanings when we ascend from the immediate relationships
to wider and wider circles." It thereby "repeatedly encompasses on the higher
level what was its contrary on the lower level." In Dravidian terminologies, by
contrast, "we find nothing of the sort, the (main) categories . . . stand in neat
distinctive opposition" (Dumont 1983: 166).

Dumont seems never to have considered a third possibility, however, which
would be the inverse of the Northern Indian case: affinity repeatedly encompassing consanguinity "when we ascend from the immediate relationships to
wider and wider circles." This is precisely the case of Amazonia, I suggested, especially in locally endogamic and cognatic societies where "prescriptive alliance"
is not based on any schema of descent, such as the Trio (Rivière 1969), Piaroa

---

3.   Cf. Viveiros de Castro 1993a, 1998b; Viveiros de Castro and Fausto 1993.

(Overing 1975), Jívaro (Taylor 1983), Yanomami (Albert 1985), and other peoples (Viveiros de Castro 1993a, and 1995).

My proposal was not entirely new. Bruce Albert, albeit not evoking the concept of hierarchical opposition, had arrived at something very similar to my own conclusion, and much of what I later wrote about the regime of Amazonian affinity was merely a systematic extrapolation of his earlier analysis.[4] Prior to this, however, the core idea had been formulated with concision by Joanna Overing apropos the Piaroa and like societies:

> We must distinguish among those societies that emphasize descent, those that emphasize both descent and alliance, and finally those that stress only alliance as a basic organizing principle. (1975: 2)

This trichotomy pointed to a case left uncovered by the two ethnographic prototypes of the time: the African systems of British anthropology (descent only) and the Australian and South Asian structures of French structuralism (descent plus alliance). One can read here, in fact, a distinction, formulated in Lévi-Straussian terminology, between the "post-elementary" systems in which alliance is ancillary to the perpetuation of descent groups (relations have no more than a regulatory role, being subordinated to independently constituted terms), the elementary systems in which the "method of classes" prevails (terms and relations are mutually constitutive), and, finally, the Amazonian "pre-elementary" structures in which the "method of relations" applies (relations subordinate and constitute terms).[5] However these contrasts may also be cast more simply in Dumontian terms and taken to distinguish between societies where consanguinity encompasses affinity, those where the two principles are in equistatutory opposition, and those where affinity encompasses consanguinity. Such a reading requires that we interpret the "descent" and "alliance" in Overing's formulation as simply the institutional elaborations of consanguinity and affinity, respectively, taken as the two basic states of the kinship nexus. If so, then saying that alliance prevails

---

4. In my 1984 thesis on the Araweté, the notion of potential affinity, in the sense that I would give to it later (see below), was already reasonably well developed; however it was undoubtedly Albert's (1985: 542–44) thesis on the Yanomami that was able to show its full sociological reach and comparative importance (which included a citation of the Araweté materials).

5. The notions of "method of classes" and "method of relations" appear in LéviStrauss 1969.

over descent as an *institutional* principle in a given society is tantamount to saying that affinity prevails over consanguinity as a *relational* principle.

In my previous works cited above, I sought to extract all ethnographically possible consequences (and perhaps a few impossible ones) from the idea of affinity as a dominant principle. I opted to call this principle "potential affinity," thereby distinguishing affinity as a *generic value* from affinity as a *particular manifestation* of the kinship nexus. The distinction implies that potential affinity as a generic value is *not* a component of kinship (unlike matrimonial, actual affinity) but its exterior condition. It comprises the dimension of virtuality of which kinship is the process of actualization.

The name with which I baptized the concept (Viveiros de Castro 1993a) was somewhat unfortunate. I contrasted "potential affinity" not only to matrimonially created "actual affinity" (e.g., the brother-in-law relation) but also to what I called "virtual affinity" (e.g., cross-cousins, terminological affines in Dravidian systems). One of the problems is that "potential" and "virtual" have been treated as synonyms in the literature and applied without distinction to the cognatic affines I labeled "virtual" (potential affines did not have a theoretical existence in their own right). Perhaps a more appropriate expression would be "meta-affinity," by analogy with the notion of "meta-siblingship" coined by Raymond Jamous (1991) to describe the kinship matrix of the Meo of Northern India. The parallel is relevant since Meo meta-siblingship (linked to the *bhai* example in the citation from Dumont above) is the consanguine equivalent of Amazonian potential affinity. Based on the Jivaroan context, Taylor (2000: 312, n.6) proposes a permutation of the terms "virtual" and "potential" that seems entirely defensible, and that for me would have the additional benefit of approximating affinity, as a generic value, to the concept of the virtual developed by Gilles Deleuze and utilized in the present article. Nonetheless, since my potential/virtual distinction has been more or less absorbed, in these terms, by the literature (see Barry et al. 2000: 721), I feel compelled to honour it, or at the very least to continue to use "potential" in the same sense with which I have employed it up to now (apart from anything else because I still find the adjective "potential" full of, as I put it then, potential). "Virtual," however, no longer seems appropriate to designate cognatic affinity. I shall try to resolve this lexical indecision and imprecision another time.

This distinction was forced on me by a number of considerations. The initial question was simple: determining what happened when we shift from the sphere of internal relations to the local group or village to the sphere of interlocal relations. In the model from *The elementary structures of kinship* (Lévi-Strauss 1969), descent was the principle responsible for the internal composition of the exchange units, while alliance configures the connections between them, thereby generating the form and continuity of the global system. In her interpretation of Piaroa social morphology, Overing took the decisive step of introjecting alliance within the units themselves, transforming it into the principle that constitutes and perpetuates local groups (the endogamic and localized kindreds common in the Guianas and elsewhere). This shift opened up a whole new horizon in terms of our understanding of Amazonian kinship universes, as well as allowing a general reconceptualization of the so-called systems of restricted exchange. But while it solved various problems, it also created new ones. Instead of descent groups linked by global formulas of alliance, we now had local groups founded on matrimonial alliance—but linked by what? If affinity was an internal mechanism, how then were external, supralocal relations expressed, given that it could not be through constructs of descent, generally non-existent or rudimentary in Amazonia, or through simple consanguinity, which is equally concentrated in the local group? Were we to adhere to the traditional view of "primitive society" as founded on kinship, we would have to conclude that Society, in many Amazonian cases, coincides with the local community: the local group is a total group. This seems consistent with the "xenophobia" (Rivière 1984: 61) described as typical of many indigenous peoples, who see non-kin and members of other groups as beings of tenuous and doubtful humanity. In this view, the outside comprises pure negativity, an absence of relation. Sociality terminates where sociability ends.[6]

One solution proposed by Amazonianists involves showing that no local group founded on intra-alliance is an island. Despite their will to autarchy, each community is (or was) at the center of a web of relations with other groups; these relations are fully, even if ambiguously, recognized by native ideology and practice. However this emphasis on the much wider sociological matrices— the "multicommunity cluster," "agglomerate," "nexus," and so on—in which the

---

6. On the difference between "sociality" and "sociability," notions usually amalgamated in Amazonian ethnology, cf. Strathern 1999: 18–19, or Edwards & Strathern 2000: 152–53.

local quasi-monads are immersed fails to solve the problem since the analysis remains inspired by a traditional theoretical concern with morphological totalization. Even a cursory acquaintance with Amazonian ethnography reveals that the "wider sociological matrices" in the region are *truly* wide, including much more than just other local groups from the same ethnic or linguistic family—and here I am not referring to other "tribes," or to the large and heterogenic pre-Colombian regional systems. The sociological matrices extend as far as the native sociologies go; and the latter muster a very diverse multitude of Others, human and non-human, a multitude that is neither sortable nor totalizable in any clear way.[7]

The implications of the above are not limited to social morphology. Consider, for example, the notion of a *political economy of persons,* proposed with frequency to describe Amazonian and other similar modes of sociality. Though certainly an interesting idea, it takes for granted precisely what it should not: that we already know in advance who these persons are. In other words, all the planet's peoples are assumed to entertain more or less the same ideas about what qualifies as a person (and what qualifies this person). But since this is patently not so, the question remains open: what might a "political economy of persons" mean in worlds like those of Amazonia where there are more persons in heaven and earth than are dreamt of in our anthropologies?[8]

Returning to the question of supralocal relations in Amazonia, we can note that they form a highly diverse mixture: statistically residual but politically

7.   The fact that, in indigenous thought, other humans can be "ethnocentrically" defined as non-human is linked by mutual implication to the fact that many non-humans are "animistically" conceptualized as human. Moreover, Amazonian ideologies commonly involve the simultaneous negation of the humanity of foreign peoples and the affirmation that they possess cultural knowledge far beyond that of the reference group. The very least that can be said of indigenous xenophobia is that it is highly ambivalent.

8.   For the concept of a *political economy of people,* cf. Wagner (1975) 1981: 24–26; Meillassoux 1975; Turner 1979b; Gregory 1982; Rivière 1984: 87–100. These authors lend different names to the concept and rely on somewhat different notions of "political economy" and "person." Their overall emphasis, however, is on the production and circulation of agents or subjects in society, not of organisms in nature. Hence there is no compelling reason to restrict the extension of "person" or "people" to our own species. This restriction, presupposed in uses of the concept, may derive from an implicit reliance on the notion of biological reproduction, which is then reproduced at a metabiological (if not metaphysical) level as the so-called "social production of persons."

strategic intermarriages (in endogamic regimes); formal friendships and trade partnerships; intercommunity ceremonies and feasts; and a latent or open state of "warfare" in which allied and enemy groups continually swap positions, a state manifested in ways varying from the shamanic combat of souls to the bellical clash of bodies, from more or less individualized vendettas to mass raids, from psychological pressure to headhunting and cannibal victims, passing through the capture of women, children and other socially valued wealth. In some cases these different modes correspond to different levels of supralocality: intervillage, interregional, intertribal, interethnic, and so on. In numerous other cases, though, they intersect, mingle or oscillate conjuncturally within the same zone. Furthermore, this relational complex spans multiple socio-cosmological spheres: animals, plants, spirits, and divinities, all circulate via myriad channels that both link them to and separate them from humans. Yet whatever the situations and personae involved, all these relations evoke the same set of values and dispositions, as attested by the common symbolism with which they are expressed: they are all inflected in the idiom of affinity. Guests and friends as much as foreigners and enemies; political allies and clients as much as trade partners or ritual companions; game animals as much as predatory spirits—all these kinds of people are awash in affinity, conceived either as generic affines or as marked versions (or sometimes inversions) of this omnipresent position.[9] The Other, in sum, is first and foremost an Affine.

It should be emphasized that this affinization of others happens despite the fact that the vast majority of actual matrimonial alliances occur within the local group. And in any event, such alliances cannot but accumulate within the local group, given that their concentration defines the "local" dimension—the village, nexus, or cluster. By this I imply that the situation changes little when we shift our focus to those Amazonian regimes that favour or prescribe village or descent group exogamy. Potential affinity and its cosmological harmonics continue to set the tone of the generic relations with non-allied groups, whites, enemies, animals and spirits.[10]

---

9. As an example of inversion, see the case of the Araweté ceremonial friends, the *apihipihã*, who are "anti-affines" without thereby being consanguines (Viveiros de Castro 1992a: 167–78).

10. The geographically local should not be mistaken for the structurally local. A single local community may perfectly well be "global" in the sense of containing—representing within itself—the entire cosmos. This is the image that one extracts, for example, from the classic ethnography of Central Brazilian societies (an

As well as these collective relations of affinity with the outside, particularized connections can (or perhaps must) also be activated, such as those that linking trade partners, ritual friends, shamans and their non-human allies, or warriors and their human victims. These personalized relations of affinity (still non-matrimonial, in the sense that they are not based on an actual, or at least intra-human, marriage tie) are a central element of indigenous cosmopolitics, serving as both evidence and instrument of the generic relation.

It was this configuration characteristic of Amazonian sociality that I called potential affinity. What matters, however, is that this "symbolic" affinity seems to embody the distinctive qualities of this mode of relation *more fully* than the actual affinal ties that constitute "the group." In the context of the local and cognatic endogamy that prevails in many of the region's societies, affinity as a particular relation is expurgated of all, or almost all, the meanings attributed to the generic version. While affinity as a generic value is an "affine-less affinity," the situation within the intra-alliance collective produces, inversely, "affinity-less affines." Cognatic affines are treated as cognates more than affines; actual affines are consanguinized at the level of attitudes; specific terms of affinity (when they exist) are avoided in favour of teknonyms that express consanguinity; spouses are conceived to become consubstantial through sex and commensality, and so forth. It can be said, therefore, that affinity as a particular relation is virtually eclipsed by consanguinity as part of the process of making kinship. As Rivière observed, "within the ideal settlement affinity does not exist" (1984: 70).

Rivière's observation undoubtedly expresses an ideal of many Amazonian communities. But I take his remark to mean that if affinity does not exist *inside* the ideal community, then it must exist somewhere else. Inside real communities, without doubt, but above all *outside* the ideal community: in the ideal exterior of the settlement, as ideal (pure) affinity. As the perspective (of the observer or the native) shifts from local relations to wider contexts—matrimonial relations and intervillage rituals, warfare and intergroup trade, hunting and interspecies shamanism—so the distribution of value is inverted and affinity becomes the generic mode of relationship. Sociality *begins* where sociability ends.

---

image that is beginning to change; cf. Ewart 2000, and below). Conversely, a set of communities linked into a network is "local" if it specifically excludes relations with other communities and, more widely, if it institutes a cosmological "outside" as immanent to its own constitution.

THE GIVEN AND THE MADE

So far we have seen how Amazonian kin collectives are related. But to proceed further another question needs to be posed: such collectives are defined and constituted in relation to what? Put otherwise, what makes these communities *local?* I suggest that local groups are defined and constituted in relation not to some global society, but to an infinite background of virtual sociality. Moreover I suggest that these collectives are made local, that is, *actual*, by extracting themselves from this infinite background and making, literally, their own bodies of kin. And these processes correspond to the concepts of affinity and consanguinity, respectively, in the Amazonian world.

What I refer to here as the *background of virtual sociality* finds its fullest expression in indigenous mythology, which records the actualization of the present state of affairs from a pre-cosmos of *absolute transparency* in which the bodily and spiritual dimensions of beings were not yet mutually hidden from each other. In this pre-cosmos, rather than any originary indifferentiation between humans and non-humans—or Indians and Whites, and so on—what prevails is a *difference* that is *infinite* but *internal* to each persona or agent (in contrast to the *finite* and *external* differences that codify the actual world).[11] Hence the regime of metamorphosis, or qualitative multiplicity, characteristic of myth: it is strictly impossible to know whether the mythic jaguar, say, is a bundle of human affects in jaguar shape or a bundle of feline affects in human shape, since mythic metamorphosis is an event or a becoming (an intensive superposition of states) not a "process" of "change" (an extensive transposition of states). The line traced by mythic discourse describes the lamination of these pre-cosmological flows of indiscernibility as they enter the cosmological process: thenceforth, the human and jaguar aspects of the jaguar (and of the human) alternate as figure and ground to each other. Absolute transparency bifurcates at this point into a relative *invisibility* (the soul) and *opacity* (the body)—relative because reversible, since the virtual

---

11. "Undoubtedly in mythic times humans were not distinguishable from animals; but among these undifferentiated beings who were set to give origin to the former and the latter, certain qualitative relations pre-existed the specificities still left in virtual state" (Lévi-Strauss 1971: 526).

background is indestructible or inexhaustible. Potential affinity reaches back into this background of metamorphic sociality implied in myth: this explains why the great origin narratives of indigenous mythologies involve figures who are paradigmatically linked by transnatural alliance: the human protagonist and the vulture father-in-law, the peccary brother-in-law, the plant daughter-in-law, and so on. Actual human kinship originates from this sphere, but it should never (because it may always) return there, at least in the absence of the socius – hence the effort manifested in practices like the couvade through which the potential connections between the newborn and pre-cosmological alterity are severed and the child acquires a specifically human opacity.

Earlier I alluded to the inversion in values that occurs when we move from proximate to more distant relations. This formulation is somewhat misleading, however. It expresses our obdurate inclination towards extensionism by implying that the movement inherent to Amazonian sociality radiates from an intimate, ordinary and quotidian sociability (where consanguinity prevails) to cosmologically wider spheres that are somewhat extraordinary in nature (where affinity holds sway). In other words, from a socially positive intimacy to a socially negative distance. This corresponds to an ego-centred model common in the West where the prototype of the relation is self-identity.[12] The Amazonian movement seems to me to travel in the opposite direction. Rather than being a metaphoric projection, a semantic and pragmatic attenuation of matrimonial affinity, potential affinity is the *source* of actual affinity and of the consanguinity generated by the latter. And that is why particular relations must be constructed through generic relations: they are outcomes, not origins. If so, then "classificatory" kinship relations cannot be seen as extensions of "real" relations; on the contrary, the latter consist of reductions of the former. In Amazonia, a close or real consanguine (which does *not* mean "biological," much less "ethnobiological") is perhaps more consanguine than a distant or classificatory

---

12. Here we can recall the *Nicomachean ethics* and its famous definition of *philia:* the Friend is "another self." As Francis Wolff (2000: 169) observes, the Aristotelian theory implies that "every relation with another, and thus every form of friendship, is founded on man's relationship to himself." The social bond presumes self-relation as origin and model.

consanguine—*but a classificatory affine is certainly more affinal than a real affine.*
This suggests that Amazonian consanguinity and affinity are not taxonomically
discontinuous categories, but zones of intensity within a single scalar field. The
movement that traverses this field is not from the proximal to the distal, from
the ordinary to the extraordinary, but the precise opposite. Something extra
must be summoned in order to bring forth the ordinary.

This is a general theoretical point. Immediate cognatic ties are required
for the fabrication of classificatory relations and categories: they function
as the material and efficient causes of kinship. But reciprocally so-called
classificatory ties are needed for the institution of these immediate ties, and
of kinship in general: they are the formal and final causes of the system,
and as such are presupposed by the first order of causality. The old quarrel
between extensionists and categorialists boils down to this question. The
former believe that fabrication (necessarily particular) also fabricates the
institution (necessarily general)—which is clearly false. The latter make
the opposite mistake, or rather simply fail to make the distinction. These
considerations will have to be developed elsewhere; I merely point out
here that the distinction between fabrication and institution could be
productively applied to another debate, namely the opposition between
"projectionist" and "immanentist" interpretations of so-called animism: the
former presume that the anthropomorphization of non-humans involves
extending human predicates to non-human entities, while the latter
reject the notion of anthropomorphism and argue that "personhood" is an
immediate and substantive property of humans and non-humans alike (or
some of them).

The real significance of the idea of affinity as the given does not reside in its
impact on kinship terminologies, but in the fact that it constitutes a privileged
instantiation of the ontological premises of Amazonian lifeworlds. The first and
foremost of these premises is: *identity is a particular case of difference.* Just as cold
is the relative absence of heat, but not vice-versa (heat is a quantity with no
negative state), so identity is the relative absence of difference, but not vice-versa. Put otherwise, only difference exists in greater or lesser intensity: this is the
nature of the measured value. Transposing this analogy to the domain of kinship—and taking "kinship" as a convenient abbreviation for what, in Amazonia,

would be better to call a *theory of generalized relationality*—we could say that consanguinity is a limit value of affinity. A limit in the strict sense of the term, since it can never be attained. What kinship measures or calculates in Amazonian sociality is the coefficient of affinity in relations, which never reaches zero, given that there can be no absolute consanguineal identity between two people, however close they may be.[13] Strictly speaking, not even individual persons are identical to themselves, since they are not really individuals—at least while alive.

Hence the cardinal rule: *there is no relation without differentiation.* In sociopractical terms, this means that the partners in any relation are related *because* they are different from each other, not *despite* being so. They are related through their difference and become different through their relation. But is this not precisely what affinity is all about? Affinity is a connection in which the terms are connected by their difference in relation to the connecting term: my wife is your sister, etc. What unites us is that which distinguishes us. This would explain why affinity is such a powerful symbol of the social nexus in Amazonia. To use Lévi-Straussian language, a symbol that far transcends the simple expression of a kinship tie; that transcends kinship as such—in fact, from where it descends. While the Western Other emerges from the realm of the indeterminate by being posed as a *brother*, that is, as someone who is connected to myself by being related in an identical way to a superior common term (the father, the nation, the church, an ideal), the Amazonian Other is determined as a *brother-in-law*, a horizontal and immanent otherness (Keifenheim 1992: 91). If we take "liberty" to be the ultimate purpose of social life, then, in the Amazonian case, the means to this end are not equality and fraternity, but difference and affinity—*liberté, différence, affinité.* Put succinctly: the Relation as similarity or the Relation as difference.

But where does consanguinity enter into all this? It needs precisely to "enter" because it is not there as a given. Since affinity is the fundamental state of the relational field, something must be done, a certain quantity of energy must be expended for zones of consanguineal valence to be able to be created. Consanguinity must be fabricated deliberately; it has to be extracted from the virtual background of affinity through an intentional and constructed differentiation from universally given difference. But if so, consanguinity can only ever

---

13. Pursuing the thermal analogy, I would say that affinity and consanguinity as expressed in kinship terminologies are conventional measures of relational temperature, but that what is being measures is the relational heat contained in affinity. A negative affinal temperature exists, namely terminological consanguinity, but not a negative affinal energy.

be the outcome of a process, necessarily interminable, of depotentializing affinity: its reduction through (and to) marriage. This, in sum, is what the concept of potential affinity means: affinity as the generic given, the virtual ground against which a particular figure of consanguine sociality must be made to appear. Kinship is undoubtedly constructed, not given, because what is given is potential affinity.

THE LINE THAT DESCENDS AND THE LINE THAT ASCENDS

We have seen then how the Indian language of hierarchical encompassment can be translated into the Melanesian language of convention and invention, the literal and the figurative, the given and the constructed. But what do we gain from this?

My recourse to the concept of hierarchical opposition was a consequence firstly of the materials with which I was initially faced: the Amazonian two-section terminologies, a type canonically described by Dumont. Since he had employed the idea of hierarchy to explain other (or indeed all) aspects of Indian society, his refusal to apply the same idea to Dravidian kinship intrigued me. All the more so since he had used the idea to mount a devastating attack on the "equistatutory" interpretations of sociocosmological dualisms proposed by Needham and his associates.[14] Dumont's argument, that every socially posed opposition always implies—in the absence of any conscious effort to equalize it—an asymmetry of value, struck me as highly convincing. It was an obvious step, therefore, to use it to mount a critique of the critic, at least in the context of Amazonian Dravidian systems.

Secondly, I saw the concept of hierarchical opposition as an interesting application of the linguistic concept of *markedness*.[15] In this sense, my thesis on affinity as hierarchically superior to consanguinity simply meant that the former is the unmarked category of Amazonian sociality, signifying the *relation* in

14. Cf. Dumont (1978a) and Needham (1973). Needham's interest in dualist symbolic classifications stemmed directly from his studies of two-section terminologies and their supposed "total structural implications."

15. On the considerable extra-linguistic yield of the notion of markedness, which originated from the Prague structuralist school, see Jakobson and Pomorska (1985). It should not be forgotten that in the marked/unmarked opposition, "marked" is, unfortunately, the lexically unmarked term and "unmarked" the marked term.

generic contexts, while the latter is a marked relational category or relational quality. Consanguinity is, before anything else, *non-affinity*.

> By this I mean that Amazonian consanguinity needs affinity in order to be defined, but the opposite is not true, since affinity is axiomatically primitive. I should emphasize that my argument does not concern the lexical structure of terminologies. This is the limited sense in which the concept of markedness first appeared in the anthropology of kinship (e.g. Scheffler 1984). Dumont's observation concerning the difference between North and South India, cited above, is also couched in purely lexical terms, although he clearly wishes to evoke something more general. In the case of Amazonia, I see no unequivocal signs of the unmarked status of affinal terms. At this level, if something is unmarked it is actually the consanguineal terms, as occurs among those "pseudo-Iroquois" terminologies that show a neutralization (in favor of sibling terms) of the consanguine/affine contrast in Gê. More commonly, though, affinal and consanguineal terms are equally primary and non-neutralizable: an equistatutory situation, were we to limit ourselves to lexical structure. Hence the Amazonian terminological landscape does not contradict Greenberg's (debatable) thesis concerning the universally marked status of affinal and cross-collateral terms (Hage 1999). But, again, my point is not lexical. It concerns rather the pragmatics of kinship usages, the range of application of the affinal and consanguineal terms, and the values manifested by these two categories. Above all, it implies that the marked status attributed to affinal terms within the kinship domain is evidence that kinship, as such, is a marked (particular) mode of sociality, in contrast to the unmarked (generic) value of the alterity embodied in potential affinity.

True, there was a distinctly Dumontian flavour to my use of the idea of markedness, insofar as it highlighted the inversion of logical dominance that occurs when one "switched level" in the consideration of a system: hence, in the case of Amazonian Dravidian systems, if we situate ourselves on the inferior level of the cognatic local group, the inferior principle becomes dominant with consanguinity encompassing affinity. The fact that this encompassment is always partial, incomplete, and continually threatened by the irruption from within of the superior general principle would be merely a sign of the secondary status of the context created by this encompassment, namely, kinship.

But it was these words, "superior" and "inferior," emerging naturally, so to speak, from within the conceptual schema of hierarchy, that seemed to provoked the most qualms among colleagues about the wisdom of applying Dumont's theories to Amazonia. The prevailing view of contemporary indigenous societies sees them as fundamentally egalitarian in terms of both their political organization and their interpersonal practice. Certainly some controversy exists over gender relations, or the historical depth and continuity of such egalitarianism, but generally speaking the manifestly non-hierarchical (in the current acceptation of the term) nature of Amazonian sociality has been stressed by many ethnographers, including myself. To this source of resistance we can add the negative aura that today envelops Dumont's ideas, denounced as a kind of orientalist despotism (a *black holism*), or the current unpopularity of terms like "hierarchy" and "structure," whose supposedly anti-processual and anti-constructivist resonances are seen as antiquated.

I have no intention of defending the word "hierarchy" here, still less of entering the debates over Dumont, India, power, colonialism, and the like.[16] Suffice to say that my use of the concept did not concern the power structures of Amazonian societies, neither proving or disproving their political egalitarianism (if this is the best term) or their emphasis on personal autonomy (ditto). Put otherwise: the hierarchical dominance of affinity over consanguinity certainly creates power differentials—between affines from adjacent generations, for example (Turner 1979b, 1984)—but it also drastically curbs the potential for the kind of political-segmentary hierarchy present in regimes where consanguinity (descent) is institutionally dominant.[17] Whatever the case, the translation of this concept into the language of the given and the constructed is proposed here as a less polemical option.[18]

---

16. See Parry (1998) for a sober evaluation that largely succeeds in "decolonizing" Dumont.

17. I am suggesting, therefore, a specific congruence between the brideservice societies described by Collier and Rosaldo (1981) and this Amazonian cosmology of potential affinity.

18. It would be equally feasible to translate Dumont's idiom of "encompassment" into Strathern's idiom of "eclipsing" (Strathern 1988; cf. Gell 1999: 41–42 for an implicit connection), a strategy that would have the same advantage as Wagner's model, namely avoiding any implication of a horizon of totalization (see below).

There are, of course, more pressing motives for resorting to this other language. We can consider, for example, the idea advanced by Overing of a variable emphasis on affinity and consanguinity, which I have proposed to retranslate as hierarchical encompassment. If we take the further step of equating this emphasis with the thesis of the differential distribution of the given, we can invest the typology in question with a more dynamic quality. The secondary principle in each configuration ceases to be conceived as merely de-emphasized and instead acquires its own sphere of activity. What does not pertain to the given is not just 'not-given,' in the sense of non-existent. It is something that must be done – done with, and to a large extent against, the given. True enough, the concept of the encompassment of the opposite already furnished a certain dynamism by underlining the bidimensionality of hierarchy, that is, the inversions of value that occur when the subordinate contexts become foregrounded (Dumont 1980: 225).[19] As we shall see, though, Dumont's model is inadequate as a description of Amazonian kinship. Moreover, the notion of encompassment is not entirely free of the implication that the encompassed principle is secondary, not in the correct sense of "coming after," but in the very incorrect sense of "less valued." Hierarchy is too readily interpretable as a linear gradient of value, which, among other things, allows the concept of value as a real structure to degenerate into an idea of value as moral sentiment (a problem that, in my view, encumbers a number of the works from the school I baptized as "the moral economy of intimacy").

But the real difficulty that the present text seeks to obviate is of another order: namely, the rooting of Dumont's approach in a problematic of *totality*. Faced by a regime of "anti-totalization" in which the outside encompassed the inside without merely creating a larger inside in the process, my application of the concept of hierarchy to the Amazonian materials had to more or less deliberately distort the original concept. The challenge here was to avoid ending up with a figure that contained the inside and the outside as different levels of a single whole, since such an outcome would be tantamount to transforming the exterior into a milieu of interiority.

This issue is important. In Dumont's hands, encompassment defines a totality within which differences are sequentially nested. In fact, such a structure lacks any outside insofar as encompassment is an operation similar to the

---

19. This important aspect of the theory went entirely unperceived by some critics of the concept of potential affinity, who seem to have taken a hierarchical structure *sensu* Dumont to comprise a classificatory taxonomy.

notorious dialectical "sublation": a movement of inclusive synthesis, of the sub-sumption of difference by identity.[20] Difference is *interior* to the whole, but also *inferior* to it. Amazonian ethnology's emphasis on the constitutive role of alter-ity, by contrast, indicates a structure in which encompassment does not produce or manifest any superior metaphysical unity. No transcendent identity exists between difference and identity—only difference all the way. The subsumption of the inside by the outside, which characterizes Amazonian cosmological pro-cesses, specifies a structure in which the inside is a mode of the outside, and as such can only be constituted by locating itself *outside* the outside. (To be true to its encompassed condition of being inside the outside, the inside has to become the outside of the outside, only achievable in precarious form.) Amazonian hi-erarchical synthesis is disjunctive, not conjunctive. Affirming that the enemy is "included in society" (see Viveiros de Castro 1992a: 282–301) does not imply that the Other is ultimately a kind of Self, therefore, but that the Self is primar-ily a figure of the Other.

In my earlier excursions through Dumontian terrains, I occasionally slipped into a simplistic application of the model, speaking of the "whole society." This was certainly a mistake. Lost somewhere between intimate sociability and ultimate sociality, "society" in Amazonia is not an object with sharply defined boundaries. Where it does seem to constitute a cardinal reification, among Central Brazilian peoples for instance, it can more accurately be described as the outcome of a process of pre-empting intradomestic sociability and interspecific sociality. This hypothesis is extrapolated from Terence Turner's well-known argument concerning the communal level of Ge societies as the transformation of domestic relations. Turner ascends from the domestic to the communal: here I suggest that we must also *descend* to this level, since the public sphere in these societies is made from elements extracted from both the domestic and the cosmic. But since the domestic is itself a particularized transformation of the cosmic, the two movements are perhaps just one and the same. Domesticity does not pertain to the given.

20. I am well aware that Dumont would disagree with this point. He frequently contrasted hierarchical encompassment to dialectic totalization. However I do not think the distinction is so easy to maintain—as its deliberate conflation by Turner (1984), for example, shows—and, in any event, neither mode of theoretically constructing the whole adequately accounts for Amazonian cosmological operations.

Allow me to elaborate further on this inclusive or internal function played by alterity. Internality in an ontological sense (alterity as a constitutive relation) is not the same thing as internality in a mereological sense (the other as part of a social or cosmological whole). In some respects, the former notion implies the very opposite of the latter. It is precisely because alterity is an internal relation in Amazonia that one can assert, without any appeal to paradox, that some of the region's societies have no interior.[21] Hence, stating that the outside encompasses the inside does not mean that the latter is (tautologically) inside the former, like a fish swimming in the ocean, but that the outside is *immanent* to the inside, like the ocean swimming inside the fish, making it a figure of (and not just in) the ocean. The corollary of this immanence is that any arbitrarily chosen point of the interior is a limit between an interior and an exterior: no absolute milieu of interiority exists. Likewise any region of the exterior is a potential focal point of interiority: in each drop of the ocean swims a virtual fish.[22]

The Dumontian language of "wholes" and "encompassments" is awkward, therefore, since it encourages a confusion between the two meanings of internality distinguished above, especially problematic where cosmological values are expressed in topological form, as in the case of the Amazonian interior and exterior. This provides another reason for us to use the alternative theoretical idiom of the given and the constructed, which has no mereological connotations.

I am not advocating that we shun any notion of the whole, as though this notion were irremediably un-Amazonian, only that we avoid succumbing to a fallacy of misplaced wholeness. Any cosmology is by definition total, in the sense that it can only think all that there is, and think it—this whole that is not a Whole, or this whole that is not a One—in accordance with a finite set of premises. It does not follow, though, that every cosmology thinks all that there is within the category of totality, or that it poses a Whole as the objective correlate of its own virtual exhaustiveness. I would venture to suggest that in Amazonian cosmologies the whole is not (the) given, nor even the sum of the given and the constructed. The whole is, rather, the part that must be constructed, that which humans must strive to make appear by reducing the given: the given as an anti-whole, or a universal differential relation.

---

21. See Viveiros de Castro 1992a: 4, 1999: 119–22.
22. Which is a way of summarizing indigenous perspectivism.

What I have in mind is something like the following structure.[23] Once supposed (given "by construction" as one says in geometry), affinity immediately poses non-affinity, since the former, the principle of difference, contains its own internal difference rather than embodying a transcendent unitary whole. Non-affinity is a purely indeterminate value, as its marked condition attests. As I discussed above, consanguinity is, before anything else, non-affinity. But for this non-affinal value to become something else—a determinate quality—it must reciprocally and actively extrude affinity from within itself, since the latter is the only *positive* value available (i.e., given). Non-affinity is internally differentiated, therefore, into affinity and non-affinity. Hence it is always possible to extract more affinity from non-affinity in order to determine the latter more perfectly as consanguinity. In fact, this has to be done because the differentiation of non-affinity reproduces affinity through the very movement of extracting or separating it from itself. The potential of differentiation is given by affinity: to differentiate from it is to affirm it through counter-effectuation. Consequently, through the reiterated exclusion of affinity at each level of contrast, consanguinity appears to include it at the next level: affinity is thereby disseminated downwards to infiltrate even the tiniest recesses of the structure. This recursive process of "obviation" (Wagner 1978) of affinity, which could also be called, to use contemporary anthropological jargon, the "construction of kinship," can only ever remain unfinished: a state of pure consanguinity is unattainable, since it would signify the death of kinship (which is what death signifies, as we shall see). It would become a sterile state of non-relationality, of *indifference*, in which the construction would self-deconstruct. Affinity is the principle of instability responsible for the continuity of the kinship life-process: "The proper functioning of the system depends on this dynamic disequilibrium, for without it this system would at all times be in danger of falling into a state of inertia," as Lévi-Strauss ([1991] 1995: 63) observed in another context—a context, as we shall soon see, very proximate to the one described here. Put simply, consanguinity is the continuation of affinity by other means (Figure 5.1).

---

23. Readers averse to the term "structure" are free to substitute a word of their choice—"process" perhaps? In the present case the outcome is exactly the same, since what this structure *structures* is a process, and what this process *processes* is a structure.

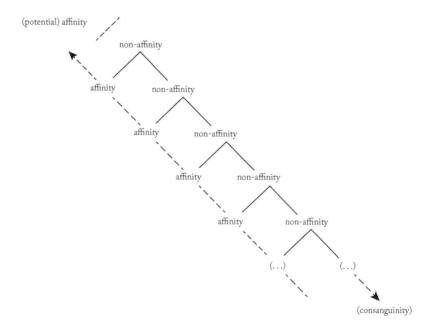

Figure 5.1. The Amazonian construction of kinship

Figure 5.1 depicts a "structuring" structure rather than a "structured" one, in the sense that it shows the conditions for the constitution of a value (kinship) rather than depicting a constituted organizational form; it describes a morphogenesis, not a morphology. This structure differs, therefore, from the Dumontian hierarchy, which articulates values determined from the outset. In fact it is more akin to what Houseman ([1984] 2015) calls an "anti-extensive hierarchy."[24] In this type of configuration, the marked "anti-extension" (non-affinity) of the unmarked dominant principle (affinity) includes the dominant principle at a lower level as its own marked version (of the anti-extension). But since the dominant principle is inherently *unmarked*, this inclusion creates an irresolvable tension that simultaneously drives the subordinate principle into increasingly

---

24. In a classic or "extensive" hierarchy (Houseman [1984] 2015) the dominant value includes its opposite within its own extension: "Man" includes "man" and "woman," etc. Since the Dumontian standard model operates on pre-determined values, it is insufficiently dynamic to render Amazonian cosmological processes. The bidimensionality of hierarchy is not enough here, since we need an operator of indetermination and recursivity. Houseman (1988) provides an insightful formulation of this argument in a different ethnographic context.

particularized actualizations and generates an ascending counter-current of ever broader generalizations, directed by and towards the dominant principle: in sum, actualization and counter-effectuation. In the diagram we can also note that each downward-branching triangle (originating in the right diagonal) *separates* two modes of the value embodied in the upper vertex, while the lower vertex of each upward-branching triangle (originating on the left diagonal) *connects* the two values located above it. As the two diagonals are oriented, both the particularizing separations and the generalizing connections are asymmetric or hierarchical, but with inverse markedness. The line that ascends is not the same line that descends:

> From virtuals we descend to actual states of affairs, and from states of affairs we ascend to virtuals, without being able to isolate one from the other. But we do not ascend and descend in this way on the same line: actualization and counter-effectuation are not two segments of the same line but rather different lines. (Deleuze and Guattari [1991] 1994: 160).

In short, the Amazonian dualism of affinity and consanguinity is in *perpetual disequilibrium.*

DISEQUILIBRIUM

This expression, perpetual disequilibrium, brings us back to the *terra firme* of Americanist ethnology. As we know, in *The story of lynx* Lévi-Strauss describes the principle impelling the Amerindian cosmological process in precisely such terms: as an unstable and dynamic dualism in perpetual disequilibrium (1991: 90, 306–16).

The name of Lévi-Strauss is often associated with an unhealthy fascination with binary, static and symmetrical oppositions. This image, though, corresponds much better to some British versions of structuralism. In fact Lévi-Strauss was the first—and from very early on—to highlight the illusory nature of the symmetry displayed by sociocosmological dualities. Suffice to recall the points set out in his 1956 article on dual organizations: the static quality of diametric dualism as a formal structure; the asymmetric values frequently attributed to the diametric partitions as lived structures; the explicit or implicit combination of diametric and concentric dualism; the derivability of the former from the latter; the triadic origin of concentric dualism, and, more generally, the derivative status of binary relations vis-à-vis ternary structures. The theme indeed was never absent from LéviStrauss' work, but it comes most evidently to the fore in *The story of lynx*, the author's last mythological study, where, notably, it is also subject to a native philosophical caution: "Amerindian thought thus gives to symmetry a negative, even evil value" ([1991] 1995: 230).

One key aspect of Lévi-Strauss' model of concentric dualism is its openness to the outside. While diametric dualisms define a self-contained whole circumscribed by an insurmountable limit, a dimensional barrier entirely heterogenic to the internal meridian line—from the system's viewpoint, its exterior simply does not exist[25]—the exterior of the concentric model is, by contrast, immanent to it: "The system is not self-sufficient, and its frame of reference is always the environment" (Lévi-Strauss 1956: 168). Here the exterior is a feature of the interior, defining the structure as a whole—or more precisely, it is the feature that actively prevents the structure from becoming a whole.[26] The exterior is relative, making the interior equally so. Such "dualism" brings indetermination to the very core of the system, rather than casting it out into the darkness of nonbeing. And here we can recall that a center is no more than the inferior limit of the infinity of circles that can be drawn around it.[27]

The dependence of concentric dualism on its own exterior anticipates another famous example of exteriorization in Lévi-Strauss' work: the *ouverture à l'Autre*, identified by the author as one of the defining features of the Amerindian bipartite ideology (1991: 16, 299 and ff). This notion of an opening to the Other stems directly from the dualism in "perpetual disequilibrium" evident in the reference myth in *The story of lynx*, the famous Tupinambá cosmogony recorded by Thevet *circa* 1554. Figure 5.1 cannot have failed to evoke in the reader's mind the schema of successive bipartitions traversing this myth from beginning to end (Figure 5.2).

---

25. The frame separating the diametric totality from its exterior belongs to the universe of the *observer* rather than the observed.

26. The exterior of the diametric figure *is* exterior *to it*; the exterior of the concentric figure *is* the exterior *of it*. On the distinction between "exterior to" and "exterior of," see Deleuze and Guattari (1980: 65).

27. A center is undoubtedly necessary to draw a circle, but without a circle there is no center, just a random point. While the central point "fabricates" the circle, the circle "institutes" the point as a center.

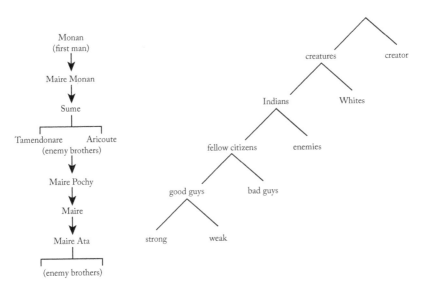

Figure 5.2. Bipartitions of the Tupinambá myth (Lévi-Strauss 1991: 76)

For these reasons it seems clear to me that the recursive dualism of 1991 is a simple transformation of the concentric dualism of 1956. A simple transformation that is far from trivial, nonetheless, since it enables us to isolate a property far less evident in the older model. The bifurcations of the Tupinambá myth initiate in the broader zone of the universe of discourse, proceeding through successively diminishing oppositions, which funnel down towards an attractor represented by the myth's pole of enunciation (the narrator's society). Translated into the concentric model, this produces an *inward movement*. As we descend the cascade of ever smaller distinctions within the dynamic schema, so we move ever closer to the center of the concentric schema, the point where the subject is located, an entity of infinite comprehension and zero extension—perfect self-identity. Yet this point is never reached, of course, since the pure identity of the center is itself purely imaginary. The center is a limit of convergence, the same limit labelled "consanguinity" in Figure 5.1.[28]

---

28. An alternative construction of the diagram in Figure 5.2 would show how it differs from the kind of diametric dualism that its patent binarism ("we" and the "others," etc.) initially appears to evoke. Imagine a square divided by a median line. A diametric reiteration of this structure would involve drawing a median perpendicular to the first, and so on successively, transforming the square into a chess board of increasingly smaller but always equal squares. Now imagine that, on

It is no coincidence, I feel, that the expression "dualism in perpetual disequilibrium" emerged in the course of *The Story of Lynx* as part of an argument closely exploring the structural dynamic of a Tupinambá myth. Reading the phrase, I had the distinct sensation that I had already encountered it somewhere else in a similar context. Returning to my book on the Araweté, I discovered that I had used the expression when commenting on a paragraph from Florestan Fernandes' classic study of Tupinambá warfare: "Despite what [Fernandes] meant to demonstrate, he ends up revealing the opposite: that the Tupinambá system was in a perpetual disequilibrium. The 'autonomy' of some could only be obtained at the expense of the 'heteronomy of others" (Viveiros de Castro 1992a: 283). On re-reading my own text, though, it immediately dawned on me that I had taken the expression from Lévi-Strauss himself, and had done so because it referred, once again, to a pertinent context. Sure enough, it can be found in *The elementary structures of kinship*, where it describes the oblique or avuncular marriage system: "the 'oblique' perspective involves a perpetual disequilibrium, each generation having to speculate on the following generation . . ." (Lévi-Strauss 1969: 447). This matrimonial form was characteristic of the Tupinambá, of course.[29] Finally, the idea that Amerindian dualisms exhibit a "dynamic disequilibrium" (Lévi-Strauss 1991: 90) revives the debate with Maybury-Lewis (1960), an author who criticized the concept of concentric dualism and suggested (1989) by way of contrast that Central Brazilian dualisms express a "dynamic equilibrium"

---

the contrary, the reiteration of the initial division involves dividing in half just one of the rectangles created by the initial division, and then just one of the rectangles of these two smaller rectangles, *ad infinitum*. The figure would look like a spectrum of increasingly fine bands tending asymptotically towards one side of the initial square, which thereby functions as an intensive attractor—a center, or more precisely a pole—for the internal divisions, rather than merely an inert limit surrounding them, as in the case of the diametric reiteration. Finally we can note that the decreasing bipartitions of the 1991 dualism, and thus the concentric schema of 1956, show no significant likeness to Evans-Pritchard's "segmentary opposition." Segmentary opposition joins-opposes entities of the same kind; it is organized around a single principle that permeates the entire structure (the conflict) and does not arise from an initial asymmetry. Neither is dualism in perpetual disequilibrium dialectical: the composition-decomposition of the structure is infinite or fractal, never stabilizing around a final pair of reconciled and unified opposites.

29.   The same passage from *The elementary structures of kinship* is cited and commented on in Viveiros de Castro 1990: 67.

(see Ewart 2000 for a survey of the polemic). The logical and historical connection between the concentricism of 1956 and the dynamism of 1991 seems to me patently clear, then, although Lévi-Strauss (1991: 311 and ff) himself never made it fully explicit.[30]

The diagrams in Figures 5.1 and 5.2 do not merely deliver the same message via different codes: they manifest the same structure. This fact will become clearer, perhaps, if we provide a concrete ethnographic interpretation for each level of the diagram of affinity/non-affinity (Figure 5.1). Figure 5.3 corresponds to one possible actualization of this structure in accordance with a repertoire of values widespread in Amazonia, in particular among the endogamic socialities of the kind first described by Peter Rivière (1984).

This diagram describes a single process encompassing both interpersonal and intrapersonal relations without interruption. The construction of the person is coextensive with the construction of sociality: both are founded on the same dualism in perpetual disequilibrium that opposes the poles of consanguineal identity and affinal alterity. Intrapersonal and interpersonal relations are, moreover, "co-intensive," since the person cannot be conceived as part of a social whole, but as a singular version of a collective—which is, in turn, an amplification of the person. In this sense, the above structure is "fractal": any distinction between part and whole becomes meaningless.[31] Hence the gap between the individualist (or particularist) societies of Guiana and the collectivist (or totalist) societies of Central Brazil may be much narrower than we once imagined.[32]

---

30. A similar expression, "dynamic dualism," was deployed by Peter Roe in *The cosmic zygote* (1982: 15–17; also see 1990), where he envisages a configuration very similar to the unstable and perpetually disequilibrated dualisms of *The story of lynx*. Once again, the context is Lévi-Straussian (and mythological, though not Tupinambá).

31. The image of fractality is taken from Wagner (1991) and Strathern (1988, 1992b); it has also been applied in a highly suggestive way to some South American materials in an article by Kelly (2001, 2005), which was, indeed, one of the immediate sources of inspiration for the present essay.

32. Here I refer to the contrast made by Peter Rivière (1984: 98) between societies possessing communal institutions, like those of the Rio Negro and Central Brazil, and the peoples of Guiana where the socius is "no more than the aggregate of individually negotiated relationships" and where "societal and individual relationships remain at the same order of complexity." This same order of *complexity*, in Rivière's argument, is in fact the same order of *simplicity*. But if, on the contrary,

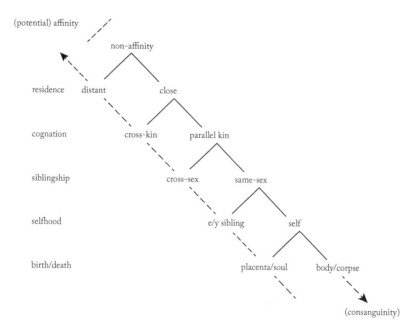

Figure 5.3. Bipartitions of Amazonian kinship

The upper region of Figure 5.3 is relatively self-explanatory: suffice to observe the inclusion in the diagram of those Sahlins-like zones or circles of sociability so often cited in ethnography (albeit imbued with very different interpretations). Its lower region requires some explication, however. The division between *junior/senior sibling* and *ego* is based on the idea that (same-sex) siblinghood in Amazonia is almost always marked by a principle of relative age, suggesting a notion of diachronic and differential repetition, rather than synchronic and total identification; nor is it free of a residual affinal potential.[33] There is more to this,

---

we take the structure to be fractal, everything changes and the idea of a "same order" signifies that societal and individual relations are *the same relations*. There is no difference of order, because difference does not pass between "individual" and "society" but passes through them equally. The *singular* and the *collective* (Strathern 1988), not the individual and society, are the true modes or moments of this complex difference.

33. Especially in the case of male twins, I would say. Consider the Araweté practice of adult brothers calling each other *he rayin-hi pihã*, which can be translated both as "my child-mother-companion" and "companion of my child-mother." In both cases, but especially if the latter translation is the more accurate, the expression means "husband of my (possible) wife." Hence two brothers see themselves to be

though. In principle it would be possible to introduce an intermediary level to the diagram—it is, *de jure*, indefinitely "intensible"—by opposing a pole labeled *twin* to the *senior/junior sibling* pole. This would bring us to the limit of interpersonal identity, a figure of merely numeric alterity between a perfectly consanguine pair: the absolute zero of relational temperature, so to speak. As Lévi-Strauss argued in the same *The story of lynx*, though, twins are not conceived as ideally identical in indigenous thought: much the opposite, they have to be differentiated. Usually, when not both killed at birth (which zeroes the score), either one twin is killed, which generates an absolute difference between them, or both are spared but distinguished by their birth order, which retransforms them into a senior/junior pairing. In indigenous mythologies, which abound with twin figures, another strategy is adopted: either different fathers are attributed to the twins (which "de-twins" them) or their character and behavior become expressly differentiated over the course of the narrative. Even when indistinguishable at birth, mythic twins always drift toward difference. Twinship reproduces the self/other polarity, posited as indelible even in this limit case of total consanguineal identity. It constitutes the *least common multiple* of Amerindian thought.[34]

Twins and their essential imparity or "oddness" allow us to pass to the level of the "person." Dropping down one level in our diagram, we can note that the placenta is frequently conceived as a double of the newborn, a kind of stillborn twin, or a non-human Other of the child (Gow 1997a: 48; Karadimas 1997: 81).[35] In some mythic traditions, such as that of the Ye'kuana, the placenta gives rise to a living and breathing rival twin (Guss 1989: 54). As for the distinc-

---

connected not through their actual co-filiation, but through their potential co-affinity – that is, via an opposite-sex relator, as two brothers-in-law do, but *the opposite way round* (Viveiros de Castro 1992a).

34. Lévi-Strauss locates the core schematism of Amerindian asymmetric dualism in the *clinamen* of imperfect twinship. The contrast made by the author between twins in European mythology (which emphasizes similarity) and Amerindian mythology (which emphasizes difference) is isomorphic with the contrast made in *The elementary structures of kinship* between the brother relationship and the brother-in-law relationship. This suggests the intrinsic continuity between the twin-centred mythology analyzed in *The story of lynx* and the mythology of affinity explored in the *Mythologiques*.

35. For North American examples, see Lévi-Strauss (1978) and Désveaux (1998). This placenta-twin theme is also common in the Malayo-Polynesian region, and possibly elsewhere.

tion between the *placenta* pole and the *body/corpse* pairing (which recalls the Greek *soma/sema* dyad), I would point out that the placenta and body are also frequently contrasted by their distinct movements in space and time, the former needing to be buried and putrefy so that the latter can grow and develop. Hence the placenta seems to be conceived as a kind of anti-corpse (C. Hugh-Jones 1979: 128–29), or as an inside-out body (i.e., as the exteriorized entrails of the child: Gow 1997). The division between *body* and *soul* manifests precisely the same polarity. Like the placenta, the soul is a separable aspect of the person, its double. In the Amazonian case, my "soul mate" is in fact my "soul twin": it is my soul, though never actually my own, since it is my "other side," which is the side of the Other. Placenta and soul, indeed, are temporally equivalent: the separation of the former marks both the possibility and beginning of life, while the separation of the latter prefigures or manifests death. The soul, like the placenta and the least common multiple of twinness, is unequivocally located at the other-affine pole of the Amazonian diagram. And here we reach the relational nucleus—the nuclear relation—of the person. While the construction of Amazonian kinship essentially involves the fabrication (and destruction) of bodies, souls are not made but given: either absolutely during conception, or transmitted with names and other pre-constituted principles, or captured "ready-to-use" from the outside. The soul is the eminently alienable, because eminently alien, dimension of the Amazonian person. Given, it can also be taken.[36]

> The world of souls and other invisible actualizations of the originary cosmic transparency (see above) is frequently designated in indigenous cosmologies by expressions signifying "the other side." This designation, at first sight analogous to our "beyond," contains a hidden symmetry: the other side of the other side is this side, meaning that the invisible of the invisible is the visible, the non-human of the non-human is the human, and so forth.

---

36. I simplify here since Amazonian ethnography recognizes numerous varieties of soul (as well as multiple souls). It seems to me, though, that a basic distinction can be made between a concept of the soul as a *representation of the body* and another concept of the soul that designates not a mere image of the body but *the other of the body*. Both ideas exist and co-exist in indigenous cosmologies, but it is the latter to which I refer when I say that the soul is given, alien and affinal. I also simplify when I identify the *personal name* as an entity of the same general kind as the soul; although this is the case in various Amazonian cultures, in others the name is a third personal principle, distinct from both the body and the soul.

The traditionally Platonic reading of indigenous body-soul dualism, which projects an opposition between appearance and essence, should therefore be abandoned in favour of an interpretation of these two dimensions as figure and ground to one another: the body's ground is the spirit, the spirit's ground is the body. The connections between this formulation and the theme of perspectivist deixis should be abundantly clear.

As we have seen, not even twins are perfectly consanguineal. Does this mean that an individual person would be reflexively so: that is, once separated from his or her original placental Other? No, I think. A living person is not an individual but *dividual*, a singularity of body *and* soul internally constituted by the self/ other, consanguine/affine polarity (Kelly 2001; Taylor 2000).[37] The composite singularity of the living is decomposed at death, which separates a principle of affinal alterity, the soul, from a principle of consanguineal identity, the body. This is the same as asserting that pure consanguinity can only be attained in death: it is the ultimate consequence of the vital process of kinship, just as pure affinity is the cosmological condition of this process. Death splits the person, or reveals its divided essence: as disembodied souls, the dead are archetypal affines (as described in the classic analysis by Carneiro da Cunha 1978). As despiritualized bodies, however, they are supremely consanguineal. Death thus releases the tension (the potential difference) between affinity and consanguinity that impels the kinship process, completing its trajectory of consanguinization—that is, its de-affinization.

The structure depicted in Figure 5.3 is oriented but cyclical, illustrating the cosmological movement of transformation of affinity/alterity into consanguinity/identity *and vice-versa*. The line that descends, however, is not the same line

---

37. My allusion to the concept of the "dividual" derives, of course, from Strathern (1988), who, developing an idea originally proposed by McKim Marriott, imbued it with a theoretical dimensions of enormous scope, applicable in Melanesia and elsewhere. Lacking the space here to fully justify my transposition, I merely point out that the Amazonian dividual (beautiful concept, ugly word) does not seem to "dividualize" along gender lines, as in Melanesia, but through the contrasts between consanguinity and affinity and/or human and non-human (these two contrasts are isomorphic). Something else to which I can only allude for now is a suspicion that the widespread uneasiness that soul/body dualities (customarily insulted as Cartesian) stir in contemporary philosophical thought may, paradoxically, derive from the subversive potential of this (divi)dualism in relation to our own individualism.

that ascends. The kinship process requires the progressive particularization of general difference through the constitution of *bodies of kin*—the singular body constructed through the kin collective and the collective constructed as a body of kin—which form the concretions of shared consanguineal identity within the universal field of potential affinity.

> The trivial critique of sociological organicism and the naturalization of the social obscures a basic dimension of Amazonian sociality. In indigenous relations worlds, the collective is something organic, or more precisely, *corporeal.* Not an organism in the sense of a functionally differentiated totality (which would be a circular definition: as Gabriel Tarde alerted us, it is not society that is an organism, but the organism that is a society) but an organic or *living* entity, a body formed of bodies, not of minds or consciences: bodies extracted from other bodies, bodies absorbed by other bodies, bodies transformed into other bodies. The emphasis on the kinship process as a "construction" of sociality expresses this *corporal imagination of the collective*, its grounding in the bodily exchanges between persons, and a conception of the person founded on a corporeal idiom. "Indigenous society" is not a collective unified consciousness, but neither is it a processual flow of individual (un)consciousnesses: it is a distributively collective body. See: Seeger, DaMatta, and Viveiros de Castro 1979; Viveiros de Castro 1979, 1996a; Gow 1991; and Vilaça 2000a, who all develop these ideas further.

However, the life process of kinship terminates each cycle with the production of an entity that is absolutely self-identical, and thus absolutely *pair-less*: the dead body of the kinsperson, the pure substantive singularity of the corpse. The other part of the person, relational rather than substantial, departs with the soul, which, as Amazonian ethnography tells us, has various posthumous destinies (alternative or sequential) of an affinal kind: it transforms into an enemy for the living kin of the deceased, or takes a non-human body as its abode, or is transmitted to non-substantial kin, or returns to an indeterminate condition of subjective principle, a kind of generic ontological equivalent, the measure of all meaningful difference in the universe. Hence the body connects kin, while the soul separates them—precisely because the soul connects non-kin (humans to non-humans), while the body separates them.[38] Body and soul perform inverse functions depending on whether we move down or up the diagram. The kinship process continues the differentiation or speciation of bodies set off at the end of the pre-cosmological period. However the residual but irreducible alterity of the soul—the "background radiation" left by the mythic Big Bang, the residual legacy of the primeval transparency between beings—prevents a complete differentiation of corporeal exteriorities. The soul assures the connection with the infinite and internal difference of the virtual pre-cosmos. Or to paraphrase Nelson Rodrigues: without a soul, you can't even suck a lollipop.

There is, of course, another end-product of the kinship process at the close of each life cycle: the procreated child, who completes the movement of consanguinization initiated by the marriage of its parents. This new dividual is never the consanguineal replica of its parents, since its body mixes their two bodies (and therefore the bodies of two brothers-in-law—see Taylor 2000), while its soul must come from a non-parent: minimally, from an anti-parent, that is, a parent of the parent (a grandparent) or an opposite-sex sibling of the parent (maternal uncle, paternal aunt).[39] Most important of all, this dividual child needs to be *made into the kin* of its kin, since in indigenous worlds substantial identifications are an outcome of social relations and not the contrary: kinship relations do not "culturally" express a "naturally" given bodily connection; bodies are created by relations, not relations by bodies, or rather, bodies are the mark left in the world when relations are consummated, when they become actualized.[40] This implies that the child needs to be de-affinized: it is a stranger, a guest to be transformed into a consubstantial (Gow 1997a; Rival 1998). The construction of kinship is the deconstruction of potential affinity; but the reconstruction of kinship at the end of each cycle must rely on the given background alterity that envelops human sociality.

---

38. Cf. Viveiros de Castro 1996c.

39. In cultures where souls—or their onomastic reifications so widespread in Amazonia—must come from the interior of the socius, they are transmitted via channels systematically distinct to those through which bodily substances circulate. As I indicated, a minimal difference can be obtained by shifting one degree in the cognatic network, i.e. positing the grandparents or cross-cousins as namers. As far as I recall, these kin are never included in the circle of abstinence when someone becomes ill and that defines the unit of communion and production of bodies. In this sense, the couvade can be seen as an anti-naming ceremony.

40. If the first postulate of Amazonian ontologies is "there is no relation without differentiation," then the second is the idea that substances derive from relations and not vice-versa. There is no space to develop this topic here.

SOME MANIFESTATIONS OF THE DIAGRAM

All the preceding argument would require a degree of fine tuning to function satisfactorily. However it is not difficult to discern already various ethnographic expressions of this Amazonian structure—expressions not necessarily codified in kinship categories. The following examples come to mind right now:

1. The model of Kalapalo relationship terminology developed by Ellen Basso (see the figure in Basso 1973: 79), which could be given a Dumontian-hierarchical twist rather than the ethnoscientific-taxonomic interpretation proposed by the author, especially if we observe the eclipsing of the sibling relation as a base idiom in favour of the cross-cousin relation as we shift from the intralocal to the interlocal and, in particular, the large inter-village rituals. It should be noted that these rituals construct "Xinguano society" as a maximally inclusive unit. In Chapter 1 of my book, *A inconstância da alma selvagem (e outros ensaios de antropologia)* (2002), we see another such example of the application of the diagram in the Upper Xingu context (Figures 1-3, p. 41), suggesting that it not only describes a sociological dynamic, as evinced in Basso's analysis, but also an ontological dynamic.

2. The systematic gender associations transmitted by the right/descending and left/ascending diagonals of the diagram in Figure 5.1, when applied to Achuar sociality. Pure consanguinity seems to be attainable only by and between women, just as pure affinity is a male condition. These divergent impulses generate a complex kinship dynamic on the interface of the system of attitudes with the terminological system, a phenomenon superbly analyzed by Taylor (1983, 2000).

3. The circulation between the *Maï* and humans in Araweté cosmology. Figure 5.4 combines two figures presented in my monograph (Viveiros de Castro 1992a: 251, 253), the direct ancestors of the structure proposed in this essay:[41]

---

41. The second diagram (Viveiros de Castro 1992a: 253), which illustrates the posthumous transformations of the person, was incorrectly interpreted by myself at the time and is now corrected through its embedding in the first diagram.

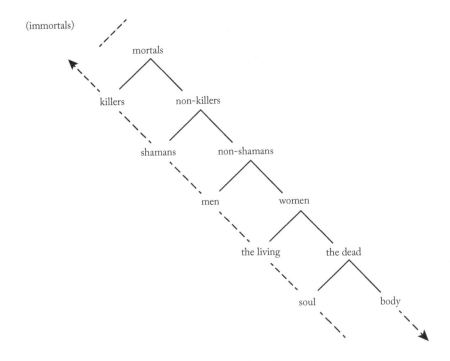

(immortals)

mortals

killers   non-killers

shamans   non-shamans

men   women

the living   the dead

soul   body

Figure 5.4. Araweté cosmological bipartitions

4. The "alternative descriptions" of Tukano sociality proposed by S. Hugh-Jones (1993). Everyday practice—and the Foodgiving House ritual which functions as its hyperbolic form—pervaded by an ethos of generalized cognation, egalitarianism, gender symmetry and group inclusion, corresponds to the descending line of the diagram.[42] The major *He* rituals, by contrast, which validate and reproduce the hierarchical and androcentric ideology (in opposition to everyday practice) of Tukano peoples correspond to the ascending line of counter-effectuation, the moment when cosmological differences are re-posited—which requires a passage through the world of infinite metamorphosis of the pre-cosmological period. Hugh-Jones associates the rites of the Food-giving House with "consanguinity" and the *He* rites with

---

42. In truth, in the case of the Food-giving House ritual (the *Dabucurí*), there is more than a symmetrization of the gender relations inherent to these societies described as highly patrilinear and patrilocal: the reference group, or the host group, is likened to a female position. This inverts the general ideological model (exacerbated in the *He/Jurupari* ritual), which posits women as the epitome of affinal exteriority and men as the epitome of consanguineal interiority.

"descent."[43] As for affinity, the author writes that "[it] contains an inherent ambiguity which depends on relative point of view" (1993: 112). In other words, it is not clearly situated, either on the side of everyday consanguinity, or that of ritual descent. I suggest, on the contrary, that it is located on both sides (as consanguinity is for Hugh-Jones, given that his "descent" is a pure consanguinity) but subject to complementary dynamics. On the ascending line taken by the *He* ritual, affinity essentially appears as potentiality: this is the affinity implied in the definition of the group as a monolithic entity, *separated* from analogous entities by differential descent, but implicitly *connected* to them by matrimonial alliance—"affine-less affinity." On the line that descends from the Food-giving House, affinity appears to be finalized, that is, effective, and thus dissolved in cognation—producing "affinity-less affines." Hence it is not so much affinity that is ambiguous, but everyday life itself, polarized as shown between the *He* and Food-giving House models.[44]

5. The foregrounding of the consanguine/affine division, occluded during the life process of kinship, which occurs in the funerary endocannibalism system of the Wari' (Vilaça 1992). It is tempting to venture that the affines of the deceased are those who must eat the corpse precisely because the latter embodies the person in its purely consanguineal phase or state; the soul of the deceased, in turn, embarks on a journey to the Beyond entirely marked by affinity, eventually transforming into a peccary that may eventually be killed and eaten by the consanguine kin of the dead. This body/peccary is, I suggest, a human anti-corpse; it is the body *of the soul*, and to this extent perfectly "other" in relation to its consanguine kin (on a very similar situation in the eschatology of the Ese Eja, see Alexiades 1999: 135).

6. The construction of Piro sociality as a "mixture of blood" (Gow 1991). Following a primeval state of pure potential affinity between different "peoples," human history unfolds as a process of kinship ("history is kinship," Gow says of the Piro). Hence we could take our diagram to describe the movement from myth (mythically given affinity) to history (historically constructed consanguinity) *and* vice-versa. This macro-process echoes recursively in the

---

43. Here what Stephen Hugh-Jones calls consanguinity, I would call cognation.

44. The above paragraph radically corrects what was stated in earlier versions of this essay on the Tukano ritual dynamic and its connection with the diagram. My thanks to Cristiane Lasmar for drawing my attention to the errors contained in the earlier versions, and for the discussion of the present (and still incomplete) formulation.

micro-oscillations between alterity and identity that inform the different stages of the life-cycle.

7. The warfare rituals of the Tupinambá and the Jívaro, which involve multiple divisions of the person (of both the killer *and* the victim) into ego-consanguineal and other-affinal halves (Viveiros de Castro 1992a: 287–92; Taylor 1993a). More generally, the Amazonian processes of incorporating the Other through the Self—which crucially presume or imply processes that involve the determination of the Self through the Other—analyzed by authors like Taylor (1985, 1993a), Vilaça (1992, 2000b), Fausto (2001) or Kelly (2001) are all particular instantiations of our structure. The meta-diagram in Figure 5.1 can be used to represent both the dynamic of predation and the dynamic of potential affinity—given that these dynamics are one and the same. Figure 5.5 outlines this translation:

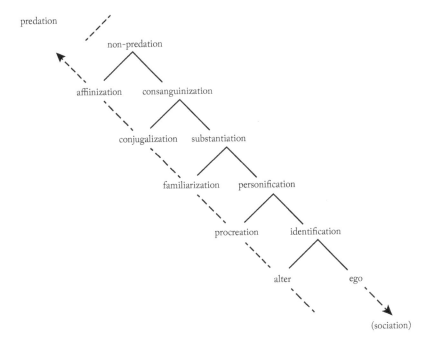

Figure 5.5. The assimilation of the Other (and the dissimilation of the self)

8. The "included thirds," those anti-affinal figures who evade the affinity/consanguinity opposition, can also be situated in the diagram. Readers of the

latter text will recall that these included thirds were defined as potential affines; next, that they were defined not only as exterior *to* kinship but as representing the exterior *of* kinship (to adopt the distinction contained in note 26, this chapter). In terms of the present diagram, I propose that these figures are located in affinal positions on the left line, but taken in this case as the *dominant line* (when the line turns from dotted to joined, so to speak). Included thirds represent affinity when this condition turns into the focus of social investment: the ascending line is the line of ritual counter-effectuation of the socius, the descending line, that of its everyday actualization. While in everyday life an (effective) affine is an inferior kind of consanguine, in the ritual environment a consanguine becomes a provisional kind of (potential) affine. Likewise, while, in everyday life, affinity must be extracted and excluded to generate a consanguineal interiority through a process of restrictive disjunction, in ritual consanguinity must be absorbed in order to connect it to its exterior conditions of possibility in a process of inclusive synthesis. More generally the ascending line is, as I stated, the line of ritual: ritual is the context par excellence for deliberate invention of the given, or the moment of the "collectivization of the innate" (Wagner [1975] 1981: n.8) and thus of the invention of nature; when the dotted line becomes joined, we shift from "counter-effectuation" (Deleuze) or "counter-invention" (Wagner) to the *inversion of invention*. Finally it is worth noting that this ascending line is continually threatening to become counter-effected beyond the controlled context of ritual: there is something like an upward push with each downward movement of the correlative line, a constant pressure to return to the virtual with each movement of actualization. Hence the danger of metamorphosis, and the theme of the deceptive nature of appearances.

9. Returning to the ethnographic examples, and by way of conclusion, I suggest that one of the most instructive applications of the diagram is the redescription of the model (or models) of Kayapó social structure elaborated by Turner (1979a, 1979b, 1984, 1992). Figure 5.6 is a partial schematization of the dimensions isolated by the author.[45]

---

45. Here I omit the constitution of intrapersonal levels in accordance with the same principles, something that has been elaborated at length by Turner (1995, for instance).

Two points can be observed in relation to this figure. Firstly, nature encompasses (in the immanent sense elucidated above) society in Ge cosmology. In fact, as Turner seems to imply in his more recent works, the ritual construction of society—its determination "counter" to its own initially derivative, marked condition as non-nature—involves the recognition and control (through internalization) of the infinite relational potential contained by the "natural" outside. But if so, Ge social structure is not a closed system, as we were made to think for so long, after all: it is much more similar to the general sociocosmological landscape of Amazonia than once imagined—or at least than I had imagined.[46]

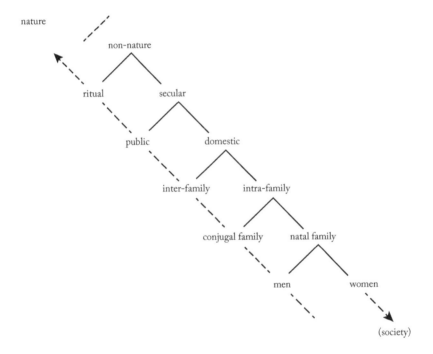

Figure 5.6. Kayapó social structure (via Turner)

---

46. An important contribution here is the thesis by Elizabeth Ewart (2000) on the Panará, which highlights the constitutive internality of the "dialectic" between Self and Other, Panará and non-Panará. Ewart suggests that the diametric dualism of the Panará is in fact a figure of concentric dualism, arguing moreover that the center (physical and metaphysical) of Panará society is the place of change and history, while the periphery is the place of stasis and permanence–which turns upside-down at least some of the grounds for the centeR/periphery dualism of the Ge.

The second point is that, arguably, in Ge cosmology women do not represent the nature pole in any relevant sense. On the contrary, the diagram suggests that a socially pure state could only be attained in a world constituted and reproduced exclusively by women. That is precisely the meaning of Ge uxorilocality, I believe.

FINAL NOTE

While some Amazonian societies (and/or their ethnographers) give considerable emphasis to the descending diagonal of my metadiagram, that is, to the vector of consanguinization that guides the kinship process, others keep their eyes firmly set on the source and general condition of this process: potential affinity. This difference in orientation within the same cosmological framework explains, I think, the contrasts and confrontations forever irrupting in regional ethnography: pacifism or bellicosity, intimate mutuality or predatory reciprocity, xenophobia or openness to the other, a this-worldly or other-worldly philosophical vision, and so on. These contrasts can but surface: they are, precisely, superficial. Despite all their intuitive salience, they are no more than partial visions of a single generic structure that necessarily flows in both directions.

But the line that ascends is still not the line that descends.

CHAPTER SIX

The Gift and the Given
Three Nano-Essays on Kinship and Magic

This paper attempts to relate three anthropological arguments about kinship. Each concerns the thorny problem of how to bypass our all-enveloping cosmology of nature and culture when describing the very province of human experience on which this dualism is supposed to be ultimately grounded. In the modem Western tradition, as we know, kinship is the primal arena for the confrontation of biological nature and cultural nurture, animal instincts and human institutions, bodily substances and spiritual relations, real facts and legal fictions, and so on. Indeed, this has been so, supposedly, ever since humans became what they are, for this divisive predicament is precisely, we are asked to believe, what makes humans *into* what they are: *Homo sapiens* (Linnæus) is *Homo duplex* (Durkheim). It is certainly no accident therefore that the most momentous anthropological reflection on nature and culture took kinship as its defining problem (Lévi-Strauss 1969), just as some of the most enlightening ethnographic accounts of this opposition in modern Euro-American settings turned to the same object (e.g., Schneider 1968; Strathern 1992a). Neither is it any coincidence that many, perhaps all, of the foundational dichotomies of the anthropology of kinship are simply particular refractions of the nature/culture schema: matriarchy and patriarchy, descriptive and classificatory, affect and right, domestic and public, filiation and descent, genealogy and category, consanguinity and alliance, and so forth. Likewise, the recent sea-changes in the

Western reflexive economy of nature and culture (Serres 1990; Latour 1991), some of them directly engaging human procreation,[1] could not fail to have profound repercussions upon anthropological discourses concerning kinship. In sum, insofar as anthropology remains essentially a disquisition on nature and culture, one is tempted to quip that it is forced to choose between studying kinship and studying nothing.

Of the three arguments that follow, the first concerns the possibility of imagining a relation between kinship and bodiliness irreducible to "biological" categories, ethno- or otherwise. The second addresses the complementary problem of how to devise a non-jural conception of kinship relatedness. Combined, the two arguments amount to a sort of "no nature, no culture" (Strathern 1980) approach to the subject. Finally and conversely, the third argument advocates a partial reclaiming of this much-maligned opposition for heuristic and comparative purposes.

FOREIGN BODIES

A few years ago, I received an e-mail from Peter Gow reporting an incident he had witnessed during a recent visit to the Piro of Peruvian Amazonia:

> A mission schoolteacher in [the village of] Santa Clara was trying to convince a Piro woman to prepare food for her young child with boiled water. The woman replied, "If we drink boiled water, we get diarrhoea." The schoolteacher scoffed, and said that the common infantile diarrhoea was caused by drinking unboiled water. Unmoved, the Piro woman replied, "Perhaps for people from Lima this is true. But for us native people from here, boiled water gives us diarrhoea. Our bodies are different to your bodies." (Peter Gow, pers. comm.)

Gow sent me this anecdote as direct evidence for my perspectival account of indigenous ontologies (Viveiros de Castro 1998a), which proposed rethinking the frequently reported Amerindian "relativism" as a natural or ontological relativism rather than a cultural or epistemological one: different kinds of persons, human as well as non-human, are distinguished by their bodies or "natures," not their spirit or "culture" (which is one and the same across the whole multiverse

---

1.   See, for example, Strathern 1992c; Franklin and Ragoné 1998; Edwards et al. 1999.

of persons). A multinaturalism, then, instead of the multiculturalism propounded by modernism.

However, rather than expressing a peculiarly Amerindian ontological tenet, the Piro woman's reply might be construed as an apt illustration of Robin Horton's general thesis (1993: 379ff) concerning the cognitive style of traditional societies, which argues that all such peoples are afflicted with "world-view parochialism." Devoid of the imperative of universalization intrinsic to the rationalized cosmologies of Western modernity, traditional world-views seem to manifest a spirit of all-pervasive tolerance which, truth be known, is nothing more than a deep indifference towards other, discrepant world-views. The "relativism" of the Piro would simply suggest that they could not care less how things are elsewhere. The woman from Gow's anecdote would seem to find a natural soul mate in the person of the Zande man who Evans-Pritchard overheard saying of Europeans: "perhaps in their country people are not murdered by witches, but here they are" ([1937] 1976: 540).

Well "perhaps" they are—I mean, perhaps the Piro woman and the Zande man were expressing the same parochialism. But perhaps not. Indeed, I think there are cogent reasons for rejecting a theory such as Horton's: the fact, for instance, that the relativistic outlook of many traditional societies—and this is certainly the case in indigenous Amazonia—is not merely inter-cultural, as he intimates, but also intra-cultural, and sometimes thoroughly reflexive. In the final analysis, such an outlook may prove totally indifferent to the alternative of either indifference (the Piro mother) or intolerance (the mission schoolteacher): indeed, I am persuaded that Amerindian ideas are refractory to any notion of culture as a system of "beliefs"—culture as a religious system, if you will[2]—and hence cannot be reliably described through the use of theologico-political concepts.

This said, the main reason for rejecting a Hortonian interpretation of the Piro dialogue is not so much the mildly ethnocentric notion of parochialism, but the very ethnocentric one of world-view. For such a notion assumes a "one nature, many cultures" ontology—a multiculturalism—which happens to be the self-same ontology implied in the schoolteacher's position. And this way the debate is over before it has even started. As Gow observed in the same e-mail:

> It would be tempting to see the positions of the schoolteacher and the Piro woman
> as representing two distinct cosmologies, multiculturalism and multinaturalism

2.   See: Tooker 1992; Viveiros de Castro 1993b; Ingold 2009.

respectively, and to imagine the conversation to be a clash of cosmologies or cultures. This would, I think, be a mistake. . . . [T]his formulation translates the conversation into the general terms of one of its parts, multiculturalism. The co-ordinates of the multinaturalist position of the Piro woman are systematically violated by the analysis. This is not, of course, to say that I believe that infants should be fed with unboiled water. It is, however, to say that ethnographic analysis cannot proceed if it is already decided what the general meaning of the encounter could be.

Like the schoolteacher, we (Gow, myself, and very likely the reader) do not believe that Piro infants should be given unboiled water. We know that human beings are made of the same stuff, over and above cultural differences; for there may be many world views, but there is only one world viewed—a world in which all human children must drink boiled water, should they happen to live in a place where infantile diarrhoea is a health hazard. The Piro may deny this fact, but their cultural "view" cannot change one iota the way things are.

Well, perhaps we know this to be the case. What we do *not* know, however, as Gow points out, are the ontological presuppositions of the Piro mother's reply. Perhaps this is another instance of Roy Wagner's paradox ([1975] 1981: 27): imagining a culture for people who do not imagine it for themselves. Be that as it may, it is certainly the case that, to continue to paraphrase Wagner (ibid.: 20), the schoolteacher's misunderstanding of the Piro mother was not the same as the Piro mother's misunderstanding of the schoolteacher.

Let me venture another reading of this incident. The argument of bodily difference invites us to determine the possible world expressed in the Piro woman's reply. In order to determine this possible world, there is no need for us to contrive an imaginary science-fictional universe endowed with another physics and another biology. Instead, what we must locate is the real problem that makes possible the world implied in the Piro woman's riposte. For there undoubtedly *is* a problem; and this problem has nothing to do with the quality of Santa Clara's water supply, and everything to do with the relation, both bodily and political, between the mother, the schoolteacher, and the child.

At a certain point in *Art and agency*, Alfred Gell remarks that the Frazerian theory of magic is wrong not because it invokes the notion of causality, but, rather, because it "impose[s] a pseudo-scientific notion of physical cause and effect . . . on practices which depend on intentionality and purpose, which is precisely what is missing from scientific determinism" (Gell 1998: 101). He concludes by saying that:

> Frazer's mistake was, so to speak, to imagine that magicians had some non-standard physical theory, whereas the truth is that 'magic' is what you have when you *do without* a physical theory on the grounds of its redundancy, relying on the idea . . . that the explanation of any given event . . . is that it is caused intentionally. (ibid.)

Gell's point can be transposed analogically to "kinship." In other words, we can say that the problem with kinship is like the problem with magic: classical anthropological renditions of non-Western forms of kinship are wrong not because they invoke the causal notion of reproduction, but, rather, because they presuppose a pseudo-scientific notion of biological causality. The mistake we have to avoid here is imagining that Amazonian peoples (for example) entertain some non-standard biological theory, like, say, Lamarckian inheritance or homuncular preformation, whereas the truth is that Amazonian kinship ideas are tantamount to a non-biological theory of life. Kinship here is what you have when you "do without" a biological theory of relationality.

Returning to the Piro argument to the effect that their bodies are different, we may observe, then, that it should be taken neither as the expression of an outlandish biological view (an "ethno-biology"); nor—should I add "of course"?—as an accurate description of an objective fact; namely, the anomalous biological makeup of Indian bodies. What the argument expresses is *another* objective fact: the fact that the Piro and Western concepts of "body" are different, not their respective "biologies." The Piro position derives not from a discrepant "view" of the same human body, but from *concepts* of bodiliness and humanness which differ from our own, and whose divergence both in extension and intension from their "homonymous" counterparts in our conceptual language is precisely the problem. For the problem is not that Amazonians and Euro-Americans give different names to (have different representations of) the same things; the problem is that we and they are not talking about the same things. What they call "body" is not what we call "body." The words may translate easily enough—perhaps—but the concepts they convey do not. Thus, to give a recursive example, the Piro concept of body, differently from ours, is more than likely not to be found within the "mind" as a mental representation of a material body without the mind; it may be, quite to the contrary, inscribed in the body itself as a world-defining perspective, just as any other Amerindian concept (Viveiros de Castro 1998a).

Peter Gow saw the anecdote as an apt illustration of my hypothesis about corporeality being the dimension Amazonians privilege when explaining the differences among kinds of people, whether those that distinguish living species (animals and plants are people in their own sphere), those that set human "ethnic groups" apart, or those that isolate bodies of kin within a larger social body.[3] If this hypothesis is correct, then the Piro mother's reply, rather than expressing a weird biological theory, encapsulates a kinship theory which is fairly characteristic of Amazonians. Bringing my correspondent's ethnography (Gow 1991) to bear upon this particular incident, we may construe the Piro woman's reply as meaning: our bodies are different from your bodies *because you are not our kin*—so do not mess with my child! And since you are not our kin, you are not human. "Perhaps" you are human to yourselves, when in Lima, say, just as we are human to ourselves here; but it is clear we are not human to each other, as our disagreement over children's bodies testifies. On the other hand, if you become our kin, you will become human, for the difference between our bodies is not a ("biological") difference which would prevent or otherwise advise against our becoming related—quite the opposite, in fact: bodily differences are necessary for the creation of kinship, because the creation of kinship is the creation of bodily difference. As Gow argues (1997a), to be human and to be kin are the same thing to the Piro—to be a person is to be a relative and vice-versa. But this is not a simple equation: the production of relatives (consanguines) requires the intervention of non-relatives (potential affines), and this can only mean the counter-invention of some relatives as non-relatives ("cutting the analogical flow" as Wagner would say), and therefore as non-human to a certain critical extent, since what distinguishes consanguines from affines are their bodily differences. If the body is the site of difference, then a difference is required in order to make bodies by means of other bodies.

Hence, Amazonian kinship is not a way of speaking "about" bodiliness, that is, about biology, ethno- or otherwise, but the other way around: the body is a way of speaking about kinship. Perhaps biology is what we get when we start believing too much in our own ways of speaking.[4]

---

3.   No metaphor intended in these two phrases, "bodies of kin" and "social body"; I
     mean them literally (Viveiros de Castro 2001; see also this volume, Chapter 5).

4.   See Schneider 1968: 115 and Wagner 1972b: 607-8.

Note that the Piro woman did not say that her people and the Limeños had different "views" of the same human body; she appealed to the different dispositional constitution of their respective bodies, not to different representational contents of their minds or souls. As it happens, the soul idiom cannot be used in Amazonia to express differences or recognize contrasts. The world is peopled by diverse types of subjective agencies, human and non-human, all endowed with the same general type of soul, i.e., the same set of cognitive and volitional capacities. The possession of a similar soul implies the possession of similar concepts (that is, a similar culture), and this makes all subjects see things in the same way, that is, experience the same basic percepts. What changes is the "objective correlative," the reference of these concepts for each species of subject: what jaguars see as "manioc beer" (the proper drink of people, jaguar-kind or otherwise), humans see as "blood"; where we see a muddy salt-lick in the forest, tapirs see their big ceremonial house, and so on. Such difference of perspective—not a plurality of views of a single world, mind you, but a single view of different worlds—cannot derive from the soul, since the latter is the common original ground of being; the difference is located in the body, for the body is the site and instrument of ontological differentiation. (Accordingly, Amazonian myths mostly deal with the causes and consequences of the species-specific embodiment of different pre-cosmological subjects, all of them conceived as originally similar to "spirits," purely intensive beings in which human and non-human aspects are indiscernibly mixed.)

The meaning of kinship derives from this same predicament. The soul is the universal condition against which humans must work in order to produce both their own species identity and their various intraspecific kinship identities. A person's body indexes her constitutive relation to bodies similar to hers and different from other kinds of bodies, while her soul is a token of the ultimate commonality of all beings, human and non-human alike: the primal analogical flow of relatedness (Wagner 1977a) is a flow of spirit. That means that the body must be produced *out* of the soul but also *against* it, and this is what Amazonian kinship is "all about": becoming a human body through the differential bodily engagement of and/or with other bodies, human as well as non-human. Needless to say, such a process is neither performable nor describable by the "genealogical method."

This does not mean, though, that the soul has only negative kinship determinations. A consideration of soul matters brings us back to magic. Gell's remarks on magical intentionality suggest that we can do more than analogically transpose anthropology's problems *with* magic to its problems *with* kinship. Perhaps the problem *of* magic is the problem *of* kinship; perhaps both are complementary solutions to the same problem: the problem of intentionality and influence, the mysterious effectiveness of relationality. In any case, it seems useful to ask ourselves whether magic and kinship have a deeper connection than that usually acknowledged in contemporary anthropological theorizing. This would help explain why it is precisely these two themes which lie at the root of our disciplinary genealogical tree: the "animism" and "magic" of Tylor and Frazer on the one hand, the "classificatory kinship" and "exogamy" of Morgan and Rivers on the other (Fortes 1969: 10ff). The reader will recall the hypothesis expounded by Edmund Leach in *Rethinking anthropology*, according to which:

> in any system of kinship and marriage, there is a fundamental ideological opposition between the relations which endow the individual with membership of a "we group" of some kind (relations of incorporation), and those other relations which link "our group" to other groups of like kind (relations of alliance), and that, in this dichotomy, relations of incorporation are distinguished symbolically as relations of common substance, while relations of alliance are viewed as metaphysical influence. (Leach [1951] 1961: 20, emphasis removed)

In sum: consanguinity and physics on one hand, affinity and metaphysics on the other.[5] Note that what Leach calls metaphysical or mystical influence need not exclude bonds of "substance"; on the contrary, it may be exerted precisely through such links (the maternally transmitted flesh-and-blood of the Kachin, for example). Or take Wagner's famous analysis of Daribi kinship: it is *because* mother's brother and sister's son share bodily substance that the former exerts a permanent influence of a "mystical" nature over the latter.[6] Note that Leach's hypothesis is not invalidated by the Daribi; according to them, fathers and sons also share bodily substance, but this does not involve any spiritual power of the former over the latter. So the correlation between bonds of alliance and magical influence does seem to obtain among the Daribi, since the mother brother's is

---

5. Here I am disregarding Leach's additional distinction between "uncontrolled mystical influence" and "controlled supernatural attack."

6. See Wagner (1967: 63–66). The author defines influence as "any relationship of dominance or control among souls" (ibid.: 46–47), but remarks (ibid.: 61) that the notion covers "natural," "social," and "supernatural" agencies (see also, ibid.: 218: "the notion of 'influence' is applicable both to social structure and religion").

a consubstantial of the sister's son, but also an affine of the latter's father, who must pay his wife's brother to counter the latter's influence over the sister's son.

In short, it is not so much "bodily substance" and "spiritual influence" as such that seem to be opposed, but what Leach defined as "relations of incorporation" and "alliance," or, as I would prefer to envisage them, relations based on similarity and relations based on difference.[7] In Amazonian kinship, the first defines a quality I will call, for comparative purposes, "consanguinity," and the second the quality of "affinity." And I think Leach's correlation is perfectly valid for Amazonia, as long as we rephrase it by saying that the body is the consanguineal component of the person and the soul is the affinal component. What we have here, then, is not so much a case of a person's affines exerting a spiritual influence over her, but, rather, of the spiritual dimension of the person herself having affinal connotations, i.e., *being* such an influence rather than suffering it. Hence this is not the same as saying that Amazonian consanguinity involves shared "physical substance" while affinity involves some *other* type of substance—a spiritual one, say—or a kind of immaterial influence of mental-intentional rather than causal-mechanical type. In fact, the distinction between a world of physical objects and a world of mental states is meaningless in Amazonian and similar ontologies (Townsley 1993). Instead there is a single analogic field of influence, to use Wagner's terms; a continuous field of magical forces that continually convert bodies into souls, substances into relations, physics into semantics, "social structure" into "religion"—and back again. In brief, a single world but a double movement.

Accordingly, while the Amazonian process of kinship essentially concerns the fabrication and destruction of bodies, individual souls are never made, but

---

7. We cannot oppose relations of group incorporation (or "unit definition," per Wagner) to relations of intergroup alliance ("unit relation") in Amazonia, since this region abounds in alliance-based collectives, where the definition of group "units" is based on the marriage alliance relations *internal* to these units. As Overing (1975) has classically demonstrated for Amazonia, group endogamy is in no way incompatible with two-section terminologies, affinal alliance, prescriptive marriage and other appurtenances of "elementary structures." Besides, it is crucial to distinguish, in Amazonia and other similar contexts, between consanguinity as a substantial condition (the fact of being cognatically related through ties mediated by procreative acts) and consanguinity as a relational determination (the fact of being a terminologically parallel or non-affinal relative). In all endogamous systems, elementary or not, one marries "consanguines," i.e., cognates (the mother's brother' daughter, say); in no elementary system, endogamous or otherwise, does one marry consanguines, i.e., non-affines (the father's brother's daughter, say).

always given: either absolutely during conception, or transmitted along with names and other pre-constituted principles, or captured ready-made from the outside. A living person is a composite of body and soul, internally constituted by a self/other, consanguine/affine polarity (Kelly 2001, Taylor 2000). This dividual entity is decomposed by death, which separates a principle of "affinal" otherness, the soul, from one of "consanguineal" sameness, the dead body. Unalloyed consanguinity can only be attained in death: it is the final result of the life-process of kinship, just as pure affinity is the cosmological precondition of the latter. At the same time, death releases the tension between affinity and consanguinity that impels the construction of kinship, and completes the process of consanguinization, i.e., de-affinization, which such a process effectively comprises (Viveiros de Castro 2001).

Just as with the "body" of the Piro anecdote, it is quite clear that Amazonian consanguinity and affinity must mean something very different to our homonymous notions. This was precisely the reason I decided to establish such a homonymy—to create a relation between the Amazonian and the Western heterogenic conceptual fields, a relation based on their difference not their similarity. Note, then, that this relation is reciprocal but oriented, since it is within Amazonian and "similar" symbolic economies (like the Melanesian one recently described by James Leach [2003]), as opposed to what might be called our own folk modernist ontology, that difference can be a positive principle of relationality, meaning both disjunction and connection (Strathern 1995b: 165), rather than a merely negative want of similarity.

GIFT ECONOMIES AND ANIMIST ONTOLOGIES

Let us tackle more directly the question of the possible co-implication of the two founding problematics of anthropology, kinship and magic. Could there be a hidden affinity between, say, prescriptive marriage and magical causation? Are the two Tylorean neologisms required by primitive (i.e., paleologic) cultures, "animism" and "cross-cousin," expressing ideas, which are, in some obscure way, germane? Put simply, does one have to practice magic to believe in mother's brother's daughter's marriage? In order to sketch the positive answers I obviously intend for these rhetorical questions, I believe we need an additional, mediatory concept in order to determine this relation more clearly. Such a concept is that of the gift.

Let us start with Chris Gregory's definition: "Gift exchange is an exchange of inalienable things between persons who are in a state of reciprocal dependence" (1982: 19). You will appreciate that this is as good a definition of gift exchange as of kinship pure and simple—taken in its affinal dimension, obviously, but also in its filiative one. For while the prototype of gift exchange in this definition is marriage exchange ("the supreme gift," etc.), procreation or generational substitution can also be conceived as a process of transmitting inalienable things—body parts and substances, classically, but also memories, narratives, connections to land (see Bamford 2009)—which create persons who thereby belong in a state of reciprocal dependence.

Marriage exchange is conceptually prototypical because all gift exchange is an exchange of persons—a personification process: "Things and people assume the social form of objects in a commodity economy while they assume the social form of persons in a gift economy" (Gregory 1982: 41). If the first definition of gift exchange made it synonymous with kinship, this one makes the concept of gift economy virtually indistinguishable from the notion of animism (Descola 1992)—the label traditionally applied to those ontological regimes in which, precisely, things and people assume the social form of persons. Perhaps, then, gift exchange, kinship and animism are merely different names for the same personification process: the economic, political and religious faces of a single generalized symbolic economy, as it were. Just as commodity production, the State and the "scientific revolution" form the pillars of our own modernist symbolic economy.

The connection between gift economy and animism is acknowledged in *Gifts and commodities*, albeit somewhat in passing. After mentioning Mauss and alluding to the "anthropomorphic quality" of gifts (1982: 20, 45), Gregory summarizes the theoretical rationale for such anthropomorphization as follows:

> [T]he social organisation of reproduction of things—gifts is governed by the methods of reproduction of people. The latter is a personification process which gives things-gifts a soul and a gender classification; thus the reproduction of things-gifts must be organized as if they were people. (ibid.: 93)

This passage rounds off a paragraph about the importance of magic for the material production (i.e., productive consumption) process in gift economies (ibid.: 92). Animism, then, would be the cosmological corollary of the gift, and magic the technology of such a cosmology. If the reproduction of gifts supposes they are people, or human-like agents, then magic is the proper way to produce them, for magic, as Gell noted, is the technology of intentionality.

But instead of taking animism as the ideology of the gift economy, as Gregory may be construed as saying, I prefer to turn the formula back-to-front: the gift is the form things take in an animist ontology. This way round—gift exchange as the political economy aspect of the semiotic regime or dispensation of animism—seems preferable to me since I believe Gregory's formulation derives in the last instance from the commodity perspective: it privileges "the economy" as the projective source of form for all human activity. Production, whether of things through productive consumption or of people through consumptive production, is the all-embracing category; human reproduction (kinship) is universally imagined as a kind of production, the better, one might say, to retroproject primitive, gift-oriented production as a kind of human reproduction. ("Material production" seems to play the same role in political economy as "biogenetic kinship" in anthropological theory.)

I believe the perspectival distortion of gift "economies" generated by apprehending them from a commodity-derived standpoint is also responsible for a conceptual slippage in Gregory's analysis between the personification process of consumptive production and the personification process involved in "giving things—gifts a soul and a gender classification." The notion of personification does not have the same meaning in the two cases—indeed, the first is a *"social form"* phenomenon, the second an *"as if"* one. Here I am intrigued by Gregory's appeal to analogical modalization when discussing magic ("the reproduction of things-gifts must be organized as if they were people"), while before, when describing the predominance of consumptive production in gift economies, he uses the concept of "social form" ("things and people assume . . . the social form of persons in a gift economy"). Now, there is surely some kind of difference between the "social form" of something and its "as if" properties; a difference of epistemological form, so to speak—or of theoretical economy. I prefer to see gift exchange, kinship and animism as different names for the same personification process, a process which is neither an "as if" phenomenon nor exactly (or exclusively) a "social form" one. The "as if" supposes an extensionist semiotics of literal and metaphorical meanings, while the notion of social form raises the question: "social" as opposed to what? To "phenomenal," assuredly (cf. Gell 1999b: 35ff); but here perhaps we come a little too close for comfort to our familiar nature/culture schema.

My interest in the relations between kinship and magic has its proximate source in a series of conversations with Marilyn Strathern, especially a discussion we had in 1998 in Brazil about intellectual property rights (IPR). In an interview she gave to Carlos Fausto and myself (Strathern et al. 1999), I introduced the IPR theme with the somewhat imprudent suggestion that the concept of "right" is the form the relation takes in a commodity economy. In a regime where things and people assume the form of objects, relations are exteriorized, detached from persons in the form of rights. All relations must be converted into rights in order to be recognized, just as commodities must have prices to be exchanged; rights and duties define the relative value of persons, just as prices define the exchange rate of things. The question that ensued was: what would be the equivalent of the notion of "right" in a gift economy? Strathern observed that this way of phrasing the problem would imply (in order to pre-serve the translative inversions between gift and commodity regimes) looking for the substantial or thing-like correlation of the gift. For some (obvious?) reason, none of us found this a very promising line of inquiry, and the subject was dropped. When she picked up the topic again in a recent paper, Strathern (2004) zeroed in on the *debt* as the gift-economy correlative of *right*, in accord-ance with Fausto's answer to my question during our conversation of six years ago: "gift is to debt as commodity is to right." Noting that this answer had been more or less anticipated by Gregory (1982: 19): "The gift economy . . . is a debt economy," Strathern then proceeded to sketch a wonderfully illuminating contrast between the intrinsic temporalities of rights (which anticipate transac-tions) and debts (which presuppose them).

While fully accepting the heuristic potential of the right/debt contrast, I venture to suggest another candidate for the conceptual role of anti-right. In the passage of *Gifts and commodities* cited by Strathern, Gregory actually under-stands that gift is to debt as commodity is to profit:

> The gift economy, then, is a debt economy. The aim of a transactor in such an economy is to acquire as many gift-debtors as he possibly can, and not to maxi-mize profit, as it is in a commodity economy. What a gift transactor desires is the personal relationships that the exchange of gifts creates, and not the things themselves. (Gregory 1982: 19)

If profit is the commodity correlative of debt, the gift equivalent of commod-ity prices would be "classificatory kinship terms" (ibid.: 16, 67–68). Gregory is referring here to the relations of prescriptive marriage exchange between cer-tain "classificatory" kinship positions, which index whole groups as transactors.

While prices describe cardinal value relations between transacted objects, kinship terms describe ordinal rank relations between the transactors themselves.

All the elements of my problem are now deployed. Kinship relations have traditionally been conceptualized by anthropology as jural relations: descent has always been a matter of rights and duties, not of natural filiation, and alliance was prescriptive, or preferential, or else a matter of choice—a whole juridical metaphysics was erected around "primitive kinship"; no need to rehearse this story.[8] Now, in a commodity economy (where things and people assume the form of objects) relations between human beings are conceived in terms of rights, which are, in a sense, prices in human form.[9] This makes the notion quite inappropriate to a gift economy, where kinship relations are not detachable from people as our rights are. By the same token, in a gift economy (where things and people assume the form of persons) relations between human beings are expressed by classificatory kinship terms—in other words, they are kinship relations. But then, relations between things must be conceived as bonds of magical influence; that is, as kinship relations in object form. The objective world of a gift "economy" is an animistic ontology of universal agency and trans-specific kinship relatedness, utterly beyond the grasp of the genealogical method—a world where yams are our lineage brothers and roam unseen at night, or where jaguars strip away their animal clothes and reveal themselves as our cannibal brothers-in-law. As Strathern once observed with pleasant irony, many nonliterate people, meaning those who happen to abide by the dispensation of the gift, "appear to see persons even where the anthropologist would not . . . [a]nd kinship may be claimed for relations between entities that English-speakers conceive as frankly improbable" (1995a: 16). Indeed, it appears that when these people talk about personification processes, well—they really mean it.[10]

---

8.   A story the reader may find in any good introduction to the anthropology of kinship, like Holy 1996.

9.   The formula is merely a transformation of something Marilyn Strathern casually remarked to me, some years ago: "the individual is the object in human form."

10.   See also Strathern (1999: 239): "[Melanesian] convention requires that the objects of interpretation—human or not—become understood as other persons; indeed, the very act of interpretation presupposes the personhood of what is being interpreted". Pages 12–14 of the same collection contain some decisive remarks on the role of magic in a relational ontology. For an insightful connection of IPR to magical conceptions, see Harrison 2002.

The modern language of rights is rooted in the early modem Big Split between the Hobbes world and the Boyle world—in other words, the moral-political and natural-physical domains.[11] Our commodity economy is equally grounded on this dual dispensation of social form versus natural force (exchange-value and use-value). Non-modern gift economies, however, having no truck with such dualities, must operate on the basis of a unified world of form and force; that is, a 'magical' world, 'magic' being the name we give to all those ontologies that do not recognize the need to divide the universe into moral and physical spheres—in kinship terms, into jural and biological relations.

I would vote for magic, then. Commodity is to jural right as gift is to magical might. So I *was* looking for the "substantial"or thing-like correlation of the gift, after all; only it was less a thing than a force, less like a material substance and more like a spiritual principle (a social form?). Or, to put it differently, I was merely looking for the way the debt is theoretically reified. Well, it is reified as the spirit of the gift, of course: as the *Hau*, the archetypal embodiment of that "anticipated outcome" which makes up the "aesthetic trap" of the gift economy (Strathern 1988: 219ff).[12] There is no need to recall that *The gift* is, among other things, a study on the pre-history of the notion of Right, and that the "general theory of the obligation" that Mauss ([1950] 1990) saw as the ultimate aim of his essay derived the juridical bond (*le lien juridique*) created by the transmission of a thing from the animate character of that thing. No need to remember, either, that the *hau* is a form of *mana*, or that *hau* and *mana* are "species of the same genus", as Mauss says somewhere. In this sense, the *hau* of *The gift* is just a special case of the *mana* of *Outline of a theory of magic:* the latter is taken to be the ancestor of the modem notion of natural force, just as *hau*-concepts are thought to lie at the root of our idea of contractual obligation.

Gregory notes a further contrast between commodity and gift-exchange:

Commodity-exchange—the exchange of unlike-for-unlike—establishes a relation of *equality* between the objects exchanged. . . . [T]he problem is to find the common measure. . . . Gift-exchange—the exchange of like-for-like—establishes an unequal relation of *domination* between the transactors. . . . [The problem here is:] who is superior to whom? (1982: 47–8).

<hr>

11. Shapin and Schaffer 1985; Serres 1990; Latour 1991.

12. For an interpretation of the *hau* that builds on the Strathernian notion of anticipated outcome (how to make the effect cause its own cause), see Gell 1998: 106-9.

He cautions that the "precise meaning of 'domination' is an empirical question." Indeed it may mean many different things; but I believe it means, first and foremost, what Leach and Wagner refer to as "influence"—magical influence. For influence is the general mode of action and relation in a world of immanent humanity. As their common etymology suggests, what the analogical "flow" carries is "influence." Immanence is fluid.[13]

I am afraid all the above comments on the gift, animism and kinship will have struck the reader as tiresomely obvious. Perhaps they are. My point was simply to call attention to the need to put back together what was pulled apart early in the history of our discipline, and seldom re-assembled since: magic and kinship, animism and exogamy. Introducing the notion of magic into the discussion is intended, in part at least, to temper our obsession with "biology"—whether for or against—when it comes to theorizing about kinship. We have known for quite a while that an anthropological theory of magic will not work if it starts out from the premise that magic is no more than mistaken physics. Neither is it helpful to imagine kinship as a weird biology. And likewise I believe there are strong reasons for not framing our conceptualization of kinship relations in general with the help of the notion of right. Kinship is not "primitive law," for just the same reason it is not "natural law." Kinship is magic, for magic is kinship.

AN AMAZONIAN CRITIQUE OF SOME NEW APPROACHES TO THE STUDY OF KINSHIP

There is a famous passage in *The elementary structures of kinship* where Lévi-Strauss contrasts the sociological properties of the "brother" and "brother-in-law" relations. Alluding to what is arguably the primal scene of structuralism, the collective affinization of a foreign band by the Nambikwara group with whom he was staying, the author writes that although the Nambikwara may occasionally use the "brother" idiom to institute bonds with non-relatives, the "brother-in-law" idiom is far more consequential:

> [T]he whole difference between the two types of bond can also be seen, a
> sufficiently clear definition being that one of them expresses a mechanical

---

13. I am alluding here to Wagner 1967 (influence), [1975] 1981 (immanent humanity), and 1977a (analogical flow).

solidarity, . . . while the other involves an organic solidarity. . . . Brothers are closely related to one another, but they are so in terms of their similarity, as are the posts or the reeds of the Pan-pipe. By contrast, brothers-in-law are solidary because they complement each other and have a functional efficacy for one another, whether they play the role of the opposite sex in the erotic games of childhood, or whether their masculine alliance as adults is confirmed by each providing the other with what he does not have—a wife—through their simultaneous renunciation of what they both do have—a sister. The first form of solidarity adds nothing and unites nothing; it is based upon a cultural limit, satisfied by the reproduction of a type of connection the model for which is provided by nature. The other brings about the integration of the group on a new plane. (Lévi-Strauss 1969: 483–84)

In short, the brother relationship is natural while the brother-in-law one is cultural. The motif pervades *The elementary structures of kinship*: consanguinity (filiation plus siblingship) is a natural given which must be limited by constructed affinity; culture or society is instituted by the normative occupation of the spaces left unguarded by natural law (mate choice as against heredity).

Even as he devalues "blood kinship" as a model for sociality, Lévi-Strauss nevertheless reasserts the robust modern Western cosmology of consanguinity as the Given and affinity as the Constructed (see Wagner [1975] 1981)—i.e., as the "nature" and "law" aspects of kinship, respectively (Schneider 1968). Indeed, he treats the distinction between consanguinity and affinity in very much the same way Fortes and so many other anthropologists before him (Delaney 1986)—not to mention Freud—conceive the difference, internal to consanguinity, between motherhood and fatherhood: the first term of each pair is associated with naturally given immanence, the second with culturally created (and culture-creating) transcendence.[14] In the best tradition of Euro-American modernity, therefore, Lévi-Strauss restates the image of civil society as emerging from the sublimational displacement (the "enterprising up")[15] of natural solidarities.

No big difference, then, between "descent theory" and "alliance theory" (Schneider 1965, 1984)? Not exactly, for structuralism did accomplish a conceptual breakthrough. Although associating consanguinity with nature and affinity

---

14. See McKinnon (2001) for an inspiring comparison between Morgan and Lévi-Strauss' "origin myths" of kinship.

15. *Sensu* Strathem (1992c), as in McKinnon (2001).

with society, Lévi-Strauss' alliance theory amounts to a conception of kinship in which affinity is as much given as consanguinity. Furthermore, in the exemplary case of elementary structures, affinity is given in exactly the same way as consanguinity; that is, as a permanent, internal and constitutive interrelationship between the partners to the marriage exchange—even if this inherence is a deed (a ruse) of Culture rather than a fact (a given) of Nature.

But such a breakthrough was not really destined to take root in the discipline, for the whole anthropology of kinship was to be shaken to its foundations in the decades following the structuralist spring (or was it an autumn?). Prescriptive marriage, for instance, was theoretically exposed as an idealized cover-up ("etic" and/or "emic") for real-life strategies, calculations, and interests—these being the current conceptual upgrades of the perduring "choice" motif. Constitutive alliance has been driven back to its traditional regulative status, the pre-given domain it regulates having now become for the most part "the Political"—this being the postmodern (no offence intended) *ersatz* of transcendent Nature. Alliance was reconstrued as sitting squarely within the domain of the constructible. More importantly, an idea such as the one expressed by Lévi-Strauss when he asserted that the sibling relationship is natural, or at least that its model is provided by nature (i.e., given), would today be flatly rejected. The whole of kinship—brothers just as much as brothers-in-law—is now seen as constructed, or rather as a "process" of construction which leaves no room for notions of the given as a natural or social "structure." Consider, for instance, the following remark from a contemporary Amazonianist. Arguing for the phenomenally constructed character of Amazonian parenthood, my colleague Laura Rival invokes "the current understanding of kinship, no longer seen as a social identity given at birth and fixed in a set of structural positions, but, rather, as a process of becoming" (Rival 1998: 628).[16] The given, the fixed and the structural are thereby lumped and dumped together in the capacious dustbin of disciplinary history. We know much better now (Carsten 2000b).

But do we really? What guarantees that our current understandings, of kinship or whatever, are more in line with, say, Amazonian understandings? Well, in the particular case of parenthood-filiation as a constructive process, rather than a given structure, one could argue that the new understanding is the end result of non-Western ideas having been successfully employed to challenge Eurocentric anthropological conceptions. But one could just as easily argue that Western

---

16. Rival is citing Carsten (1995: 223).

views themselves have changed, and this independently of any enlightenment dispensed by anthropology. Perhaps, rather, it is a number of specific historical developments such as the new reproductive technologies and certain general cultural trends like the current infatuation with "creativity" and "self-fashioning" that explain anthropology's sudden realization that nothing is "given at birth." And if this is so, we are in no better position than our anthropological forebears, as far as non-Western understandings are concerned.

Be that as it may, the purpose of this paper is not to dispute the current insights of anthropology. Besides, I harbor no anti-constructionist feelings, and am not going to start appealing now to "intractable" or "indisputable" facts of life. My point is simply that there is no *a priori* reason for supposing that Amazonians share our understandings—past or present—of kinship. There is particularly no reason for supposing that all aspects of what we call kinship are understood by Amazonians as equally constructible or "processual." Rival's generic mention of kinship glosses over possible differences internal to this province of human experience.

My argument should by now be obvious. Let us take one of the major conceptual dichotomies of Western kinship practice and theory, the consanguinity/affinity dichotomy of Morganian (and structuralist) fame, and combine it with Wagner's distinction between the innate and the constructed, as formulated in *The invention of culture* ([1975] 1981). This procedure generates four possible cases.

1. The standard model

Consanguinity is the province of the given: it is an innate, passive property of the human relational matrix, its essential bodily substrate. Affinity is active construction: it is differentiating choice, affective or political, and inventive freedom. This is the Western standard model, the well-known cosmology of nature and law, status (substance) and contract (code), theoretically universalized by many as "human kinship." In its comparative developments, this model implies that the cultural constructions placed upon consanguineal relations are severely limited, oscillating around a powerful natural attractor represented by maternity, sibling solidarity and the nuclear family. Affinity, on the other hand, is supposed to vary more freely, ranging from primitive compulsory marriage to modern love-based unions; it reveals itself as "intractable" only in its negative connection to consanguinity, that is, in the incest prohibition.

The standard model conceives consanguinity as an internal relation derived from procreation (see Bamford 2009). The procreative links and resulting corporeal similarities among "blood" kin are (or were until very recently) conceived to make up the unchangeable, ineffaceable, originally constitutive aspects of a person's identity insofar as s/he is thought of "in relation" to other persons.[17] To use the biological metaphor, kinship is primarily a genotypic, rather than phenotypic, property of persons. The genotype (the body as Substance) is ontologically deep-sealed, unmodifiable by any of the active relations through which the phenotype (the body as Subject) engages with the world. Affinal connections on the other hand are purely external, regulative relations between already-constituted persons, binding reciprocally independent partners. So "biological" continuities are our own concrete metaphor of internal relatedness, while real (i.e., social) relations are seen as external and regulative (Schneider 1984: 188).

This is a drastic simplification, of course (Carsten 2001). When it comes to modern Western conceptions of kinship, "biology is never the full story" (Edwards and Strathern 2000: 160), and genetic transmission still less so (Edwards 2009). Lived consanguinity always evinces a complex interdigitation of "social" and "biological" dimensions, and the latter are just as likely to be accepted as rejected as the basis of a relationship. Still, the simplification holds to a very important extent, for there are limits to the combinations of social and biological attributes inherent to our cosmology. A choice always exist as to whether or not biology is made the foundation of relationships, but there is no choice about making relationships the foundation of biology—this is impossible. The code of conduct may prevail over substance, but it cannot create substance. It is admissible for the relation not to proceed from substance, but not that it precedes substance. An adoptive son may be more of a "son" than a natural one, but there is nothing that can make him a natural son. Biological connections are absolutely independent of social relations, but the reciprocal does not hold. Even though biology may not be destiny, or the full story, it will always be necessity, because it is history; through it, time is irreversibly inscribed in the body: "contained within the bodies of living human beings is a protracted history of procreative events extending back in time from the present to the remote past" (Bamford 2009: 170).

---

17. Contrast with Bamford's (2009: 173) subtle observation concerning the Kamea: "Unlike Euro-Americans, the Kamea make a sharp distinction between what goes into the making of a person in a physical sense and what connects them through time as social beings."

If consanguinity embodies the procreative causes of kinship, affinity is an effect of marriage or its analogues. And it is precisely as a consequence of conjugality that affinity can be said to be constructed. The true "construction" is conjugality, the outcome of choice; the affinal kin resulting from conjugality are "given" *a posteriori*, as the spouse's consanguines or as consanguines' spouses. Hence the possibility of situating, in the standard model, affinity along with consanguinity on the side of the given, in contrast to freely "chosen" constructed relationships, such as love, friendship, spiritual kinship, etc. Hence also the contemporary tendency to separate conjugality from affinity, in order to root more firmly, as it were, the former on the soil of affective choice. "I did not marry your relatives"—this was a formula frequently voiced in my country a generation ago, when it sounded amusing because of its wishfully-thought utter counterfactuality; nowadays, however, it is beginning to ring ever more true.

To summarize, let us say that the kinship content of the Given, in the standard model, is a constitutive relation of consubstantial similarity inscribed in the body and resulting from procreation. The form of the Constructed is a relation established by free choice, expressing the spiritual complementarity of the individuals entering into it; such complementarity (or difference), embodied in conjugality, results in procreation. Put together, these two dimensions of given substance and constructed choice are the condition of possibility of the "diffuse, enduring solidarity" found at the root of human sociality.

2. The constitutive model

Here both dimensions are seen as given, the first naturally (and thence socially, once sanctioned by culture), the second socially (but also in a sense naturally, since it evinces the essence of human sociality). This corresponds in effect to the structuralist conception of "primitive" kinship, especially as expressed in the concepts of elementary structure and prescriptive marriage: both the consanguineal and affinal areas of an elementary kinship structure are treated, by the persons abiding by it, as "given at birth." In such a model, affinity is not created by marriage, but the other way around: we do not see as affines those whom we marry, but, rather, marry those whom we have always seen as affines (or construe as having always seen as affines—since we marry them now).

Now, one might wish to emphasize—were one willing to conflate constitutive and regulative understandings and read the model in a "prescriptive" key—the debt of the structuralist model to the traditional view of primitive society as a rule-dominated, no-choice universe, as well as to the "Durkheim-Saussure hypothesis" (as it were) which sees human action as the automatic enactment of a transcendent set of cultural instructions (a cultural genotype of sorts). But one could also argue—and with much more reason, I think—that this model displays a thoroughly relational or non-substantivist view of kinship, since it implies "that persons have relations integral to them (what else is the specification of the positive marriage rule?)" (Strathern 1992c: 101).[18] Above all, we can observe that although both dimensions of kinship are "given" in this model, they are not given in the same way and at the same logical time. For the Lévi-Straussian concept of the incest prohibition means strictly no more (nor less) than this: affinity is prior to consanguinity—it comprises its formal cause. There are no consanguines before the inception of the idea of exchange; my sister only becomes a "sister" when I apprehend (or anticipate) her as a "wife" for someone else. Men do not "exchange women," and women are not there *for* exchange: they are created *by* exchange. As are men. Indeed, as a matter of fact (or rather, a matter of right), it is never a case of some people (men) exchanging some other people (women): marriage is a process whereby people (men and women) exchange kinship *relations,* as Lévi-Strauss suggested a while ago ([1956] 1983: 91),[19] or *perspectives,* as Strathern put it more recently (Strathern 1988: 230 *et passim,* 1992c: 96–100; 1999: 238–40).

3. The constructive model

Both dimensions are treated here as the result of socio-practical processes of relating; that is, they are conceptualized as equally constructed by human agency. Kin ties are not given at birth—not even birth is given at birth (see Rival 1998 on the *couvade).* Instead, they are "created" or "produced" by purposeful acts of feeding, caring, sharing, loving, and remembering.[20] The

---

18. And what, one may ask, is a positive marriage rule if not the kinship-terminological inscription of the aesthetic of the "anticipated outcome" (Strathern 1988)?

19. Kinship *relations,* it should be noted, not kinship *rights* ("over people," "over the reproductive capacity of women," etc).

20. The "production" idiom is evoked here simply to recall its role as a variant of the "construction" idiom, the main difference being that "production" builds that much-frequented metaphorical bridge between "kinship" and "political economy," sometimes allowing the former to be derived from certain politico-economical givens.

overwhelming theoretical emphasis rests upon the socially created nature of consanguineal relations, in particular the parent-child ties; it is considered unnecessary to argue that affinal ties are also socially created. This constructionist model seems to be the currently dominant anthropological understanding of kinship; it has also been attributed, causally or consequentially, to many—perhaps all—non-Western peoples. It has largely emerged as a reactive inversion of the preceding position, although it could be argued that it is as old as anthropology itself, having been adumbrated by authors as different as McLennan and Durkheim. But it has also reacted to some contemporary competing understandings of kinship in (then) socio-biological and (now) psycho-evolutionary terms, which propound a particularly imperialistic version of the Given: genotypic consanguinity not only determines phenotypic behavior vis-à-vis "relatives," it also governs "affinal" choices (i.e., mating) in the best interest of gene replication.

Partisans of the constructionist model devote much attention to "optative" and "adoptive" relations, as well as to extra-uterine, post-natal modes of creating or validating bonds of consubstantiality. Adoptive kinship, milk kinship, spiritual kinship, commensality, co-residence and so forth are shown to be considered by many peoples as equal to, and often more valued than, relations based on the sharing of pre-natally produced bodily substance. Kinship, in short, is made, not "given by birth" (Carsten 2000a: 15; Stafford 2000: 52). Note that "kinship" here essentially means consanguinity—filiation and siblingship—not affinity: the latter seems to be already regarded as a kind of "fictive consanguinity," and as I remarked earlier, the question of the possibility of something like a "fictive affinity," that is, a relation of affinity not based on a "real" marriage alliance, fails even to see the light of day. Apparently, to argue that affinity is socially constructed would be deemed redundant—a telling presupposition.

The primary target of the constructionist model is the notion of biologically given relatedness. It aims to show that, when it comes to kinship, "the world of made" is as good as, and often better than, "the world of born." But under closer scrutiny, it is impossible to avoid the conclusion that the equation at the base of the Western standard model still remains in force—the equation between "biological," "given," and "non-negotiable," on the one hand, and "social," "constructed," and "optative," on the other. The notion of "substance" may have been theoretically extended from the sphere of the given to that of the constructed (Carsten 2001)—but that is about it. Biology ("sex," "birth," etc.) is still the given in the constructive model; it simply carries less value than the constructed

("gender," "feeding," etc.) dimensions of kinship. Some peoples may even entirely ignore the given, entertaining a "nothing is given, all is made" type of ontology—but no people would have something other than biologically-grounded
consanguinity as the given.[21] Why not, though?

Nowadays, social constructionism's dominance is under siege on multiple
fronts. The model just evoked is being hit by a volley of criticisms, the more
hostile of them coming from the camp of those I would dub "natural instruc-
tionists"—cognitivistic-minded anthropologists, their associates and fellow-
travellers. Virtually all of the criticisms, however, amount to restatements of
the old modernist ontology of natural universals and cultural particulars. "Kinship," "gender," and "person," among many other concepts, have been victimized
by these somewhat reactionary reconstructions. In the face of the "nothing is
given" banner waved by the constructionists, these reactions content themselves
in reaffirming the universal content of the Given, "given" certain universals—be
they physico-material ("nature"), psycho-cognitive ("human nature"), or phenomenological (the "human condition"). Back to case one.

In total disagreement with these rejections of the social constructionist
stance, I assume that what is pre-historical and generic is that something is
always presupposed as given, not its specification. What is given is that *something* has to be given—that some dimension of human experience must be constructed (counterinvented) as given.[22] And *that* is about it.

So one possibility is left, given the parameters chosen "by construction," for
the present experiment.

4. The Amazonian model

The remaining possibility is the converse of the first one. Here we find affinity
as a given, internal and constitutive relation, and consanguinity as constructed,
external and regulative. This, I suggest, is the value distribution present in the
Amazonian relational world. If the privileging of the fraternal idiom in our
own model of sociality (we are all brothers in something, sociality is fraternity

---

21. See Bamford (2007: 57–58): "Despite the novelty of these newer formulations ... they
    continue to rest upon two underlying ideas: first, that kinship is a bond of substance;
    and second, that it unites two or more people in a 'physical' relationship."

22. I believe I'm following Wagner ([1975] 1981) here. For a similar criticism of the
    constructive model, see Leach (2003).

writ large) derives from the given character of consanguinity for ourselves, then the analogous privileging of the affinal bond by Amazonians would point to affinity as the given dimension of kinship there. Likewise, if affinity is seen as constructed in our social tradition, then consanguinity has a good chance of standing as the non-innate dimension of Amazonian kinship. If all this happens to be true, then Lévi-Strauss was not correct in arguing that the brother relationship is natural, i.e., given and socially sterile, while the brother-in-law one is cultural, i.e., constructed and socially fecund. As far as Amazonians are concerned, I would say that the opposite is true: affinity is natural, consanguinity is cultural. (It is precisely because affinity is seen as a *natural* given by the Nambikwara, I would argue, that they treated it as socially *fecund*, resorting to it when constructing a relation with the foreign band.)

I am stretching the meanings of "natural" and "cultural" here, to be sure; but that is the whole point of this exercise. Amazonian affinity cannot be "natural" in exactly the same sense as our consanguinity—that is, given as a deep-sealed organismic condition, although it does entail important bodily determinations.[23] It is not a given in *The elementary structures of kinship* sense, either, although it does incorporate "prescriptive alliance" as one of the possible consequences of a wider cosmopractical structure. Affinity is the given because it is lived and conceived as an ontological condition underlying *all* "social" relations. Affinity, in other words, is not something that comes after prior natural relatednesses; rather, it is one of the primordial givens from which the relational matrix ensues. It belongs as such to the fabric of the universe.[24] So, if we wish to continue to think of affinity as cultural or conventional, we must also realize that "human" culture, for Amazonians (and others), is a trans-specific property, belonging to the province of the universal and the "innate"—or what we might as well call

---

23. Cannibal determinations, for instance; see Viveiros de Castro 1993b.

24. It is worth remembering that the protagonists of the major Amerindian origin myths, as abundantly illustrated in Lévi-Strauss' *Mythologiques* (1964, 1967a, 1967b, 1971), are related as affines. Our own Old World myths seem to be haunted, on the other hand, by siblingship and parenthood, particularly fatherhood. Not to put too fine a point on it, we had to steal culture from a divine father, while Amerindians had to steal it from an animal father-in-law. "Mythology" is the name we give to other people's discourses on the innate. Myths address what must be taken for granted, the initial conditions with which humanity must cope and against which it must define itself by means of its power of invention. In the Amerindian worlds, affinity and alliance/exchange, rather than parenthood and creation/production, would thus comprise the unconditioned condition.

the natural.[25] By the same token, Amazonian consanguinity is experienced as constructed, but not only (or always) as an instituted set of jural categories and roles, a "social structure." Consanguinity is constructed more or less along the lines of the current understanding of kinship: in the phenomenal sense of being the outcome of meaningful intersubjective practices. It is "culture," then—it is, for example, history (Gow 1991). This has nothing to do with choice, as in our own notions of the constructed. Humans have no option but to invent and differentiate their own bodies of kin; for this, too, follows from the conventional givenness of affinity.[26]

EPILOGUE

Let me conclude by insisting that consanguinity and affinity mean very different things across the four cases summarized above. In each configuration they highlight possibilities that are downplayed or subsumed by the meanings they assume in the other configurations. Hence, my decision to stick to these two words in the face of a lived world quite foreign to the constellation of ideas we express by them was not taken just for the sake of the debate—much less because I believe "that our words consanguinity and affinity have some universal value" (Leach [1951] 1961: 27)—but in order for us fully to appreciate the extent of such foreignness. Indeed I think that one of the most rewarding anthropological experiments is the anti-Fregean trick of forcing unfamiliar "references" onto familiar "senses," the subverting of the conceptual regime of everyday notions-making the right mistake, so to speak.[27] To my mind, this sort

---

25. See Wagner 1977b; Viveiros de Castro 1998b.

26. The reader is asked to note that, although I have been using a Wagnerian frame (adapted from *The invention of culture*) here to redistribute the Lévi-Straussian "affinity/consanguinity" pair in relation to the contrast between the "given" and the "constructed," the resulting inversion is *not* identical to the inversion proposed by Wagner himself in *The curse of Souw* (Wagner 1967) for the equivalent pair "exchange/consanguinity." In the latter book, the relevant parameters are the functions of "unit definition" and "unit relation," not the given and the constructed.

27. To paraphrase the editors' description of the theoretical task of *Relative values* (Franklin and McKinnon 2001: 7), my purpose is also "to open up" the categories of consanguinity and affinity and "examine how [they] can be put to use in ways that destabilize the 'obviousness' of [their] conventional referents, while expanding the scope of [their] purchase as well."

of controlled equivocality is the stuff of which anthropology is made. And this, after all, is what "kinship" is all about.

The reader will have noticed that my two intermediary cases (the "constitutive" and the "constructive") were not directly associated with culturally-specific instantiations. They are theoretical constructs developed within anthropology by a sort of internal dialectic that took off through a negation of the Western viewpoint. Perhaps one might find ethnographic examples of these two cases, though I suspect this would be a far from easy task. If my general argument is correct, the opposition between consanguinity and affinity—as with any conceptual dualism not submitted to deliberate, reflexive equalizing—is inherently unstable, and tends to fall into a marked/unmarked distribution: you cannot have both affinity and consanguinity as given, or both as constructed.[28] Such asymmetry can be seen even within the theoretical constructs that apparently impose the same value upon both poles: the structuralist "constitutive" model obviously privileges affinity as the truly interesting "given"—since the model reacts against an artificialist and individualist conception of sociality—while the constructive model tends to concentrate on consanguinity as the critically interesting "constructed"—for the model opposes naturalized views of kinship. Therefore, should the symmetrical character of the relation between the "Western" and the "Amazonian" models look a tad too neat, I invite the reader to see the latter as an analytical cross between the structuralist model, from whence it draws the notion of affinity as the given, and the constructionist model, from whence it draws the idea of consanguinity as processual construction.

But there is a critical subtext here. I take the Constructive model to be a particularly strong version (a terminal transformation of sorts) of the Standard model, since it does "no more" than extend to consanguinity the constructed status traditionally given to affinity in modern Western kinship ideology. Thus the Constructive model would be describing (or prescribing) what we might call, in Lévi-Straussian terms, a post-complex kinship system, where the element of "choice," which in complex systems characterizes only the affinal dimension, ideally defines the consanguineal one as well. This seems to be pretty much in

---

28. "The precipitation of one [semiotic] modality [i.e., literal or figurative] by the other follows from the fact that their complementarity is essential to meaning. And the interpretive separation of one modality from the other, assuring that the actor's intention will conform to the lineaments of literal or figurative construction, *but not both, or neither, or something else,* emerges as the crucial factor in the construction of human experience" (Wagner 1977b: 392, emphasis added).

phase with recent transformations in the Western culture of kinship (Strathern 2001), since we have now begun to be able to choose (or imagine we can, and perhaps must choose) both the kind of children we want to have, thanks to the new reproductive technologies—the transcription of the old nonliterate "analogical kinship" into the digital genealogical alphabet of DNA—and the kind of parents and siblings we prefer, by way of the new optative solidarities and alternative families. We can now offer ourselves the luxury of two *entirely* different genealogies, one consisting of (biological) relatives without (social) relatedness, the other of relatedness without relatives.[29] Having divided the world into what one is obliged to accept and what one can/must choose—a very peculiar cultural reading of the formal distinction between the given and the constructed—our contemporary social sensibility has become obsessively impelled by a desire to expand the latter domain, indeed, we seem to have finally arrived. We succeeded so well that our predicament is now one of being obliged to choose (Strathern 1992c: 36–38). And *there* we have our own postmodern Given; a sort of dialectical vengeance.[30] The contrast has thereby become absolute, between our state of forced choice and the "choosing to be obliged" characteristic of gift-based socialities. In a way, the constructive model represents the final hegemony of consumptive individualism, which has taken possession of the intrinsically anti-individualist (because relational) field of kinship. This expansion of the sphere of constructiveness of human kinship has, to my mind, an essential connection to our "own particular brand of magic"—technology. Whence the ideologically central character of cultural enterprises like the new reproductive technologies

---

29. "Relatedness without relatives one might say"—Strathern (2002: 44). The contrast with the relatives without relatedness of the new optative families is my own authorship. Here Strathern is discussing, via J. Dolgin, the practico-ideological generalization of the concept of genetic kinship, which establishes entirely "a-moral" links between individuals; the latter have now simply become the carriers of infra- and supra-individual biological units. The relatedness without relatives of bio-kinship contrasts both with the "traditional" family founded on the naturalization of cultural norms and with the contemporary optative family based on affective choice. This postmodern fission of "kinship"—again, of consanguinity—has an interesting parallel in the fission of affinity one finds in Amazonia, where "affines without affinity" stand in opposition to an "affinity without affines" (Viveiros de Castro 2001: 24).

30. As Sartre would have phrased it, our human "essence" consists in being "condemned to freedom." Of course he was not thinking of self-customized late-capitalist productive consumption, but well, history also takes its own liberties

or the Human Genome Project in our present civilization. Kinship still has its magic.

Conversely, I believe the Amazonian model is only accessible by way of a theoretical construct, which emphasizes the givenness of affinity in human kinship—the "Constitutive" model. Or rather, I see in the Amazonian model an image of a pre-elementary system, since one might argue that the classic (Lévi-Strauss 1969) concept of "elementary structures" held that marriage exchange relations necessarily take place between groups defined by a rule of consanguineal recruitment. In truth, my "Amazonian" schema may be taken as a radical version of the structuralist constitutive model; as I remarked above, what does the concept of "incest prohibition" ultimately mean, if not the idea that all consanguinity must be a consequence of affinity?

If this is the case, then we can start to understand why incest is often associated, in Amazonian languages and cosmologies, with processes of metamorphosis—that is, the transformation of the human body into the body of an animal. Kinship, in Amazonia, is a process of constructing a proper human body out of the primal analogic flow of soul-matter in which humans and animals interchange their bodily forms unceasingly. Incest inverts this process (Coelho de Souza 2002), "unrelating" us to other humans and taking us back to where we came from—the pre-cosmological chaos described by myth. But this, in the appropriate context, is exactly what magic and ritual are supposed to do.

ACKNOWLEDGMENTS [FROM THE ORIGINAL]

I would like to thank Marilyn Strathern, James Leach, Sandra Bamford, Marcela Coelho de Souza, Peter Gow, Susan McKinnon and David Rodgers for variously inspiring, causing, shaping, improving, supporting, criticizing and otherwise debugging this paper.

CHAPTER SEVEN

Immanence and Fear

Stranger-Events and Subjects in Amazonia

TRANSLATED BY DAVID RODGERS

ADDITIONS TO THE ORIGINAL TRANSLATED BY IRACEMA DULLEY

Things being thus arranged,
as for those who rise, in their totality,
it is to their future nourishment they
turn the attention
of their gaze, all of them;
and as the attention of their gaze is
turned to their future
nourishment,
so they are those who exist, all of them.

– Mbyá prayer, in Pierre Clastres,
Society against the state, 1989

"Imagine you are standing at the podium about to deliver a public lecture. Your voice cuts into the silence and you begin. No moment is so sheer, so existentially chilling." Our colleague Michael Lambek opened an inaugural lecture at the LSE with these words a short time ago (Lambek 2007: 19). This situation, and the fear that consumes us as we face the problem of a beginning, is overwhelmingly familiar to any academic, however seasoned and however sure he or she may be of the quality of the lecture about to be delivered. If the speaker is an anthropologist, perhaps at this moment another fear at (or of) beginning will come to mind, one situated at the outset of the sequence of circumstances that led to him or her standing at the podium "now":

> Imagine yourself suddenly set down surrounded by all your gear, alone on a trop-ical beach close to a native village, while the launch or dinghy which has brought you sails away out of sight. (Malinowski 1922: 4)

The sequence of circumstances is self-similar—ontogenesis repeats phylogen-esis—in the same way that this famous "imagine" of Malinowski takes all of us back to the anxiety-ridden initial moments of our own field research, marking the historical instauration of the very idea of fieldwork, its originary, and hence radically imaginary, narrative moment.

I highlight the "imagine" in the two quotations above because both convey the intrinsic connection between fear, origin and imagination. As we know, a minimal amount of imagination is needed to be afraid. Even the so-called in-stinctive fears, the "animal fears," are but acts of imagination embedded in the ethogram of our species through a painful originary and immemorial learning, as we have learned from Friedrich Nietzsche and Samuel Butler. Since we need to learn, to have learned, to be afraid. For example, I have recently learned to be afraid of the fear that others have of me when I manifest my intention to cross some of the multiple fractal borders constituting the geopolitical ecology of the present. (I am no longer afraid of planes; I am now afraid of airports.) If the border is, in diverse ways, the place of danger and fear *par excellence*, it is equally clear today that the contemporary world is anything but a world with-out borders—the famous "final frontier" of *Star Trek* is the universal moleculari-zation of the frontier. Crapanzano (2003: 14) suggests that today everywhere is a frontier, that is, a border or limit that cannot be crossed. Imagine the fear that constitutes living today in the "centre" of a world that is nothing but fron-tiers and terms, horizons and closure. The end of the world is now everywhere, while its true centre is nowhere, which happens to be the inverse of the classical definition of the infinite. It is thus to be concluded that we are approaching the anthropological zero—as a limit.

But it is possible to laugh about some fears and, even more so, about some imaginations. In fact, if there is an idea that can be thought of as truly comi-cal today with its mixture of naiveté and presumption it is the belief of our immediate ancestors, the "moderns," that Progress—the advancement of technology and science, the revelation of the mysteries of the cosmos and the organism, the expansion in the free circulation of things, people and ideas, the spread of literacy and the state of law—would dissipate the pervasive state of fear in which our more distant ancestors (or our contemporary "pre-moderns") lived. As is well-known, they lived in fear: fear of other humans, fear of nature, fear of death, fear of the dead, fear of whatever is new, fear of everything. The light of reason, arriving to dispel the darkness of superstition and its imaginary terrors, and science, arriving to lessen the impotence of humans in the face of the real dangers of the world, would finally allow us to attain a state of safety and knowledge, a calm state of non-fear. We would fear nothing because we understood everything; and what could be improved, would be. It is unnecessary to dwell on the point that this prophecy has proven to be relentlessly and tragicomically wrong.

Other people's real fears of imaginary monsters have given way to a frightening proliferation of imaginary fears of real monsters among us. These fears are "imaginary" insofar as they are generated and managed by a gigantic political economy of the image, the "cinematic mode of production" that defines late capitalism (Beller 2006)—the monsters and dangers among us being "real" insofar as they are capable of constantly escaping images. We have even started to define our civilization as a true Fear System. Take, for example, Ulrich Beck's "risk society" (1992). This is a society organized around risks created by itself, frightened of its capacity to annihilate its own conditions of existence—a society, that is, which is afraid of itself (this, I believe, is what is dubbed reflexive modernization). It seems that the spread of "Reason" has ruthlessly increased our reasons for being afraid. That is, if reason has not itself become the very thing to be feared. And it was we who enjoyed the pleasure of complacently ironizing the fears of the "poor primitives": they were afraid of other men, afraid of the natural forces. Precisely we, who are in perpetual—if justified—panic of the fierce fourth-world immigrants as well as of the inexorable global warming. An unexpected proof of Latour's thesis: we have really never been modern.

I have no intention of using my remaining pages to entertain you with images of all too familiar fears. Instead, I wish to talk about a "risk society" of an entirely different kind, a risk society in which risk is experienced not as a threat to the conditions of existence of a social form but as an existential condition of the social form itself—an existential condition of possibility: its reason for being, its mode of becoming. In short, I wish to talk about the forms of fear in the

native societies of Amazonia, or more precisely, about another way of relating to
fear exemplified by these societies.

In a marvellous article published in *Society against the state*, Pierre Clastres
(1989: 129–50) asked: what do Indians laugh about? By analogy, I wish to ask:
what are Indians afraid of? The response is, in principle (and only ever in principle…), simple: they laugh at and fear the same things, the same ones indicated
by Clastres: things such as jaguars, shamans, whites and spirits—that is, beings
defined by their radical alterity. And they are afraid because alterity is the object
of an equally radical desire on the part of the Self. This is a form of fear that,
far from demanding the exclusion or disappearance of the other in order for
the peace of self-identity to be recuperated, necessarily implies the inclusion or
incorporation *of* the other or *by* the other (*by* also in the sense of "through"), as
a form of perpetuation of the becoming-other that is the process of desire in
Amazonian socialities. Without the dangerous influx of forces and forms that
people the exterior of the *socius*, the latter would inevitably perish from a lack of
difference. In order to live according to desire—to "lead a good life"(vivir bien)
as it is said that Indians like to say—it is first necessary to enjoy living on the
edge.

PUDENDA ORIGO

Let us begin again. If, as Nietzsche claimed, all historical beginnings are lowly
or despicable, then it makes sense to begin down below—precisely with the
"bodily lower stratum," in the Bakhtinian sense. I recommence then with a ven-
erable Brazilian proverb (Iberian, I believe) which tells us, *mirabile dictu*, that:
"*Quem tem cu tem meed,*" "Anyone with an asshole feels fear." What this saying
means is not completely agreed upon. I have already found various extravagant
hypotheses (on the internet, where else?) concerning, for example, the need
to be continually on the lookout for the risk of being raped and sodomized.
Personally, I have never heard it used in a sexually paranoid sense. What the
proverb underlines is actually the common human predicament defined by the
sufficient relation between being anatomically equipped with an anus and being subject to the emotion of fear. Presumably, this is a way of saying that fear
(like the anus) is not something we are likely to be proud of or parade, yet it
remains undeniably part of us and fulfils the humble but indispensable function
of helping in the afflictions of life. This profound definition of fear through its

juxtaposed correlation with a literally fundamental anatomical condition is, we should note, unmarked from the viewpoint of gender. The anus is that "private part" equally shared by males and females; having balls makes no difference when one is afraid. . . . It is also unmarked from the viewpoint of species, given that the anus (or its equivalent) is part of the body plan of many animal orders. This suggests an image of fear as an essentially democratic emotion: organic, corporeal, animal, universal. Everyone is afraid of something—the mouth of the enemy, for example, and perhaps above all else the mouths of animals that prey on our own species:

> The Arawaks [of the Guiana region] have a saying, *hamáro kamungka turuwati* (lit. 'everything has [its own] tiger [jaguar]'), as a reminder of the fact that we should be circumspect, and on our guard, there always being some enemy about. (Roth 1915: 367)

But while anyone with an asshole feels fear, we have not all always possessed this remarkably convenient organ. There is an anus origin myth, told by the Taulipang Indians of Guiana and recorded in 1905 by Koch-Grünberg (in Medeiros 2002: 57), which is well worth retelling here. It will lead us back to fear along some unexpected paths.

PU'IITO, HOW PEOPLE AND ANIMALS RECEIVED THEIR ANUS

> In the deep past, animals and people lacked an anus with which to defecate. I think they defecated through their mouths. Pu'iito, the anus, wandered around, slowly and cautiously, farting in the faces of animals and people, and then running away. So the animals said: "Let's grab Pu'iito, so we can divide him up between us!" Many gathered and said: "We'll pretend that we're asleep! When he arrives, we'll catch him!" So that's what they did. Pu'iito arrived and farted in the face of one of them. They ran after Pu'iito, but couldn't catch him and were left trailing behind.
>
> The parrots Kuliwaí and Kaliká got close to Pu'iito. They ran and ran. Finally they caught him and tied him up. Then the others who had been left behind arrived: tapir, deer, curassow, Spix's guan, piping guan, dove. . . . They began to share him out. Tapir eagerly asked for a piece. The parrots cut a large piece and

threw it to the other animals. Tapir immediately grabbed it. That's why his anus is so huge.

The parrot cut a small, appropriately-sized piece for himself. The deer received a smaller piece than tapir's. The doves took a little piece. Toad arrived and asked them to give him a piece too. The parrots threw a piece in his direction, which stuck on his back: that's why even today the toad's anus is on his back.

That was how we acquired our anuses. Were we without them today, we'd have to defecate through our mouths, or explode.

Koch-Grünberg makes the following comment about this story: "Pu'iito is undoubtedly the weirdest personification of which we have record," an observation likely to receive the hearty endorsement of any reader.

The myth of Pu'iito immediately brings to mind a passage from *Anti-Oedipus* on the collective investment of the organs in the primitive territorial machine:

> The mythologies sing of organs-partial objects and their relations with a full body that repels or attracts them: vaginas riveted on the woman's body, an immense penis shared by the men, an independent anus that assigns itself a body without anus. . . . (Deleuze and Guattari 1972: 142–43)

Deleuze and Guattari add that "it is the collective investment of the organs that plug desire into the socius," and that:

> [o]ur modern societies have instead undertaken a vast privatization of the organs. . . . The first organ to suffer privatization, removal from the social field, was the anus. It was the anus that offered itself as a model for privatization. (ibid.)

Pu'iito is one of the many Amerindian myths relating to speciation, that is, the process through which a virtual proto-humanity separates out into the different corporalities of the contemporary world. The history of Pu'iito describes the original, common condition of mythic beings in their pre-corporal, or rather, pre-organic—and yet an anthropo-morphic and anthropo-logical state—a state in which the anus was a person (a spiritual angelic anus, so to speak). It narrates the moment when the organ in question leaves its "intensive" existence, as a part identical to its own (w)hole, and is "extensified," collectively invested and distributed (shared) among the animal species. (In this sense, the Brazilian proverb with which I began refers to the socialized, intermediary phase of the anus, its post-actualized yet pre-privatized moment.) We should note that the myth does not involve giving each individual an identical anus that is his/her *own* in the sense of his/her private property; instead it involves giving the representatives of each future species an organ that is *specific* to it—in other words, one that characterizes each species as a distinct multiplicity. We are not yet within the regime of general equivalence. Still, every species shall have an anus because, as the myth endeavours to explain *in fine*, every species has a mouth. And it is through the mouth that the most decisive relations between the species in the post-mythic world take place—through inter-corporal predation.

AN EYE FOR A TOOTH, A TOOTH FOR AN EYE

The pre-cosmological world described by Amerindian myths is a world completely saturated with personhood. A Yawanawa (Panoan of Western Amazonia) story begins: "in that time there was nothing, but people already existed" (Carid Naveira 1999). The emergence of the species and the stabilization of the food chain (processes described in the myths), have not extinguished this originary universal personhood; they have merely put it into a state of dangerous non-appearance, that is, a state of latency or potentiality. Every being encountered by a human over the course of producing his or her own life may suddenly allow its "other side" (a common idiom in indigenous cosmologies) to eclipse its usual non-human appearance, actualizing its latent humanoid condition and automatically placing at risk the life of the human interlocutor. The problem is particularly acute because it passes through the mouth: "A shaman in Iglulik once told Birket-Smith: *'Life's greatest danger lies in the fact that man's food consists entirely of souls'*" (Bodenhorn 1988: 1; my emphasis).

This is not, then, equivalent to the contemporary fear that our food is composed of "transgenic organisms," but a fear of the latency—of quite other hybrids, transontological intentionalities, non-organic lives—that are just as dangerous as our modern poisons (or even more) as inducers of corporal metamorphoses, as abductors of souls. The theme is fairly well known. Cannibalism is, for the native peoples of America, an inevitable component of every act of manducation because everything is human, in the sense of *capable of being* human: background humanity is less a predicate of all beings than a constitutive uncertainty concerning the predicates of any being. This uncertainty does not implicate merely the "objects" of perception, and it is not a problem of attributive judgment; still less is it a problem of "classification." The uncertainty includes the subject, in other words, it includes the subject condition of the human actant who is exposed to contact with the radical alterity of these other people, people who, like any other people, claim for themselves a sovereign point of view. Here we approach one of the origins of Amerindian metaphysical fear. It is impossible not to be a cannibal; but it is equally impossible to establish a consistently one-way active cannibal relation with any other species—they are bound to strike back. Everything one eats is "soul-food" in the Amerindian world, and therefore threatens life: those who eat souls shall be eaten by souls.

In sum, these are worlds where humanity is immanent, as Roy Wagner puts it; that is, worlds where the primordial takes human form; which does not make it in any sense comforting, much the opposite: there where all things are human, the human is something else entirely. And there where all things are human, nobody can be certain of being unconditionally human, because nobody is—including ourselves. In fact, humans have to be capable of "deconditioning" their humanity in certain conditions, since the influx of the non-human and becoming-other-than-human are obligatory moments of a fully human condition. The world of immanent humanity is also (and for the same reasons) a world of the immanence of the enemy.

Irving Hallowell (1960: 69–70) makes an observation that recurs in many Amerindian ethnographies:

> My Ojibwa friends often cautioned me against judging by appearances. . . I have since concluded that the advice given me in a common sense fashion provides one of the major clues to a generalized attitude towards the objects of their behavioural environment—particularly people. It makes them cautious and suspicious in interpersonal relations of all kinds. The possibility of metamorphosis must be one of the determining factors in this attitude; it is a concrete manifestation of the deceptiveness of appearances.

Do not judge by appearances. . . I presume this warning is issued in virtually all cultural traditions since it belongs to that universal fund of popular wisdom that includes many similar maxims. This wisdom is well grounded in a sense, or rather, in many different culturally specific senses. But Hallowell is saying a bit more than "appearances deceive" in the abstract: he says that the caution about the deceptiveness of appearances applies especially to dealings with persons, and further, that the notion of metamorphosis is a crucial factor. Indeed, if persons are the epitome of what should not be judged by appearances, and if all (or almost all) types of beings are people, we can never take appearances at face value. What appears to be a human may be an animal or a spirit; what appears to be an animal or human may be a spirit, and so on. Things change—especially when they are persons. This has very little to do with our own familiar epistemological warning, "not to trust our senses." What cannot be "trusted" is people, not our senses. Appearances deceive not because they differ from the essences presumed (by us) to be concealed behind them, but because they are, precisely, appearances, i.e. apparitions. Every apparition demands a recipient, a subject to whom it appears. And where there is a subject, there is a point of view. Appearances deceive because they carry embedded within themselves a particular point of view. Every appearance is a perspective, and every perspective "deceives."

The question of distrusting appearances introduces to us the third organ relevant to determining what we could call the "transcendental conditions" of fear in Amerindian socialities: the eye. Here I need to return to a typical motif of indigenous cosmopraxis, one about which I have already written so exhaustively that the reader might be already familiar with it. I refer to Amerindian "cosmological perspectivism," the idea according to which each species or type of being is endowed with a prosopomorphic or anthropomorphic apperception, seeing itself as a "person," while it sees the other components of its own eco-system as non-persons or non-humans. Some are seen as prey animals or predatory animals (everything has its own jaguar), or as spirits (invariably cannibal, or sexually voracious). Other components of the eco-system are seen as artefacts of one's self-own culture: jaguars see humans as peccaries, and see the blood of the prey that they kill as maize beer; the dead see the crickets as fish, the tapirs see the salt licks where they gather as large ceremonial houses, etc. (Much of what I say here about animals can also be said about the dead since, in various aspects, animals are like the dead and the dead are like animals. That is, the dead are not human.) Thus, each species occupies "in" culture the position that humans (that is, the humans' humans) see themselves as occupying in relation to the rest of the cosmos. Hence, it is not just a question of each species identifying itself as a culturally defined humanity: perspectivism also means that each species possesses a particular way of perceiving alterity, a "consensual hallucination" device which makes it see the world in a characteristic way.

This perspectival divergence of the species is frequently attributed to the quality of eyes possessed by each species. The Ye'kuana of Venezuela say: "Each people have their own eyes. . . . The people [humans] can't understand the anacondas

because they have different eyes . . ." (Civrieux 1985: 65–66). The theme is omnipresent in mythology, where magical eyewashes, the swapping of eyeballs and
other ophthalmological tricks produce effects out of radical transformations of
the perceived world—a sure sign that the protagonists have crossed some kind of
ontological barrier (from species to species, living to dead, etc.).

Having different eyes, however, does not mean seeing "the same things" in a
different "way"; it means that you don't know what the other is seeing when he
"says" that he is seeing the same thing as you: we do not understand anacondas.
The problem is one of perceptive "homonymy," not "synonymy." Perspectivism
is not a trans-specific multiculturalism stating that each species possesses a particular subjective "point of view" of a real objective, unique and self-subsistent
world. It is not Anthropology 101—"various cultures and one nature." Perspectivism does not state the existence of a multiplicity of points of view, but the
existence of the point of view as a multiplicity. There is just "one" point of view,
the one which humans share—like the anus—with every other species of being:
the point of view of culture. What varies is the objective correlative of the point
of view: what passes through the optic nerve (or digestive tube) of each species,
so to speak. In other words, perspectivism does not presume a Thing-in-Itself
partially apprehended by the categories of understanding proper to each species.
I do not believe that the Indians imagine that there is a thing-in-itself which
humans see as blood and jaguars see as beer. There are not differently categorized self-identical substances, but immediately relational multiplicities of the
blood-beer, salt lick-ceremonial-house, cricket-fish type. There is no *x* which is
blood for one species and beer for the other: there exists a blood-beer which is
one of the singularities characteristic of the human-jaguar multiplicity.

What *defines* these perspectival multiplicities is their incompatibility. A human and a jaguar cannot be people at the same time; it is impossible to experience blood as beer without having-already-become a jaguar. Perspectivism
states that each species sees itself as people. However, it also states that two
species cannot see each other simultaneously as people. Each species has to be
capable of not losing sight, so to speak, of the fact that the others see themselves
as people and, simultaneously, capable of forgetting this fact—that is, of "no
longer seeing it." This is a particularly important point for humans when they
kill to eat. But although we need to be able "not to see" the animals that we
eat as they see themselves, sometimes it might be interesting, useful, and even
necessary to see how certain animals see and to see them as they are seen by
other animals: to cure humans made sick by the spirit of a certain animal species

(when the shaman must negotiate with the members of the aggressor species); to invest oneself with the predatory capacities of the jaguar or anaconda in order to attack enemies; to know how our world appears when seen from above (the sky) or below (the depths of the river), and so on.

George Mentore (1993: 29) provides a concise formula for the cosmopraxis of the Waiwai of the Guianas: "the primary dialectic is one between seeing and eating." This observation reminds us of that perspectival multiplicity is the correlate of the generalized cannibalism that defines the indigenous cosmopolitical economy. This complex combination between seeing and being seen, eating and being eaten, commensality and inter-perceptuality is abundantly illustrated in the ethnographic record. Consider, for example, the following:

> According to the informant, a jaguar of any species that devours a human being, firstly eats the eyes of its victim, and very often is content with this. In actuality, the eye here does not represent the organ of vision, but a seminal principle which the jaguar thereby incorporates into itself. (Reichel-Dolmatoff 1973: 245)

That this really involves eating the "seminal principle" is not something I would unhesitatingly swear by. However it is quite a good example of the "primary dialectic between seeing and eating." Consider also, from Eduardo Kohn's thesis on the Ávila Runa of Peru:

> Several myth images explore how perspectivism can reveal moments of alienation and the break down of self-knowledge. This is evident in the myth regarding juri juri demons [*Aotus* sp., nocturnal primates with enormous bulging eyes]. . . . This myth begins with an episode in which ten hunters make fun of the monkeys they have hunted and are punished for this by the juri juri demon. This demon eats their eyes out while they are sleeping. (Kohn 2002: 133)

The author also records:

> When [jaguars] encounter people in the forest they are always said to make eye contact. . . . I should also note that one of the ways in which people acquire jaguar souls is through an application of a jaguar canine or incisor tooth dipped in hot peppers to the tear duct. Jaguar teeth that are intact and have not yet developed hairline fractures contain the souls of jaguars. People can absorb this—with the aid of hot peppers—through the conduit of the eyes. (ibid.: 203)

In other words: an eye for a tooth, a tooth for an eye. Miguel Alexiades (1999: 194), discussing the *edosikiana*, spirits encountered by the Ese Eja of Bolivia, writes: "the *edosikiana* are invisible to everyone except the shaman: anyone who sees an *edosikiana* is devoured by it." Interestingly, "seeing" here is "being seen" and, consequently, being devoured. In other cases, it is necessary to see so as not to be seen. This theme is frequent in the Amazonian hunting folklore, indeed, it is a Pan-Amerindian theme, which is also found in the popular tradition of many other peoples. In circumpolar cultures it is, as we know, fundamental. It also appears in Medieval Europe:

> [A] man who encounters a wolf has one chance in two of escaping: he needs to see the wolf first. The latter then loses its aggressiveness and flees. If the wolf perceives the presence of the man first, though, the latter will become paralyzed and will end up being devoured; even if, with a stroke of luck, he manages to escape, he will remain dumb for the rest of his days. (Pastoureau 1989: 167)

An interesting permutation of the senses: if you are seen first instead of seeing, you will become mute. . . . What needs to be remembered is that there is more in perspectivism than meets the eye; there is an entire theory of the sign and communication.

THE HEART OF THE LONELY HUNTER

Joana Miller, in her recent dissertation defended at the Museu Nacional in which she analyzes the importance of body decorations in the constitution of human personhood among the Nambikwara of Central Brazil, cites an indigenous explanation for the danger of a person losing his or her body ornaments. Asked for the reason behind this fear, a young man with some experience of city life replied that his ornaments,

> were like white people's ID cards. When white people lose their ID, the police arrest them, arguing that without their identity card, they are nobody. The same happens when the spirits of the forest steal the ornaments of the Nambiquara. They hide them in holes in the forest and the soul (*yauptidu*) of the person becomes stuck in the hole as a result. The person becomes sick and no longer recognizes his or her kin. Without their ornaments, they are nobody. (Miller 2007: 171)

"No longer recognizing kin" means no longer occupying the human perspective; one of the most important signs of metamorphosis (and every illness is a metamorphosis, especially when caused by soul abduction) is not so much the change in appearance of the self in the eyes of others, but the change in the perception by the self of the appearance of others, detectable by these others by a change in the behaviour of the subject in question: the sick person loses the capacity to see others as conspecifics, that is, kin, and begins to see them as the animal/spirit who captured his or her soul sees them—typically, as prey. This is one of the reasons why a sick person is dangerous.

But the point of more interest to me in this explanation is the relation between indigenous ornaments and the ID card, a fundamental object in the Brazilian state's system for controlling the population. The Nambikwara necklaces and bracelets are "like" the ID cards of white people because this document, as the Indians perspicaciously perceived, is "like" an ornament—it is a humanization device. While the person who "lost" her ornaments, that is, had them stolen by the spirits, no longer recognizes her kin, the person who lost her ID card is no longer recognized by the state, and can thus be "stolen"—arrested—by the police and separated from her kin.

The crucial comparison made by the young Nambikwara man, I suggest, is that between the police and the spirits. The police, like the spirits, are always on the lookout for the chance to transform *somebody* into a *nobody* and then make them disappear. Here we are approaching what seems to me to be the context *par excellence* for experiencing fear in indigenous Amazonia: entry into a "supernatural" regime. I use this term to designate a situation in which the subject of a perspective, or "self," is suddenly transformed into an object in the perspective of another being. Irrespective of its apparent species-specific identity this other being is revealed to be a spirit by the act of assuming the master position of the dominant perspective, thus submitting the human to its definition of reality. This definition of reality is one in which the human, by definition, is not human—it is a prey animal of the spirit, which devours the ex-subject in order to redefine the latter as its conspecific (a sexual partner, or an adopted child).

This is the "war of the worlds" that forms the backdrop to Amerindian cosmopraxis. The typical confrontation takes place in the encounter outside the village between a person who is alone (a hunter, a woman collecting firewood, etc.) and a being that at first sight looks like an animal or person—sometimes a relative (living or dead) of the subject. The entity then interpellates the human: the animal, for example, speaks to the hunter, protesting against his treatment of

itself as prey; or it looks "strangely" at him, while the hunter's arrows fail to in-
jure it; the pseudo-relative invites the subject to follow it, or to eat something it
is carrying. The reaction to the entity's initiative is decisive. If the human accepts
the dialogue or the invitation, if he or she responds to the interpellation, the
person is lost: he/she will be inevitably overpowered by the non-human subjectivity, passing over to its side, transforming him/herself into a being of the same
species as the speaker. Anyone responding to a "you" spoken by a non-human
accepts the condition of being its "second person" and when assuming, in turn,
the position of "I" does so already as a non-human. The canonical form of these
encounters, then, consists in suddenly finding out that the other is "human," or
rather, that *it is the other that is human*, which automatically dehumanizes and
alienates the interlocutor. As a context in which a human subject is captured
by another cosmologically dominant point of view, where he/she becomes the
"you" of a non-human perspective, Supernature is the form of the Other as
Subject, implying an objectification of the human "I" as a "you" for this Other.

This, in sum, would be the true meaning of the Amerindian disquiet over
what is hidden behind appearances. Appearances deceive because one can never
be sure whose or which is the dominant point of view. One can never be sure,
that is, which world is in force when one interacts with the Other.

I spoke of the lethal "interpellation" of the subject by a spirit. The Althus-
serian allusion is deliberate. I see these supernatural encounters in the forest,
where the self is captured by an other, and defined by it as its "second person,"
as a kind of indigenous proto-experience of the State. That is, a premonition of
the fateful experience of finding out that you are a "citizen" of a State (death and
taxes . . .). In an earlier work, I argued that the constitutive problem of Western
modernity, namely, solipsism—the supposition that the other is merely a body,
that it does not harbor a soul like that of the self: the absence of communication as an anxiety-ridden horizon of the self—had as its Amazonian equivalent
the (positive or negative) obsession with cannibalism and the affirmation of the
latent transformability of bodies. In a cosmos totally impregnated with subject-
hood, the dominant supposition-fear is that what we eat are always, in the final
analysis, souls: an excess of communication, the dangerous transparency of the
world.

Here I wish to suggest that the true equivalent of the "indigenous category
of the supernatural" are not "our" extraordinary or paranormal experiences (alien
abductions, ESP, mediumship, premonition), but the quotidian experience, perfectly terrifying in its very normality, of existing under a State. The famous poster

of Uncle Sam with his finger pointing in your face, looking directly at anyone who allowed their gaze to be captured by him, is for me the perfect icon of the State: "I want you." An Amazonian Indian would immediately know what this evil spirit is talking about, and, pretending not to hear, would look elsewhere.

I do not know what the presuppositional experience of citizenship is like in Canada or Japan, but in today's Brazil, I can assure you, everyone (still!) feel a tingle of fear on being stopped by the police—a highway patrol, for example—and asked to hand over his/her "documents" for inspection. Maybe "authorities" and the really rich do not experience such a fear; but these are not people: they are functions and officials of the State and/or Capital. This is quite different for a common mortal (and the more common one is, the more mortal one gets). Even if his/her documents are perfectly in order, even if you are a completely innocent person (and who is completely innocent?), it is impossible not to feel a cold shiver down your spine (i.e., right down to another part of the body mentioned earlier) upon being confronted by the Forces of Order. This is not simply derived from the fact that the police in Brazil are often corrupt and brutal, and that the citizen's innocence and a clean record do not guarantee very much there. Since we feel the same fear (once more, I can only speak of my own experience and of the environment familiar to me) on having our passport examined by Immigration in a foreign country, on crossing the metal detectors found in public buildings across the planet, on disembarking in an absolute non-place such as an international airport, on seeing the banknote we used to make a purchase checked for its authenticity by the shop assistant, on seeing yourself caught by a CCTV camera, and so on. Clearly, all of us almost always escape. Almost always nothing happens: or more exactly, *something always almost-happens*. This is precisely how the subjectivities that wander the forest are typically experienced by the Indians—they are usually only almost-seen, communication is almost-established, and the result is always an almost-death. The almost-event is the Supernatural's default mode of existence. We need to have almost-died to be able to tell.

But what is this experience of uncertainty and helplessness that we feel when faced by the incarnations of the State or, in the case of the Indians, the incarnations of spirits? We could begin by establishing that the modern State is the absence of kinship; this is effectively its principle. Peter Gow observed that the jaguar, the typical antagonist of the natives of Amazonia in these (almost-) lethal supernatural encounters is, for the Piro, "the very antithesis of kinship" (2001: 106). Old people tell Piro children:

You should never joke about the jaguar. That one is not like our mothers and fathers, who are always saying, 'Watch out, I'm going to hit you, I'll hit you,' but never do. No, the jaguar is not like that. That one just kills you! (ibid.: 110)

And here we are. It is no mere coincidence that the large felines are found as imperial symbols just about everywhere, including in indigenous America. And, if the Jaguar-State is the antithesis of kinship it is because kinship is, somehow, the antithesis of the State. Even where kinship groups and networks are firmly ensconced in the State it is through these very networks that powerful lines of flight enable an escape from the state apparatus. In regions where, on the contrary, kinship is assembled into a machine capable of blocking the coagulation of a separate power, as in the Clastrean societies of Amazonia, it (kinship) is less the expression of an "egalitarian" molar philosophy than a perspectivist cosmology where the humanity of the subject is always molecularly at risk, and where the ever-present challenge is to capture inhuman potencies without allowing oneself to be totally dehumanized by them. The problem is "how to make kin out of others" (as Vilaça 2002 put it)—because kin can only be made out of others; conversely, one must become-other to make kin. While the Piro say that you should never joke about the jaguar, we have mentioned Clastres's observation that the myths that make the Indians laugh the most tend to put the jaguars in particularly grotesque situations. The jaguar is the antithesis of kinship and yet, at the same time, the epitome of beauty for the Piro—the beauty of alterity and the alterity of beauty. To avoid being devoured by the jaguar, one need know how to assume its point of view as the point of view of the Self. And here is the crux of the problem: how to let yourself be invested with alterity without this becoming a seed of transcendence, a basis of power, a symbol of the State, a symbol, that is, of a symbol.

THE ENEMY AS IMMANENCE

If we accept my recontextualization of the concept of Supernature, much of what traditionally falls under this rubric must be left out. "Spirits" or "souls," for instance, do not belong to this category, as such; everything that performs the role of antagonist in the perspectival war of the worlds "becomes" a spirit or soul. From this perspective, much of what would not normally be classed as supernatural (for us), must be thus so redefined.

We can take our earlier example of hunting. Hunting is, in a sense, the su-preme supernatural context—from the perspective of both animals (when the hunter succeeds) and humans (when things go wrong and the hunter becomes prey). Warfare and cannibalism are other obvious contexts that can be construed as "supernatural." The analogy between shamans and warriors has often been highlighted in Amerindian ethnographies. Warriors are to the human world what shamans are to the wider universe: commutators or conductors of per-spectives. Shamanism is indeed warfare writ large: this has nothing to do with killing as such (though shamans often act as spiritual warriors in a very literal sense), but rather with the commuting of ontological perspectives; another kind of violence, a "self-positivized violence," in the words of David Rodgers (2004).

Indigenous warfare belongs to the same cosmological complex as shaman-ism insofar as it involves the embodiment, by the self, of the enemy's point of view. Likewise, the intention behind Amazonian ritual exo-cannibalism is to incorporate the subject-aspect of the enemy who, rather than being shaman-istically de-subjectified as in the case of game animals, is hyper-subjectified. Sahlins (1983: 88) writes that "cannibalism is always 'symbolic', even when it is 'real'." With his leave I rewrite the formula thus—all cannibalism is "spiritual", especially when it is "corporeal."

The subjectification of human enemies is a complex ritual process. Suffice to say here that it supposes the complete identification of the killer with the victim, precisely in the same way as shamans become the animals whose bodies they pro-cure for the rest of the group. Killers obtain crucial aspects of their social and met-aphysical identities from the person of the victim—names, surplus souls, songs, trophies, ritual prerogatives—but in order to do this, they must first become the enemy. A telling example of this enemy-becoming can be found in Araweté war songs, in which a killer repeats words taught to him by the spirit of the victim dur-ing the ritual seclusion that follows the killing: the killer speaks from the enemy's point of view, saying "I" to refer to the self of the enemy and "him" to refer to him-self. In order to become a full subject (for the killing of an enemy is a precondition to adult male status in many an Amerindian society), the killer must apprehend the enemy "from the inside," that is, as a subject. The analogy with the perspectival theory, according to which non-human subjectivities see humans as non-humans and vice-versa, is obvious. The killer must be able to see himself as the enemy sees him—as, precisely, an enemy in order to become "himself," or rather, a "myself."

The prototypical manifestation of the Other in Western philosophical tradi-tion is the Friend. The Friend is an other but an other as a "moment" of the self.

If the self finds its essential political determination in the condition of friend-ship this is only because the friend, in the well-known Aristotelian definition, is an other self. The self is there from the start, at the origin, and as origin. The friend is the condition of alterity back-projected, as it were, under the condi-tioned form of the subject. As Francis Wolff (2000: 169) remarks, "the Aristo-telian definition supposes a theory according to which every relation with an Other, and hence every mode of friendship, finds its grounding in the relation-ship of man to himself." The social nexus presupposes self-relation as its origin and model. The connection with modern ideas of property is obvious. To quote Marilyn Strathern quoting someone else quoting yet another source:

> Davis and Naffine (2001: 9) quote the observation, for instance, that western property is based on self possession as a primordial property right which grounds all others. This axiom holds whether or not the self-owning individual is given in the world (being ultimately owned by God, Locke) or has to fashion that condition out of it (through its owns struggling, Hegel). (Strathern 2006: 23n57)

The Friend, however, does not ground an "anthropology" only. Given the his-torical conditions of constitution of Greek philosophy, the Friend emerges as intrinsically implied in a certain relationship to truth. The Friend is a condi-tion of possibility for thought in general, an "intrinsic presence, a live category, a transcendental lived condition" (Deleuze and Guattari 1991: 9). Philosophy requires the Friend, *philia* is the constitutive relation of knowledge.

Very well. The problem, from the standpoint of Amerindian thought—or rather, from the standpoint of our understanding of this thought, is the fol-lowing: what does a world where it is the foe, not the friend, that functions as a transcendental lived condition look like? That was, after all, the real question behind the theme of perspectivism: if the concept of "perspectivism" is nothing but the idea of the Other as such, what is it like to live in a world constituted by the enemy's point of view? A world where enmity is not a mere privative com-plement of "amity", a simple negative facticity, but a *de jure* structure of thought, a positivity in its own right? And then—what regime of truth can thrive in this world where distance connects and difference relates?

The Other has another important incarnation in our intellectual tradition besides that of the Friend. It is consubstantial to a very special, actually, a very singular personage: God. God is the proper name of the Other in our tradi-tion (interestingly, "the Other"—"the enemy"—is one of the euphemisms for the devil; this goes a long way to explaining how otherness is conceived by us). God is the Great Other, being at the same time the one who guarantees the absolute reality of reality (the Given) against the solipsism of consciousness; and the Great Self, the one who warrants the relative intelligibility of what is perceived (the Constructed) by the subject. God's major role, as far as the destiny of Western thought is concerned, was that of establishing the fundamental divide between the Given and the Constructed, since, as Creator, he is the origin point of this divide, that is, its point of indifferentiation. It is here, I believe, that the true Fear of God originates—philosophically speaking of course.

It is true that God no longer enjoys the limelight of history (rumour has it he is preparing a triumphal return). But before he died, he took two providential measures: he migrated to the inner sanctum of every individual as the intensive, intelligible form of the Subject (Kant's Moral Law), and he exteriorized himself as Object, that is, as the infinite extensive field of Nature (Kant's starry heaven). Culture and Nature, in short, the two worlds in which Supernature as originary otherness divided itself.

Well then, to conclude. What is the truth regime proper to a radically non-monotheistic world such as the Amerindian worlds? What is the form of the Great Other in a world which is foreign to any theology of creation? I am not referring to a world created by the retreat of the Creator, such as our modern world, but a radically uncreated world, a world without a transcendent divinity. My answer to these difficult questions, given the space I have to develop it, will be mercifully short, and will simply repeat the gist of everything I said so far: the world of immanent humanity is also a world of immanent divinity, a world where divinity is distributed under the form of a potential infinity of non-human subjects. This is a world where hosts of minuscule gods wander the earth; a "myriatheism," to use a word coined by the French micro-sociologist Gabriel Tarde, Durkheim's fiercest—precisely—enemy. This is the world that has been called animist, that is, now to use the terms of our inanimist tradition, a world where the object is a particular case of the subject, where every object is a subject *in potentia*. Instead of the solipsistic formula "I think, therefore I am" the indigenous cogito must be articulated in animistc terms, as in, "It exists, therefore it thinks." But there, where on top of this the Self is a particular case of the Other, such "animism" must necessarily take the form of—if you excuse the pun—an "enemism": an animism altered by alterity, an alterity that gets animated insofar as it is thought of as an enemy interiority: a Self that is radically Other. Hence the danger, and the brilliance, of such worlds.

PART III

Cosmological Perspectivism in Amazonia and Elsewhere

(Four Lectures given in the Department of Social Anthropology, University of Cambridge, February–March 1998)

Preface to the Lectures

These lectures contain the first English language rendering of an article that was written in 1996 and published in Brazil that same year. While being translated into English (Viveiros de Castro 1998a), the article mutated into the backbone of a longer text that I read, in four installments, at the Cambridge Department of Social Anthropology in 1998. It was my intention to later consolidate and expand these lectures in a detailed monograph. Since such a work, over the past thirteen years, has not yet managed to emerge from the womb, and perhaps may never do so, I accepted an invitation from Hau to publish the lectures' original content in the Masterclass Series. That content appears here, departing in no significant way from the typescript deposited at the Haddon Library in April of 1998. Any change found in the text can be almost entirely attributed to the thorough copy editing and rectification of my defective English, a process carried out by Bree Blakeman and Holly High, whom I thank. I deleted only a few passages that I today judge infelicitous, and I restored a few sentences that I had suppressed in the original typescript.

The lectures circulated, in their "Haddon version," among a number of colleagues who worked at the time on similar themes. One of these colleagues was Philippe Descola, whose comprehensive treatise *Par-delà nature et culture*, published in 2005 [English translation published in 2013 —Ed.], carries out a sustained dialogue with the material that I presented in Paris on three or four occasions between 1995 and 2001. This is not the appropriate context for a return to the dialogue with Descola, which, in truth, has never fallen silent (Latour 2009). Nor do I have the intention of intervening in the many other debates ignited by the arguments outlined in the lectures and in several subsequent articles. For that very reason, I have not added any references to materials published after 1998. HAU's gesture, here, aims at documenting one of the earliest stages in the articulation of the theme of Amerindian perspectivism, or multinatural perspectivism, a theme whose repercussions in the discipline proved somewhat surprising (at least to me).

I have also not filled the text's obvious bibliographic lacunae, which result from faulty scholarship. One such omission that cries out for remediation—a remediation I strove to provide in later works—is the nearly-complete absence of any reference to Roy Wagner's *The invention of culture* ([1975] 1981). I only perceived this book's relevance to my argument at a later date. Another instance, only slightly less embarrassing, is the lack of a closer engagement with *The gender of the gift* (1988) and other works of Marilyn Strathern, in which the theme of the exchange of perspectives had already been masterfully developed.

The only change worthy of note is the restoration of a passage from the first lecture—the subsections "Cosmology" and "Cognition"—that was not included in the version deposited in the Haddon Library. This passage was initially omitted because, at the time, it consisted of a string of half-baked paragraphs written in a mix of Português-English, which were quickly glossed over in my oral presentation. The restored passage has had its Portuguese segments translated by Gregory Duff Morton, whom I thank (again!).

In the Haddon version, I give thanks to the following colleagues: Stephen Hugh-Jones, Marilyn Strathern, Peter Gow, Philippe Descola, Bruno Latour, Michael Houseman, Tânia S. Lima, Aparecida Vilaça, Marshall Sahlins, Tim Ingold, Martin Holbraad, Morten Pedersen, Carrie Humphrey, Peter Rivière, Joanna Overing. Here I would like to also acknowledge the Cambridge Department of Social Anthropology for the warm welcome with which they honored me, and for their highly stimulating engagement, which opened new intellectual perspectives for me. With reference to the present moment, I must thank HAU's Editor-in-Chief, Giovanni da Col, who suggested that these lectures be published in HAU's Masterclass Series and that Roy Wagner be invited to introduce them [Wagner's Introduction is now included as an Afterword in this volume —Ed.], and I must also thank Justin Shaffner, who actually talked me into it, Stéphane Gros, Carna Brkvovic, Mylene Hengen, Juliette Hopkins, Henrik Hvenegaard, Luis Felipe Rosado Murillo, and Philip Swift.

I warn that some of the positions expressed in these lectures no longer correspond exactly to what I think, or, at least, to the way in which I would express myself today. The only virtue of their first official publication, insofar as I can name myself judge of the matter, comes from the fact that they now serve as foundation for a heretofore-unpublished introduction [see Afterword, this volume —Ed.] by Roy Wagner, whose generosity exceeds the limits of any possible acknowledgement from me. It will not be the first time that the preface is worth much more than the book.

EDUARDO VIVEIROS DE CASTRO

CHAPTER EIGHT

Cosmologies
Perspectivism

Can the anthropological theorist justifiably deny theoretical insight to his subjects?
– Irving Goldman, *The mouth of heaven* (1975)

The subject of these lectures is that aspect of Amerindian thought which has been called its "perspectival quality" (Århem 1993) or "perspectival relativity" (Gray 1996): the conception, common to many peoples of the continent, according to which the world is inhabited by different sorts of subjects or persons, human and non-human, which apprehend reality from distinct points of view. I shall try to persuade you that this idea cannot be reduced to our current concept of relativism (Lima 1995, 1996), which at first it seems to call to mind. In fact, it is at right angles, so to speak, to the opposition between relativism and universalism. Such resistance by Amerindian perspectivism to the terms of our epistemological debates casts suspicion on the robustness and transportability of the ontological partitions which they presuppose. In particular, as many anthropologists have already concluded (albeit for other reasons), the classic distinction between nature and culture cannot be used to describe domains internal to non-Western cosmologies without first undergoing a rigorous ethnographic critique. That critique, in the present case, implies a dissociation and redistribution of the predicates subsumed within the two paradigmatic sets that traditionally oppose one another under the headings of "Nature" and "Culture": universal and particular, objective and subjective, physical and social, fact and value, the given and the instituted, necessity and spontaneity, immanence and transcendence, body and mind, animality and humanity, among many more.[1]

Such an ethnographically-based reshuffling of our conceptual schemes leads me to suggest the expression "multinaturalism" to designate one of the contrastive features of Amerindian thought in relation to modern "multiculturalist" cosmologies. Where the latter are founded on the mutual implication of the unity of nature and the multiplicity of cultures—the first guaranteed by the objective universality of body and substance, the second generated by the subjective particularity of spirit and meaning—the Amerindian conception would suppose a spiritual unity and a corporeal diversity.[2] Here, culture or the subject would be the form of the universal, whilst nature or the object would be the form of the particular.

This inversion, perhaps too symmetrical to be more than a speculative fiction,[3] must be developed by means of an analysis of Amerindian cosmological categories enabling us to determine the contexts we can call "nature" and "culture." The dissociation and redistribution of the predicates subsumed by such categories, therefore, is not enough: the latter must be dessubstantialized

---

1. Each one of these paired predicates plays a role in the syncretic master opposition between nature and culture, but their relative importance in our tradition has varied. There have also been some major inversions of the correlative pairing of the predicates. Thus, as Nieztsche remarked somewhere, in the modern world nature is necessity, culture is freedom; in Classical Greece, on the other hand, nature was freedom (*phusis* is that which grows *sponte sua*), while culture was rule and necessity (*nomos*, "law").

2. This idea is hardly new—it has been variously hinted at by a number of Americanists, as I discovered after having written the first version of my argument. Thus, Goldman, in his brilliant reanalysis of Boas' Kwakiutl materials, sketches the contrast: "Scientific materialism postulates the consubstantiality of matter, primitive religions that of life and the powers of life" (1975: 22; see also 182–83, 200, 207). Even closer to my point, as will become clear, is this recently published remark by Andrew Gray on Arakmbut (Peruvian Amazonia) concepts of body and soul: "The physical property of the body separates a person from all others, whereas the soul is a dynamic, invisible substance which is constantly seeking contact outside. . . . The effect is a total contrast to the occidental view of the soul as the unique and essential aspect of a person because, for the Arakmbut, whereas the body gives a distinct form to a person, the *nokiren* [soul] reaches out in dreams to others—not just humans but also species and spirits" (Gray 1997: 120). The present lectures are a sustained effort to draw out all the consequences of observations such as these, by connecting them to the theme of perspectivism.

3. Such fictions have their uses, as argued and demonstrated by Strathern (1988).

as well, for in Amerindian thought, it is not simply that the categories of nature and culture have other contents to their Western counterparts, they also have a different status. They are not ontological provinces, but rather refer to exchangeable perspectives and relational-positional contexts; in brief, points of view.

Clearly, then, I think that the distinction between nature and culture must be subjected to critique, but not in order to reach the conclusion that such a thing does not exist. There are already far too many things which do not exist. The flourishing industry of criticisms of the Westernising character of all dualisms has called for the abandonment of our conceptually dichotomous heritage, but to date the alternatives have not quite gone beyond the stage of wishful unthinking. I would prefer to gain a perspective on our own contrasts, contrasting them with the distinctions actually operating in Amerindian perspectivist cosmologies.

PERSPECTIVISM IN AMAZONIA AND ELSEWHERE

The initial stimulus for the present reflections were the numerous references in Amazonian ethnography to an indigenous theory according to which, the way humans perceive animals and other subjectivities that inhabit the world—gods, spirits, the dead, inhabitants of other cosmic levels, meteorological phenomena, plants, occasionally even objects and artefacts—differs profoundly from the way in which these beings see humans and see themselves.

Typically, in normal conditions, humans see humans as humans and animals as animals; as to spirits, to see these usually invisible beings is a sure sign that the "conditions" are not normal. Animals (predators) and spirits, however, see humans as animals (as prey), to the same extent that animals (as prey) see humans as spirits or as animals (predators). By the same token, animals and spirits see themselves as humans: they perceive themselves as (or become) anthropomorphic beings when they are in their own houses or villages and they experience their own habits and characteristics in the form of culture—they see their food as human food (jaguars see blood as manioc beer, vultures see the maggots in rotting meat as grilled fish etc.), they see their bodily attributes (fur, feathers, claws, beaks) as body decorations or cultural instruments, they see their social system as organised in the same way as human institutions are (with chiefs, shamans, ceremonies, exogamous moieties etc.). This "to see as" refers literally to percepts and not analogically to concepts, although in some cases the emphasis is placed more on the categorical rather than on the sensory aspect of the phenomenon; in any case, the shamans, masters of cosmic schematism (Taussig 1987: 462–63) and dedicated to communicating and administering these cross-perspectives, are always there to make concepts tangible and instuitions intelligible.

In sum, animals are people, or see themselves as persons. Such a notion is virtually always associated with the idea that the manifest form of each species is a mere envelope (a "clothing") which conceals an internal human form, usually only visible to the eyes of the particular species or to certain transspecific beings such as shamans. This internal form is the soul or spirit of the animal: an intentionality or subjectivity formally identical to human consciousness, materializable, let us say, in a human bodily schema concealed behind an animal mask.

At first glance then, we would have a distinction between an anthropomorphic essence of a spiritual type, common to animate beings, and a variable bodily appearance, characteristic of each individual species but which rather than being a fixed attribute is instead a changeable and removable clothing. This notion of clothing is one of the privileged expressions of metamorphosis—spirits, the dead and shamans who assume animal form, beasts that turn into other beasts, humans that are inadvertently turned into animals—an omnipresent process in the "highly transformational world" (Rivière 1994) proposed by Amazonian ontologies.[4]

This perspectivism and cosmological transformism can be seen in various South American ethnographies, but in general it is only the object of short commentaries, and seems to be quite unevenly elaborated. In South America, the cosmologies of the Vaupés area are in this respect highly developed (see Århem 1993, 1996; Reichel-Dolmatoff 1985; Hugh-Jones 1996), but other Amazonian societies also give equal emphasis to the theme, such as the Wari' of Rondônia (Vilaça 1992) and the Yudjá of the Middle Xingu (Lima 1995). It can also be found, and maybe with even greater generative value, in the far north of North America and Asia, as well as amongst a few hunter-gatherer

---

4.   This notion of the body as clothing can be found among the Makuna (Århem 1993), the Yagua (Chaumeil 1983: 125-27), the Piro (Gow pers. comm.), the Trio (Rivière 1994), and the Upper Xingu societies (Gregor 1977: 322). The notion is very likely pan-American, having considerable symbolic yield for example in Northwest Coast cosmologies (see Goldman 1975 and Boelscher 1989), if not of much wider distribution. I return to this them in Lecture 4 (Chapter 11, this volume).

populations of other parts of the world.[5] Outside these areas, the theme of perspectivism seems to be absent or inchoate. An exception could be the Kaluli of Papua New Guinea's Southern Highlands, who have a cosmology quite similar in this respect to the Amerindian ones. Schieffelin (1976: chapter 5) and Sahlins (1996: 403) reminded me of this parallel. Interestingly, Wagner (1977: 404) characterized Kaluli cosmology as "bizarre"—by Melanesian standards of course, for it would sit rather comfortably in Amazonia.[6]

Perspectivism in the literature: Some examples

The notes and quotations below are an aleatory sample of the ethnographic record about our subject (other references will be given as the argument unfolds).

(1)   Pierre Grenand (1980: 41–42), on the Wayãpi of French Guiana: A man who falls in the subterranean world is seen by its denizens, who are giant sloths, as a kinkajou. "For humans, animals are animals; for animals [who are humans for themselves, presumably], humans are animals." But for the Sun and the Moon, both humans and animals are animals (humans are monkeys).

(2)   Fabíola Jara (1996: 68-74), on the Akuryió of Surinam: Vultures go "fishing" on earth; the maggots on rotten meat are their fish. For the spirits living on the river bottom, fishes are forest animals; land animals are seen by them as birds. The "banana" of the tapir is an inedible fruit of the forest; the forest floor is the hammock of tapirs; in the village of tapirs, identical to a human one, "manioc" can be seen (the leaves tapirs eat), etc. These Akuryió myths, like many other references to animal perspectivism (e.g., Hallowell

---

5.   See for example, Saladin d'Anglure (1990) and Fienup-Riordan (1994) on the Eskimo; Nelson (1983) and McDonnell (1984) on the Koyukon, Kaska; Tanner (1979), Hallowell (1960), Scott (1989), and Brightman (1993) on the Ojibwa, Cree; Goldman (1975) on the Kwakiutl; Guédon (1984a, 1984b) on the Tsimshian; Boelscher (1989) on the Haida. See also, the following remarkable studies by Howell (1984, 1996) on the Chewong of Malaysia, and Hamayon (1990) on Siberia.

6.   Note, however, Wagner's writing on Melanesian notions of the "innate," which has throw light on Amerindian materials (Brightman 1993: 177–85; Fienup-Riordan 1994: 46–50). This suggests that the "perspectivism" found in native America is a possibility in Melanesia, although only (?) actualized by the Kaluli.

1960: 63; Lévi-Strauss 1985: 151), can be read as lessons in natural history, presenting a detailed account of the ethnogram of different species. The motif of human-animal parallelisms suggests, furthermore, that Amerindians conceive of something like an abstract, pan-specific behavioral schema which includes humans: culture is human nature, just as animal nature is culture. However, perspectivism cannot be reduced to—even if it may be derived from—a sort of generalized analogical ethology (with more than a grain of Western-scientific truth in it, by the way). It applies to other beings besides animals, like the dead, spirits, chthonian and celestial races, plants, artefacts and so on. It often has important cosmographic connotations, as noted in items 3, 5 and 8 below. And in many cases the theme has no obvious naturalistic references, as in the long Matsiguenga myth analyzed by Renard-Casevitz (1991: 16-27).

(3)   Gerald Weiss (1972: 170) on the Campa of Peru:

And what is the nature of the universe in which the Campa find themselves? It is a world of semblances; for example, what to us is the solid earth is airy sky to the beings inhabiting the strata below us, and what to us is airy sky is solid ground to those who inhabit the strata above. It is a world of relative semblances, where different kinds of beings see the same things differently; thus humans eyes can normally see good spirits only in the form of lightning flashes or birds whereas they see themselves in their true human form, and similarly in the eyes of jaguars human beings look like peccaries to be hunted.

(4)   Aparecida Vilaça (1998: 4) on the Wari' of Rondônia (Brazil):

Humanity is defined by the possession of a spirit or soul. Animals endowed with spirit are considered as "people," "human." They have a human body that shamans can see; they live in houses, drink maize beer and eat their food roasted and boiled. All "human" animals have culture, the same culture of the Wari'. That is why they hunt, kill enemies, use fire to prepare their food, cultivate maize etc. This, however, is the way they [the animals] see things. The Wari' know the jaguar kills its prey with tooth and claw, and eats it raw. But for the jaguar, or rather, from the jaguar's point of view (shared by shamans, but not by the rest of the Wari'), he kills his prey with arrows like the Wari' do; he takes the prey home, gives it to his wife and tells her to cook it.

(5)   Marie-Françoise Guédon (1984a: 142), on the Tsimshiam (NW Coast):

There are stories of human beings transformed into salmon, or snails, or mountain goats and living a human-like life with the salmon, snails, or mountain goats
... and looking at the humans as we look at the supernatural beings, the *naxnoq*.
... So, we are to the animal what the powers of the spirit are to us. For example,
consider a hunter shooting a sea lion; from the point of view of the sea lions,
who are living in houses with their human-like families, the sea lion which has
been struck by the arrow becomes sick; so it needs a shaman, a sea lion shaman
to cure a sea lion from the spirit arrow of a *naxnoq*, who is the human hunter.

(6)   Robert Brightman (1993: 44–47), on the Rock Cree (Canada). Com-
       menting a myth opposing wolverines' and wolves' behaviors and percep-
       tions, the author sketches a lapidary characterization of perspectivism:

These scenes typify epistemological themes that resonate in other myths, in
dreams, and in Cree reflections on the quality of their waking perceptions.
Beings or selves of two different species or kinds may have radically different
perceptions and understandings of the same events in which both partici-
pate. More specifically, individuals or selves of one species or kind experience
individuals of other species as different from themselves in appearance and
practices. The experience that each "self" has of the "other" may be, however,
radically different from the experience that the "other" has of its own appearance and practices. Further, selves of different species or kinds may each experience *themselves* in similar or identical terms: as users of fire, speech, and
manufactured objects. . . . Crees speculate that modern animals, whatever they
may look like to humans, experience themselves as participating in the same
appearances and behaviours that Crees understand themselves to possess.

See also pp. 163–85 of Brightman's outstanding monograph, to which I
shall be making less mention than it obviously deserves (I still have to give
it a closer reading).

(7)   Out of America: Signe Howell (1996: 139), on the Chewong of Malaysia:

A large number of myths concern deceptive relations between different species
of personages. Thus there are stories in which human personages appear in the

cloak of animals, and stories where animals, plants or spirits appear in human cloak. An added complication is that non-human personages may appear in human bodies when they are "at home," in "their own land," thus expressing the fundamental equality between all species of personages.

Howell's (1984) monograph on the Chewong is a pioneering study of a perspectivist cosmology remarkably evocative of Amerindian themes.

(8)   The *Mythologiques*, of course, include abundant materials relevant to our theme. But it is in *La potière jalouse* that Lévi-Strauss deals more direct-ly with it. It appears there in connection with the notion of *"le monde à l'envers,"* the world as seen by the denizens of other cosmic levels (1985: 134–42, 149–52): for the red-haired anusless chthonian dwarves who feed on the smell of foods, wasps are enemy Indians, hares are jaguars; their day or summer is our night or winter and vice-versa. (Lévi-Strauss takes the chthonian dwarves, present in many Amerindian mythologies, to be a spa-tial translation of the arboreal fauna). In Arapaho mythology, the dwarves speak the same language as humans, but with the meaning of words sys-tematically inverted, a theme that reappears in the Chinook idea (1985: 152) that the language of the dead is to that of the living as figurative is to literal. (Compare this to the "twisted language" used by Yaminahua shamans when dealing with the spirit world, see Townsley [1993].) More generally, Lévi-Strauss observes the connection between perspectivistic themes and the many-layered universes so common in native America, and identifies the "reciprocity of perspectives" as a characteristic of Amer-indian myths: *"la réciprocité de perspectives où j'ai vu le caractère propre de la pensée mythique . . ."* (1985: 268).[7]

---

7.   "The reciprocity of perspectives, where I perceived the singular character of mythical thought." The theme of perspectivism is absent from *Histoire de Lynx*. But we can find there many references (Lévi-Strauss 1991: 97–100, 113–16, 127, 131, 216) to skin-changing or clothes-changing as inter-specific metamorphosis, and to human-animal marriages as deriving from the "two-sided" nature of mythic animals (part human, part beast). I am far from having completed my survey of Amerindian materials concerning perspectivism; among other interesting Amazonian references not used in the present lectures, see Journet (1995: 193–94) (Curripaco); Nimuendaju (1952: 113, 117–18) (Tukuna); Gallois (1984/85: 188) (Wayãpi); Osborn (1990: 151) (U'wa).

(9)   The most insightful exploration of a perspectivist cosmology is to be found
      in Tânia S. Lima's thesis on the Yudjá (Juruna) of Eastern Amazonia
      (1995; 1996). The richness and complexity of Lima's analyses makes any
      summary mention of her data inappropriate. I can only refer the reader to
      her work; it was one of my major inspirations, even if my extrapolations
      would not necessarily meet her approval.[8]

ETHNOGRAPHIC CONTEXT

Some general observations are necessary. In the first place, perspectivism does
not usually involve all animal species (besides covering sundry other beings), or
does not involve them to the same extent. The emphasis seems to be on those
species which perform a key symbolic and practical role such as the great predators, the rivals and enemies of human beings, and the main species of prey for
humans: one of the central dimensions, possibly even the fundamental dimension, of perspectival inversions refers to the relative and relational statuses of
predator and prey (Vilaça 1992: 49-51; Århem 1993: 11-12; see also Howell
1996: 133).

    Personhood and "perspectivity"—the capacity to occupy a point of view—is
then a question of degree and/or context (Hugh-Jones 1996; Gray 1996: 141–
44; see also Howell 1996: 136), rather than an absolute, diacritical property of
some species and not of others. Some non-human beings evince this attribute
in a more consequential manner than others; as a matter of fact, many of them
have powers of agency far superior to humans and in this sense are "more persons" than the latter (Hallowell 1960: 69). On the other hand, the question of
non-human personhood has an essential *a posteriori* dimension: the possibility
that a thus far insignificant type of being turns out to be a prosopomorphic
agent capable of affecting humans is always open—context and personal experience are decisive here.

---

8.   The notions of "perspective" and "point of view" play a central role in some of my
     previous work, but there the main focus was on intra-human dynamics (Viveiros
     de Castro 1992a: 64-66, 68, 343 n.16, 344 n.22, 248-51, 256-59; see also Viveiros
     de Castro 1996a, 1998). The thesis of Vilaça (1992) and especially that of Lima
     (1995) showed me that it was possible to generalize these notions both in terms
     of extension and comprehension, and made me look deeper into the ethnographic
     record.

In the second place, to affirm that non-human beings are persons capable of a point of view is not the same as affirming that they are "always" persons, that is, that humans' interactions with them are always predicated on a shared personhood. I am not referring here to any "dual attitude" to animals or nature in general, that is, to a distinction between practical cognition and religious ideology.[9] If there is any duality—and there is indeed—it belongs primarily to persons themselves (human and non-human), not to the attitudes towards them, for these are but a consequence of the two-sided nature of persons. It has nothing to do with reality vs. illusion, economy vs. ideology, or practice vs. theory: it derives from a distinction between visible and invisible, objective and subjective, affects and percepts. The personhood of animals (and of humans) is in effect a question of context; but contexts cannot be imported ready-made from our own intellectual context—they must be defined in Amerindian terms.

Finally, it is not always clear whether spirits or subjectivities are being attributed to each individual animal, and there are examples of cosmologies which deny consciousness to postmythical animals (Overing 1985: 249ff; 1986: 245-46) or some other spiritual distinctiveness (Viveiros de Castro 1992a: 73-74; Baer 1994: 89)—but it is also far from clear whether this constitutes "animality" as a unified domain opposed to "humanity." (I believe it does not; see below.)[10] Be that as it may, the notion of animal spirit "masters" ("mothers of the game," "master of the white-lipped peccaries" etc.) is widely spread throughout the continent. These spirit masters, clearly endowed with a type of intentionality-based agency analogous to that of humans, function as hypostases of the animal species with which they are associated, thereby creating an intersubjective field for human-animal relations even where empirical animals are not spiritualized.

We must remember, above all, that if there is a virtually universal Amerindian notion, it is that of an original state of undifferentiation or "undifference" (don't mistake this for "indifference" or "sameness") between humans and animals, described in mythology:

---

9. For instance, Tanner (1979) and Karim (1981). See Bloch ([1985] 1989) for a generalization of this argument, which smacks of the classical distinction between "technical" and "expressive" aspects of action.

10. In the Araweté case (Viveiros de Castro 1992a), for example, non-Araweté humans have the same spiritual handicap as animals (their souls do not go to the celestial paradise).

[What is a myth?] If you were to ask an American Indian it is extremely likely that he would answer: it is a story from the time when humans and animals did not distinguish themselves from one another. This definition seems to me to be very profound. (Lévi-Strauss and Eribon 1988: 193)

Myths are filled with beings whose form, name and behavior inextricably mix human and animal attributes in a common context of intercommunicability, identical to that which defines the present day intrahuman world. Myth is thus the vanishing point of Amerindian perspectivism, where the differences between points of view are at the same time anulled and exacerbated: this gives it the character of an absolute discourse. In myth, every species of being appears to others as it appears to itself (as human), while acting towards others as if already showing its distinctive and definitive nature (as animal, plant or spirit). All the beings which people mythology, manifest this ontological entanglement or crossspecific quality which makes them akin to shamans (an analogy which is explicitly made by some Amazonian cultures).[11] Myth speaks of a state of being where bodies and names, souls and affects, the I and the Other interpenetrate, submerged in the same immanent presubjective and preobjective milieu, the demise of which (ever incomplete, always undone) is precisely what the mythology sets out to tell.

The "end" of this primordial immanence is, of course, the well-known separation of culture and nature which Lévi-Strauss showed to be the central theme of Amerindian mythology. But such separation was not brought out by a process of differentiating the human from the animal, as in our own evolutionist mythology. *The original common condition of both humans and animals is not animality, but rather humanity.* The great separation reveals not so much culture distinguishing itself from nature but rather nature distancing itself from culture: the myths tell how animals lost the qualities inherited or retained by humans. Humans are those who continue as they have always been: animals are ex-humans, not humans ex-animals.[12] As Father Tastevin tersely remarked with

---

11. "The Earth's present animals are not nearly as powerful as the originals, differing as much from them as ordinary humans are said to differ from shamans. . . . The First people lived just as shamans do today, in a polymorphous state . . ." (Guss 1989: 52).

12. Brightman (1983: 40, 160) and Fienup-Riordan (1994: 62) discuss similar ideas in a North American context. For Amazonia, see also Jara 1996: 92–94 (Akuryó) and Guss (1989: 40) (Ye'kuana). Schiefflin (1976: 94–95) reports the same for the Kaluli of New Guinea.

regard to the Cashinahua: "Contrary to Spencer, they deem animals to have
descended from man and not man from animals" (in Lévi-Strauss 1985: 14).
In the cosmology of the Campa, humankind is the substance of the primordial
plenum or the original form of virtually everything, not just animals:

> Campa mythology is largely the story of how, one by one, the primal Campa
> became irreversibly transformed into the first representatives of various species
> of animals and plants, as well as astronomical bodies or features of the terrain. .
> . . The development of the universe, then, has been primarily a process of diver-
> sification, with mankind as the primal substance out of which many if not all of
> the categories of beings and things in the universe arose, the Campa of today
> being the descendants of those ancestral Campa who escaped being transformed.
> (Weiss 1972: 169–70)[13]

In sum, "the common point of reference for all beings of nature is not humans as a species but rather humanity as a condition" (Descola 1986: 120). This
distinction between the human species and the human condition—analogous
to that between "humankind" and "humanity" made by Ingold (1994; see below)—should be retained. It has an evident connection with the idea of animal
clothing hiding a common spiritual "essence" and with the issue of the general
meaning of perspectivism.

There is one further well-known aspect of Amazonian mythologies which
deserves to be mentioned. I am thinking of the rarity of the idea of creation
ex nihilo in Amazonian cosmogonies. Things and beings usually originate as a
transformation of something else (a *trans*-formation, not an *in*-formation, by
which I mean the creative imposition of mental form over passive and inert
matter)—in the case of animals, as I have noticed, as the transformation of a
primordial, universal humanity.[14] Wherever we do find notions of creation—al-

---

13. The notion that the "I" (humans, Indians, my tribe) is the historically stable term in
    the distinction between the "I" and the "other" (animals, white people, other Indians)
    appears as much in interspecific differentiation as in intraspecific separations, as can
    be seen in the various Amerindian myths of origin of white people. The others used
    to be what we are and are not, as amongst ourselves, what we used to be. Thus it can
    be perceived how very pertinent the notion of "cold societies" can be: history does
    indeed exist, but it is something that happens only to others.

14. This point has often been made for other non-Western cosmologies. See, for
    instance, Gell (1995: 23) on Polynesia: "Polynesian thought about the universe

most never *ex nihilo* anyway, but as the fashioning of some prior substance into a new type of being—it seems to me that what is stressed is the imperfection of the end product; the typical Amerindian demiurge (often because of the misdeeds of his trickster twin brother) always fail to deliver the goods.

In like manner to this transformed rather than created nature, culture is not a matter of invention, but of transference (of "tradition," then). In Amerindian mythology, the origin of cultural implements or institutions is canonically explained as a borrowing, a transfer (violent or friendly, by stealing or by learning, as a trophy or as a gift) of prototypes of these institutions or implements such as already possessed by animals, spirits, or enemies. The origin and thereby the essence of culture is acculturation.

I would like to call your attention to the difference between the idea of creation-invention and the idea of transformation-transference, and to associate the creation idea to the metaphor of *production*: of production as a kind of weak version of creation, but at the same time as its model, as the archetypal mode of action in—or rather, upon and against—the world. I borrowed this contrast from François Jullien (1989a, 1997), but I am using the notion of transformation in a sense very different from Jullien's, who is concerned with Chinese ideas of efficaciousness. I am referring to production as the imposition of mental design over formless matter. By the same token, I would associate the idea of transformation to the metaphor of *exchange*. An exchange event is always a transformation of a prior exchange event; there is no absolute beginning, no absolute initial act of exchange—every act is a response, that is, a transformation of an anterior token of the same type. Now, creation-production is our archetypal model of action—the heroic or epic model of action, as Jullien observes, which dates from the Greeks and which is still very much alive: let us recall our current obsession with "agency" and "creativity"—while transformation-exchange would probably fit better

---

differed from Judæo-Christian 'creationist' thought in that it was predicated, not in the creation of the universe *ex nihilo* by God, but on the initial existence of everything in an all-embracing plenum or tightly-bound continuum. The creative epoch occurred as a process of 'differentiation' within this pre-existing plenum. . . ." As I have just observed, the Amerindian plenum, differently from the more "naturalistic" Polynesian cosmogonies, is human: humanity is the form of the primordial continuum. On the relevance of the mythological theme of the continuum in Polynesian cosmologies—a theme originally developed by Lévi-Strauss (1964) precisely in a Polynesian-Amerindian comparative context—see the remarkable book by Schrempp (1992).

the Amerindian and other nonmodern worlds.[15] The exchange model of action supposes that the other of the subject is another subject, not an object; and this, of course, is what perspectivism is all about (Strathern 1992d: 9–10). In the creation paradigm, production is causally primary, and exchange its encompassed consequence; exchange is a "moment" of production (it "realizes" value) and the means of *re*-production. In the transformation paradigm, exchange is the condition for production (without the proper social relations with the nonhuman world, no production is possible: production is a type or mode of exchange), and production the means of "re-exchange"—a word we certainly do not need, for exchange is by definition re-exchange. Production creates, exchange changes.[16]

I would venture a further remark on this contrast: the idiom of production applied to what lies without the source domain of material production—like when we speak of the production of persons, of social reproduction, of "consumptive production" as if it meant the production of subjects rather than simply of humans organisms, etc.—is necessarily "metaphorical"; it is as metaphorical, at least, as the idiom of exchange when applied to the engagement between human and nonhuman beings. To speak of the production of social life makes as much, or as little, sense as to speak of the exchange between humans and animals. Historical materialism is on the same plane as structural perspectivism, if not at a further remove from "the native's point of view."

It is also worth pointing out that Amerindian perspectivism has an essential relation with shamanism, and with the valorization of hunting as the archetypal mode of practical interaction with the nonhuman world. The association between shamanism and this "venatic ideology" is a classic question (for Amazonia, see Chaumeil 1983: 231–32; Crocker 1985: 17–25). I stress that this is a matter of symbolic importance, not ecological necessity: full-blown horticulturists such as

---

15. I do not mean to imply that this obsession is a "mistake," only that we "late Moderns" seem to be particularly haunted by that aspect of Being (though not too willing to extend it to nonhuman beings).

16. Production is about projection (productive consumption) and introjection (consumptive production). Exchange is about commutation and transmutation (two notions which could perharps be correlated with the two Strathernian modes of personification, mediated and unmediated exchange). Production has a beginning (creation), but has no end (reproduction, the endless dialectics of ablation and sublation); exchange, on the other hand, has no beginning—the "anticipated outcome" as the form of the gift (Strathern 1988: 221–23) makes any beginning appear as a response—it can, however, have an end (relationships can be terminated).

the Tukano or the Yudjá, who couldn't have less of a "hunter-gatherer" disposition (and who in any case fish more than they hunt), do not differ much from circumpolar hunters in respect of the cosmological weight conferred on animal predation, spiritual subjectivation of animals, and the theory according to which the universe is populated by extra-human intentionalities endowed with their own perspectives. In this sense, the spiritualization of plants, metereological phenomena or artefacts seems to me to be secondary or derivative in comparison with the spiritualization of animals: the animal is the extra-human prototype of the Other, maintaining privileged relations with other prototypical figures of alterity, such as affines (Erikson 1984: 110–12; Descola 1986: 317–30; Århem 1996).[17] This hunting ideology, as I said, is also and above all an ideology of shamans, insofar as it is shamans who administer the relations between humans and the spiritual component of the extra-humans, since they alone are capable of assuming the point of view of such beings and, in particular, are capable of returning to tell the tale.[18]

THEORETICAL CONTEXT

Before we proceed to examine the ethnography, I should address some likely disputable points. I am prompted to this by an awareness that substantive arguments about "how 'natives' think" (as opposed to arguments about how other anthropologists think), and especially arguments that appeal explicitly to a contrast with Western intellectual traditions as an expository device (as opposed to those wherein such contrast is willy-nilly left embedded in the very process of describing and analyzing), are mandatorily prefaced by a wealth of qualifications, apologies, and disavowals. I suppose I have to abide by the current protocol, on pain of being convicted of uncouthness or worse—of naiveté. The major qualm I must do my best to appease concerns the nature and purpose of

---

17. In the cultures of Western Amazonia, however, especially those in which hallucinogens of botanical origin are widely used, the personification of plants seems to be at least as important as that of animals.

18. It is worth noticing that in those Amazonian societies where shamanism as an institution (as opposed to a general cosmological stance) is weakly developed, if present at all, the theme of perspectivism seems barely sketched. The Gê-speaking societies of Central Brazil are a case in point. The basic idea, however, is very much present among some Gê—see the story of Umoro's death below (Lecture 4; Chapter 11 in this volume).

this overall contrast between Amerindian and modern Western cosmologies. But I would also like to say something about the relation between what I shall be doing here and contemporary theories of human cognition.

Cosmology

By applying the labels "perspectivism" or "multinaturalism" to "Amerindian cosmologies" and contrasting it to a "Western cosmology," I am bound to be accused of two complementary faults (among others). It might be said that I am over-differentiating these two poles, and perhaps even essentializing them, that is, of proposing yet another Great Divide theory, and that I am under-differentiating each of them internally—the Amerindian one by treating, say, the Kayapó and the Tsimshian as birds of a feather who flocked together just yesterday from Siberia, and the Western one by lumping under this label an ungodly bricolage of histories, languages, cultures, intellectual traditions, discursive practices, genres, and what have you.

   Great Divide theories, i.e., polarities and other "othering" comparative devices, have had a bad press lately. The place of the other, however, can never remain vacant for too long. As far as contemporary anthropology is concerned, the most popular candidate for the position appears to be anthropology itself. Firstly, in its formative phase (never completely outgrown), anthropology's main task was to explain how and why the primitive or traditional other was wrong: savages mistook ideal connections for real ones and animistically projected social relations onto nature. Secondly, in the discipline's classical phase (which lingers on), the other is Western society/culture. Somewhere along the line—with the Greeks? Christianity? the Reformation? the Enlightenment? Capitalism?—the West got everything wrong, positing substances, individuals, separations, and oppositions wherever all other societies/cultures rightly see relations, totalities, connections, and embeddednesses. Because it is both anthropologically anomalous and ontologically mistaken, it is the West, rather than "primitive" cultures that requires explanation: the Occident was an Accident. And, thirdly, in the post-positivist (still very much desiderative) phase of anthropology, first Orientalism, then Occidentalism, is shunned: the West and the Rest are no longer seen as so different from each other. On the one hand, we have never been modern (this is true) and, on the other, no society has ever been primitive (this is very true as well). Then who is wrong, what needs explanation? (Someone *must* be wrong, something *has* to be explained.) Our anthropological forebears, who made us believe in tradition and modernity, were wrong—and so the great polarity now is between anthropology and the real practical/embodied life of everyone, Western or otherwise. In brief: formerly, savages mistook (their) representations for (our) reality; now, we mistake (our) representations for (other peoples') reality. Rumor has it we have even been mistaking (our) representations for (our) reality when we "Occidentalize."

But once the blame games and guilt trips are over, what is left? The present writer, probably because he is stuck in anthropology's second stage, does believe there are striking differences between our modern official, hegemonic ontology—a precipitate of the Cartesian, Lockian, and Kantian reformations (i.e., epistemologizations) of previous ontologies—and the cosmologies of many "traditional" peoples, such as those I am most familiar with: Amazonian Indians. I take it this belief is not contradictory with the idea that "we have never been modern"; for the belief that we have been, or still are, modern (a belief that created, among many other things, the very category of "belief") is distinctive of modernity, and as such is related to a number of epistemo-political consequences, as shown by Latour (1991, 1996a).[19] (I should also remark that some of the most forceful deconstructors of Great Divides show a propensity to rebuild them along different fault lines. Goody [1996] is the most obvious example. Showing himself very much in phase with recent geopolitical realignments, he duly chastises orientalisms, sneers at the "hot/cold" contrast etc., but quickly replaces these "othering" devices by a number of coincident divides—the hoe and the plough, bridewealth and dowry, the oral and the written etc.—which simply transform the East/West polarity into a North/South one.)[20]

I have to say in my defence that the decision to concentrate on some similarities internal to (but not exclusive to) the Amerindian domain and on an overall contrast with the modern West is mostly a question of choice of level of

---

19. A tripartition similar to the one proposed above is to be found in Latour (1996b); but my connecting thread is different from Latour's. What makes our three states comparable is their common emphasis on fetishism and reification.

20. "The Munchkins told Dorothy that there were four witches in Oz. The ones from the North and South were good, but those from the East and West were bad." So Orientalism and Occidentalism are politically incorrect in the Land of Oz, too—but Goody's "meridionalism" would be quite all right. As an Americanist, I have always found Goody's contrasts between "Eurasia" and "Black Africa" interesting but somewhat arbitrary. In many respects, such as political organization and kinship ideology, Europe and "Black Africa" look quite similar, and quite different from Amazonian forms.

generality; it has no "essentialist" value. Had I chosen instead to emphasize the commonality of human thought processes—about which I would not have much to talk about—or, conversely, the uniqueness of each Amerindian culture—in which case there would be no reason to stop talking—I would have to deliver a very different series of lectures. Let me just observe that these options I have not followed are actually far more liable to carry essentialist presuppositions.

The word "Amerindian" refers here to a limited number of native cultures from Lowland South America (mainly from Western Amazonia) and from septentrional North America (Northwest Coast, N. Athapaskan, N. Algonquian, Eskimo). These limits are the limits of my ignorance: I am not conversant with the ethnology of other, more southerly parts of North America. I am not including the Mesoamerican and Andean regions in my synecdoche, either. Generally speaking, I am at a quite unsafe remove from the ethnographic realities discussed here. My own fieldwork with the Araweté of Eastern Amazonia was certainly a crucial inspiration for the pages that follow, but these are based on the work of other ethnographers, sometimes on secondary sources already of an analytical and interpretive nature; more often than not, I shall be commenting on comments rather than on indigenous statements and narratives.

It should be quite obvious that the Kwakiutl and the Cree are not "the same thing," let alone the Kwakiutl and the Tukanoans. Both of the major regions from which I take my examples exhibit marked internal differences in social morphology, economic and political structure, ceremonial life, religion, and so on. As with many of my colleagues, I have been much intrigued by some Amazonian contrasts, and have even been suspected of "reifying" some of them (between central Brazil and Amazonia, for example).[21] Be that as it may, with the present lectures I shall be moving up in the reification scale. They are an effort to tackle themes and problems that would allow me to make sense of some of these differences by identifying a sort of cosmological background from which they could be shown to emerge (as opposed to a cosmological horizon into which they should be resorbed). In this I am simply following the lead of Lévi-Strauss, who in his *Mythologiques* provided a forceful demonstration of the historical unity of indigenous America. The ethnographic and thematic grounds I shall be covering are a small subset of the *Mythologiques'* universe.

---

21. See, for instance, Overing (1981, 1983–84, 1988); Rivière (1984); Viveiros de Castro (1992a, 1993b); Hugh-Jones (1992, 2001); Descola (1992); Henley (1996a, 1996b); Fausto (1997).

I must also stress that there is not a hint of comparison in the present endeavor; there is only generalization. The materials I refer to, culled from a small sample of texts (I did not engage in a collation of different sources on the same groups—no internal, "critical" comparison as well), are used as a springboard for a thought-experiment consisting in abstracting and generalizing a set of ideas about subjects and objects, bodies and souls, humans and animals, and then sketching what could be called the "virtual ontology" underlying these abstracted generalizations.

Lévi-Strauss famously described indigenous America as "*un Moyen âge auquel aurait manqué sa Rome*" (1964: 16).[22] He might have added: and a Greece as well, were it not for the fact that his own work shows the remarkable unity of the Amerindian world when we leave the socio-political for the mythico-philosophical plane. There was no Greece of course, and no identifiable Plato or Aristotle: there was no one, in particular, to oppose "myth" and "philosophy." But the thought-experiment that follows may be read as outlining a sort of imaginary identikit picture of an Amerindian philosophy who would stand to indigenous mythopoeisis as Cartesian or Kantian ideas, say, stand to what I am calling the "modern West." If the analogy strikes you as too far-fetched, then what about this one:

> I have not authored a "perspective" on Melanesian society and culture; I have hoped to show the difference that perspective makes . . . I have not presented Melanesian ideas but an analysis from the point of view of Western anthropological and feminist preoccupations of what Melanesian ideas might look like if they were to appear in the form of those preoccupations. (Strathern 1988: 309)

Now, it would very likely be argued—after Bourdieu (1972) and his strictures against the "theoricist" misrepresentation of the practical-embodied life of all peoples, Westerners included—that such an endeavor is meaningless, for people do not act out philosophical systems or cosmologies: the first belong to a very specialized type of discourse characteristic of higher civilizations, and the second are fanciful constructs of anthropologists unduly modeled on the former. The peoples of the world live through practice, in practice, and for practice. Any "plausible" anthropological theory must begin with this principle: that the phenomena that it studies differ radically from itself, not only in their contents, but also in their form and even in their reason for being. All anthropological

22. "Middle Ages which lacked a Rome."

theory must be a theory of practice. And practice and its behavioral precondi-
tions (which go by various names—schemata, presuppositions, premises, scripts,
habitus, relational configurations, etc.—the important criterion here being that
the name must *not* be a word that resembles "culture" or "structure") are quin-
tessentially nonpropositional.[23] What "goes without saying" (Bloch 1992) is the
stuff social life is made of. We study the opposite of our study; nothing is more
different from an anthropological theory than the practice of a native.

Thus anthropologists find themselves sometimes obliged to make embarrassing compromises in order to be able to say anything at all about this stuff
that goes without saying. Take, for example, the brilliant analysis of Yaminahua
shamanic knowledge carried out by Graham Townsley (1993). The paper's thesis is that

> Yaminahua shamanism cannot be defined by a clearly constituted discourse of
> beliefs, symbols or meanings. It is not a system of knowledge or facts known, but
> rather an ensemble of techniques for knowing. It is not a constituted discourse
> but a way of constituting one. (Townsley 1993: 452)

In other words, the author stands against the traditional anthropological understanding of shamanism—shamanism as the expression of a traditional indigenous cosmology (Townsley 1993: 450). At the same time, however, he ad-
mits that, to account for this "constituting discourse" that constructs meaning
from the actual experience of ritual (practice, practice), "it will *first* be necessary to discuss some of the basic Yaminhaua *ideas* about the *constitution of the
world* which provide the *framework* for shamanism . . ." (Townsley 1993: 452,

---

23. Bourdieu's strictures, of course, did not prevent him from bodying forth that
prodigious oxymoron, the "theory of practice," the intended self-irony of which—if
any were intended—was entirely lost on the ensuing flock of pratice theorists. In like
manner, Brunton (1980) and similar expostulations against the anthropological "will
to order" in cosmological analyses seem to be slightly deficient in reflexivity. Even as
they denounce the socio-professional pressures and rewards leading anthropologists
to exaggerate the conceptual orderliness of non-Western cosmologies, they forget
to mention the even more pressing and enticing incentives towards "critical"
originality, deconstruction of other analytical styles by using some version of
the "ethnocentrism" argument—a fickle weapon, given its intrinsic rebounding
potential—and the unveiling of (preferably unconscious) "political" motivations.
There is thus more sociological order (and academic calculus) in Brunton's decision
to reveal cosmological disorder than he seems prepared to acknowledge.

emphasis mine). Such ideas involve concepts like *yoshi*, i.e. "spirit, or animate essence," and certain subtle native theories (my word) of language that seem to me fairly explicit. On the whole, all of this, these "basic ideas" about the "constitution of the world," are quite similar to that which once got called, in the bad old days, "cosmology," "ontology," or even "culture."

It seems to me, all in all, that we have to resolve our highly ambivalent attitude concerning the propositional content of knowledge. Contemporary anthropology, both in its phenomenological-constructionist and in its cognitive-instructionist guises, has proven notable for insisting on the severe limitations of this model when it comes to dealing with intellectual economies of nonmodern, nonwritten, nontheoretical, nondoctrinal—in short, non-Western type. Anthropological discourse has embroiled itself in the paradoxical pastime of heaping propositions on top of propositions arguing for the fundamentally nonpropositional nature of other peoples' discourses. We count ourselves lucky when our natives display a blissful disdain for the practice of self-interpretation, and even less interest in cosmology and system. We're probably right, since the lack of native interpretation has the great advantage of allowing the proliferation of anthropological interpretations of this lack. Simultaneously, the native's disinterest in cosmological order fosters the production of neat anthropological cosmologies in which societies are ordered according to their greater or lesser inclination towards systematicity (or doctrinality, or whatever). In sum, the more practical the native, the more theoretical the anthropologist. Let us also not forget that the nonpropositional mode is held to be characterized by a constitutive dependency on its "context" of transmission and circulation. This makes it the exact opposite (supposedly, it goes without saying) of scientific discourse—a discourse whose aim is precisely universalization. All of us are context-bound, but some are so much more context-bound than others.

My issue here isn't with the thesis of the quintessential nonpropositionality of untamed thought, but with the underlying idea that the proposition is in any sense a good model of conceptuality in general. The proposition continues to serve as the prototype of rational statements and the atom of theoretical discourse. The nonpropositional is seen as essentially primitive, as nonconceptual or even anticonceptual. Naturally, such a state of affairs can be used both "for" and "against" this nonconceptual Other: the absence of rational-propositional concepts may be held to correspond to a superpresence of sensibility, emotion, sociability, intimacy, relational-cum-meaningful engagement in/with the world, and what not. For or against, though, all this concedes way too much to the proposition, and reflects a totally archaic concept of the concept, one which continues to define it as the subsumption of the particular by the universal, that is, as essentially a movement towards classification and abstraction. Now, rather than simply divorcing, for better or worse, the concept from "cognition in practice" (Lave 1988), I believe we need to discover the infraphilosophical, i.e., the vital, within the concept, and likewise (perhaps more importantly) the virtual conceptuality within the infraphilosophical. What kind (or "form") of life, in other words, is virtually projected by ideas such as the Cartesian Cogito or the Kantian synthetic a priori? (Recall Wittgenstein's indignation against the petty spiritual life presumed by Frazer's interpretations of primitive rites.) And in like manner, what sort of virtual conceptuality pulsates within Amazonian shamanic narratives, Melanesian initiation rituals, African hunting traps, or Euro-American kinship usages? (Think of the ludicrously stunted conceptual imagination presumed by many an anthropological expatiation upon wild thought.) We need a little less by way of context and much more by way of concept.

Cognition

The style of analysis instanced in these lectures has been repeatedly assailed by anthropologists who favor so-called cognitive approaches. I will not examine their arguments in detail. Let me just say I think the materials presented here have little to expect from, and little to contribute to, cognitivist theories and concerns. Cognitivism belongs to my field of objects, not tools. It is something I shall be contrasting (more or less explicitly) with Amerindian ideas, not the standard of evaluation of these ideas or the instrument for their analysis. In other words, my problem is not that of Bloch (1989), i.e., that of showing how humans move (upwards and backwards, so to speak) "from cognition to ideology"—and how anthropology followed, historically, the inverse direction, leaving the dark ages of ideology to enter the enlightened era of cognition—but rather that of treating cognition *as* "ideology," the Western ideology of cognition.

Let me resort to an analogy to illustrate my contention that the materials presented here have little to do with cognitivist preoccupations. Consider the following trenchant remarks by Pascal Boyer on structuralism. (I am using Boyer as a target because, if we are to refer to anthropological cognitivism, we must go for the real McCoy, not some recent convert—and because I greatly admire his work.) These are his words:

Structuralist descriptions of cultural realities are generally based on strong assumptions about supposedly universal patterns of thinking. From a psychological
viewpoint, however, such claims are generally unconvincing. . . . For instance,
structuralism assumes that the most important aspect of conceptual structure is
binary opposition. . . . Psychological research, however, has never found anything
of the sort in the mental representations of concepts and categories. . . . Binary
oppositions . . . play virtually no part in these representations. . . . In the same
way, a central tenet of the Lévi-Straussian analysis of myth is that these same
binary oppositions are crucial to the memorisation and transmission of stories.
Again, however, empirical research in this domain has uncovered many complex
processes to do with the reorganisation of stories in memory . . . none of which
have anything to do with structuralist oppositions. In so far as it is making claims
about the "human mind," structuralism seems to be pointing to realities which
elude any psychological description. (1993: 16–17)

Now, in the same article whence this dismissal of the psychological substance
of binary opposition was extracted, we can also behold a dichotomous tree, used
by Pascal to demarcate his own theoretical tribe from the rest of anthropology:

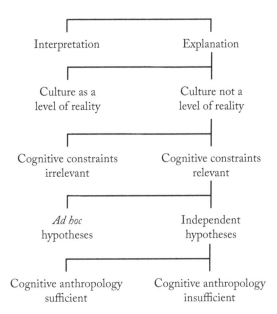

Figure 8.1. Five choices in the study of religious symbolism (from Boyer 1993: 7)

I do not know about the human mind in general, but Boyer's manifestly has some sort of commerce with binary oppositions, and his mental representations of concepts and categories do seem to resort to this type of device after all. As for myself, and contrary to whatever empirical research has uncovered, I must say I found the binary tree above quite useful for memorizing Boyer's place in the cast of characters of his theoretical mythology. (There would be other things to observe about this tree, like the nobly pure vertical line connecting directly the "explanation" root above down to the branch on which Pascal is perched.)

My point here, let me be very clear about it, is *not* to prove that Boyer is wrong about structuralism, and that the human mind does feature binary opposition as its central conceptual mechanism. For all I know, he is probably right. But it is also a fact that some of his thought *contents*—his thoughts about cognitive anthropology, its relationships to other anthropological styles, the encompassing dualism of "interpretation" and "explanation" etc.—if not his thought *processes*, seem definitely to have been cast into a binary mold, as shown by the tree above. Nothing strange about that. Our intellectual tradition abounds in dichotomies. Boyer's tree, for example, has solid roots in both Plato and Aristotle, and we are certainly not an exception: from the Chinese *yin/yang* to the Bororo *aroe/bope*—both dualities, it should be remarked, very different from any Western construct—any anthropologist could recall dozens of examples to the effect that we are not alone in imagining dual principles and using them as master schemes for ontology-building.[24] So the human *mind* may not have binary opposition as the basic building material of its "mental representations." . . . But many human *cultures*, or if you wish, many historically specific intellectual traditions, obviously use dualistic schemes as their conceptual skeleton key.

What can we conclude from that? At the very least, that cognitive psychology cannot tell us much—certainly not the whole story—about higher-level, collective "mental" constructs such as cosmologies or philosophical systems. Conversely, we are led to suspect that the anthropological analysis of these objects may have little to tell us about the human mind—in this respect, the ambitions of structuralism, and indeed of much of classical anthropology, may have been a bit too grand—and still less about the ultimate nature of reality (Gell 1992). In short, I believe that there is a gap here, which, far

---

24. My point here is simply that "binary thought" is not a side effect of the alphabet (see the Bororo; Crocker 1985), nor dualism an exclusive property of Western theological or philosophical traditions (see Jullien 1993 on China).

from having been bridged by neocognitive anthropology, has only been made wider.[25]

My real problem with cognitivism, however, concerns its central concept, that of "mental representation." It is of course perfectly feasible to account for the perspectivist cosmologies of Amerindians with the help of the concept of mental representation. But one of the contentions in what follows is that a representationalist account of these cosmologies seriously misrepresents, if one may say so, the Amerindian point of view. My aim here, anyway, is not to *explain* this point of view, that is, to find its causes (cognitive, economic, and what have you); it is rather to *explicate* it: to explore its consequences and follow its implications.

WORDS

I would like to close this general introduction to our subject with some miscellaneous remarks on my use of certain words or concepts. I shall proceed from the more "abstract" or merely definitional to the more "concrete" and substantial.

Subject and object

These dangerous words are used here in a purely—but metaphorically—pragmatic, indexical, or pronominal sense. "Subject" is the semiotic position correlated with the capacity to say "I" in a real or virtual *cosmological* discourse. "Object," by the same token, is that which is "talked" about. As will become clear in the following lectures, I am relying essentially on Benveniste's seminal work on "subjectivity in language" as expressed in the pronominal set (1966a, 1966b). I use "person" as a synonym of "subject," when wishing to mark the fact that persons are "objects" capable of acting as "subjects." This notion of "person" is equally pronominal, and can also be derived from Benveniste. My metaphors come, therefore, from semiosis, not production or desire: there is no dialectics of "self" and "other" intended, for there is no synthesis and coproduction, but rather alternation and disjunction, that is, exchange (of perspectives). The possible

---

25. *Ideas* like "the mind" or "the ultimate nature of reality," however—in the sense that they are historically constituted, culturally determined, collective intellectual products—are perfect examples of those objects that anthropology *can* claim as falling (among others) within its proper field of study.

connections of my "subject" and "object" to the concepts of "objectification," "personification," and "reification" such as developed, for instance, by Strathern (1988) are left open for further exploration.

Body and soul

I shall be here using the words "soul" and "spirit" as partial synonyms to refer to the subjective, volitional-intentional invisible component of persons associated to, but detachable from, the visible bodily forms that characterize each species. I shall also be calling "spirits" some entities of Amerindian worlds that do not have a stable, normally visible bodily form, evincing in a superlative manner the metamorphic capacity proper to all persons (Hallowell 1960: 69): spirits are, in a sense, more-than-human persons, or meta-persons.

I am aware that the words "soul" and "spirit" have quite distinct connotations in our tradition, especially in their more philosophical usages. Also, an exact interlingual translation of these two words, even between closely related languages, is a very difficult task (Wierzbicka 1989).[26] Be that as it may, my somewhat loose usage of "soul" and "spirit" is based on the sentiment that these words span a continuous semantic space (as suggested for instance by the fact that the adjectival form associated to "soul" is "spiritual"). This common space is separated by a marked discontinuity from the one covered by notions such as "body," "matter," and (in its modern, nonphilosophical usages) "substance."

As to "body" versus "soul," let me firstly observe that there is a curious asymmetry in anthropological attitudes towards them. When we translate the indigenous words that correspond to our notions of "soul," "spirit," "vital principle" etc., we usually spend whole pages to comment on their glosses, cushioning these in warnings about the inadequacy of the available notions in the target-language. On the other hand, our "mind" seems perfectly at ease when translating the words that correspond to "body"—sometimes we do not even bother to write the relevant word in the source-language. It is as if the concept of body were evident, because universal, whilst the concepts of "soul," "spirit" etc. were supremely culture-specific, and therefore ultimately non-translatable. This asymmetry when dealing with the semantic aspect of "body" and "soul" is a

---

26. Portuguese and English vernaculars, for instance, feature a third substantive of the same semantic family—"*mente*" and "mind"—that exists in French only as an adjective, "*mental.*" The corresponding substantive, as you know, is "*esprit.*"

symptom of their asymmetric status in our ontology: the body is common, is what connects us to the rest of reality, whilst the soul is what separates and distinguishes. Solipsism (a standard "modernist" philosophical obsession), therefore, is not only *caused* by the soul—by its absolute singularity—but *affects* first and foremost the concept of soul. Another source of this difficulty in translating the words for "soul" may be this: how does one translate what "does not exist"? One must not only translate, but explain and justify—two things "body" would supposedly not need.

In the wake of the pervasive dichotomy between a dichotomous West and a nondichotomous Rest, the notorious "mind-body dualism" (Pauline, Augustinian, or Cartesian—but also Kantian and Durkheimian, of course: cf. the *Homo duplex*) became the sitting duck of anthropologists as well, who thus belatedly joined the anti-dualist sentiment of post-Kantian philosophy (Lovejoy 1960). It is now de rigueur to state that Amerindians (or Melanesians, Africans, non-Westerners, nonmodernist cultures, nonacademic Westerners) do not "have" such a thing. Very well—I am an anti-dualist myself. But a conceptual duality needs not imply a metaphysical dualism. It is one thing to argue that Amerindians do not separate body and spirit the way "we" do, and quite another that they make no distinction whatever between body and spirit. To take the first argument (which is quite true) as entailing the second (which is patently false) is unfortunately a very common rhetorical practice nowadays. All the available ethnographic evidence indicates that the distinction between body and spirit (or analogue qualities and states) plays a central role in Amerindian cosmologies, and indeed in all shamanic cosmologies. The whole problem, of course, consists in determining the nature of this distinction, and the referents of "body" and "spirit" in the Amerindian context.

This same analytico-rhetorical *non sequitur*, this slippage from "not like here" to "not at all there," afflicts all the other conceptual pairs I shall be concerned with: humans/animals, nature/culture, subject/object etc.[27] For it will not do simply to argue that "body" and "soul" (especially "soul," for today we all love "body") and their opposition are modernist or Western constructs and accordingly should be shunned. This is linguistic "fetishism," a typical Western disease (modern and post-), incidentally: the prison-house of language, etc.[28] This is, in fact, simple-minded linguistic-cultural relativism. It is better to follow here the

27. Such slippage sets the stage for those privative oppositions characteristic of "Great Divide" theories.
28. Both the disease *and* the diagnosis are "typically Western."

lead of Amerindian perspectivism and be aware that the same signs may stand for entirely different things: the dictionary of the jaguar also contains the concept of "manioc beer," and it has the same signification as in a human dictionary (a tasty and nutritious liquid substance that makes you drunk)—but jaguars use it to refer to what we call "blood." Why not treat "body" and "soul" (and "nature," "culture," etc.) in like manner, in our analytical language?

Perspective

Considering all that has been written about the visual bias of our philosophical tradition, it might seem hazardous to lay such stress upon the notion of perspective, this hyper-Western, supremely modernist, "sightist" metaphor. But then, "what . . . does the anthropologist do in the face of deliberate provocations to vision?" (Strathern 1994: 243).[29] All I can do here is observe that most Amerindian cultures evince a visual bias of their own: vision is the model of perception and knowledge (Mentore 1993); many indigenous languages feature evidentials that distinguish between direct knowledge (obtained by sight) from hearsay knowledge; shamanism is laden with visual concepts (Gallois 1984–85; Townsley 1993); in many parts of Amazonia, hallucinogenic drugs are used as a "deliberate provocation" *of* visions; more generally, the distinction between the visible and the invisible (Kensinger 1995: 207; Gray 1996: 115, 177) seems to play a major ontological role; we might also recall the emphasis on the decoration and exhibition of bodily and object surfaces, the use of masks, etc. (See Gow 1997b for a detailed and insightful analysis of vision in an Amazonian culture.)

In some cases, the notion of "perspective" or "point of view" is literally and indigenously expressed. Consider this passage by Guédon:

> One of the first Tsimshian women I have met who is still involved today in shamanism has explained to me that it is not the *atiasxw* [the healer's helper, the embodiment of his gift: an object that serves as the shaman's tool] as object that matters but the methods used to place the power in proper focus with the help of the *atiasxw*. In her case, her power is the rope. One may think that a rope can be

---

29. In the face of non-Western cultures that show a visual bias, the anthropologist can, for instance, argue that Western tradition emphasizes the verbal rather than the visual (e.g., Wagner 1987: 57). And indeed, the "mirror of nature" (Rorty 1980), for all its ocularity, is always cast in writing.

used to tie or to pull, but hers is not a material rope, it is an *atiasxw*, that is, as she explains it, a *"point of view."* If she is looking at a sick person in a normal way, she knows she cannot get through (not only to the sick person but also to herself), that there is nothing she can do to help the person. Her idea is to shift the point of view: she would imagine herself as a rope, "a big rope of light going from way, way back to way, way in the future. As a rope I can do something. I can be there as a rope and there would be that other rope (the patient) with a big knot (the disease). . . ." We may note that she is not actually transformed into a rope. . . . The *atiasxw* is simply used as a point of view. (1984b: 204)

It might be argued that this woman had been "exposed" to Western idioms and concepts, is probably literate, and a very sophisticated person. Perhaps. Be that as it may, she chose this particular notion of a point of view; she did not say the rope was a metaphor, a symbol, or a manner of speaking. Indeed, the rope was definitely *not* a manner of speaking.

The Wari' of Brazilian Amazonia, who are very likely unaware of what "point of view" means in Portuguese, also emphasize sight, and here directly in the context of human/animal perspectival differences:

Shamans possess two simultaneous bodies, one human, the other animal. They can alternate their points of view by manipulating their sense of sight. When he wishes to change his vision, a shaman rubs his eyes for a few seconds: if he was seeing humans as animals—this being the point of view of his animal body— then he starts seeing them as humans; if he was seeing some particular animal as a person, then he will start seeing it as an animal and will then feel free to kill and eat it.[30] The problem, as Topa explained to me, is that these different points of view alternate too quickly, and a shaman always runs the risk of suddenly realizing that the animal he had just killed was actually some relative of his. . . . Orowan, who is a shaman, told me he made this "mistake" once, while he was in his jaguar body: he killed and ate a man because he saw him from the jaguar's point of view, as an enemy or game. (Vilaça 1998: 25–26)

30. A shaman cannot kill or eat the body of the animal species which he shares. Some shamans see *all* soul-endowed animals as people—and are accordingly very poor hunters because the majority of the species hunted by the Wari' are in this category. This reputation of shamans as poor hunters due to their "species-androgyny," is also found among the Cashinahua (Kensinger 1995: 211), and among the Akuryó (Jara 1996: 92–94), where shamans are not allowed to hunt for this very reason.

This same emphasis on the eyes and sight is clearly expressed in the most developed non-Amerindian example of perspectivism, the Chewong of Malaysia:

> Much of Chewong morality is expressed through directives involving food which in turn are predicated upon how each species actually sees reality. This is directly attributable to the quality of their eyes, which are subtly different in each case. The way one species sees another is dependent upon what constitutes food for them. Thus, when human beings see a monkey's body they see it as meat; when a tiger sees a human body it sees it as meat. A *bas* (a group of harmful spirits) upon seeing human *ruwai* perceive it as meat, and so on. (Howell 1996: 133)[31]

In those Amazonian cultures where one finds the notion of multiple personal souls, the eyes are usually endowed with a soul of their own, and this eye soul is often the "true soul." This is what Mentore says of the Waiwai (Caribs of Guiana):

> Besides the body as a whole, only the eye possesses a distinct soul. . . . At death, when detached from their corporeal self, the body soul remains on the earthly plane, while the eye soul rises to the first ascending plane of *kaup* (the celestial spirit world) . . . to know, that is, to be human, is "to see" in all its various forms. (1993: 31)

The same idea can be found among the Peruvian Aguaruna (Jívaro): there are two human souls, an eye soul residing in the pupil—this is the one that goes to the celestial world after death—and the demon-shadow *iwanch* that remains on earth under various animal guises (Brown [1986] 1993: 55).

Among the Panoans these ideas are present in a rather more elaborated form (Kensinger 1995; Townsley 1993; McCallum 1996). In a nice prefiguration of the theory of cognitive modularity, the Cashinahua assign different modes of knowledge to different organs: skin, ears, eyes, liver, hands, genitals, etc. (see Kensinger 1995: ch. 22). This modular knowledge is associated with different

---

31. Shamans and laypersons are also distinguished on the basis of their eyes: the former have cold, the latter hot eyes. This Chewong connection between food and sight, besides illustrating the already mentioned idea that perspectivism is crucially concerned with the relational statuses of predator and prey, brings to mind a remark by Mentore (1993: 29) on the Waiwai of Guiana: "the primary dialectics is one between seeing and eating."

souls: thus skin knowledge, an attribute of the skin soul, has as its object "the natural world," it is knowledge of "the jungle's body spirit," the visible, sensory aspect of things; hand knowledge refers to bodily skills, ear knowledge to social behaviour, the genitals are the source and the site of knowledge of mortality and immortality, and so on. These different bodily-based types of knowledge appear to be subsumed by a generalized "body spirit" which encases the person as an outer skin (so skin-knowledge would be the dominant synecdoche). To this body knowledge the Cashinahua oppose eye knowledge, an attribute of the eye-soul, also called the "true soul" or "real spirit." This is the module which allows one to see "the true nature of people and things that make up the natural world"; it is "knowledge of the supernatural" (Kensinger 1995: 233). The eye soul is the immortal part of the person; it is the agent in dreams and drug-induced hallucinatory experiences. McCallum (1996: 32) describes the eye soul as "a kind of person within the person"—a metaphoric or iconical double then, as opposed to the metonymical and indexical partial souls of the other organs.

This may suffice as evidence for the importance of vision in Amerindian cosmologies and justify my appeal to the notion of "perspective." I must stress, however, that the salience of these visual idioms should not make us disregard the fact that there is more to the concept of perspective than meets the eye, and that Amerindian perspectivism uses perceptual differences to express conceptual ones: the epistemological language of "seeing/knowing" the world is at the service of an ontology. What is at stake there is the relation between different ontological, not epistemological, perspectives. These differences may be expressed in visual terms, but differences are not visual as such: they are relational. (You do not "see a difference"—a difference is what makes you see.) The point, in short, is that perspectives do not consist in representations (visual or otherwise) of objects by subjects, but in relations of subjects to subjects. When jaguars see "blood" as "manioc beer," the terms of the perspectival relation are jaguars and humans: blood/beer is the "thing" which relates (separates) jaguar and human "persons." As Strathern has shown (1988, 1992), the exchange of perspectives or points of view need not be cast in visual language, or concern vision as such. And perspectives are "about" exchange, for they relate subjects or persons.

Animal

In what follows, "animal" is to be understood in the distributive, not the collective sense: each and any (nonhuman) animal species, not the animal kingdom, let alone animality as opposed to humanity. The available ethnographic evidence suggests that Amerindian cosmologies do not feature a general, collective concept of "animal" as opposed to "human." Humans are a species among others, and sometimes the differences internal to humanity are on a par with species-specific ones: "The Jívaro view humanity as a collection of natural societies; the biological commonality of man interests them far less than the differences between forms of social existence" (Taylor 1993b: 658).

If this is true, then at least one basic meaning of the standard opposition between nature and culture must be discarded when we move to Amerindian contexts: nature is not a domain defined by animality in contrast with culture as the domain of humanity. The real problem with the use of the category of "nature" in these contexts, therefore, lies not so much with the fact that animals also have (or are in) "culture," but rather with the assumption of a *unified* nonhuman domain (Gray 1996: 114). Our essentialist "nonhuman" is there a contextual "not-human"; "it" has no overarching, common substantive (even if privative) definition: taxonomical or ethological similarities apart, each nonhuman species is as different from all the others as it is from humans.

It is indeed rare to find Amerindian languages possessing a concept co-extensive with our concept of "(nonhuman) animal," although not uncommon to find terms which more or less correspond to one of the informal meanings of "animal" in English: relatively big land animals, typically nonhuman mammals—as opposed to fish, birds, insects and other life-forms.[32] I suspect that the majority of indigenous words which have been rendered as "animal" in the ethnographies actually denote something analogous to this. Let me give some examples.

The Gê word *mbru*, which is usually translated as "animal," and sometimes used as a synecdoche for "nature" (Seeger 1981), is literally neither fish nor fowl, for it does not subsume these life-forms: it refers prototypically to land animals, and has the pragmatic and relational sense of "victim," "prey," or "game," and in *this* latter sense may also be applied to fish, birds, etc.[33] The Wari' (Txapa-

---

32. I am aware that there are such things as "covert categories," i.e., nonlexicalized conceptual forms. But my contention is that in the majority of (possibly all) Amazonian cases there is *no* submerged notion meaning "nonhuman animal" (in our sense of "animal").

33. I asked Anthony Seeger to check the meaning of *mbru*—which he had translated as "animal" in his books on the Suyá—on a recent visit to this Gê-speaking society of Central Brazil. This is what he wrote to me on his return:

kuran) word applied to "animals," *karawa*, has the basic meaning of "prey," and as such may be applied to human enemies: the contrastive pair *wari'/karawa*, which in most contexts may be translated as "human/animal," has the logically encompassing sense of "predator/prey" or "subject/object"—humans (Wari,' i.e., *wari'*) can be the *karawa* of predators—animal, human, and spiritual—who are in their predatory function or "moment" defined as *wari'* (Vilaça 1992). In these two cases, then, the words supposedly referring to "animal" as the "nonhuman" actually appear to have the sense of "prey" or "game" (and are typically applied to land mammals insofar as these are the typical or ideal form of prey for humans). Such concepts of "animal" have a narrower extension than our zoological concept, and a logically more abstract, relational and perspectival, comprehension.

But if what has been called "animal" means first and foremost "prey," "game," or simply "meat," in some other cases it signifies exactly the opposite: inedible spirit.[34] The Yawalapíti (Upper Xingu Arawak) call *apapalutapa-mina* a variety of animals, the majority of them land creatures—and all of them, with one

---

"I asked about what the word '*mbru*' means, and was quite surprised by the answer. I was talking with one of the most thoughtful speakers of Portuguese, a man of about 50, and the oldest male Suya, about 65. I asked about what *mbru* was. The response was that it meant animal. I asked, then, if fish were *mbru*, and they said no. They said that everything that swims in the water is '*tep*' (fish), everything that walks or locomotes (as in snakes) on land is *mbru*, and that everything that flies is '*saga*' (bird). I said, then, what about snakes. They said snakes are *mbru kasaga* (bad or ugly game), like frogs and lizards, and other things. I asked about wasps, which they said are *sag-kasaga* (bad or ugly birds). They said in old Suya songs, the *jacaré* (alligator), or *mi*, is called '*te-we-mi-ji*' proving that its classification as a 'fish' or watery animal is an old one. This classification had never occurred to me, so I tried it out on someone else who said 'of course, that's the way it is.' Now, there are some contradictions. One curing chant I collected turns out to call the jacare '*mbru-taw*' or game. There is a word *simbru* (*nyimbru* 'my,' *nimbru* 'your,' *simbru* 'his' . . .) that no one could give me a direct translation for. I believe it means 'my game' in the sense of 'my killed prey.' The word is used to refer to fish, game, and dead birds. It is also used to refer to the cockroaches killed by a wasp (the wasp's '*simbru*'). In this form, the word does mean 'prey' as you suggested when we talked."

I am grateful to my teacher Tony Seeger for this detailed explanation.

34. Thus the Araweté word *ha'a*, "meat" or "flesh" (the Araweté have no general word for "animal"), is the cognate of the sixteenth century Tupinamba word *so'o*, which seems to have meant "game animal." Curiously enough, the Tupinamba word for "deer" is *soo asu*, lit. "big game," in a strict analogy to the Anglo/German "deer/tier," and to the Anglo/French "venison/venaison," which derives from the Latin verb for "hunting" (see also Spanish/Portuguese "venado/veado," deer).

exception, considered unfit to be eaten by Xinguanos.[35] The proper Xinguano diet is fish, and some avian species. The word *apapalutapa-mina*, which is on the same level of contrast as the words for "bird" and "fish," derives from the word *apapalutapa*, "spirit" (meta-person evincing dangerous powers), followed by the modifier *-mina*, which denotes something like "nonprototypical member of a class," "inferior token of a type," but also "of the substance/nature of [the concept modified]" (Viveiros de Castro 1978). Thus, "land" animals and all mammals are "spirit-like," "quasi-spirits," "sub-spirits. . . ."[36] This is quite similar to a Barasana conception (Hugh-Jones 1996) according to which game animals are referred to as "old fish"—"old" (or "mature") having here a superlative-excessive connotation. If the Tukanoans think of game as "super-fish," then, implying that these are a particularly potent and dangerous type of fish, the Yawalapiti think of game animals as "sub-spirits": and whilst the Tukanoans are able symbolically to reduce the game they eat to "fish," the Xinguanos, who do not eat game, cannot de-spiritualize these animals and accordingly are empirically reduced to eating (mostly) fish. We may perhaps extend the scope of the Amazonian continuum of edibility (within the meat domain) proposed by Hugh-Jones, then, making it go from fish to spirits, not only to human beings. The Tukanoans start conceptually from the "fish" pole, defining game as a sub-class of it; the Yawalapíti start from the other pole, having game as a sub-class of spirits. This suggests that spirits are the supremely inedible species of being in the cosmos—what makes them the supreme cannibals.

35. See Viveiros de Castro (1978) for an analysis of Yawalapíti concepts about "animals" and a tentative explanation of the (apparently paradoxical) dietary exception—*Cebus* monkeys, which are considered fit to be eaten "because they look like humans." All mammals, including aquatic ones, are *apapalutapa-mina*.

36. The prototypical (the "chief" of) *apapalutapa-mina* is the jaguar, which in Xinguano mythology is the ancestor of humans. Upper Xingu mythologies often oppose land, water and sky domains, making humans and *apapalutapa-mina* share a common origin as opposed to fish and birds.

CHAPTER NINE

Culture
The Universal Animal

I would like to start with a recapitulation of the substantive points made last Tuesday. The purpose of these lectures is to follow the implications of Amerindian "perspectivism": the conception according to which the universe is inhabited by different sorts of persons, human and nonhuman, which apprehend reality from distinct points of view. This conception was shown to be associated to some others, namely:

(1) The original common condition of both humans and animals is not animality, but rather humanity;

(2) Many animals species, as well as other types of "nonhuman" beings, have a spiritual component which qualifies them as "people"; furthermore, these beings see themselves as humans in appearance and in culture, while seeing humans as animals or as spirits;

(3) The visible body of animals is an appearance that hides this anthropomorphic invisible "essence," and that can be put on and taken off as a dress or garment;

(4) Interspecific metamorphosis is a fact of "nature"—not only it was the standard etiological process in myth, but it is still very much possible in present-day life (being either desirable or undesirable, inevitable or evitable, according to the circumstances);

(5)   Lastly, the notion of animality as a unified domain, globally opposed to that of humanity, seems to be absent from Amerindian cosmologies.

Let us go back to the conception that animals and other ostensibly nonhuman beings are people.

ANIMISM, OR THE PROJECTION THESIS

You will have probably noticed that my "perspectivism" is reminiscent of the notion of "animism" recently recuperated by Philippe Descola (1992, 1996) to designate a way of articulating the natural and the social worlds that would be a symmetrical inversion of totemism.[1] Stating that all conceptualisations of non-humans are always "predicated by reference to the human domain" (a somewhat vague phrasing, it should be said), Descola distinguishes three modes of "objectifying nature":

(1)   *Totemism*, where the differences between natural species are used as a model for social distinctions, that is, where the relationship between nature and culture is metaphorical in character and marked by discontinuity (both within and between series);

(2)   *Animism*, where the "elementary categories structuring social life" organize the relations *between* humans and natural species, thus defining a social continuity between nature and culture, founded on the attribution of human dispositions and social characteristics to "natural beings";

(3)   *Naturalism*, typical of Western cosmologies, which supposes an ontological duality between nature, the domain of necessity, and culture, the domain of spontaneity, areas separated by metonymic discontinuity.

The "animic mode" is characteristic of societies in which animals are the "strategic focus of the objectification of nature and of its socialisation," as is the case among indigenous peoples of America. It would reign supreme over those social morphologies lacking in elaborate internal segmentations; but it can also

---

1.   Descola's inspirational articles on Ameridian "animism" were one of the proximate causes of my interest in perspectivism.

be found coexisting or combined with totemism, wherein such segmentations exist, the Bororo and their *aroe/bope* duality being such a case.

Descola's theory of animism is yet another manifestation of a widespread dissatisfaction with the unilateral emphasis on metaphor, totemism, and classificatory logic which characterises the Lévi-Straussian concept of the savage mind. This dissatisfaction has launched many efforts to explore the dark side of the structuralist moon, rescuing the radical theoretical meaning of concepts such as participation and animism, which have been repressed by Lévi-Straussian intellectualism.[2] Nonetheless, it is clear that many of Descola's points are already present in Lévi-Strauss. Thus, what he means by "elementary categories structuring social life"—those which organize the relations between humans and natural species in "animic" cosmologies—is basically (in the Amazonian cases he discusses) kinship categories, and more specifically the categories of consanguinity and affinity. In *La pensée sauvage* one finds a remark most germane to this idea:

> Marriage exchanges can furnish a model directly applicable to the mediation between nature and culture among peoples where totemic classifications and functional specializations, if present at all, have only a limited yield. (Lévi-Strauss 1962a: 170)

This is a pithy prefiguration of what many ethnographers (Descola and myself included) came to say about the role of affinity as a cosmological operator in Amazonia. Besides, in suggesting the complementary distribution of this model of exchange between nature and culture and totemic structures, Lévi-Strauss seems to be aiming at something quite similar to Descola's animic model and

---

2. To remain on an Americanist ground, I might mention: the rejection of a privileged position for metaphor by Overing (1985), in favour of a relativist literalism which seems to be supported by the notion of belief; the theory of dialectical synecdoche as being anterior and superior to metaphoric analogy, proposed by Turner (1991), an author who like other specialists (Seeger 1981, Crocker 1985) has attempted to contest the interpretations of the nature/culture dualism of the Gê-Bororo as being a static opposition, privative and discrete; or the reconsideration by Viveiros de Castro (1992a) of the contrast between totemism and sacrifice in the light of the Deleuzian concept of becoming, which seeks to account for the centrality of the processes of ontological predation in Tupian cosmologies, as well as for the directly social (and not specularly classificatory) character of interactions between the human and extra-human orders.

its contrast with totemism. To take another example: Descola mentioned the Bororo as an example of coexistence of animic and totemic modes. He might also have cited the case of the Ojibwa, where the coexistence of the systems of *totem* and *manido* (evoked in *Le totemisme aujourd'hui*) served as a matrix for the general opposition between totemism and sacrifice (developed in *La pensée sauvage*) and can be directly interpreted within the framework of a distinction between totemism and animism.

I would like to concentrate the discussion on the contrast between animism and naturalism, for I think it is a good starting point for understanding the distinctive stance of Amerindian perspectivism. I will approach this contrast, however, from a different angle than the original one. Descola's definition of "totemism" also deserves some comments, which I shall present for your consideration after contrasting animism and naturalism.

Animism could be defined as an ontology which postulates the social character of relations between humans and nonhumans: the space between nature and society is itself social. Naturalism is founded on the inverted axiom: relations between society and nature are themselves natural. Indeed, if in the animic mode the distinction "nature/culture" is internal to the social world, humans and animals being immersed in the same sociocosmic medium (and in this sense, "nature" is a part of an encompassing sociality), then in naturalist ontology, the distinction "nature/culture" is internal to nature (and in this sense, human society is one natural phenomenon among others). Animism has "society" as the unmarked pole, naturalism has "nature": these poles function, respectively and contrastingly, as the universal dimension of each mode. Thus animism and naturalism are hierarchical and metonymical structures.

Let me observe that this phrasing of the contrast between animism and naturalism is not only reminiscent of, or analogous to, the famous gift/commodity one: I take it to be the *same* contrast, expressed in more general, noneconomic terms.[3] This relates to my earlier distinction between production-creation (naturalism) and exchange-transformation (animism).

In our naturalist ontology, the nature/society interface is natural: humans are organisms like the rest, body-objects in "ecological" interaction with other bodies and forces, all of them ruled by the necessary laws of biology and physics;

---

3.   "If in a commodity economy things and persons assume the social form of things, then in a gift economy they assume the social form of persons" (Strathern 1988: 134 [from Gregory 1982: 41]). The parallels are obvious.

"productive forces" harness, and thereby express, natural forces. Social relations, that is, contractual or instituted relations between subjects, can only exist internal to human society (there is no such thing as "relations of production" linking humans to animals or plants, let alone political relations). But how alien to nature—this would be the problem of naturalism—are these social relations? Given the universality of nature, the status of the human and social world is unstable, and as the history of Western thought shows, it perpetually oscillates between a naturalistic monism ("sociobiology" and "evolutionary psychology" being some of its current avatars) and an ontological dualism of nature/culture ("culturalism" and "symbolic anthropology" being some of its recent expressions).

The assertion of this latter dualism, for all that, only reinforces the final referential character of the notion of nature, by revealing itself to be the direct descendant of the theological opposition between nature and supernature. Culture is the modern name of spirit—let us recall the distinction between *Naturwissenschaften* and *Geisteswissenschaften*—or at the least it is the name of the compromise between nature and grace. Of animism, we would be tempted to say that the instability is located in the opposite pole: there the problem is how to deal with the mixture of humanity and animality constituting animals, and not, as is the case among ourselves, the combination of culture and nature which characterize humans; the problem is to differentiate a "nature" out of the universal sociality.

Let us return to Descola's tripartite typology.[4] Given the nature/culture polarity, Descola distinguishes three "modes of identification" (these being our familiar triad of totemism, animism, and naturalism), then three "modes of relation" (predation, reciprocity, protection), then an indefinite number of "modes of categorization" (left nameless and undetermined); the combinatorial possibilities within and across the three modes are not totally free. Now, I believe that the absence of any specification of the "modes of categorization" is more than a temporary vacancy (but I can always be surprised, of course); it points to a conceptual problem related to the definition of "totemism" used by Descola.

The typology seems to suggest, correctly I think, that the preeminence of the nature/culture opposition in our anthropological tradition derives from the joint

---

4.   Let me say I have nothing against typologies as such, which I deem an important step in anthropological reasoning: typologies are like rules—we need them in order to break them. And butterfly collecting is a most honorable and rewarding occupation—if carried with ecological circumspection—unjustly reviled by one of our eminent forebears.

privilege of the totemic and naturalist modes, both characterized by dichotomy and discontinuity (the first supposedly typical of "savage thought," the second of "domesticated thought"). Descola's emphasis on the logical distinctiveness of the animic mode—a mode he considers to be far more widespread than totemism—is intended to correct this distortion; it also destabilizes the totemism/naturalism divide and the nature/culture dualism common to both modes.

Descola appears to adopt an institutional reading of totemism, whilst Lévi-Strauss had taken it as a mere example of the global style of the savage mind; the cognitive form exemplified by totemism is considered by Lévi-Strauss as much more important than the contingent conceptual and institutional contents to which it is applied. We are accordingly led to infer that animism is also conceived by Descola in an institutionalist key, and that it would be then possible to reabsorb it in the sacrificial pole of the famous Lévi-Straussian contrast between totemism and sacrifice, if we interpret it as a general cognitive distinction and not in terms of its somewhat ill-chosen institutional labels.

If I am right in drawing these conclusions, where does totemism stand? Totemism seems to me a phenomenon of a different order from animism and naturalism. It is not a system of *relations* between nature and culture as is the case in the other two modes, but rather of *correlations*. Totemism is not an ontology, but a form of classification—it would not belong, therefore, to the category of "modes of identification," but rather to that, left vacant by Descola, of "modes of categorization." The totemic connection between the natural and the social series is neither social nor natural—it is purely logical and differential. By the same token, this connection is not metonymic and hierarchical as is the case with animic and naturalist modes of relating and defining nature and culture—it is a metaphoric and equipollent relation. This would explain why totemism, as a form of classification, can only be found in combination with animic systems: even the classical totemisms suppose more than a set of symbolic correlations between nature and culture; they imply a relationship of descent or participation between the terms of the two series (Lévi-Strauss called this latter relationship the "imaginary side" of totemism—but this does not make it any less real, ethnographically speaking).[5]

---

5.   Totemic orderings can also be found in combination with naturalist schemes, as shown by modern genetics and its correlations between genotypical and phenotypical differences (the "more natural" series of the genome and the "more cultural" series of its expressions), or by linguistics—the formal model of Lévi-Straussian totemism—with its vast repertoire of differential correlations between signifier and signified, physico-acoustical and mental-conceptual series, etc.

In sum, I believe that the really productive contrast is the one between naturalism and animism as two inverse hierarchical ontologies. Totemism, as defined by Descola, seems to be a different phenomenon. However, let us suspend our judgement till we explore more fully the notion of animism, for it may be the case that totemism and animism reveal themselves to be related by more significant similarities and differences.

PROBLEMS WITH PROJECTION

The major problem with Descola's inspiring theory, in my opinion, is this: can animism be defined as a projection of differences and qualities internal to the human world onto nonhuman worlds, as a "socio-centric" model in which categories and social relations are used to map the universe? This interpretation by analogy is explicit in some glosses on the theory, such as that provided by Kaj Århem: "if totemic systems model society after nature, then animic systems model nature after society" (1996: 185). The problem here is the obvious proximity with the traditional sense of animism, or with the reduction of "primitive classifications" to emanations of social morphology; but equally the problem is to go beyond other classic characterizations of the relation between society and nature.

I am thinking here of Radcliffe-Brown's 1929 article on totemism, where he presents the following ideas (1952: 130–31):

(1)   For "primitive man" the universe as a whole is a moral and social order governed not by what we call natural law but rather by what we must call moral or ritual law.

(2)   Although our own explicit conception of a natural order and of natural law does not exist among the more primitive peoples, "the germs out of which it develops do exist in the empirical control of causal processes in technical activities"—we find here the "germs" of Leach's distinction between technical and expressive aspects of action, and perhaps also of Bloch's distinction between cognition and ideology.

(3)   Primitive peoples (in Australia, for example) have built between themselves and the phenomena of nature a system of relations which are essentially similar to the relations that they have built up in their social structure between one human being and another.

(4)   It is possible to distinguish *processes of personification* of natural phenom-
       ena and natural species (which "permits nature to be thought of as if it
       were a society of persons, and so makes of it a social or moral order"), like
       those found amongst the Eskimos and Andaman Islanders, from *systems
       of classification* of natural species, like those found in Australia and which
       compose a "system of social solidarities" between man and nature—this
       obviously calls to mind Descola's distinction of animism/totemism as well
       as the contrast of *manido/totem* explored by Lévi-Strauss.

Some ethnographers of hunter-and-gatherer economies have appealed to the
ideas of an extension of human attributes to nonhumans and a metaphorical
projection of social relations onto human/nonhuman interactions. Such arguments have been put forth as weapons in the battle against the interpretation of
these economies in ethological-ecological terms (optimal foraging theory, etc.).
As Ingold (1996) most convincingly argued, however, all schemes of analogical
projection or social modeling of nature escape naturalist reductionism only to
fall into a nature/culture dualism which, by distinguishing "really natural" nature
from "culturally constructed" nature, reveals itself to be a typical cosmological antinomy (in the original Kantian sense) faced with infinite regression. The notion
of model or metaphor supposes a previous distinction between a domain wherein
social relations are constitutive and literal and another where they are representational and metaphorical. Animism, interpreted as human sociality projected
onto the nonhuman world, would be nothing but the metaphor of a metonymy.[6]

---

6.   In the article referred to above, Radcliffe-Brown also proposed, in contrast to the
     Durkheimian idea of a "projection of society into external nature," that "the process
     is one by which, in the fashioning of culture, external nature, so called, comes to
     be incorporated in the social order as an essential part of it" (1952: 130–31). This
     is an interesting anti-metaphorical remark, which Lévi-Strauss (1962c: 84–89)
     interpreted quite unfairly as a kind of utilitarian argument. Radcliffe-Brown's point
     reappears almost *verbatim* in Goldman (who does not mention Radcliffe-Brown's
     article): "To Durkheim . . . it was easy to imagine that 'primitive' people projected
     their own natures onto the rest of nature. It is far more likely that *Homo sapiens*
     sought to understand himself and all other realms of nature through a dialectic
     of interchange, of understanding the outer world in terms of his own nature and
     his own nature in terms of the outer. If Kwakiutl attribute human qualities to the
     grizzly bear, they have also learned to define and to regulate their own qualities
     of physical strength and fearlessness in terms of their knowledge of the bear. . . .
     Kwakiutl do not merely project themselves on the outer world. They seek to incorporate it."
     (1975: 208; emphasis added).

The idea of an animist projection of society onto nature is not in itself a problem, if one abides by the doctrine of "particular universalism" (the term comes from Latour [1991]), which supposes the privileged access of one culture—our culture—to the only true, real Nature. This particular universalism would be, says Latour, the actual cosmology of anthropology, being in force even among those who have "cultural relativism" as their official creed. It would also be the only possibility of arresting the infinite regression that Ingold rightly sees in the relativist cliché: "Nature is culturally constructed." Particular universalism brings such regression to a halt because it subordinates the Nature/Culture dualism to an encompassing naturalism, according to which our culture is the mirror of nature and other cultures are simply wrong. But all forms of constructionism and projectionism are unacceptable if we are decided not to let "animism" be interpreted in terms of our naturalist ontology.

Allow me a further comment on Latour's idea that particular universalism is the practical ideology of anthropologists—their official or theoretical one being cultural relativism. While agreeing with Latour, I would just remark that the really characteristic relativism of anthropologists seems to consist less in a clandestine appeal to particular universalism than in a kind of distributive inversion of it, which carefully distinguishes culture (as human nature) from (cosmological) nature. Since every culture studied by anthropology is typically presented as expressing (and recognizing) some deep hidden truth of the human condition—a truth forgotten or denied by Western culture, like, for instance, the very inseparability of nature and culture—the sum total of these truths leads to the dismaying conclusion that all cultures, except precisely the (modern) Western, have a kind of privileged access to human nature, what amounts to granting Western culture an *underprivileged* access to the universe of culture. Maybe this is the price we feel we have to pay for our supposedly privileged access to non-human nature.

Now, what is Ingold's solution to these difficulties he found in the projection argument? Against the notion of a social construction of nature and its implied metaphorical projectionism, he proposes an ontology founded on the immediate "interagentive" engagement between humans and animals prevailing in hunter-gatherer societies. He opposes our cognitivist and transcendental cosmology of "constructed nature" to a practical, immanent phenomenology of "dwelling" (*sensu* Heidegger) in an environment. There would be no projection of relations internal to the human world onto the nonsocial, i.e., natural domain, but rather an immediate interspecific sociality, at the same time objective and subjective, which would be the primary reality out of which the secondary, reflective differences between humans and animals would emerge.

Ingold's inspirational (and influential) ideas deserve a discussion I cannot develop here. In my opinion, his perspicacious diagnosis of metaphorical projectionism is better than the cure he propounds. For all their insightfulness, these ideas illustrate the inversion of "particular universalism" I alluded to above. Ingold never makes it quite clear whether he takes Western constructionism to be absolutely false (that is, both unreal and malignant)—I feel he does think so—or just inadequate to describe other "lived worlds," remaining true as the expression of a particular historico-cultural experience. But the real problem lies not with this. My structuralist reflexes make me wince at the primacy accorded to immediate practical-experiential identification at the expense of difference, taken to be a conditioned, mediate, and purely "intellectual" (that is, theoretical and abstract) moment. There is here the debatable assumption that commonalities prevail upon distinctions, being superior and anterior to the latter; there is the still more debatable assumption that the fundamental or prototypical mode of relation is identity or sameness. At the risk of having deeply misunderstood him, I would suggest that Ingold is voicing here the recent widespread sentiment against "difference"—a sentiment "metaphorically projected" onto what hunter-gatherers or any available "others" are supposed to experience—which unwarrantably sees it as inimical to immanence, as if all difference were a stigma of transcendence (and a harbinger of oppression). All difference is read as an opposition, and all opposition as the *absence* of a relation: "to oppose" is taken as synonymous with "to exclude"—a strange idea. I am not of this mind. As far as Amerindian ontologies are concerned, at least, I do not believe that similarities and differences among humans and animals (for example) can be ranked in terms of experiential immediacy, or that distinctions are more abstract or "intellectual" than commonalities: both are equally concrete and abstract, practical and theoretical, emotional and intellectual, etc. True to my structuralist habitus, however, I persist in thinking that similarity is a type of difference; above all, I regard identity or sameness as the very negation of relatedness.

The idea that humans and animals share personhood is a very complicated one: it would be entirely inadequate to interpret it as if meaning that humans and animals are "essentially the same" (and only "apparently" different). It rather means that humans and animals are, each on their own account, *not* the same—they are *internally* divided or entangled. Their common personhood or humanity is precisely what permits that their difference to be an *inclusive*, internal relation. The primordial immanence of myth (never lost, ever threatening) is not absence of difference, but rather its pervasive operation in a "molecular" mode (Deleuze and Guattari 1980), as difference not yet "molarized," i.e., speciated. Immanence is not sameness, it is infinite difference: it is (molar) difference preempted by (molecular) difference.

Among the questions remaining to resolve, therefore, is the one of knowing whether animism can be described as a figurative use of categories pertaining to the human-social domain to conceptualize the domain of nonhumans and their relations with the former, and if not, then how should we interpret it. The other question is: if animism depends on the attribution (or recognition) of human-like cognitive and sensory faculties to animals, and the same form of subjectivity, that is if animals are "essentially" human, then what in the end is the difference between humans and animals? If animals are people, then why do they not see us as people? Why, to be precise, the perspectivism? We might also ask if the notion of contingent corporeal forms (clothing) is properly described in terms of an opposition between appearance and essence. Finally, if animism is a way of objectifying nature in which the dualism of nature/culture does not hold, then what is to be done with the abundant indications regarding the centrality of this opposition to South American cosmologies? Are we dealing with just another "totemic illusion," if not with a naïve projection of our Western dualism? Is it possible to make a more than synoptic use of the concepts of nature and culture, or are they merely "blanket labels" (Descola 1996) to which Lévi-Strauss appealed in order to organize the multiple semantic contrasts in American mythologies, these contrasts being irreducible to a single massive dichotomy?

ETHNOCENTRISM, OR THE REJECTION THESIS

In a well-known essay, Lévi-Strauss observed that for savages, humanity ceases at the boundary of the group, a notion which is exemplified by the widespread auto-ethnonym meaning "real humans," which in turn implies a definition of strangers as somehow pertaining to the domain of the extra-human. Therefore, ethnocentrism would not be the privilege of the West, but a natural ideological attitude, inherent to human collective life. The author illustrates the universal reciprocity of this attitude with an anecdote:

> In the Greater Antilles, some years after the discovery of America, whilst the Spanish were dispatching inquisitional commissions to investigate whether the natives had a soul or not, these very natives were busy drowning the white people they had captured in order to find out, after lengthy observation, whether or not the corpses were subject to putrefaction. (Lévi-Strauss [1952] 1973: 384)

From this parable, Lévi-Strauss derives the famous paradoxical moral: "The barbarian is first and foremost the man who believes in barbarism," which, as Aron (1973) noted, may be taken to imply that the anthropologist is the only nonbarbarian on the face of the earth. Some years later, in *Tristes tropiques*, Lévi-Strauss (1955: 82–83) was to retell the case of the Antilles, but this time he underlined the asymmetry of the perspectives: in their investigations of the humanity of the Other, whites appealed to the social sciences, whereas the Indians founded their observations in the natural sciences; and if the former concluded that Indians were animals, the latter were content to suspect that the whites were divinities. "In equal ignorance," says our author, the latter attitude was more worthy of human beings.

The anecdote reveals something else, as we shall see; something which Lévi-Strauss came close to formulating in the *Tristes tropiques* version. But its general point is quite obvious: the Indians, like the European invaders, consider that only the group to which they belong incarnates humanity; strangers are on the other side of the border which separates humans from animals and spirits, culture from nature and supernature. As matrix and condition for the existence of ethnocentrism, the nature/culture opposition appears to be a universal of social apperception.

At the time when Lévi-Strauss was writing these lines, the strategy for vindicating the full humanity of savages was to demonstrate that they made the same distinctions as we do: the proof that they were true humans is that they considered that they alone were *the* true humans. Like us, they distinguished culture from nature and they too believed that *Naturvölker* are always the others. The universality of the cultural distinction between Nature and Culture bore witness to the universality of culture as human nature. In sum, the Lévi-Straussian answer to the question of the Spanish investigators was positive: savages do have souls. (Note that this question can be read as a sixteenth-century theological version of the "problem of other minds," which continues to this day to feed many a philosophical mouth.)

But now, in these poststructuralist, ecologically-minded, animal-rights-concerned times, everything has changed. Savages are no longer ethnocentric or anthropomorphic, but rather cosmocentric or cosmomorphic. Instead of having to prove that they are humans because they distinguish themselves from animals, we now have to recognize how *in*-human *we* are for opposing humans to animals in a way they never did: for them nature and culture are part of the same sociocosmic field. Not only would Amerindians put a wide berth between themselves and the great Cartesian divide, which separated humanity from animality, but their views anticipate the fundamental lessons of ecology which we are only now in a position to assimilate (as argued by Reichel-Dolmatoff [1976], among many others). Before, the Indians' refusal to concede predicates of humanity to other men was of note; now we stress that they extend such predicates way beyond the frontiers of their own species in a demonstration of "ecosophic" knowledge (the expression is Århem's [1993]) which we should emulate in as far as the limits of our objectivism permit. Formerly, it had been necessary to combat the assimilation of the savage mind to narcissistic animism, the infantile stage of naturalism, showing that totemism affirmed the cognitive distinction between culture and nature; now, as we have seen, animism is attributed once more to savages, but this time it is proclaimed—though not by Descola, I hasten to note—as the correct (or at least "valid") recognition of the universal admixture of subjects and objects, humans and nonhumans, to which we modern Westerners have been blind, because of our foolish, nay, sinful habit of thinking in dichotomies. Against the *hubris* of modernity, the primitive and postmodern "hybrids," to borrow a term from Latour (1991).[7]

---

7.   Latour has provided here only the term, not the target: I do not intend his work to be identified with anything I say in this paragraph. By the way, there is another familiar variant of this change in the way "we" think "they" think. At the time *La pensée sauvage* was written, it was deemed necessary to assert, and to provide abundant illustration thereto, that primitive peoples were endowed with a theoretical cast of mind, showing an authentic speculative interest in reality—they were not moved by their bellies and other such purely practical considerations. But this was when "theory" was not a word of abuse. Now, of course, everything has changed. These peoples have returned to practice; not, it goes without saying, to practice because of an incapacity for theory (well, the "oral vs. written" or the "cosmological disorder" schools would disagree here), but to practice as anti-theory. Be that as it may, not all contemporary primitive peoples seem to agree with our current interest in practice; perhaps because they are no longer primitive (but have they ever been?). So, in Fienup-Riordan's latest book (1994: xiii), we can read the following introductory remark from a Yup'ik man: "You white people always want to know about the things we do, but it is the rules that are important."

It looks like we have here an antinomy, or rather two paired antinomies. For either Amerindians are ethnocentrically stingy in the extension of their concept of humanity, and they "totemically" oppose nature and culture; or they are cosmocentric and "animic" and do not profess to such a distinction, being (or so has been argued) models of relativist tolerance, postulating a multiplicity of points of view on the world.[8]

I believe that the solution to these antinomies lies not in favoring one branch over the other, sustaining, for example, the argument that the most recent characterization of Amerindian attitudes is the correct one and relegating the other to the outer darkness of pre-afterological anthropology. Rather, the point is to show that the thesis as well as the antithesis of both antinomies are true (both correspond to solid ethnographic intuitions), but that they apprehend the same phenomena from different angles; and also it is to show that both are "false" in that they refer to a substantivist conceptualization of the categories of nature and culture (whether it be to affirm or negate them) which is not applicable to Amerindian cosmologies.

THE SUBJECT AS SUCH: FROM SUBSTANTIVE TO PERSPECTIVE

Let us return to the observation by Lévi-Strauss about the widespread character of those ethnic self-designations which would mean "real humans" or some suchlike myopic conceit. The first thing to be considered is that the Amerindian words which are usually translated as "human being" and which figure in those self-designations do not denote humanity as a natural species, that is, *Homo sapiens*. They refer rather to the social condition of personhood, and—especially when they are modified by intensifiers such as "true," "real," "genuine"—they function less as *nouns* than as *pronouns*. They indicate the position of the subject; they are enunciative markers, not names. Far from manifesting a semantic shrinking of a common name to a proper name (taking "people" to be the name of the tribe), these words move in the opposite direction, going from

---

8.   The uncomfortable tension inherent in such antinomies can be gauged in Howell's recent article (1996) on the Chewong of Malaysia. Chewong cosmology is paradoxically—but the paradox is not noticed—described as "relativist" (ibid.: 133) and as "after all . . . anthropocentric" (ibid.: 135). A double mislabelling, at least if carried to the Amerindian universe.

substantive to perspective (using "people" as a collective pronoun "we people/ us"; the modifiers we translate by adjectives like "real" or "genuine" seem to function much like self-referential emphases of the type "we ourselves"). For this very reason, indigenous categories of identity have that enormous variability of scope that characterizes pronouns, marking contrastively Ego's immediate kin, his/her local group, all humans, humans and some animal species, or even all beings conceived as potential subjects: their coagulation as "ethnonyms" seems largely to be an artefact of interactions with ethnographers and other identity experts such as colonial administrators. Nor is it by chance that the majority of Amerindian ethnonyms which entered the literature are not self-designations, but rather names (frequently pejorative) conferred by other groups: ethnonymic objectivation is primordially applied to others, not to the ones in the position of subject. Ethnonyms are names of third parties, they belong to the category of "*they*," not to the category of "*we*."[9] This, by the way, is consistent with a widespread avoidance of self-reference on the level of onomastics: personal names are not spoken by their bearers nor in their presence; to name is to externalise, to separate (from) the subject.[10]

9.   An interesting transformation of the refusal to onomastic self-objectification can be found in those cases in which, since the collective-subject is taking itself to be part of a plurality of collectives analogous to itself, the self-referential term signifies "*the others*." This situation occurs primarily when the term is used to identify collectives from which the subject excludes itself: the alternative to pronominal subjectification is an equally relational auto-objectification, where "I" can only mean "the other of the other": see the *achuar* of the Achuar, or the *nawa* of the Panoans (Taylor 1985: 168; Erikson 1990: 80–84). The logic of Amerindian auto-ethnonymy calls for its own specific study. For other revealing cases, see: Vilaça (1992: 449–51), Price (1987), and Viveiros de Castro (1992a: 64–65). For an enlightening analysis of a North American case similar to the Amazonian ones, see McDonnell (1984: 41-43).

10. It has become quite fashionable to drop traditional Amerindian ethnonyms, usually names given by other tribes or by whites, in favor of more politically correct ethnic self-designations. The problem, however, is that self-designations are exactly this, *self*-designations, which when used by foreigners produce the most ludicrous referential problems. Take the case of the Campa, who call themselves "*ashaninka*," and who accordingly are now called "Ashaninka" by well-meaning NGO people (I thank Peter Gow for this example). The root *shaninca* means "kinsperson"; *ashaninca* means "our kinspeople." This is what Campa people call themselves as a collectivity when contrasting themselves to others, like *viracocha*, "Whites," *simirintsi*, "Piro," etc. It is easy to imagine how strange it may sound to the Campa to be called "our kinspeople" by a *viracocha*, a white person, who is anything but a relative. It is more or less like if I were to call my friend Stephen "I," because that's what he calls

Thus self-references such as "people" mean "person," not "member of the human species"; and they are personal pronouns registering the point of view of the subject talking, not proper names. To say, then, that animals and spirits are people, is to say that they are persons, and to personify them is to attribute to nonhumans the capacities of conscious intentionality and agency which define the position of the subject. Such capacities are objectified as the soul or spirit with which these nonhumans are endowed. Whatever possesses a soul is a subject, and whatever has a soul is capable of having a point of view. Amerindian souls, be they human or animal, are thus indexical categories, cosmological deictics whose analysis calls not so much for an animist psychology or substantialist ontology as for a theory of the sign or a perspectival pragmatics. (In a previous version of this argument, I used the expression "epistemological pragmatics" where now I prefer to talk of perspectival pragmatics. This is because in the meantime I developed a deep mistrust of "epistemological" interpretations of Amerindian ontological tenets.)

So, every being to whom a point of view is attributed would be a subject; or better, wherever there is a point of view there is a subject position. While our constructionist epistemology can be summed up in the Saussurean formula: *the point of view creates the object*—the subject being the original, fixed condition whence the point of view emanates—Amerindian perspectival ontology proceeds along the lines that the *point of view creates the subject*; whatever is activated or "agented" by the point of view will be a subject.[11]

This is why terms such as *wari'* (a Txapakuran word), *masa* (a Tukanoan word) or *dene* (an Athapaskan word) mean "people," but they can be used for—and therefore used by—very different classes of beings: used by humans they denote human beings; but used by peccaries, howler monkeys, or beavers, they self-refer to peccaries, howler monkeys, or beavers (Vilaça 1992; Århem 1993; McDonnell 1984).

As it happens, however, these nonhumans placed in the subject perspective do not merely "call" themselves "people"; they *see* themselves anatomically and culturally as *humans*. The symbolic spiritualization of animals would imply its imaginary hominization and culturalization; thus the anthropomorphic-anthropocentric character of indigenous thought would seem to be unquestionable.

---

himself, while "Stephen" is a name which someone else gave to him, and which other people, rather more frequently than he himself, use to refer to him.

11. This idea comes from Deleuze's book on Leibniz (1988: 27): "Such is the foundation of perspectivism. It does not express a dependency on a predefined subject; on the contrary, whatever accedes to the point of view will be subject." The Saussurean formula appears on the beginning of the *Cours de linguistique générale*.

However, I believe that something quite different is at issue. Any being which vicariously occupies the point of view of reference, being in the position of subject, sees itself as a member of the human species. The human bodily form and human culture—the schemata of perception and action "embodied" in specific dispositions—are deictics, pronominal markers of the same type as the self-designations discussed above. They are reflexive or apperceptive schematisms ("reifications" *sensu* Strathern) by which all subjects apprehend themselves, and not literal and constitutive human predicates projected metaphorically (i.e., improperly) onto nonhumans. Such deictic "attributes" are immanent in the viewpoint, and move with it. Human beings—naturally—enjoy the same prerogative and therefore see themselves as such: "Human beings see themselves as such; the Moon, the snakes, the jaguars and the Mother of Smallpox, however, see them as tapirs or peccaries, which they kill" (Baer 1994: 224).

We need to have it quite clear: it is not that animals are subjects because they are humans (humans in disguise), but rather that they are human because they are subjects (potential subjects). This is to say *culture is the subject's nature*; it is the form in which every subject experiences its own nature. Animism is not a projection of substantive human qualities cast onto animals, but rather expresses the logical equivalence of the reflexive relations that humans and animals each have to themselves: salmon are to (see) salmon as humans are to (see) humans, namely, (as) human. If, as we have observed, the common condition of humans and animals is humanity not animality, this is because "humanity" is the name for the general form taken by the subject.

Let me make two remarks by way of conclusion. The attribution of human-like consciousness and intentionality (to say nothing of human bodily form and cultural habits) to nonhuman beings has been indifferently denominated "anthropocentrism" or "anthropomorphism." However, these two labels can be taken to denote radically opposed cosmological outlooks. Western popular evolutionism, for instance, is thoroughly anthropocentric, but not particularly anthropomorphic. On the other hand, animism may be characterized as anthropomorphic, but it is definitely not anthropocentric: if sundry other beings besides humans are "human," then we humans are not a special lot. So much for primitive "narcissism."

Marx wrote of man, meaning *Homo sapiens*:

> In creating an objective world by his practical activity, in working-up inorganic nature, man proves himself a conscious species being.... Admittedly animals also

produce. . . . But an animal only produces what it immediately needs for itself or its young. It produces one-sidedly, while man produces universally. . . . An animal produces only itself, whilst man reproduces the whole of nature. . . . An animal forms things in accordance with the standard and the need of the species to which it belongs, whilst man knows how to produce in accordance to the standards of other species. (Marx [1844] 1961: 75–76, *apud* Sahlins 1996: 400n17)

Talk about "primitive" narcissism. Whatever Marx meant by this idea that man "produces universally," I would like to think he is saying something to the effect that man is the universal animal—an intriguing idea. (If man is the universal animal, then perhaps each animal species would be a kind of particular humanity?). While apparently converging with the Amerindian notion that humanity is the universal form of the subject, Marx's is in fact an absolute inversion of it: he is saying that humans can "be" any animal—that we have more being than any other species—whilst Amerindians say that "any" animal can be human— that there is more being to an animal than meets the eye. "Man" is the universal animal in two entirely different senses, then: the universality is anthropocentric in the case of Marx, and anthropomorphic in the Amerindian case.[12]

The second remark takes us back to the relationship between animism and totemism. I have just said that animism should be taken as expressing the logical equivalence of the reflexive relations that humans and animals each have to themselves. I then proposed, as an example, that salmon are to salmon as humans to humans, namely, human. This was inspired by Guédon's paragraph on Tsimshiam cosmology:

If one is to follow the main myths, for the human being, the world looks like a human community surrounded by a spiritual realm, including an animal kingdom with all beings coming and going according to their kinds and interfering with each others' lives; however, if one were to go and become an animal, a salmon for instance, one would discover that salmon people are to themselves as human beings are to us, and that to them, we human beings would look like *naxnoq* [supernatural beings], or perhaps bears feeding on their salmon. Such

---

12. Be that as it may, Marx's notion of an universal animal—capable of "producing in accordance with the standards of other species" (whatever this means)—is an accurate anticipation of another universal metaphorical being. I am referring of course to the universal machine, the machine capable of simulating (i.e., reproducing) any other machine: the Turing-Von Neumann computer.

translation goes through several levels. For instance, the leaves of the cotton tree falling in the Skeena River are the salmon of the salmon people. I do not know what the salmon would be for the leaf, but I guess they appear what we look like to the salmon—unless they looked like bears. (1984a: 141)

Therefore, if salmon look to salmon as humans to humans—and this is "animism"—salmon do not look human to humans and neither do humans to salmon—and this is "perspectivism."

If such is the case, then animism and perspectivism may have a deeper relationship to totemism than Descola's model allows for. Why do animals (I recall that by "animals" I always mean: each animals species) see themselves as humans? Precisely because humans see *them* as animals, and see *themselves* as humans. Peccaries cannot see themselves as peccaries (and then speculate that humans and other beings are really peccaries behind their species-specific clothing) because this is the guise in which peccaries are *seen* by humans.[13] If humans see themselves as humans and are seen as nonhuman (as animals or spirits) by animals, then animals must necessarily see themselves as humans. Such asymmetrical torsion of animism contrasts in an interesting way with the symmetry exhibited by totemism. In the case of animism, a correlation of reflexive identities (human : human :: animal : animal) serves as the substrate for the relation between the human and animal series; in the case of totemism, a correlation of differences (human ≠ human :: animal ≠ animal) articulates the two series. It is curious to see how a correlation of differences (the differences are identical) can produce a reversible and symmetric structure, while a correlation of similarities (similarities differ, for animals are similar to humans because they are *not* humans) produces the asymmetric and pseudo-projective structure of animism.

---

13. This would be *our* version of "perspectivism," namely, the critical stance regarding anthropomorphism (here crucially and mistakenly conflated with anthropocentrism) as a form of projection. It was advanced two and half millenia ago by Xenophanes, who memorably said (though what he meant is very much open to debate) that if horses or oxen or lions had hands, they would draw the figures of the gods as similar to horses, oxen or lions—a point which reappears under many guises in Western tradition, from Aristotle to Spinoza, from Hume to Feuerbach, Marx, Durkheim, etc. Characteristically, our problem with "anthropomorphism" relates to the projection of humanity into divinity, not animality.

CHAPTER TEN

Nature
The World as Affect and Perspective

Let us start with a recapitulation of the points made in the last lecture. In it, I discussed Descola's trichotomy of animic, totemic, and naturalistic modes of articulation of "nature" and "culture." I drew a contrast between animism and naturalism as inverse hierarchical ontologies, and pointed to the problematic status of totemism within Descola's typology. I then discussed the two major problems with the idea of a metaphorical projection of social relations onto nature: firstly, its close similarities to anthropological theories (particularly to Durkheimian sociological symbolism) that have lost their usefulness or at least their appeal; secondly, the infinite regression which haunts the relativist cliché "nature is culturally constructed," and the implicit recourse to particular universalism, in Latour's sense, as the only means to stop such regression. In the second section of the lecture, evoking the parable about the Spaniards and the natives of the Antilles in the sixteenth century, I noted an antinomy in our characterization of Amerindian attitudes toward difference: either ethnocentrism, which would deny the predicates of humanity to other humans, or animism, which would extend such predicates to nonhumans and would furthermore (in its contemporary, relativist rendering) endow these nonhuman persons with species-specific perspectives on reality. In the final section, I pointed to the pronominal rather than substantive quality of Amerindian supposedly ethnocentric self-designations. I then proposed that the human bodily shape and cultural habits that constitute the self-percepts of all species of persons (human and nonhuman) are deictical or pronominal attributes analogous to these self-designations. After drawing a contrast between our constructionist motto: "the point of view creates the object," and the perspectival formula: "the point of view creates the subject," I proposed a definition of culture as being the subject's nature. "Culture" would be the auto-anthropological schema, in the Kantian sense (today we would call it the "embodiment"), of the first-person pronouns "I" or "me." I concluded by contrasting Western anthropocentrism to Amerindian anthropomorphism, and argued that the latter is the logical entailment of perspectivism: since humans see themselves as humans and see animals as animals (or as spirits), animals can only see themselves as humans and see humans as animals (or as spirits). Humanity is a reflexive property of the subject position, it is the universal mirror of nature (in a totally different sense from Rorty's, though—it is the mirror in which nature sees *itself*).

Our problem today is to determine the notion of nature in Amerindian ontologies.

THE OBJECT AS SUCH: WHY A PERSPECTIVE IS NOT A REPRESENTATION

In our last lecture we argued that what has been called "animism" is not the narcissistic projection of humanity onto nature, but rather a consequence of the fact that the Amerindian world comprises a multiplicity of subject-positions. Today we shall discuss the usual interpretation of this perspectival cosmology as a form of relativism.

The label "relativism" has been frequently applied to cosmologies of the Amerindian type; usually, it goes without saying, by anthropologists who have some sympathy for relativism, for not many of us would be prepared to impute to the people one studies a preposterous philosophical belief. Among those who have spoken of an indigenous relativism, I could recall: F. M. Casevitz for the Matsiguenga, McCallum for the Cashinahua, Gray for the Arakmbut, Århem for the Makuna, Overing for the Piaroa; outside of Amazonia, there is Howell for the Chewong. I will single out for discussion Århem's analysis of the cosmology of the Makuna, for he puts the question in concise and precise terms. After describing the elaborate perspectival universe of this Tukanoan people of Northwestern Amazonia, Århem observes that the notion of multiple viewpoints on reality implies that, as far as the Makuna are concerned, *"every perspective is equally valid and true"* and that *"a correct and true representation of the world does not exist"* (1993: 124, emphasis added).

Århem is right, of course; but only in a sense. For one can reasonably surmise that as far as *humans* are concerned, the Makuna would say that there is only one correct and true representation of the world indeed. If you start seeing, for instance, the maggots in rotten meat as grilled fish, like vultures do, you are in deep trouble. Perspectives should be kept separate. Only shamans, who are so to speak species-androgynous, can make them communicate, and then only under special, controlled conditions. In the same spirit as Århem's, Howell wrote that for the "relativist" Chewong, "each species is different, but equal" (1996: 133). This is also true; but it would be probably truer if we inverted the emphasis: each species is equal (in the sense that there is no species-independent, absolute point of view), but different (for this does not mean that a given type of being can indifferently assume the point of view of any other species).

This is not my point, however. Here is the real point: is the Amerindian perspectivist theory in fact asserting a multiplicity of *representations* of the same world, as Århem maintains? It is sufficient to consider ethnographic evidence to perceive that the opposite applies: all beings see ("represent") the world in the *same* way—what changes is the *world* that they see. Animals impose the same categories and values on reality as humans do: their worlds, like ours, revolve around hunting and fishing, cooking and fermented drinks, cross-cousins and war, initiation rituals, shamans, chiefs, spirits. . . . "Everybody is involved in fishing and hunting; everybody is involved in feasts, social hierarchy, chiefs, war, and disease, all the way up and down" (Guédon 1984a: 142). If the moon, the snakes, the jaguars, and the Mother of Smallpox see humans as tapirs or white-lipped peccaries (Baer 1994), it is because they, like us, eat tapirs and peccaries, people's food. It could only be this way, since, being people in their own sphere, nonhumans see things *as* "people" do. But the things *that* they see are different: what to us is blood, is maize beer to the jaguar; what to us is soaking manioc, the souls of the dead see as rotting corpse; what we see as a muddy waterhole, the tapirs see as a great ceremonial house . . .

This idea may at first sound slightly counter-intuitive, for when we start thinking about it, it seems to collapse into its opposite. Here is how Weiss (1972), for instance, described the Campa world, in a passage I have already quoted (emphasis added):

It is a world of relative semblances, *where different kinds of beings see the same things differently*; thus humans' eyes can normally see good spirits only in the form of lightning flashes or birds whereas they see themselves in their true human form, and similarly in the eyes of jaguars human beings look like peccaries to be hunted. (1972: 170)

While this is also true in a sense, I believe Weiss does not "see" the fact that different kinds of beings see the same things differently only as a *consequence* of the fact that different kinds of beings see different things in the same way. For what counts as "the same things"? Same for whom, which species? The notion of "the thing in itself" haunts Weiss' formulation.

Another way of interpreting this perspectival ontology in relativist terms can be seen in the ethnographies of Renard-Casevitz (1991) or Gray (1996). These authors consider it to be the extension beyond the species border of a characteristically Amerindian (in the case of Gray) or universal (in the case of Renard-Casevitz) sociological relativity, according to which differences of gender, age and kinship status lead to different visions of society.[1] My problem with this idea is that it trivializes the question. *Contra* Gray, I would observe that such sociological relativity is a property of human relational life; Amerindian can hardly be said to have a monopoly on it. *Contra* both Gray and Renard-Casevitz, I would observe that, granting that perspectivism is the application of such relativity beyond the species border, we still have to account for the crucial question of perceptual differences—or rather, referential differences—for sociological relativity certainly does not imply that men and women, for instance, actually see things differently. Or rather, women and men *do* "see" things differently; what they do *not* do, precisely, is to see different things as if they were the same: men and women are genders of the same species.[2]

---

1.   Gray (1996: 280) explicitly, but in my opinion unconvincingly, distinguishes his "relativity" from any notion of "cultural relativism."

2.   Species differences rather than gender differences function as the "master-code" of Amerindian cosmologies; the main æsthetic (in Strathern's sense) here is one of anthropomorphism and theriomorphism, rather than one of andromorphism and gynomorphism (Fienup-Riordan 1994: 49; Descola 1996). If such is the case, then we could perhaps see in the human/animal original (but not bygone) mythic "undifference" an exact equivalent of the basic androgyny which Strathern (1988) detected in Melanesian gender ideologies. The possibility of conflating these two aesthetics is actualized in those Amerindian cosmologies in which shamans are defined as andronygous or "third sex" beings (Saladin d'Anglure 1989), and, more

Renard-Casevitz realizes that perspectivism is not a case of "relativism," even though she describes it in these terms (1991: 11). Discussing a Matsiguenga myth in which the protagonists travel to different villages inhabited by people—probably spirits—who call "fish," "agouti," or "macaws" (proper food for humans) the snakes, bats, or balls of fire they eat, she observes:

[The myth] affirms that there are transcultural and transnational norms, which are in force everywhere. Such norms determine the same likes and dislikes, the same dietary values and the same prohibitions or aversions . . . The mythical misunderstandings derive from visions out of phase [*visions décalées*], not from barbarian tastes or an improper use of language. (ibid.: 25–26)

However, she concludes that:

This setting in perspective [*mise en perspective*] is just the application and transposition of universal social practices, such as the fact that a mother and a father of X are the parents-in-law of Y. This variability of the denomination as a function of the place occupied explains how A can be both fish for X and snake for Y. (ibid.: 29)

The problem, of course, is that this universalization of sociocultural positional relativity—its application to the difference between species—has the paradoxical consequence of making human (Matsiguenga) culture natural, i.e., absolute: everybody eats "fish," and nobody eats "snake."

Renard-Casevitz's analogy between kinship positions and what counts as fish or snake for different species, however, is intriguing. Let us engage in a thought experiment. Kinship terms are open, relational pointers; they belong to that class of nouns that define something in terms of its relations to something else (linguists certainly have a name for these words). Concepts like "fish" or "tree," on the other hand, are proper, self-contained substantives: they are applied to an object by virtue of its self-subsisting, autonomous properties. Now, what seems to be happening in Amerindian perspectivism is that substances named by substantives like "fish," "snake," "hammock," or "canoe" are somehow

---

generally, in those cosmologies which frame hunter/prey relationships in terms of erotic seduction (e.g., Holmberg 1969: 240; Murphy 1958: 39; McCallum 1989: 155; Descola 1986: 322ff.; Désveaux 1988: 199).

used as if they were relational pointers, something halfway between a noun and a pronoun, a substantive and a deictic. (There is supposedly a difference between "natural kind" terms such as "fish" and artefact terms such as "hammock"—we shall come to this shortly.) You are a father only because there is another person whose father you are: fatherhood is a relation, while fishness is a intrinsic property of fish. In Amerindian perspectivism, however, something would be "fish" only by virtue of someone else whose fish it is.

But if saying that crickets are the fish of the dead or that mud is the hammock of tapirs is like saying that Isabel's son Michael is my nephew, then there is no "relativism" involved. Isabel is not a mother "for" Michael, from Michael's "point of view" in the usual, relativist-subjectivist sense of the expression: she is the mother *of* Michael, she's really and objectively Michael's mother, and I am really Michael's uncle. This is a genitive, internal relation—my sister is the mother *of* someone, our cricket the fish *of* someone—not a representational, external connection of the type "X is fish *for* someone," which implies that X is "represented" as fish, whatever X is "in itself." It would be absurd to say that, since Michael is the son of Isabel but not mine, then Michael is not a son "for me"—for indeed he is, the son of Isabel precisely.[3]

Now imagine that all Amerindian "substances" were of this sort. Suppose then that just as siblings are those who have the same parents, then conspecifics would be those which have the same fish, the same snake, the same hammock, and so on. No wonder, then, that animals are so often conceived as affinally related to humans in Amazonia. Blood is to humans as manioc beer to jaguars in exactly the same way as a sister to me is a wife to my brother-in-law. The many Amerindian myths featuring interspecific marriages (as the Sharanahua one transcribed below), and discussing the difficult relationships between the human (or animal) in-marrying affine and his/her animal (or human) parents-in-law, simply compound the two analogies into a single complex one. We begin to see how perspectivism may have a deep connection with

---

3.   In *Process and reality* Whitehead makes the following remark: "It must be remembered that the phrase 'actual world' is like 'yesterday' or 'tomorrow', in that it alters its meaning according to standpoint" (this quotation appears as an epigraph in Latour 1994). Now, a standpoint is not an opinion or a construction; there is nothing "subjective," in the usual sense of the term, in the concepts of "yesterday" and "tomorrow," or of "my mother" and "your brother"—they are *objectively* relative or relational concepts. The actual world *of* other species depend on their specific standpoint.

exchange—not only how it may be a type of exchange, but how exchange itself may be defined in terms of perspectives, as exchange of perspectives (Strathern 1988, 1992d).

We would thus have a universe that is a hundred percent relational—one in which individual substances or substantial forms are not the ultimate reality. In any case, in this universe there would be no distinctions between primary and secondary qualities of substances (to evoke an old philosophical contrast), or between brute facts and institutional facts, to evoke John Searle's (1995) basic ontological duality.

Searle, as you recall, opposes brute facts or objects, the reality of which is independent of human consciousness—like gravity, mountains, trees and animals (all "natural kinds" belong to this class)—to institutional facts or objects, like marriage, money, axes, and cars, which derive their existence, identity, and efficaciousness from the culturally-specific meanings given to them by humans. Note that Searle's book I am referring to here is pointedly entitled *The construction of social reality* (1995), not "The social construction of reality." Natural facts are *not* constructed, social facts (including statements about brute facts) are. In this overhauled version of the old nature/culture dualism, cultural relativism applies to cultural objects, and is balanced by natural universalism, which applies to natural objects.

Searle would argue, I suppose—if he were to bother with what I am saying—that what I am actually saying is that for Amerindians all facts are of the institutional, mental variety, and that all beings, even trees and fish, are like money or hammocks, in that their only reality (as money and hammocks, not as pieces of paper or of string) derives from the meanings and uses subjects attribute to them. This would be nothing but relativism, Searle would observe—and an extreme, absolute form of relativism at that.

One of the implications of the Amerindian animic-perspectival ontology is, indeed, that there are no autonomous, natural facts, for what we see as "nature" is seen by other species as "culture," i.e., as institutional facts—what we see as blood, a natural substance, is seen by jaguars as manioc beer, an artefact; our mud is the hammock of the tapirs and so on. But these institutional facts are here *universal*, something that is quite foreign to Searle's alternatives, and that cannot therefore be reduced to a type of constructionist relativism (which would define all facts as being of the institutional type and then conclude that they are culturally variable). We have here a case of *cultural universalism*, which has as its counterpart what could be called *natural relativism*. It is this inversion of our pairing of nature to the universal and culture to the particular that I have labelled "perspectivism."

You remember the famous saying: "If a lion could talk, we could not understand him" (Wittgenstein 1958: 223; compare this with the remark of Xenophanes evoked earlier on in a footnote). This is indeed relativism. For Amerindians, lions, or rather jaguars, not only can talk, but we are perfectly able to understand what they *say*—they "speak of" exactly the same things as we do—although *what* they mean (what they are "talking about") is another matter. Same representations, different objects; same meaning, different reference. This is perspectivism.

(Multi)cultural relativism supposes a diversity of subjective and partial representations, each striving to grasp an external and unified nature, which remains perfectly indifferent to those representations. Amerindian thought proposes the opposite: a representational or phenomenological unity which is purely pronominal or deictic, indifferently applied to a radically objective diversity. One single "culture," multiple "natures"—one epistemology, multiple ontologies. Perspectivism implies multinaturalism, for a perspective is not a representation.

A perspective is not a representation because representations are a property of the mind or spirit, whereas the point of view is located in the body. The ability to adopt a point of view is undoubtedly a power of the soul, and nonhumans are subjects in so far as they have (or are) spirit; but the differences between viewpoints (and a viewpoint is nothing if not a difference) lies not in the soul. Since the soul is formally identical in all species, it can only see the same things everywhere—the difference is given in the specificity of bodies.[4]

---

4.   Representations are a property of the spirit: indeed, if we are to follow Ernest Crawley (1909), who presented the most clever intellectualist alternative to the Tylorean dream-theory of the soul, the notion of "soul" is the precursor of the notion of "representation." For Crawley, the idea of the soul was first applied to the *object*, not to the subject—it was born when primitive man reflected on the difference between actual perception and memory, the thing present and its image in absentia; the personal soul was a secondary, late application of the distinction between perception and memory to the self. (Thus Crawley's theory of the soul is thoroughly non-Cartesian as well.) It was a long time, according to Crawley, before the representation ceased to share the reality "out there" with the thing, and was made to dwell "in here"; then the notion of the soul was replaced by ideas of "representation" and "mind." Thus representations not only are *in* the spirit, they *are* spirit, or they are now what the spirit was then. (I thank Laura Rival for calling my attention to Crawley's book.)

This brings us back to the questions I raised when discussing Descola's typology: if nonhumans are persons and have souls, then what distinguishes them from humans? And why, being people, do they not see us as people? Here are my answers. Animals see in the *same* way as we do *different* things because their bodies are different to ours. I am not referring to physiological differences—as far as that is concerned, Amerindians recognize a basic uniformity of bodies—but rather to *affects*, in the old sense of dispositions or capacities which render the body of every species unique: what it eats, how it moves, how it communicates, where it lives, whether it is gregarious or solitary. . . . The visible shape of the body is a powerful sign of these affectual differences, although it can be deceptive, since a human appearance could, for example, be concealing a jaguar-affect.[5]

Thus, what I call "body" is not a synonym for distinctive substance or fixed shape; it is an assemblage of affects or ways of being that constitute a habitus. Between the formal subjectivity of souls and the substantial materiality of organisms, there is thus an intermediate plane which is occupied by the body as a bundle of affects and capacities and which is the origin of perspectives. The common, transpecific spirit has access to the same percepts, but species-specific bodies are endowed with different affects—and that is why we have multinaturalism. It would be more precise to say that all spirits are equipped with the same concepts, and *therefore* with the same percepts—this identification of concepts to percepts (or rather, the determination of percepts by concepts) being the only truly "relativistic" aspect of Amerindian cosmology. But it leads here to transspecific similarity, not difference. It would be even more precise, perhaps, to say that each type of affectual singularity—each type of body—has a different perceptual apparatus ("different eyes," as the Chewong put it [Howell 1984]), while the common soul has a single conceptual repertoire. That is why we would have identical perceptions caused by different things: different things modify different bodies identically.

5. In contrast to our own preoccupation with exhaustive morphologico-genetical classifications, I believe that Amerindian ethnobiological knowledge is less concerned with genetic continuity or morphological similarity than with affects and behaviors. This is not (necessarily) related with differential emphases on theory vs. practice, etc. Given the changeability of form, i.e., the "highly transformational world" presupposed by Amerindian ontologies, behavior is a better guide than appearances, as Rivière (1994) remarked in an analogous context. Indeed, the body is behavior rather than visible shape.

The difference between bodies, however, is only apprehendable from an exterior viewpoint, by an other since, for itself, every type of being has the same form (the generic form of a human being). Bodies are the way in which alterity is apprehended as such. In normal conditions we do not see animals as people, and vice-versa, because our respective bodies (and the perspectives which they allow) are different. Thus, if "culture" is a reflexive perspective of the subject, objectified through the concept of soul, it can be said that "nature" is the viewpoint which the subject takes of other body-affects; if culture is the subject's nature, then *nature is the form of the other as body*, that is, as the object for a subject. Culture takes the self-referential form of the first-person pronoun "I/me" or "we/ us"; nature is the form of the "third person," actually of the nonperson or the object, indicated by the impersonal pronoun "it/them" (Benveniste 1966a, 1966b).

If, in the eyes of Amerindians, the body makes the difference, then it is easily understood why, in the anecdote told by Lévi-Strauss, the methods of investigation into the humanity of the other employed by the Spanish and the natives of the Antilles showed that intriguing asymmetry. For the Europeans, the issue was to decide whether the others possessed a soul; for the Indians, the aim was to find out what kind of body the others had. For the Europeans the marker of difference in perspective is the soul (are Indians humans or animals?); for the Indians it is the body (are Europeans humans or spirits?). The Europeans never doubted that the Indians had bodies (animals have them too); the Indians never doubted that the Europeans had souls (animals and spirits have them too). What the Indians wanted to know was whether the bodies of those "souls" were capable of the same affects as their own—whether they had the bodies of humans or the bodies of spirits, non-putrescible and protean. In sum: the ethnocentrism of the Europeans consisted in doubting whether other bodies have the same souls as they themselves; Amerindian ethnocentrism in doubting whether other souls had the same bodies.

Allow me to recall another famous anedocte, which can perhaps be read in exactly the same sense as that of Lévi-Strauss. This one concerns Maurice Leenhardt, the French Protestant missionary and anthropologist, and New Caledonians:

> Once, wanting to assess the mental progress of Canaques I had taught for many years, I risked the following suggestion [to Boesoou, a sculptor and old friend of L.'s]: "In short, we introduced the notion of spirit to your way of thinking?" And he objected, "Spirit? Bah! You didn't bring us the spirit. We already knew

the spirit existed. We have always acted in accord with the spirit. What you've brought us is the body." (Leenhardt 1960: 263)[6]

I suppose, like Jean-Pierre Vernant (1986), that this man was talking about the Christian body, the fleshed, desiring, postlapsarian body, the common lot and predicament of humankind and all mortal creatures. But I also think that more important than the flesh of this body brought by Leenhardt is its form: what was brought was the universal body, the body as the form of the universal. Leenhardt thought he had brought the spirit, because his message was that the Kanak were human—but the universality of the Christian message annexed the Kanak to humanity only on the condition of separating them from the rest of creation, which is only body. The Kanak, however, already had the spirit in a far more universal sense than the Christian one. What they did not have, precisely, was the universal body.[7]

Let us hear yet another indigenous voice, featuring this same intriguing entanglement of Christianity and the body. It comes from an article by Denise Fajardo (1997), who is currently doing fieldwork among the Trio, Caribs of the Guiana region. The following is a reflection by a Trio man about how Christianity changed his attitudes (emphasis added):

> I was born here, this is my land, I am a real Trio; but now we are mixing with the Kaxuyana because God so wished. God ordered us to go and bring this people out from the forest, then the Kaxuyana came and we are all mixed now, we don't fight anymore. God tells us not to fight, not to kill; I want all of them [the K.] as my kin. Because now I know my head; before, I did not want to be with other people, other groups, because they were not my kin. *But now I have become a Christian, then I think that these other groups are my kin, they have the same body as I have, the same life.*[8]

---

6. The translation comes from the English version (1979: 164). See Clifford ([1982] 1992: 172) on this famous retort, which I first read in Vernant (1986).

7. Leenhardt himself had a very different interpretation of the anedocte: he took the "body" conveyed by his teaching as meaning the individuating, particularizing body, capable of stopping the universal participation of the spirit and disengaging the person from the sociomythic domain, providing it with an interiority, etc.

8. I take it the remark was made in Portuguese.

Note that the Christian message is, here, about sharing the same body, not the same immortal soul. The Kaxuyana are not "brothers in Christ," spiritual conspecifics of the Trio (much less brothers "in culture," which, by the way, they are)—they are brothers in life, that is, brothers in body.

As Ingold has stressed (1991, 1994), the status of humans in Western thought is essentially ambiguous: on the one hand, humankind is an *animal species* amongst others, and animality is a domain that includes humans; on the other hand, humanity is a *moral condition* which excludes animals. These two statuses, we might add, coexist in the problematic and disjunctive notion of "human nature." In other words, our cosmology postulates a physical continuity and a metaphysical discontinuity between humans and animals, the former making of humankind an object for the natural sciences, the latter making of humanity an object for the "humanities." Spirit or mind is our great differentiator: it raises us above animals and matter in general, it distinguishes cultures, it makes each person unique before his/her fellow beings. The body, in contrast, is the major integrator: it connects us to the rest of the living, united by a universal substrate (DNA, carbon chemistry) which, in turn, links up with the ultimate nature of all material bodies—so there is something like a "modern participation," which is physical participation. In contrast to this, Amerindians postulate a metaphysical continuity (a.k.a. "primitive participation") and a physical discontinuity between the beings of the cosmos, the former resulting in animism, the latter in perspectivism: the spirit or soul (here not an immaterial inner substance but rather a reflexive form—no "interiority") integrates, the body (not an extended material organism but a system of intensive affects—no "exteriority") differentiates.

The counterproof of the singularity of the spirit in our cosmologies lies in the fact that when we try to universalize it, we are obliged—now that supernature is out of bounds—to identify it with the structure and function of the brain. The spirit can only be universal (natural) if it is (in) the body. It is no accident, I believe, that this movement of inscription of the spirit in the brain-body or in matter in general—artificial intelligence, Churchland's "eliminative materialism," Dennett-style "functionalism," Sperberian cognitivism etc.—has been synchronically countered by its opposite, the neo-phenomenological appeal to the body as the site of subjective singularity. Thus we have been witnessing two seemingly contradictory projects of "embodying" the spirit: one actually reducing it to the body as traditionally (i.e., bio-physically) understood, the other upgrading the body to the traditional (i.e., cultural-theological) status of "spirit."

The contrast I have just made, between physical and metaphysical continuities and discontinuites is, I grant, much overdrawn and simplistic. It might be argued, for instance, that in our tradition, if the body is what connects us to the rest of the material world it is also something that *separates* us, each of us, from the rest of the world. By the same token, the spirit is what distinguishes but also what allow us to reach beyond our bodily limits and to communicate with our fellow humans. (Furthermore, as the conventional metaphor goes, we can change our minds, not our bodies.) Conversely, it could be noted that the body is the great differentiator in Amerindian ontologies but at the same time it is the site of interspecific metamorphosis; the soul or spirit, on the other hand, is what assimilates every type of being but at the same time is what must be kept separate (the commerce of nonhuman souls is dangerous for humans).

I will not parry these objections by resorting to dialectics. I would just distinguish the body (our "body") as concept—the concept of "body" that assimilates the human body to all other extended material objects[9]—from the body as experience. In the first sense, the spirit or "mind" is *an organ of the body;* in the second sense, however, the hierarchy is inverted: the body is an organ of the spirit. The subjective singularity of the body-as-experience is of the same ontological quality as counsciousness itself, it is the support of the famous *qualia* of the philosophers of mind. It is in this sense, and in this sense only, that the body is what distinguishes—here, however, it is not the extended body that is acting, but rather the spirit under cover of the body. I suppose the same type of reasoning could be applied to our notion of spirit, and to the Amerindian notions.

Be that as it may, one of the clearest evidences for the differentiating and singularizing role of the spirit in our cosmology comes from the thought experiments made in science fiction novels or in philosophical essays about uploading the mind, transfering your memories to other bodies etc. (In Dennett and Hofstadter [1981] you will find amusing discussions of these topics.) We can easily imagine a situation in which our "souls" (or minds, or neural networks, or memories) enter into other bodies, but the inverse situation doesn't even make sense. As far as we are concerned, the "I" is located in our soul, not in our body as an extended material object.

---

9.   The use of "body" as the name for the general physical object is, in itself, revealing. Physics describe a world of "bodies" that behave according to "laws"—this would sound quite anthropomorphic if held by any "savage."

CARTESIAN ANIMALS AND TURING MACHINES: FROM NO MIND TO NO BODY

If we consider the amount of ritual exorcism and abuse directed to his name and ideas in the writings of contemporary anthropologists and philosophers, we must conclude that Descartes is the biggest nasty around. His mind/body and humans/animal dualisms are the choice example of the so-called "persistent Western dicothomies" which everyone in our line of business—not to speak of the philosophy of mind trade—loves to deconstruct and delights in showing that the such-and-such just "don't have." Anthropologists working on the nature/society question, in particular, denounce the wrong-headedness of the Cartesian human/animal divide, whilst describing how premodern people all over the planet conceive of, and engage in, a practical, intersubjective involvement between humans and animals. By means of his wrong-headed dualism of mind vs. body, Descartes separated humanity from animality, man from nature—yet another proof of the blindness of Western civilization to that universal intersubjective sociality of living things which savages rightly affirm. So: *contra* the modern, Cartesian animals-machines, postmodern animals, just like premodern ones, are subjects. They are subjects not because they have cognitive capabilities similar to ours, be it noted, but because we all share the same embodied awareness of being-in-the-world.

For some contemporary philosophers, on the other hand, computers are the epitome of what humans are *not*. Turing machines can perhaps calculate, but they cannot really think. Computers are not human because they have no real bodies: they are incapable of intuition, they may have some sort of understanding but no sensibility, they have syntax but no semantics, rules but no habitus, energy states but no consciousness, and so forth. Such is the rationale of "embodiment" theory.

Those anthropologists who strive to demolish the human/animal divide belong, generally speaking, to the same ideological tribe as those philosophers who deny humanity to Turing machines (a tribe that we could loosely call "the neo-phenomenologists"). How come? This is what I think has happened: now that animals have a very dim presence in our life, we can afford to consider them as potential co-subjects and/or to appreciate their co-subject status in other cultures. The human/animal divide is no longer important to us. The human/machine interface, on the other hand, is what really counts: even animals have been turned into machines (think of dairy factories). So, the function of "Other" has shifted from animals to machines, and above all to those machines that may be conceived as having minds—computers. When animals were still the "Other," Western thought separated them from us on the grounds that they had no souls—they were just bodies, and bodies were just machines, or more precisely, clocks. This is Descartes (a very simplified version of the whole story of course). Now, however, when machines are no longer just clocks, but objects that are getting very close to being thinking things or potential subjects—the universal machine, the Turing-VonNeumann computer, replicating and reproducing man the universal animal (Marx)—we deny them humanity by saying that our quintessential uniqueness dwells in our "phenomenal" body, not in a disembodied, unextended, Cartesian mind. (Is this Darwinian human/animal continuity made thinkable thanks to the Industrial Revolution?)

So, Descartes set humans off from animals on the grounds that we are mind plus body, while they are only body: man *versus* (animals + machines). Our contemporary neo-phenomenologists of "embodied practice" distinguish humans from machines (computers) on the grounds that we are mind plus body, while they are only mind, or a simulacrum of it: (man + animals) *versus* machines.

We should keep the savages out of this quarrel. To begin with, if my conjecture has any sense, the anti-Cartesians of today (I mean the "practice" anti-Cartesians, not the "physicalists," mind-is-brain fellows) are indulging in the very same differencing of Man from something else, just as Descartes is supposed to have done. The something has changed, that is all: the anti-subject of today is the Turing machine, not the Cartesian machine-like animals. *Plus ça change* . . . Anthropocentrism is harder to kill than one might think. And this shows, by the bye, that anthropocentrism is the very opposite of anthropomorphism, as I said in the last lecture. For Amazonian Indians, computers would qualify as subjects just as well as animals do—if manioc grinders or canoes are people, having humanoid "embodiments" in the spirit world, why shouldn't computers?

The discourse about "embodiment," therefore, may be actually expressing the very opposite of what is intended by those who champion it. Such discourse strongly suggests an upgrading of the body to the traditional status of "mind"— it spiritualizes the body rather than embodies the mind. Computers, after all, cannot be human because they are just matter, have no spirit ("body" in today's parlance).

THE SUBJECT AS OBJECT: FROM SOLIPSISM TO CANNIBALISM

The idea that the body appears to be the great differentiator in Amazonian cosmologies—that is, as that which unites beings of the same type to the extent that it differentiates them from others—allows us to reconsider some of the classic questions of the ethnology of the region in a new light.

Thus, the now old theme of the importance of corporeality in Amazonian societies (which much pre-dates the current "embodiment" craze: see Seeger, DaMatta & Viveiros de Castro 1979) acquires firmer foundations. For example, it becomes possible to gain a better understanding of why the categories of identity—be they personal, social, or cosmological—are so frequently expressed through bodily idioms, particularly through food practices and body decoration. The universal symbolic importance of food and cooking regimes in Amazonia shows that the set of habits and processes that constitute bodies is precisely the location from which identity and difference emerge. It would be enough to recall the mythological "raw and the cooked" of Lévi-Strauss; but we may also evoke the Piro idea that what literally (i.e., naturally) makes them different from white people is the "real food" they eat (Gow 1991); the food avoidances which define "corporeal" rather than corporate groups among the Jê of Central Brazil (Seeger 1980); the basic classification of beings according to their eating habits among the Matsiguenga (Baer 1994); the ontological productivity of commensality, similarity of diet and relative condition of prey-object and predator-subject among the Pakaa-Nova (Vilaça 1992); or the omnipresence of cannibalism as the "predicative" horizon of all relations with the other, be they matrimonial, alimentary or bellicose (Viveiros de Castro 1993a).

The same can be said of the intense semiotic, especially visual, use of the body in the definition of personal identities and in the circulation of social values. As Mentore (1993: 29) wrote of the Waiwai, "the primary dialectics is one between seeing and eating"—perspectivism and predation, then; this could be extended to most of Amazonia. The connection between this overdetermination of the body (particularly of its visible surface) and the restricted recourse in the Amazonian *socius* to objects capable of supporting relations—that is, a situation wherein social exchange is not usually mediated by material objectifications such as those characteristic of gift and commodity economies—has been pinpointed by Terence Turner, who has shown how the human body therefore must appear as the prototypical social object. However, the Amerindian emphasis on the social construction of the body cannot be taken as the culturalization of a natural substrate (*contra* Turner 1980, Mentore 1993, Rivière 1994), but rather as the production of a distinctly human body, meaning *naturally* human. Such a process seems to be expressing not so much a wish to de-animalize the body through its cultural marking, but rather to particularize a body still too generic, differentiating it from the bodies of other human collectivities as well as from those of other species. The body, as the site of differentiating perspective, must be differentiated to the highest degree in order to completely express it.

The human body can be seen as the locus of the confrontation between humanity and animality, but not because it is essentially animal by nature and needs to be veiled and controlled by culture. The body is the subject's fundamental expressive instrument and at the same time the object *par excellence*, that which is presented to the sight of the other. It is no coincidence, then, that the maximum social objectification of bodies, their maximal particularization expressed in decoration and ritual exhibition is at the same time the moment of maximum animalization (Goldman 1975: 178; S. Hugh-Jones 1979; Seeger 1987; Turner 1991, 1995), when bodies are covered by feathers, colors, designs, masks, and other animal prostheses. Man ritually clothed as an animal is the counterpart to the animal supernaturally naked. The former, transformed into an animal, reveals to himself the "natural" distinctiveness of his body; the latter, free of its exterior form and revealing itself as human, shows the "supernatural" similarity of spirit.

The model of spirit is the human spirit, but the model of body are the bodies of animals; and if from the point of view of the subject, culture takes the generic form of "I" and nature of "it/they," then the objectification of the subject to itself demands a singularization of bodies—which naturalizes culture, i.e., embodies it—whilst the subjectification of the object implies communication at the level of spirit—which culturalizes nature, i.e., supernaturalizes it. Put in these terms, the Amerindian distinction of nature and culture, before it is dissolved in the name of a common animic human-animal sociality, must be re-read in the light of somatic perspectivism.

As a clinching argument in favor of this idea that the model of body are animal bodies, I would observe that there are virtually no examples, in Amerindian ethnography, of animals dressing up as humans, that is, assuming a human body as if it were a clothing. All bodies, including the human body, are thought of as garments or envelopes; but you never see animals donning this human "clothing." What you see are humans donning animal clothes and becoming animals, or animals shedding their animal clothing and revealing themselves as humans. The human form is, as it were, the body within the body, the naked primordial body—the "soul" of the body.

It is important to note that these Amerindian bodies are not thought of as given but rather as made. Therefore, an emphasis on the methods for the continuous fabrication of the body (Viveiros de Castro 1979); a notion of kinship as a process of active assimilation of individuals (Gow 1991) through the sharing of bodily substances, sexual and alimentary—and not as a passive inheritance of some substantial essence—and a theory of memory which inscribes it in the flesh (Viveiros de Castro 1992a). The Amerindian *Bildung* happens in the body more than in the spirit: there is no "spiritual" change which is not a bodily transformation, a redefinition of its affects and capacities.

Although I cannot pursue this point further here, let me just remark that much of what we would tend to associate with the "mind," such as "culture" and "knowledge," is considered by Amerindians to be an attribute of the body, as something that happens in, to, and through the body. The clearest example is shamanism, which we would consider as the "spiritual" activity par excellence, but which Amerindians see as a bodily condition. "For the Yaminahua . . . shamanism resides primarily, not in a type of thinking nor in a set of facts known, but in a condition of the body and its perceptions" (Townsley 1993: 456). Let us also recall that the use of hallucinogenic drugs as a means of "spiritual" communication with the invisible side of things plays a major role in much of Amazonian shamanism, and that to take those drugs is a very bodily experience, as remarked by Peter Gow (pers. comm.). Besides shamanism, however, many other faculties and skills that we associate with the "spirit" or "mind" are seen in bodily terms. Take language, for instance. This is what Jean Monod (1987: 114) wrote of his experience among the Piaroa:

> When you come to the Piaroa and you want to learn their language, the first thing they tell you is that you must share their food. When you have made some progress and the difficulties begin to be serious, they tell you that the only way to overcome them is by marrying a Piaroa woman. If you decline the suggestion, then they say: "take some *yopo* [*Datura*, an hallucinogenic drug], the language shall come along with the vision . . ."

We come now to a difficult question. While the *duality* of body and soul is obviously pertinent to these cosmologies—as I said, all shamanistic cosmologies operate on the basis of this major distinction—it cannot be interpreted as an ontological *dualism*. Let me cite Graham Townsley (1993: 456), on what he calls the Yaminahua "model of cognition":

> One of the keys to [shamanic] knowledge seems to me to lie exactly in an image of the person and knowing subject which ... has no place for "mind" (as an inner storehouse of meanings, thought and experience quite separate from the world), and associates "mental" events with animate essences which can drift free from bodies and mingle with the world, participating in it much more intimately than any conventional notion of "mind" would allow.

This lack of a place for "mind" has two important implications: (1) there are no representations in this universe, but only perspectives; (2) there is no *ontological* dualism of spirit (or "meaning") versus matter (or "things"); there is no such thing as a "nonphysical" (mental) world, and therefore there is no "physical" world. That is why, as many ethnographers have remarked, Amerindians take thinking and acting as coextensive; thoughts and actions happen in the same ontological space; the meaningful and the material are aspects of one single reality. Townsley once more:

> This conversion of the meaningful into the material is, of course, unthinkable from the standpoint of a model of cognition which places all meaning operations in a "mind," something interior to the person which leaves the material world unaffected. From this standpoint, not even the often mentioned idea of "illocutionary force," or any speech act or narrative which changes the world by redefining it or changing people's perception of it, could possibly encompass the sheer physicality of transformations claimed by shamanism. . . . [F]rom the very different standpoint of the Yaminahua model of cognition, the idea that experiences and meanings can be embedded in the non-human world is a less problematic one. It is the concept of a type of perceiving animate essence shared by the human and non-human alike, creating for them a shared space of interaction, which opens up the "magical" arena of shamanism. (ibid.: 465)

Body and soul, therefore—animal bodies and human souls—are not related as matter to mind, things to representations. They simply distinguish between the affectual and the perceptual, the particular and the universal. Let me rephrase the whole point: bodies are not things, souls are not representations; by the same token, *both* body and soul are not things (for there are no anti-things, i.e., representations), and they are not representations either (for there are no anti-representations, i.e., things). Body and soul are, precisely, perspectives: the body is the site of perspectives; the soul, that which the point of view has put in the subject position.

As bundles of affects and sites of perspective, rather than material organisms, bodies "are" souls, just, incidentally, as souls and spirits "are" bodies. The dual (or plural) conception of the human soul, widespread in indigenous Amazonia, distinguishes between the soul (or souls) of the body, reified register of an individual's history, site of memory and affect, and a "true soul," pure, formal subjective singularity, the abstract mark of a person (e.g., Viveiros de Castro 1992a; McCallum 1996). On the other hand, the souls of the dead and the spirits which inhabit the universe are not immaterial entities, but equally types of bodies, endowed with properties—affects—*sui generis*. Indeed body and soul, just like nature and culture, do not correspond to substantives, self-subsistent entities or ontological provinces, but rather to pronouns or phenomenological perspectives.

The performative rather than given character of the body, a conception that requires it to differentiate itself "culturally" in order for it to be "naturally" different, has an obvious connection with interspecific metamorphosis, a possibility suggested by Amerindian cosmologies. We need not be surprised by a way of thinking which posits bodies as the great differentiators yet at the same time states their transformability. Our cosmology supposes a singular distinctiveness of minds, but not even for this reason does it declare communication (albeit solipsism is a constant problem) to be impossible, or discredits the mental/spiritual transformations induced by such processes as education and religious conversion; in truth, it is precisely because the spiritual is the locus of difference that conversion becomes necessary (the Europeans wanted to know whether Indians had souls in order to modify them). Bodily metamorphosis is the Amerindian counterpart to the European theme of spiritual conversion.[10]

10. The rarity of unequivocal examples of spirit possession in the complex of Amerindian shamanism may derive from the prevalence of the theme of bodily metamorphosis. The classical problem of the religious conversion of Amerindians (Viveiros de Castro 1993b) could also be further illuminated from this angle; indigenous conceptions of "acculturation" seem to focus more on the incorporation and embodiment of Western bodily practices (food, clothing, interethnic sex) rather than on spiritual assimilation ("beliefs").

In the same way, if solipsism is the phantom that continuously threatens our cosmology—raising the fear of not recognizing ourselves in our "own kind" because they are not like us, given the potentially absolute singularity of minds—then the possibility of metamorphosis expresses the opposite fear, of no longer being able to differentiate between the human and the animal, and, in particular, the fear of seeing the human who lurks within the body of the animal one eats. (Our traditional problem is how to connect and universalize—individual substances are given, relations have to be made—the Amerindians' is how to separate and particularize—relations are given, substances must be defined. You will certainly recall Roy Wagner's [(1975) 1981, 1977b] formulation of this contrast.)[11]

Hence the importance, in Amazonia, of dietary rules linked to the spiritual potency of animals: the past humanity of animals is added to their present-day spirituality hidden by their visible form in order to produce an extended set of food restrictions or precautions, which either declare inedible certain animals that were mythically cosubstantial with humans, or demand their desubjectivization by shamanistic means before they can be consumed (neutralizing the spirit, transsubstantiating the meat into plant food, semantically reducing it to other animals less proximate to humans), under the threat of illness, conceived of as a cannibal counter-predation undertaken by the spirit of the prey turned predator, in a lethal inversion of perspectives which transforms the human into animal.[12] The phantom of cannibalism is the Amerindian equivalent to the problem of solipsism: if the latter derives from the uncertainty as to whether the natural similarity of bodies guarantees a real community of spirit, then the

---

11. "The Tsimshian world view concerns the ability of beasts, objects and all living things to communicate with beings of different species and kinds.... As a rule, one does not voice anything important in clear terms, for anything which is thought, and, more especially, anything which is spoken aloud, can be reclaimed in some way by other people, human or not. Nothing is hidden" (Guédon 1984a: 141). Besides illustrating the ontological continuity of thought and deed we have mentioned, this remark also illustrates the Amerindian problem with the excess of communication: nothing is hidden, given the universal permeability of the spirit. See also Fienup-Riordan (1994: 46): "If the fundamental existential problem of the Hobbesian individual was to forge a unity out of the natural diversity of humankind, Eskimos traditionally viewed themselves as confronted with an originally *undifferentiated* universe in which the boundaries between the human and the non-human, the spiritual and the material, were shifting and permeable."

12. See Crocker (1985) (Bororo); Overing (1985, 1986) (Piaroa); Vilaça (1992) (Wari'); Århem (1993), Hugh-Jones (1996) (Tukanoans).

former suspects that the similarity of souls might prevail over the real differences of body and that all animals that are eaten might, despite the shamanistic efforts to de-subjectivize them, remain human. This of course does not prevent us having among ourselves more or less radical solipsists, such as the relativists, nor that various Amerindian societies be purposefully and more or less literally cannibalistic.[13]

As we have remarked, a good part of the shamanistic work consists in de-subjectivizing animals, that is transforming them into pure, natural bodies capable of being consumed without danger. In contrast, what defines spirits is precisely the fact that they are inedible; this transforms them into eaters par excellence, i.e., into anthropophagous beings. In this way, it is common for the great predators to be the preferred forms in which spirits manifest themselves, and it is understandable that game animals should see humans as spirits, that spirits and predator animals should see us as game animals, and that animals taken to be inedible should be assimilated to spirits (see above, Lecture 1, Chapter 8 in this volume).

There is another classic theme in South American ethnology that could be interpreted within the argumentative framework of these lectures: that of the sociological discontinuity between the living and the dead (a theme first developed in the classic monograph of Maria Manuela Carneiro da Cunha [1978]). Contemporary Amazonian societies do not have anything similar to the "ancestor cults" to be found in other parts of the world. Of course, they may recognize mythical or historical forebears, founders of clans, "original people," and so on. But these societies do not usually transform the dead into ancestors (let us not forget ancestors have to be made, not simply "conceived"), they do not divide themselves internally in terms of affiliation to specific dead people, and they do not pay any cult to dead forebears just because they are dead. The general attitude is one of treating the dead as fundamentally other to the living: to die is to pass to the "other side"; the ontological difference between the living and

---

13. In Amazonian exo-cannibalism, rather than desubjectivization, as is the case with game animals (see Viveiros de Castro 1992a: 290–93; 1996b: 98–102; Fausto 1997), what is intended is the incorporation of the subject-aspect of the enemy (who is accordingly hyper-subjectivized, in much the same way as that described by Harrison [1993: 121] for Melanesian warfare). Amazonian cannibalism is, for me, a form of "unmediated exchange" (Strathern 1988), being the basic schematism of "ontological predation"—the assumption of the enemy's perspective as a condition of personification.

the dead is more radical than any sociological difference obtaining among the living. In fact, the difference between the living and the dead is very commonly expressed in terms, precisely, of the two fundamental differences obtaining in this social world: the dead are assimilated to affines and to enemies.

Now, the fundamental distinction between the living and the dead is made by the body and precisely not by the spirit. Death is a bodily catastrophe which prevails as differentiator over the common "animation" of the living and the dead. Amerindian cosmologies dedicate equal or greater interest to the way in which the dead see reality as they do to the vision of animals, and as is the case for the latter, they underline the radical differences vis-à-vis the world of the living. To be precise, being definitively separated from their bodies, the dead are not human. As spirits defined by their disjunction from a human body, the dead are logically attracted to the bodies of animals; this is why to die is to transform into an animal, as it is to transform into other figures of bodily alterity, such as affines and enemies.[14] As a matter of fact, if the soul of animals is conceived as having a human bodily form, it is not surprising that the soul of humans may be conceived as having an animal body, or entering into one.

In this manner, if animism affirms a subjective and social continuity between humans and animals, its somatic complement, perspectivism, establishes an objective discontinuity, equally social, between live humans and dead humans. Religions based on the cult of the ancestors seem to postulate the inverse: spiritual identity goes beyond the bodily barrier of death, the living and the dead are similar in so far as they manifest the same spirit. We would accordingly have superhuman ancestrality and spiritual possession on one side, animalization of the dead and bodily metamorphosis on the other.[15]

I would like to conclude with an image that will be pursued in our next, and final, lecture. It is as if—the image was contrived by myself—the different species of being that inhabit the perspectivist world were split into front and back halves or sides. Each type of being can only see its front half—and it always looks human (we ourselves look human to us). This front half is the soul. Each type of being, on the other hand, can only see the back half or far side of those

---

14. See Pollock (1985: 95) (Kulina); Schwartzmann (1988: 268) (Panara); Vilaça (1992: 247–55) (Wari'); Turner (1995: 152) (Kayapó); Gray (1996: 157–78, 178) (Arakmbut).

15. See Fienup-Riordan (1994: 49) on the correlations of these three different "master codes": human/animal in native America, male/female in Melanesia, and ancestors/ descendants, or the dead and the living, in "Africa."

species to which it does not belong—this back half is the body, and it looks like an animal. (Instead of the "one-legged gender" of Melanesia [Strathern 1994] we would have here the "two-sided species.") This would mean that the body of each species is invisible to that species, just as its soul is invisible to other species.[16] The problem, therefore, is: how can one see one's own "far side"? How does it feel to be under the gaze of a nonhuman being? These are some of the questions for the next lecture.

---

16. I have just discovered that this image of mine, although not directly based on any Amerindian template, can at least be found in other cosmologies. "The general Polynesian word for 'god', *atua* . . . is based on the morpheme *tua*, which means 'back', or the far, invisible side of any object. . . . The *atua* (spiritual element) of the person was the *tua* (back) of the person . . ." (Gell 1995: 36). The back and front sides of my image are here reversed, but the idea that body and spirit are like the front and back sides of an object is the same. In this connection, it is perhaps worth remarking that many languages express change, transformation, becoming, or metamorphosis by words the basic meaning of which is "turning (over)" or "flipping."

CHAPTER ELEVEN

Supernature
Under the Gaze of the Other

Today's is the final lecture of our series of four. Last Tuesday I contrasted relativism and perspectivism, arguing that the former supposes a multiplicity of subjective and partial representations of an external and unified nature, while the latter proposes a representational or subjective unity which is applied to an objective multiplicity, generated by bodily differences. I then proposed a definition of the body as a system of affectual dispositions, not to be confused with the body as organism or substance. My argument was that the body, being the origin of perspectival differences, cannot be the object of self-perception (for self-perception is always anthropomorphic), but rather appears only in the eye of the alien beholder, that is, from another species' point of view. This led me to a definition of nature as being the form of the other as body. Nature would be the schema of the pronominal "third person," the deictic position of the thing or the object.

The idea that the body is the site of difference in Amerindian aesthetic provided me with an explanation for the assymetry manifested in the anedocte reported by Lévi-Strauss. I then discussed briefly how we have been witnessing two complementary projects of "embodying" the soul, both starting from the same modern desideratum of overcoming Cartesian dualisms: the positivist project that reduces the soul to "body" as traditionally (i.e., bio-mechanically) understood; and the phenomenological one that upgrades the body to the traditional (i.e., cultural-theological) status of "spirit," and accordingly replaces

Cartesian animals by Turing machines as the paradigm of nonhumanity. (I did *not* discuss the problems faced by the positivist project, for I suppose you are familiar with them. Anyway, the latest book of John Searle's [1997]—one my favorite contemporary indigenous informants on these matters, as you may have noticed—provides abundant food for thought in this connection.)

In the final section of the lecture I approached some classic questions of Amazonian ethnology, such as the importance of food practices and bodily decoration, from the vantage point of this concept of the body. I sketched a discussion of the human body as the site of a complex interaction between humanity and animality, arguing that the ritual animalization of the human body derives from the invisibility of a species' body for itself: de-totalized and abstracted as colors and designs, animal "natural" bodies must be used to give the body of humans its distinctive "cultural" appearance, thus serving as the tools for particularizing a generic (universal) form.

I then stressed the ontological continuity between body and soul in Amerindian thought—for this duality is not similar to our radical body/soul dualism—and contrasted our concern with solipsism and its complementary figure, spiritual conversion, both derived from the just-mentioned discontinuity, to the Amerindian obsession with cannibalism and its complementary figure, bodily metamorphosis, both predicated on the idea that, if animals are human in spirit, then humans may become animals in body. I remarked that our problem was how to connect and universalize; the Amerindian one, how to separate and particularize. Eating, therefore, is a dangerous act, because it involves a major philosophical risk—something that, in our culture, had to wait for the advent of psychoanalysis to be recognized. Amerindians do not need to be reminded that no man is an island; quite the contrary.

Today we shall examine a number of questions to which we only alluded in the past lectures, before we proceed to offer an acceptable interpretation for the category of "supernature" in the Amerindian context. Let us start by having a closer look at the notion that bodies are mere envelopes, appearances that hide a spiritual essence. How can we save the phenomena?

SAVING THE APPEARANCES

The doctrine of animal "clothing," according to which animal bodies are visible shapes animated by normally invisible spiritual agencies, is directly linked to the notion of metamorphosis, which is probably one of the most difficult Amerindian notions to translate in our received ontological language. Amerindian metamorphosis is *imagined*, in the "literal" sense of this word, as a clothes—or skin-changing act in which humans and spirits put on the body of animals, or animals take off their bodies and appear in human form. Any body, the human body included, is imagined as being the outer shell of a soul. This notion is to be found all over the Americas. In some native languages, the term for "body" also means "envelope" or "casing," and as such is applied to things like baskets, shoes, clothes, hats, houses, and so on—all these things are the "body-envelope" of something else. Referring to the Kwakiutl aesthetic of containers, Goldman wrote:

> Among supernatural treasures, the house comes within the special category of containers that includes canoes, boxes, dishes, and animal skins. The idea that all forms of life and forms of vital force occupy a house or some container is widespread in North and South America. . . . The Kwakiutl speak of the body as the "house of the soul" . . . (1975: 64)

We should observe that such images are not restricted to indigenous America. They play a major role, for instance, in (neo-)Platonic, Gnostic, and Christian doctrines. In these traditions, the general idea of the body as *container* became the very specific one of the body as *constrainer:* the body as the prison of the soul (see some references in Sahlins 1996: 423). The notion of the body as a type of casing, however, can also be found in the many non-Western (and non-Amerindian) traditions where "skin" is used as the standard term for "body," although it is far from evident that the concept of "skin" is everywhere understood mainly in terms of "casing." As a matter of fact, it is far from evident what a "casing" may signify. The Kwakiutl speak of the body as the house of the soul, but also take houses, boxes, and other containers to be "supernatural treasures." (The container not the content as the real, or rather, surreal, treasure. Curious idea.)

How are we to reconcile the idea that the body is the site of differentiating perspectives with the opposition between "appearance" and "essence," which frames the overwhelming majority of interpretations of Amerindian ontologies? Our problem here is the classic one of deciding what "appearance" means. The idea of the body as a casing or shell may at first sight deprive it of any intrinsic efficaciousness, suggesting images evocative of the familiar "ghost-in-the-machine," or giving it a zombie-like quality. Let us hear Gray (1996: 142), for instance, on the Arakmbut of Peruvian Amazonia: "The anatomy of the body is not a functioning system but a visible casing which operates only when animated by the potent presence within it of the *wanokiren* (soul)." Gray also wrote: "The invisible world provides life to the visible world which would otherwise consist of dead matter. I was once shown a dead animal and told that the difference between the corpse and life was the soul" (1996: 115). Townsley, in the same vein, quotes a Yaminahua saying that "without the *wëroyoshi* [eye soul], this body is just meat" (1993: 455).

This seems to leave us with a purely material, inert body animated by an efficacious spiritual principle. However, let us not forget that we are talking of cosmologies which held that the attributes of the species one eats—the meat one eats—pass on to the eater. These attributes, as Townsley understands it, reside in the soul; and indeed, I mentioned in the last lecture that the shamanistic desubjectivization or despiritualization of animals is often an indispensable measure to make them fit to be eaten. But then we have a problem, for the souls of all species are identical, and identically humanoid. How could they be responsible for the specificity of the species? Townsley copes with the difficulty by appealing to the notion of paradox and ambiguity. The concept of "soul" in Yaminahua thought would be eminently ambiguous and paradoxical: it would be a generalized, supra-sensory anthropomorphic type of entity, but also what gives all species their particular qualities; it would be free-floating but intimately attached to the individual, and so on. He is probably right about ambiguity and paradox, but I would like to try a bit harder before resigning myself to this conclusion.

Gray himself points to one possible way of solving the difficulty (1996: 115–16). He observes that Arakmbut spirits and souls, although being the animating principle of visible bodies, receive themselves form from the visible world. The body and the soul operate on each other; one would provide the "form," the other the "energy." The body for the Arakmbut, says Gray, is both shape and matter. He then evokes the Aristotelian form/matter distinction, observing that form in Aristotle means far more than shape. The Aristotelian form is the *soul*—the soul is the form or entelechy of the body; the notion of potentiality or potency applies essentially to formless matter. Gray then suggests that "for Aristotle, form and shape are part of the soul, whereas for the Arakmbut they are part of the body." I think this is a very interesting suggestion, especially because it can be read in the same sense as my own argument! For Aristotle—as a matter of fact, in most of our tradition—the form is the soul, and the soul is difference, that which gives unity and purpose to a being; body is matter, and matter is sameness and indifference. For the Arakmbut, on the other hand, difference of form—perspective—is located in the body. The soul or spirit would be pure potentiality, that is, formless universality (or rather, uniform universality: the human form). As to "form" and "shape" being both attributes of the body, I would just observe that these must be carefully distinguished, if not in Aristotle at least in the Amerindian context, for as we shall see the shape does not coincide with the form; the shape is a sign of the form, its form of appearance, and as such may deceive. Metamorphosis would not be, in this sense, a shape-changing process, but, strictly speaking, a form-changing one. My notion of the body as a system of affectual dispositions can perhaps be related to this idea of the body as efficacious form.

Let us return to the image of the body as a type of clothing. It has proved rich in misunderstandings. The most egregious one is to take clothing as something unimportant, inert, and ultimately false. I believe that nothing could be further from the Indians' minds when they speak of bodies in terms of clothing. It is not so much that the body is clothing, but rather that clothing is body. We are dealing with societies which inscribe efficacious meanings onto the skin, and which use animal masks (or at least know their principle) endowed with the power metaphysically to transform the identities of those who wear them. To put on mask-clothing is not to conceal a human essence beneath an animal appearance, but rather to activate the powers of a different body.

Let me quote Irving Goldman, on masks and animal skins:

> In ritual the mask stands for the essential form of the being who is depicted or incarnated. Kwakiutl recognize a hidden reality behind the mask, but also insist that the mask be the only reality ordinarily exposed to mankind. . . . The animal skin is also a form, a garment that originally converts a human inner substance into animal form. . . . From the mythical perspective, the skin is the animal's essential attribute from which, however, it is separable, in the way in which soul separates from body. When, in myth, animals give their skins to humans they offer with them their characteristic animal qualities. . . . Thus the animal skin . . . which . . . Boas renders more blandly as "blanket," is like a mask. . . . For the Kwakiutl a mask is a disguise only in the ultimate metaphysical sense of being an appearance behind which is a deeper reality. The mask . . . is imagined as the visible outer form of all life. In myth the animals that deal with persons wear their forms as full body masks or coverings when they are behaving as animals, and remove them when diving for power or dancing in the Winter Ceremonial.

They then appear in a human inner form. Basically, the mask stands for natural diversity, the inner form for consubstantial unity. As naturalists the Kwakiutl are far from disparaging natural diversity, and the mask for them is no mere outer trapping. Outer is as essential as inner. (1975: 124–25)

Going back to Amazonia: Peter Gow tells me that the Piro conceive of the act of putting on clothes as an animating of the clothes. The emphasis would seem to be less on covering the body, as it is among ourselves, but rather on the gesture of filling the clothes, activating them. In other words, to don clothing modifies the clothing more than it does the body it clothes. Goldman (1975: 183) remarked that "the Kwakiutl masks get 'excited' during Winter dances." And Kensinger (1995: 255), speaking of the Amazonian Cashinahua, observed that feathers belong to the "medicine" category.

Thus, the animal clothes that shamans or sorcerers use to travel the cosmos are not fantasies but instruments: they are akin to diving equipment, or space suits, and not to carnival masks. The intention when donning a wet suit is to be able to function like a fish, to breathe underwater, not to conceal oneself under a strange covering. In the same way, the bodily "clothing" which, among animals, covers an internal "essence" of a human type, is not a mere disguise, but their distinctive equipment, endowed with the affects and capacities which define each animal.

Irving Hallowell (1960), in a justly famous analysis of Ojibwa ontology, took the clothing idiom as pertaining to the context of post-contact rationalizations. The rendering of bodily metamorphosis as the donning of a garment was attributed by Hallowell to the growing skepticism of the Ojibwa towards their traditional "world-view," or as a way of explaining to skeptical Euro-Americans what would be experienced, in the indigenous ontology, as direct bodily metamorphosis. I deem Hallowell to be wrong here. It would be a curious, and anyway a telling, coincidence that so many different Amerindian—groups, from Alaska to Amazonia, should appeal to exactly the same rationalization. Hallowell was misled perhaps by his own native understanding of what clothing is—something that veils and disguises the "naked truth." But I think Hallowell could not grasp the force of the indigenous idiom for two other more important reasons. Firstly, because of his insistence on the argument that for the Ojibwa "outward appearance is an incidental attribute of being." Metamorphosis, therefore, would not only be possible, but—this is my conclusion, not Hallowell's—also trivial, for nothing would really change when a being changed its form.

Secondly, because of his implicit belief that metamorphosis is in fact *impossible*, or rather, that it could only be a *belief*, a representation of the Ojibwa. The clothing idiom served indeed as a rationalization, but for the anthropologist.

Hallowell makes an observation which recurs in many Amerindian ethnographies:

> My Ojibwa friends often cautioned me against judging by appearances....I have since concluded that the advice given me in a common sense fashion provides one of the major clues to a generalized attitude towards the objects of their behavioral environment—particularly people. It makes them cautious and suspicious in interpersonal relations of all kinds. The possibility of metamorphosis must be one of the determining factors in this attitude; it is a concrete manifestation of the deceptiveness of appearances. (1960: 69–70)

Do not judge by appearances! I presume this warning is issued by virtually all cultural traditions, for it belongs to that universal fund of popular wisdom which includes many similar maxims. It belongs here because it is true, of course—in a sense; or rather, in many different, culture-specific senses.[1] Appearances may indeed deceive, because appearances hide what is not apparent; in order for something to appear, something else must disappear. But what appearances hide is not necessarily the truth (a point forcefully made by Marilyn Strathern in her analysis of self-decoration in Mount Hagen [1979]).

Hallowell, however, is saying a bit more than that "appearances deceive" in the abstract. He says that the caution about the deceptiveness of appearances applies above all to dealings with persons, and that the notion of metamorphosis has something to do with it. Indeed: if persons are the epitome of what should not be judged by appearances, and if every type, or most types, of beings are persons, you must never take appearances at their face value. What appears as a human may be an animal or a spirit, what appears as an animal or human may be a spirit, and so on. Things change—especially when they are persons.

This has very little to do with our familiar epistemological warning "not to trust our senses." Be that as it may, appearances have other and more important

---

1.   "One of the best known Melanesian axioms must be that appearances deceive, and the unitary identity sets the stage for the revelation that it covers or contains within itself other identities" (Strathern 1988: 122). This is quite close, though not identical, to the Amerindian sense of the deceptiveness of appearances.

functions than that of deceiving. My impression is that in Amerindian narratives which take as a theme animal "clothing" the interest lies more in what these clothes do rather than what they hide. Besides this, between a being and its "appearance" (its visible shape) is its body, which is more than just that—and the very same mythical narratives relate how appearances are always "unmasked" by bodily behavior which is inconsistent with them. (Take for instance this remark by Ann Fienup-Riordan [1994: 50] about Eskimo animal transformation myths: "The hosts invariably betray their animal identity by some peculiar trait during the visit. . . .") In short: there is no doubt that bodies are discardable and exchangeable, and that "behind" them lie subjectivities which are formally identical to humans. But the idea is not similar to our opposition between appearance and essence; it merely manifests the objective permutability of bodies which is based in the subjective equivalence of souls.

THE OTHER SIDE: DO ONTOLOGICAL DUALISMS EXIST?

What about the soul, then? Gray's discussion of Aristotle among the Arakmbut continued as follows:

> For Aristotle and Aquinas the one-way transformation of potentiality into actuality leads to a hierarchical system, whereas the Arakmbut have a more egalitarian reciprocal relationship where form and shape pass to the invisible world and life or energy passes to the visible world. . . . The spirit is consequently an animating potentiality which, when meeting shape and form, constitutes a living being. The effect is a dual causality operating between the visible and invisible worlds. (1996: 116)

I do not particularly like the notion of *energy* (as a moniker for "invisible efficacious substance"), which has been long and widely used to translate "primitive" notions, in Amazonia and elsewhere. I do not like it because it does no more than provide difficult native concepts with an equally mysterious gloss. It would not do to render, say, "spirit" or "*mana*" as "energy" for the simple reason that "energy" already means "*mana*" for the anthropologist who uses this word. Energy is a *mana*-concept, or rather *the* mana-concept of our physically-minded modern tradition: the old "matter/spirit" opposition gave way to "matter/energy," with "energy" doing pretty much the same job as the old "spirit."

Mauss and Hubert, however, in their well-known essay on magic (1950), did use the notion of energy in a very interesting, and I believe rarely noticed, sense: they say that *mana* is analogous to our notion of potential energy. Potential energy, in the dictionary I have in my computer (*American Heritage Dictionary*), is defined as "the energy of a particle or system of particles *derived from position, or condition, rather than motion*. A raised weight, coiled spring, or charged battery has potential energy" (emphasis mine). Mauss and Hubert say in their essay that the concept of *mana* is nothing but the idea of the differences of potential between things, the idea that different categories of things and persons are, precisely, different. (That is how Mauss managed to extract energy from primitive classifications; a remarkable feat.)

Suppose, then, that the spirit as "energy" or "life" (vital energy) of Gray's definition could be understood in this sense of *potential*, that is, *positional* and *differential* energy. This would be consistent with Gray's emphasis on spirit as "potentiality" (although being quite different from Aristotelian *dunamis*). But if this is the case, whence came the difference of potential? From the only source of difference in this ontology, I would argue—from the perspectival and differential body. Potential or spiritual energy would itself be derived from formal energy, energy which is "contained" in bodily form, due to the difference in "position or condition"—in affect—of each type of body relative to other bodily forms. Aristotle's scheme, therefore, is not entirely adequate, even when inverted, to account for Amerindian notions of body and soul. The notion of potentiality or power—which plays such an important role in Amerindian doctrines of metamorphosis—cannot be defined here independently of the notions of difference and form. "Essence," spiritual essence, is a function of "appearance," of bodily form.

The vocabulary of "essence" and "appearance" is more evocative of Plato than of Aristotle. Plato, as a matter of fact, is far more often evoked in Amerindian ethnography than his eminent successor. I am thinking of the common "Platonic" rendering of the difference between souls as ideas or archetypes and bodies as copies or simulacra in Amerindian ontologies.[2] The idea that Amerindians live in a universe where visible appearances are illusory, the "true reality" being hidden, invisible and spiritual, and accessible only in dreaming, trance, and hal-

---

2.   Viveiros de Castro (1978) and Crocker (1985) mention "Platonism" directly (see also Kan 1989: 117, 323n.1). But Harner (1972), Bastos (1975), S. Hugh-Jones (1979) and Guss (1989), for instance, can be read in this same general sense.

lucination, is to be found in quite a number of ethnographies.[3] Animals are "really" human, so the story goes; their animal shape is just an illusion. It is also commonly said that the spiritual world is peopled by pure archetypes of earthly objects, ideal embodiments of animals, artefacts etc. These ideal entities are usually associated with the names of things, for names and souls are often identified in Amerindian ontologies. This spiritual world is sometimes tellingly referred to as "the other side," an expression that can be found among cultures as different as the Trio of Surinam, the Piro of Peruvian Amazonia, and the Kwakiutl and Tsimshian of the Northwest Coast (Rivière in Koelewijn 1987: 305; Gow 1997; Goldman 1975: 102, 168; Guédon 1984b: 183).

A thorough discussion of this Platonic interpretation of "the other side" would take us far beyond the limits of our lecture. Gray's analysis of bodily form and spiritual energy has already given us some reasons to doubt its adequacy. He speaks, as you recall, of a "dual causality" and of a "more egalitarian" relationship between the visible and the invisible, both of which are of course incompatible with the strictly one-way Platonic distinction between the intelligible and the sensible. We might add that the anthropomorphic aspect or quality of the invisible archetypes is utterly non-Platonic: the Platonic Idea of triangle is absolutely and uncompromisingly triangular, but the Jaguar of the "other side," while embodying the concentrated essence of jaguarhood, is also human.

The dual causality of Gray is more than simply causal, or it is perhaps something different—it is a case of dual, mutual expression, rather than causality—and the relationship between the visible and the invisble is more than egalitarian—it is fundamentally reversible, for it is a matter of perspective. Let us hear a Sharanahua (Panoan) myth told in Janet Siskind's *To hunt in the morning* (1973: 138–40):

> A man built a hunting blind next to the shore of the lake, and one day as he was concealed there he saw a tapir spirit carrying genipa on its back. As the man watched, the tapir threw the genipa fruits one after another into the lake.

---

3.   Harner's (1972: 134) is the most extreme version of the idea: "The Jívaro believe that the true determinants of life and death are normally invisible forces which can be seen and utilized only with the aid of hallucinogenic drugs. The normal waking life is explicitly viewed as 'false' or 'a lie', and it is firmly believed that truth about causality is to be found by entering the supernatural world or what the Jívaro view as the 'real' world, for they feel that the events which take place within it underlie and are the basis for many of the surface manifestations and mysteries of daily life."

The water began to splash, and rising from the water was Snake-Spirit, Snake-Woman. She was beautiful, with long hair, and having received the genipa, she came to the tapir, and the man watched as the tapir stood over her and copulated with her. The man became excited, and he wanted to do the same. Then Snake-Woman returned, splashing, to the deep water, and the tapir left, and the man ran to gather genipa, lots of it.

He had heard Snake-Woman ask the tapir how soon he would return and had heard the answer, so in that number of days he went to the lake and, just like the tapir, threw the genipa fruits, one after another into the water. He hid himself and watched as Snake-Woman, splashing, appeared. She searched around and said, "Where are you?" And as she searched the man grabbed her around the ribs.

As the man listened to her snake speech he was frightened, but she coiled around him and pulled him toward the lake. He grabbed her and now she changed and was beautiful, then she became huge, up to the sky. She kept changing and transforming until she became his size. Now he saw her lovely paint and he desired her. Now they stood together, and she said, "Who are you? You are afraid, but I want to be with you."

"You don't have a husband?" he asked.

"No, I don't."

Then they copulated over and over, like the tapir, yes, in that way they copulated. "Let's go," she said, "I have no husband." She gathered leaves and rubbed and squeezed them into his eyes. Then he could see deep in the lake a huge house. As they were going to the house, they encountered her people moving within the deep. He saw all kinds of fish—*boca chica* came, sting ray threatened him with his tail, *tunofo*, holding his throwing spear, asked, "What are you doing, *chai*?"[4] He saw the evil alligator with his spear. Underwater spirits, hairless underwater spirits. Then he saw his father-in-law, an old man with frightening paint. His mother-in-law was the same. Down there the man and Snake-Woman kept copulating.

The old father-in-law was taking *shori* [ayahuasca], lots of them were taking it. "I want to take it with you," the man said to his wife.

"You must never take it," she said. "My father taught me to take it, but you must not."

But, despite her words, he took it, and he got drunk on *shori*. And then he saw! His father-in-law's frightening paint, he was a huge snake! His wife drunk-

---

4.   *Chai*: same-sex cross-cousin, brother-in-law.

enly clinging to him was a snake! "The snake wants to eat me!" he screamed.
"A snake is not eating you," she said.

His father-in-law blew on him. His wife blew on him. "Human," she said, "I told you not to, but you took *shori*. I will not eat you. I am holding you." She kept blowing on him until he was no longer drunk.

Now her people were angry at him for what he had said, but he saw Ishki [the catfish] in his small house, making a feather hat. "Ishki, Ishki, *chai ishta* [dear, little cousin], what are you doing?"

"I'm making my feather hat, *chai*," said Ishki. "Your many children and your wife are sad and weeping for you, *chai*."

The underwater spirits were swimming back and forth, looking for him, and Ishki said, "I'll take you back, dear *chai*. Hold onto my hair. We'll go to your home."

The underwater spirits kept threatening and asking Ishki what he was doing and what his *chai* was saying. But Ishki said nothing and went splashing away with the man holding onto his hair. Ishki left the man standing by the lake and swam away, pursued by the fish spirits grabbing at him. He swam and swam, Ishki, dear *chai*, until he came to his house, and there he hid with all his children.

Thus, Snake-Spirit, my father told me long ago, and I listened.

Shori is a drug that makes you see the invisible "other side" inhabited by pure spiritual essences. When you drink it you see animals, plants or spirits as cultured humans living in villages, etc. The juice put into the man's eyes by the Snake-woman can be considered a version of this drug (probably the snakes' version of it), for it allowed him to see his animal affines as humans. But when he later insists on taking *shori* while living at the other side, the invisible reality he sees is that his "human" affines are "actually" snakes.

The lesson of the myth (there are other lessons of it, drawn by Siskind) is clear. The invisible of the invisible is the visible: the other side of the other side is this side. If the body hides the soul, then the soul hides the body as well: the "soul" of the soul is the body, just like the "body" of the body is the soul. Nothing is hidden, in the end (recall Guédon's remark: "nothing is hidden"), because there is no ontological dualism. Sides are contextually occulted by sides, essences eclipse appearances and appearances eclipse essences; each side is a sign of the other, as Tânia Lima (1996) insightfully argued with regard to Juruna perspectivism—a sign, indeed, of the Other. Such reversibility does not mean that, as far as humans are concerned, reality is isotropic. As I observed about

K. Århem's notion of perspectivism, humans have no choice about which side they are on. If you start seeing things like the other half does, there is a strong possibility you are dead—the visit of the human to the bottom of the lake in the Sharanahua myth has an unmistakable connotation of death. Unless, of course, you're a shaman, endowed with eyes in your "other" (your far) side.

The death of Umoro

The following text appeared in May 3, 1996 as a letter to the editor of *Folha de São Paulo*, an influential Brazilian newspaper which occupies more or less the same ideological space as *The Guardian*.[5] Its author is Megaron Txukarramãe, a Kayapó man (the Kayapó are a Gê-speaking society of Central Brazil) who was then the head of the FUNAI branch under the jurisdiction of which is the Xingu Indigenous Park. The affair to which it refers (and which for some reason was brought to the attention of *Folha de São Paulo*) is a rather murky one. Umoro, a young man who was the son of Raoni, the chief of the Xingu Kayapó (and also Megaron's mother's brother), died amongst the Kamayurá, a Tupian-speaking group of the southern area of the Xingu Park. Umoro had gone there to be treated by Takumã, the Kamayurá chief and a very powerful shaman. While he was living with the Kamayurá, Umoro killed two villagers, and sometime later he died. The Brazilian doctors concluded that his death was the consequence of an epileptic seizure. The Kayapó were of a somewhat different opinion, as might be expected. I transcribe Megaron's letter (emphases added):

> In 7 April an article was published by Emmanuel Neri on the death of Umoro, son of Chief Raoni. We would also like him to report about other people. We, the Kayapó of Mato Grosso and Xingu, have seen many people who the Kamayurá killed. Chief Takumã, Kanato, Aritana and Kotok ordered many people to be killed. While they were killing their own people, we did nothing, because it was a problem amongst themselves. Now they ordered Umoro to be killed for no reason. Why didn't they tell Raoni about the killing? Our people heard them speaking by radio. And the Xingu Funai staff also did nothing. *The story that Umoro killed two people is true. Except that he did this without knowing what he was doing, because of a cigarette that the shaman gave him when he was having an epileptic crisis. He became worse and did not recognize anyone. He thought he was killing animals.*

---

5.   This was written in 1998. Things have changed a lot in Brazil since this time.

When he returned to normal he was very sad. Raoni thought that Takumã was going to cure him with roots. This is why he left Umoro under the responsibility
of the Kamayurá. Takumã, Kanato and Sapain are great sorcerers. They must
already be making sorcery against the Kayapó. This is why people must know
who these guys are. Takumã is frightened and keeps saying that the Kayapó are
going to kill everyone in the Xingu. Lies. The Kayapó won't fight against anyone.
Raoni is going to the place of Umoro's death to perform shamanism. Umoro's
spirit will say how and why he died. As there are three Kamayurá involved in the
death, he will say their names.

This story, a forceful illustration of the very real (and actual) politico-cosmo-
logical consequences of seeing things from "the other side," calls immediately
to mind *The Bacchae.* As Umoro, Agave kills a human being, her son Pentheus,
"thinking she was killing an animal" (1579–1675). And when she returned to
normal she was "very sad . . ." (1732–48). Because Pentheus wished to see what
he shouldn't (1095–97; 1231–32)—the maenads becoming like animals, gir-
dled with snakes, breast-feeding the young of wild beasts (955–64), and showing symptoms of epilepsy (1522–24)—and because he refused to "see" what he
should—that Dionysus was a god—he is seen as *he* shouldn't—like a wild beast
(a young lion), and killed accordingly. The female garments in which Pentheus
is dressed by Dionysus are an animal clothing (a fawn's skin, like the maenads:
same color as a lion's hide). Pentheus' *hubris* was to think Western reason was
reality-exhaustive: "Asians aren't Greeks—what do they know?" (661). And Indians, as we know, are Asians—even if between Lybia and Siberia there is a lot
of ground (recently covered by Carlo Ginzburg in his intriguing *Storia notturna*
[1991]).

METAMORPHOSIS

We must now face the question of metamorphosis. My point here will hardly
surprise you, I am afraid: I take metamorphosis as just a synonym for "perspective," or rather, for the exchangeability of perspectives characteristic of Amerindian ontologies.

Fritz Krause, in a little-known article sub-titled "The motive of the container and the principle of form" (Krause 1931), discusses Northwest Coast and
Northwestern Amazonian materials concerning masks and metamorphosis. His

argument is that these peoples are fundamentally nonanimist, for they consider the bodily form, not the spiritual essence, as the principle of being and as the means of metamorphosis. This is not the occasion to give Krause's article the discussion it deserves (it anticipates many of the arguments of the present lectures).[6] Let me just focus on one particular point. Krause insists that when the Kwakiutl, for instance, don masks, they conceive of the act as a real metamorphosis of the human mask-bearers into the beings "represented" (the word is Krause's) in the masks. He writes: "They do not simply represent these spiritual beings . . . but are really transformed into them. . . . The actions carried by the masked dancers are not just symbolic, but are understood rather as totally realistic . . ." This recalls Hallowell's idea that the Ojibwa believed in direct bodily metamorphosis, and that the "clothing" idiom was a recent rationalization.

You may have noticed a slight paradox in Krause's rendition of the process: the masked dancers *do not represent* the beings *represented* in the masks, but are "actually" transformed into them. Perhaps we should say they represent themselves as not representing the spiritual representations? This is a familiar conundrum. Krause and Hallowell force the Indians to choose between two branches of an alternative which has absolutely no place in native ontologies: metamorphosis must be *either* a representation *or* a reality. And both authors are themselves forced to conclude that the Indians represent as being a reality what is in reality a representation.[7]

Goldman (1975), commenting on the same question, is far subtler. Discussing Kwakiutl impersonations of spirits, he observes: "The impersonators are artifice, but the power brought by the spirits is genuine . . . the impersonators are not genuine spirits but genuine impersonators of spirits." I quite like this idea of "genuine impersonation." It reminds me of the remarks of Deleuze and Guattari (1980) on the subject of becoming: firstly, when a human becomes an animal, the animal may be imaginary, but the becoming is real (so the object of becoming may be a "representation," but not the act itself); secondly, when a human becomes an animal, the animal necessarily becomes something else (a different type of human, perhaps); and thirdly, in the act of becoming what changes is not the subject, but the world. Deleuze and Guattari speak of, say, jaguar-becoming

---

6. Krause's article was brought to my attention by a short note in Boelscher's book (1989: 212 n.10).

7. Latour's recent book on *faitiches* (1996b) effects a masterful demolition of this forced choice.

in such a sense that "jaguar" is an aspect of the verb "to become," not its object: to jaguar-become is not the same as to become a jaguar. In this sense, "to become" is an intransitive verb—just like "to exchange," by the way.

Let me quote once more the remarkable analysis of Tsimshian cosmology by Guédon:

> The animals and the spirits, like all non-human beings, have powers that are not readily available to humans. Humans have powers that are not possessed by or not available to animals and spirits. All are part of the same invisible network which affects any being. A noticeable aspect of that network is the transformation which affects any being of importance or the ability to transform which is granted together with power. Transformation is a sign of power. *When two worlds or two points of view are meeting,* as when salmon people and the human people recognize each other, the power manifests itself in some of the salmon being able to transform into humans and some of the humans being able to transform into salmon. . . . One of the gifts that a shaman . . . may acquire, for instance, is the ability to recognize in a floating log a double-headed land otter or a double-headed snake-like creature, which could also be used as a canoe. *Transformation then is not so much a process as a quality corresponding to multiple identities or to multiple points of view or realities focused on one entity.* (1984a: 142, emphases added)

I consider this last remark very profound. It moves me to speculate that the opposition between being and becoming, in Amerindian thought, is not equivalent to that between "structure" and "process" (much less to that between "essence" and "appearance," or "reality" and "representation"), but rather to that between univocal identity and plurivocal multiplicity. Transformation or becoming is a "quality," not a process—it is an instantaneous shift of perspectives, or rather the entangled, nondecidable coexistence of two perspectives, each hiding the other in order to appear, like those figure-ground reversals we are familar with, or like the flipping over of the front and back halves of the "two-sided species." The real opposition here is that between essences (expressed in many deceitful appearances) and apparitions (which make different essences communicate). Metamorphosis occurs at the meeting point of two perspectives, as Guédon observed. In this case, then, it would be probably more accurate to say that transformation is not a process but a relation. Nothing "happened," but everything has changed. No motion, no "process," no "production"; just position and condition, that is, relation—to recall the definition of potential energy.

The notion of "power," so important in Amerindian (especially North American) cosmologies, is always evoked in the context of metamorphosis. "Metamorphosis to the Ojibwa mind is an earmark of 'power'," says Hallowell (1960: 163). Let us hear Goldman on the Kwakiutl:

> When animals and humans touch they exchange powers; when they separate they reflect each other—humans appears as animals and animals as humans. Myth portrays the animals in their houses, holding winter dances or seeking supernatural powers by diving into deep waters in the guise of humans. Humans are portrayed in ritual in the guise of animals as they seek and portray powers. (1975: 185)

Or Guédon again, on the same vein: "The most powerful people are those who are able to 'jump' from one reality to the other; these are the shamans. When a contact is established between one layer and another, power is present" (1984a: 142). So, the touching or meeting of perspectives manifests, or signifies, power. Power—power as potential—I would say, is the quality of relations. And relations are not representations, they are perspectives.

THE OBJECT AS SUBJECT: I AM A PERSON MYSELF, TOO

Having examined the differentiating component of Amerindian perspectivism, it remains for us to attribute a cosmological "function" to the transspecific unity of the spirit. This is the point at which a relational definition could be given for a category that nowadays has fallen into disrepute (at least since Durkheim, truth be told), but whose pertinence seems to me to be unquestionable: the category of supernature.[8]

---

8.   The standard (to the point of triteness) argument against the use of the notion of "supernature" goes more or less like this: since "primitives" have no concept of natural necessity, of nature as a domain regulated by necessary physical laws, there is no sense in speaking of supernature, for there is no supraphysical domain of causality. It is all very well. But many of those who object to the notion of supernature keep using the notion of nature as a domain of indigenous cosmologies, and have no problem with the opposition between nature and culture, either as a supposedly "emic" distinction of native cosmologies, or as an "etic" ontological partition. Also, as I have observed in our first lecture, many of the traditional functions of "supernature" have been absorbed, in the discourse of modernity, by the concept of "culture."

Apart from its usefulness in labeling "hyper-uranian" cosmographic domains, or in defining a third type of intentional beings occurring in indigenous cosmologies, which are neither human nor animal (I refer to "spirits"), the notion of supernature may serve to designate a specific relational context and a particular phenomenological quality, which is as distinct from the intersubjective relations that define the social world as from the "interobjective" relations with other bodies.

Following the analogy with the pronominal set (Benveniste 1966a, 1966b) we can see that between the reflexive "I" of culture (the generator of the concept of soul or spirit) and the impersonal "it" of nature (marking the relation with bodily alterity), there is a position missing, the "you," the second person, or the other taken as other subject, whose point of view is the latent echo of that of the "I." I believe that this analogy can aid in determining the supernatural context. The typical "supernatural" situation in an Amerindian world is the meeting in the forest between a human—always on his/her own—and a being which is at first seen merely as an animal or a person, then reveals itself as a spirit or a dead person and speaks to the human. These encounters can be lethal for the interlocutor who, overpowered by the nonhuman subjectivity, passes over to its side, transforming him/herself into a being of the same species as the speaker: dead, spirit or animal. He/she who responds to a "you" spoken by a nonhuman accepts the condition of being its "second person," and when assuming in his/her turn the position of "I" does so already as a nonhuman. The canonical form of these supernatural encounters, then, consists in suddenly finding out that the other is "human," that is, that *it* is the human, which automatically dehumanizes and alienates the interlocutor and transforms him/her into an prey object, that is, an animal. As a context wherein a human subject is captured by another cosmologically dominant point of view, wherein he/she is the "you" of a nonhuman perspective, *supernature is the form of the other as subject*, implying an objectification of the human I as a "you" for this other. It is revealing, in this connection, what the Achuar Jívaro studied by Anne-Christine Taylor (1993) recommend as the basic method of protection when you encounter an *iwianch*, a ghost or spirit in the forest. You must say to the ghost: *"I, too, am a person!"* You must assert your point of view: when you say that you, too, are a person, what you really mean is that you are the "I," you are the person, not the other. "I, too, am a person" means: I am the real person here.

This would be the true significance of the "deceptiveness of appearances" theme: appearances deceive because one is never certain whose point of view is dominant, that is, which world is in force when one interacts with other beings.

If we accept this recontextualization of the category of supernature, much of what traditionally falls under this rubric must be left out: spirits or souls, for instance, do not belong *as such* to it. On the other hand, much which would not fall under this same rubric should be thus redefined. Take hunting, for instance. Hunting is the supreme supernatural context—from the perspective of animals. Warfare and cannibalism, and I refer to that Amerindian form of warfare and cannibalism which has as its object the assimilation of the subject-position of the enemy, and which has as one of its consequences the embodiment by the self of the enemy's perspective (Viveiros de Castro 1992a), is another obvious context which should be conceived as "supernatural."

Let me conclude by saying that the meeting or the exchange of perspectives is a dangerous business. The analogy between shamans and warriors has often been pointed to in Amerindian ethnographies. Warriors are to the human world what shamans are to the universe at large: commutators or conductors of perspectives. Shamanism is indeed warfare writ large; this has nothing to do with violence (though shamans often act as spiritual warriors in a very literal sense), but rather with the commuting of ontological perspectives. Only shamans, multinatural beings by definition and office, are always capable of transiting the various perspectives, calling and being called "you" by the animal subjectivities and spirits without losing their condition as human subjects, and accordingly they alone are in a position to negotiate the difficult "paths" (Townsley 1993) that connect the human and the nonhuman Amazonian worlds. In this sense, if modern Western multiculturalism is relativism as public policy, then Amerindian multinaturalism is perspectivism as cosmic politics.

We must appreciate the fact that these two cosmological outlooks are mutually incompatible. A pair of compasses must have one of its legs fixed, so the other can move around it. We have chosen the leg corresponding to nature as our pivot, letting the other describe the circle of cultural diversity; Amerindians seem to have chosen to fix the leg corresponding to culture, thus making nature subject to inflection and continuous variation. Absolute relativism, the pretension to move both legs of the compasses at the same time, is, so to speak, geometrically impossible, and accordingly philosophically unstable. Since no one, fortunately—not even those who have been accused of professing it—appears to believe in absolute relativism, we need not loose any sleep over it.

Let us not forget, however, that if the tips of the compasses' legs are apart, they are joined at their roots; the distinction between nature and culture literally hinges on (to stick to our metaphorical compasses) a preobjective and presubjective starting point that, as Latour has shown, is present in the modern West only as untheorized practice—for so-called theory is the work of purification and separation of unified practice into opposed principles, substances, or domains: into nature and culture, for instance. Amerindian thought, on the other hand—all "savage" or mythopoeic thought, I dare say—has taken the opposite route. For the object of mythology, this discourse which Lévi-Strauss called "absolute" while also remarking that it was characterized by a fundamental "reciprocity of perspectives," is situated precisely at the vertex whence the separation of nature and culture originates. At this vanishing point of all perspectives, absolute motion and infinite multiplicity are indistinguishable from frozen immobility and primordial unity.

CONCLUSION: ONTOLOGIES, FROM SIMPLE-MINDED TO FULL-BODIED

Perspectivism can be seen as a kind of radical polytheism (or rather, henotheism) applied to a universe which recognizes no *ontological* dualism between body and soul, created matter and creator spirit. I am led to ask whether our naturalistic monism is not the last avatar of our monotheistic cosmology.[9] Our ontological dualisms derive in the last instance from the same monotheism, for they all derive from the fundamental difference between Creator and creature. We may have killed the Creator some time ago, but just to be left with the other half, the unity of which had been given precisely by the now-absent God. For God prepared science (Funkenstein 1986): the transcendence of transcendence created immanence. This birthmark can be seen in the modern efforts to dispose of all dualisms: our monistic ontologies are always derived from some prior duality, they consist essentially in the amputation of one of the poles, or in the absorption (linear or "dialectical") of the amputed pole by the remaining one. A truly primary monism, anterior and exterior to the Great Divide between Creator and creature, is something that seems out of our reach. Supposing this is a legitimate desideratum—for who needs monism, after all? I guess my image of the compasses was not very apt: it contrasted and connected forms of dualism to a basic monism from which they were supposed to emerge. But the real "lesson"

---

9. A point recalled by Latour (1991) and Sahlins (1996)—to mention two recent works of an anthropological nature.

to be drawn from Amerindian perspectivism is that the relevant conceptual pair may be monism and pluralism: multiplicity, not duality, is the paired complement of the monism I am hinting at. Virtually all the attacks on Cartesian and other dualisms seem to consider that "two" is already too much—we need "just one" (principle, substance, reality, etc.). As far as Amerindian cosmologies are concerned, my feeling is that two is not enough.

My problem with the notion of relativism, or with the opposition between relativism and universalism, derives from the concept which lies behind these categories and oppositions: the concept of representation. And my problem with the concept of representation is the ontological poverty that this concept implies—a poverty characteristic of modernity. The Cartesian rupture with medieval scholastics produced a radical simplification of our ontology, by positing only two principles or substances: unextended thought and extended matter. Such simplification is still with us. Modernity started with it: with the massive conversion of ontological into epistemological questions—that is, questions of representation—a conversion prompted by the fact that every mode of being not assimilable to obdurate "matter" had to be swallowed by "thought." The simplification of ontology accordingly led to an enormous complication of epistemology. After objects or things were pacified, retreating to an exterior, silent and uniform world of "nature," subjects began to proliferate and to chatter endlessly away: transcendental egos, legislative understandings, philosophies of language, theories of mind, social representations, logic of the signifier, webs of signification, discursive practices, politics of knowledge—you name it. And anthropology of course, a discipline plagued since its inception by epistemological angst. The most Kantian of all disciplines, anthropology seems to believe that its paramount task is to explain how it comes to know (to represent) its object—an object also defined as knowledge (or representation). Is it possible to know it? Is it decent to know it? Do we really know it, or do we only see ourselves as through a glass, darkly? No way out of this maze of mirrors and this mire of guilt.[10] Reification or fetishism is our major care and scare: we began by accusing savages of doing "it," now we accuse ourselves (or our colleagues) of doing "it": confusing representations with reality. So we are afraid of our own polarity, and our most capital sin—I would have said original sin were it not so

---

10. "Will anthropology never escape from original sins? Or is it that anthropologists, so unlike the people they study, are the mindless victims and last witnesses of 'culture' as an essentialized and deterministic system?" (Sahlins 1996: 425).

unoriginal—is to mix the ontological kingdoms separated by this greatest of all divides.

The impoverishment continues. We have left to quantum mechanics the mission to ontologize and problematize our boring dualism of representation versus reality—ontology was annexed by physics—but within the very strict limits of the "quantum world," unaccessible to our "intuition," i.e., our representations. On the macroscopic side of things, cognitive psychology has been striving to establish a purely representational ontology, that is, a natural ontology of the human species inscribed in our mode of representing things (our cognition). This would be the final step: the representational function is ontologized in the mind, but in the terms set by the simple-minded ontology of mind *versus* matter. And the game goes on and on: one side reduces reality to representation (culturalism, relativism, textualism); the other reduces representation to reality (cognitivism, sociobiology, evolutionary psychology). Even phenomenology, new or old—especially the "phenomenology" invoked by anthropologists of late—can be seen as an ashamed surrender to epistemology: the notion of "lived world" is an euphemism for "real world for a subject," that is, "known world," "represented" world—nothing to do with physics, of course. Real reality is the (still virtual) province of quantum gravity or superstring theorists. But if you care to listen to these custodians of "ultimate" reality, you would be surprised—there is no stuff at the heart of matter, just form, that is, relation. What are we to do with the "materialist ontologies" which are time and again touted as the cure for our epistemological hypochondria? I do not know. All I know is that we need richer ontologies, and it is high time to put epistemological questions to rest.

Facts force you to believe *in* them; perspectives encourage you to believe *out* of them

ROY WAGNER

One of the basic axioms of science studies, or at least Thomas Kuhn's (1962) version of them, is that one does not recognize a paradigm shift when one sees one. To say that Eduardo Viveiros de Castro has introduced a new *perspective* into a discipline that had already inflated its old ones out of recognition would simply reiterate the jejune and intellectually bankrupt game of cynical "toler-ance" the insincere agreement to disagree that has by now taken the place of Boas' relativism. To say that what one makes of a paradigm shift is a matter of what "paradigm" one happens to be engaged in is like saying that one needs to *have* a perspective in order to understand what a perspective is. But why would an anthropologist bother to go to the field if they actually *believed in* their cul-ture? Postmodernism was a desperate, last ditch effort to take a perspective on one's own perspective—a work of spite done out of jealousy or worse—and it was the kiss of death.

The strength of Viveiros de Castro's essays—and especially of the four lec-tures comprising Part III of this volume—is that we no longer have to worry about apathy at all; we are *engaged*. "On the planet where I come from (e.g., Earth)," says the protagonist Genly Ai in Ursula Le Guin's novel *The left hand of darkness,* "I was taught that truth is a matter of the imagination" (1969: 1). By this standard, Viveiros de Castro's perspectivism is the *right hand of light*. We have no perspectives that are not completely *imagined* ones; that is, perspectives do not exist all by themselves in nature any more than *numbers* do, or logical propositions. It is questionable whether even the most self-possessed creator god would be able to recognize what a perspective is, being at the other end of the learning curve, or have enough critical distance to ask such questions. "Belief" is something that human beings have invented, along with perspectives, paradoxes, numbers, gods, cultures, and torture devices, to say nothing of scientific paradigms. To me, these magisterial essays are the benchmark of twenty-first-century anthropology, not so much a new beginning as a figure-ground reversal of the old one, and figure-ground reversal, as I have observed elsewhere (Wagner 1987), is the "second power," the self-exponential, of trope, and as such it is the sole arbiter of human perception.

COSMOLOGIES: PERSPECTIVISM

There are already far too many things which do not exist. — Lecture 1, p. 197[1]

We assume that other people are talking, even though we do not understand their language; we assume other people are in a relationship, even though they may only be copulating. To forestall what would be the most obvious criticism of perspectivism, it is unnecessary to ask oneself how other people and even animals really perceive; we can never know, for one thing. That they *might* see themselves in others of their kind is enough to surfeit the analogy, for it shows at least that they can not only perceive analogy but actually perceive through and by analogic means; and therefore perceive the fact that they *are* perceiving perception analogically. And if it be objected that they are only *talking* as if they could, that is the proof in the pudding, for talk is the very metier of the analogical.

---

1.   Editor's note: passages in italics are quotes from the body of Viveiros de Castro's own text in Chapter 8 (Lecture 1), Chapter 9 (Lecture 2), Chapter 10 (Lecture 3), and Chapter 11 (Lecture 4), unless otherwise noted.

[B]easts that turn into other beasts, humans that are inadvertently turned into animals— an omnipresent process in the "highly transformational world" (Rivière 1994) proposed by Amazonian ontologies. — Lecture 1, p. 198

We might just simply take "human" then as meaning "the organic ground state of a conventional mode of perceiving," since human beings have virtually monopolized that sort of thing in their literatures. They do not simply *state* it, they *publish it abroad*, like howler monkeys, so to speak. *All morphs are anthropomorphic, and therefore all anthropomorphs are morphic. Morphism: chiasmus: the fact of a fiction is the fiction of a fact*, the symbol that is both analogy and reality at once. *Allogasm.*

Outside these areas, the theme of perspectivism seems to be absent or inchoate. An exception could be the Kaluli of Papua New Guinea's Southern Highlands, who have a cosmology quite similar in this respect to the Amerindian ones. Schieffelin (1976: ch. 5) and Sahlins (1996: 403) reminded me of this parallel. Interestingly, Wagner (1977: 404) characterized Kaluli cosmology as "bizarre"—by Melanesian standards of course, for it would sit rather comfortably in Amazonia. — Lecture 1, p. 199

Of that we may be sure, for the Daribi have an even less bizarre one—the *hoabidi* shaman who transforms into a feature of the landscape when he dies, and when I described this to a Tuyuka shaman on the Rio Negro in 2011, he told me the Tuyuka living in Colombia have something like that. Otherwise "bizarre" is rather an understatement for what we learned of Kaluli cosmology from the work of Steven Feld (1982). Basically, it is an *eargasm*. Feld as well as Schieffelin (1976) characterized the Kaluli landscape as a *soundscape*, that is, fundamentally acoustic rather than visual. Feld confirms this by noting that Kaluli musicians have the facility of "echolocating" human words by coordinating the overtones produced by their drumbeats, and thus transforming the *spoken world* of everyday experience via the acoustic figure-ground reversal of overtoning on their drums into a 3-D polyphonic echo-space. This is as much a transformation product of figure-ground reversal as a seventeenth-century landscape painting is of the "point of view" transformation between (perspectival) foreground and background.

"The experience that each 'self' has of the 'other' may be, however, radically different from the experience that the 'other' has of its own appearance and practices." — Lecture 1, p. 201 (Quote from Brightman 1993)

That the "self act" or acted self is a pretense that one engages in the presence of *others* is an *imitation* that could not have been learned otherwise is the basis of all psychotherapy. Emulation of the other is the emulation of emulation itself, just as learning to think by analogy forms the analogy of analogy in and of itself. That *the body of the soul is the soul of the body* is the chiasmatic bow-drill that kindles the fires of the world's shamanism.

> *Humans are those who continue as they have always been: animals are ex-humans, not humans ex-animals.* — Lecture 1, p. 205

The idea that animals have descended from humans rather than the reverse is not only the message of the beginning of the *Tao Te Ching* (I, 2): "The named was the mother of the myriad creatures," but also a commonplace assumption of most New Guinea highlanders, who maintain that birds of paradise acquired their brilliant plumage by imitating their own (human) dancing decorations. This even applies to *technology*: the white man has invented a new kind of airplane, that does not need wings at all, but can fly the whole way along the ground, where it *really matters*.

> *In sum, "the common point of reference for all beings of nature is not humans as a species but rather humanity as a condition" (Descola 1986: 120).* — Lecture 1, p. 206

Much of the discussion here calls Descola's "common point of reference for all beings of nature" into question. Is it really "humanity as a condition" or might it have more subtle, underdetermining aspects, such as the *zhac* of the Northern Athabascans? As Edie Turner reports (pers. comm.),

> the *zhac* of an animal is its aplomb, or "pride of motion," the self-assured spontaneity with which it performs the motions that are definitive of its species. Watch a brown bear fishing: his *zhac* is the smartness with which he slaps the salmon out of the water. A rabbit has no *zhac*—that is its power. Human beings are not born with *zhac*, we have to learn it.

Writing a book like *The savage mind* (1966), or a ballet like Prokofiev's *Romeo and Juliet*, could be taken as examples of learned human *zhac*. No wonder they call athletes "jocks."

The inverse zhac of the Australian dreaming.

Sea traveling Polynesians, as well as central desert Australian aborigines (according to Myers 1986) treat the canoe or the moving pedestrian as the static point of reference for the apparent motion of the sea or the landscape around them; hence Ayers Rock for instance, "comes into appearance" as one approaches it and "goes out of appearance" as one passes it by. Daribi seem to have the same idea; there is a spell to "make the sun wait for one on the other side of the Bosia River," so that one does not arrive after dark. Does this mean that these Pacific peoples have a retro-version of the Northern Athabascan *zhac* concept?

> *I would like to call your attention to the difference between the idea of creation-invention and the idea of transformation-transference, and to associate the creation idea to the metaphor of* production: *of production as a kind of weak version of creation, but at the same time as its model, as the archetypal mode of action in—or rather upon and against—the world. . . . By the same token, I would associate the idea of transformation to the metaphor of* exchange. — Lecture 1, p. 207

These are agentive correlatives of the reality of the *active subject*—the inversive and manipulative transposition of the normally passive human subject that must surely have molded the evolving human form. One thinks of the opposable thumb on the hand, the lowering of the human larynx into the deep throat, and the aroused genital organs as a bipartisan "opposable thumb" leverage between individuals "upon and against" each other to effectuate the re-production of the species. In the light of *creation-invention* and *transformation-transference*, brilliant ideas, both of them, *objects eat each other* in the act of exchange, but also *exchanges eat each other* in the shape of objects. Any *objections?* I thought *knot* (words eat each other in the shape of *puns*), for knots eat each other in the shape of *string*, but strings also eat each other in the shape of knots. Do objects sometimes come together to exchange human beings, as the ergatively-pitched language of Lévi-Strauss might imply?

> *To speak of the production of social life makes as much, or as little, sense as to speak of the exchange between humans and animals. Historical materialism is on the same plane as structural perspectivism, if not at a further remove from "the native's point of view."* — Lecture 1, p. 208

Or is it really that a *metaphor*—the invisible transformation of a word into another word—verbal endo-cannibalism, is the social life of a language too poor to afford a dictionary (lexicon)? No matter: it takes a metaphor to put a word into perspective, and also a perspective to put a word into the dictionary. There are whole peoples, such as the Yekuana of the Orinoco, whose conventions of word-usage absolutely *forbid* the use of metaphor, and one of these, the Rauto, who live on the south coast of New Britain, consider the open expression of metaphor as something childish, not worthy of adult attention. This is according to Thomas Maschio's *To remember the faces of the dead* (1994), a magnificent but totally ignored masterpiece. Maschio elucidates the Rauto conception of *makai*, in which the responsible adult is obliged to resist the temptation to turn a sudden insight into a metaphor, and instead fold it back into their larger thoughts until it becomes a *memory*—*to remember the faces of the dead*.

The Native American "futures" market.

A cosmology is always a *miniature*, like a small-scale model in Lévi-Strauss' (1966: 23–4) sense, and an ethnography is a miniature of that miniature, just as a *myth* is a miniature of the (real or fictional) *happening* it recounts. The process of *thinking about cosmology* (reducing it to the *scale* of one's thoughts) is one of *reducing* one thing to another, and therefore an *infinite regression* of the miniaturization process. ("I could show thee infinity in a nutshell," says Hamlet.) By this measure the secret of historical time is not that it "passes," or is *past*, but that it keeps getting smaller and smaller as more and more miniatures are made of it, until it finally disappears into the dot of the (historical) *period* . . .

> *On the one hand, we have never been modern (this is true) and, on the other, no society has ever been primitive (this is very true as well). Then who is wrong, what needs explanation?* — Lecture 1, p. 210

Let me guess. Benjamin Franklin was the first "media magnate," and with his newspaper chain created two great revolutions, the American and the French. America in the revolution invented a successful, working submarine; an effective machine gun was used in the Civil War; Custer's men were wiped out by *repeating carbines*; both cowboys in the West and Civil War soldiers subsisted on *canned foods*; early computers and television were used in World War II, etc. Americans have remained riveted on the same spot—the cutting edge of technological innovation throughout their "history" (which was not a history at all but a media-*invention*): *we* invented *progress*; *they* invented *regress*. Americans have relied upon a kind of backward-parallactic view to generate their sense of their own placement among the world's peoples, and for most of its existence anthropology has counted more Americans on its roster than those of any other nation. Taking a survey? Pick an *American* as your surveyor.

> *Both of the major regions from which I take my examples exhibit marked internal differences in social morphology, economic and political structure, ceremonial life, religion, and so on.* — Lecture 1, p. 212

Aboriginally the lower Mississippi was like the lower Amazon, with "white cities" all along its banks; centralized and often socially stratified state forms (often called "chiefdoms" for want of a better term) stood in place of what the very naive might want to call "civilizations," but to what purpose? The "four civilized tribes," Cherokee, Creek, Chickasaw, and Choctaw, were the last creative peoples to inhabit the American Southeast, and when the Cherokee actually laid claim to the title they were evicted ("with major prejudice") by Andrew Jackson. Luckily both of my children are part Choctaw.

> *There was no Greece of course, and no identifiable Plato or Aristotle: there was no one, in particular, to oppose "myth" and "philosophy."* — Lecture 1, p. 213

The real "Rome" of Meso American civilization, the League of Mayapan (Hunac Ceel was its "Caesar") and the Toltec conurbations of highland Mexico, were so completely *shamanic* in their ideological and conceptual infrastructures (possibly like ancient Mesopotamia) that any comparison with classical antiquity is beside the point.

> *[L]ive through practice, in practice, and for practice.* — Lecture 1, p. 213

Was the *ritual practice* of Graeco-Roman religious politics—even as late as the Punic wars—any less shamanic than that of the Mayans? The first thing you saw in approaching *either* Athens or Tenochtitlan was an elevated rostrum (Acropolis, Templo Mayor) covered with garish, multicolored murals and monuments, and plumed columns of smoke rising from the sacrificial fires.

My issue here isn't with the thesis of the quintessential nonpropositionality of untamed thought, but with the underlying idea that the proposition is in any sense a good model of conceptuality in general. — Lecture 1, p. 215

This is proven again and again in the propositions of Wittgenstein's *Tractatus*: the proposition is a good model of logic, but logic itself is not a good model of a *proposition*. The best example of this is Proposition 4.121:

> Propositions cannot represent logical form: it is mirrored in them. What finds its reflection in language, language cannot represent.
> What expresses *itself* in language, we cannot express by means of language. Propositions show the logical form of reality. They *display* it.

Hence propositions are *wrong* for the same reason that they are *right*, but also *right* for the same reason that they are *wrong*. This means that they are *chiasmatic*, exactly like Lévi-Strauss' *canonic formula for myth* (Lévi-Strauss 1963: 228), something that is "reflected" in Karl Kraus' aphorism: an aphorism is "either a *half-truth* or a *truth-and-a-half*" (cited in Timms 1986: 88; emphasis added).

So the human mind *may not have binary opposition as the basic building material of its "mental representations"* . . . *But many human* cultures, *or if you wish, many historically specific intellectual traditions, obviously use dualistic systems as their conceptual skeleton key.* — Lecture 1, p. 218

Heretofore the problem with *dualities* as tools or playthings of organized thought has been that they have been applied only to marginal or trivial examples. They are never really engaged with the central dichotomizations that rule human form and action: those of *gender* and *laterality* (see Wagner 2001: chapter 4). Gender twins us *outward* into two distinctive body-types, called "male" and "female" for convenience; laterality twins us *inward* into two distinctive *sides* of the same organism, called "right" and "left" for the sake of orientation. The relation of the two is *chiasmatic*, both to themselves and to others, like Wittgenstein's propositions and like Lévi-Strauss' myths. These are the "hero twins" of the Mayan *Popol Vuh*, which was an attempt to make a comprehensive world-picture or cosmology of them.

*The possible connections of my "subject" and "object" to the concepts of "objectification,"
"personification," and "reification" such as developed, for instance, by Strathern (1988)
are left open for further exploration.* — Lecture 1, pp. 219–20

The biggest mistake about subject and object is to argue for a difference between
them; the second biggest is to argue for a similarity between them. By contrast
the differences between time and space, or body and soul, are easy ones. For
instance time is the difference between *itself* and space; space is the *similarity*
between them (cf. Wagner 2001: xv).

*Solipsism (a standard "modernist" philosophical obsession), therefore, is not only caused
by the soul—by its absolute singularity—but affects first and foremost the concept of the
soul.* — Lecture 1, p. 221

Solipsism is a mental disorder akin to paranoia and owes its origin to an unful-
filled need for independent confirmation for what it suspects but cannot prove.
Scientific method, which owes a certain amount of its authority to paranoia, is
a *physical* disorder based on the unwarranted assumption that there is nothing
inside of us that could guarantee absolute certainty (of this I am certain). Perhaps Heidegger (not one of my favorite philosophers and no match for Wittgenstein) could help us here and suggest some experiment by which we might
prove our Being (*Dasein*) by *unabhängig*, or independent means (cf. Heidegger
2001: 183). (Perhaps not—no such thing has ever been seen in the Black Forest,
with the possible exception of *Schwarzwälder Kirschtorte*.)

*This is, in fact, simple-minded linguistic-cultural relativism. It is better to follow here the
lead of Amerindian perspectivism and be aware that the same signs may stand for entirely
different things . . .* — Lecture 1, pp. 221–22

Eduardo is quite correct here (as usual), though a radical scission between the
phenomenal (*tonal*) and noumenal (*nagual*) as practiced by Meso-Americans
was indeed a provocative sticking-point of medieval theology (philosophy) as
debated at the University of Paris in the twelfth century. The subversive school
of Nominalism (*things have no properties saving in the names we give to them*),
supported by its disciples Roscellinus (*the Three Persons of the holy Trinity are
nothing but mere names*, flatus vocis) and Pierre Abelard, who introduced the

dialectic in his masterful *Sic Et Non*, was eclipsed by Platonic *Realism* (sic!) in the formulation of the holy Sacrament (1215), but later resurrected by the anti-theology of John Wycliffe: *We have no need of the visible church.* (Nor, Roscellinus would be bound to agree, the *audible* one either.)

> *"[W]hat . . . does the anthropologist do in the face of deliberate provocations to vision?" (Strathern 1994: 243).* — Lecture 1, p. 222

Mozart "heard" the key of A as *red*, and that of E major as "a bright sunny yellow," Beethoven said that B minor was *black*, and according to Sibelius F major is "a dark, metallic green," and D major "a dull ochre yellow." These "visions" of some of the greatest composers of all are neither *optical* nor *acoustic*, but, by partaking of both venues at once, *synaesthetic*. There is some indication from his personal diary that Sibelius wrote his Fifth Symphony (which is to me an evanescent silvery blue) as part of a shamanic engagement with the wild swan, which kept appearing to him physically throughout the course of the composition of that magnificent work. What does all this have to tell us about synaesthesia in its relation to shamanic "journeying" as well as the inherent "shamanism" of the great artistic traditions? Some of the best "journeys" of all are symphonic ones.

> *These different bodily-based types of knowledge appear to be subsumed by a generalized "body spirit" which encases the person as an outer skin (so skin-knowledge would be the dominant synecdoche).* — Lecture 1, p. 225

A totally *comprehensive*, "cover all bases" cosmology both implies and is implied by a *consensus sensorium*, a self-integral unity of all the senses acting together and as one—something that is no longer shamanic nor cosmological but in fact incapable of being categorized. The ultimate root of all metaphor is *holographic* (Wagner 2001: chapters 1 and 2), like the "holes" in the Vedic Hindu Net of the Lord Indra, in which subject may only be distinguished from object by divine intercession (imagine an *epistemological* Holy Sacrament). That is taking the counsel of the "Lord of Appearances" that the holes in the Net are not holes at all, but, understood in the proper perspective, "perfect jewels that reflect one another perfectly."

> *Humans are a species among others, and sometimes the differences internal to humanity are on a par with species-specific ones.* — Lecture 1, p. 226

Historically speaking, *pace* Descola, *laude* Lévi-Strauss, the term "animal" may be traced to *anima*, meaning "mind," and not to some superficial distinction (e.g., nature/culture) made within that domain.

> *The Wari' (Txapakuran) word applied to "animals," karawa, has the basic meaning of "prey," and as such may be applied to human enemies...* — Lecture 1, pp. 226–27

Wari in cross-cultural perspective. The Daribi term *nizimeniaizibi*, (Wagner 1972a: 95–96) literally "the lineage of creatures without hair, fur, or feathers," refers directly to creatural *immortality*. Nonetheless, it is something of a slur, as when biased and unthinking foreigners refer to the French as "frogs." The Dugum Dani (West Papua) term *wari* does indeed attribute that property to those of European descent, identifying them with snakes, frogs, tadpoles, etc., but without bias toward the descendants of the Franks (e.g., the *Ferengi*).

> *The Tukanoans start conceptually from the "fish" pole, defining game as a sub-class of it.* — Lecture 1, p. 228

In my limited experience the Tukanoans (Tuyuka—personal interview with a shaman at Manaus, August, 2011) derive all animate creatures including themselves from *fish living in milk, mammary spermatophytes*, an embryonic conflation that reminded me (as I suggested to my confrere) of the undifferentiated human-animal prototypes that inhabited the Australian Aborigine *Dreaming* epoch. Likewise, the rather ingenious Tukanoan marriage rule (linguistic exogamy?), with its tightly interwoven economy of sacred and secular dualities, resembles nothing so much as an Australian Aborigine "four section system." I had no time to point this out to my generous hosts on the Rio Negro, as the occasion was subject to heavy press-coverage, but I did present them with a CD of the most wonderful didgeridoo music I have ever heard, basically the chanting and dancing of a "dreamtime" engineered specifically for the lactose-intolerant.

CULTURE: THE UNIVERSAL ANIMAL

> Animism, *where the "elementary categories structuring social life" organize the relations* between *humans and natural species, thus defining a social continuity between nature*

and culture, founded on the attribution of human dispositions and social characteristics to
"natural beings." — Lecture 2, p. 230 (Referring to Descola 1992, 1996)

Terms like *animism,* which in the days of Edward Burnett Tylor made reference to
mind and *soul* (1958: chapter XI), do not easily suffer comparison with antithetical
categorizations, since products of mind are intrinsically subject to that which subjects them. To what is *anima* to be contrasted? Already subjected by their inclusion
in the discourse itself, none of these dualities can be seen to signify or operate independently of that discourse, or to be immune to the inherent *passivity* that characterizes all subjected elements. Both nature and culture are the *capta* of the routine
process of thinking of them: "The *named* was the mother of the myriad creatures."

Animism has "society" as the unmarked pole, naturalism has "nature": these poles function,
respectively and contrastingly, as the universal dimension of each mode. Thus animism and
naturalism are hierarchical and metonymical structures. — Lecture 2, p. 232

In other words, Lao Tzu's "myriad creatures" could also be seen as the mother
of "The named," as in those "just so" stories wherein some primordial human
intellect is seen to be wandering about the environment deriving designations
for creatures from the sounds they emit or the images they project. And if crystalline objects were proven to possess intelligence as well as structure and reproductive capabilities, anthropology might be saddled with a term like "itemism"
as well as "totemism."

(Lévi-Strauss called this latter relationship the "imaginary side" of totemism—but this
does not make it any less real, ethnographically speaking.) — Lecture 2, p. 234

If there is a quarrel between classificatory and image-inductive epistemology, it
is one to which metaphor is appropriate, and if there is no quarrel between classificatory and image-inductive epistemology, it is *still* one to which metaphor is
appropriate, given that there is no metaphor for metaphor itself other than "the
imaginary," and if there were, we would still have to *imagine* it. (See Wagner
2010: 8; "metaphor is language's way of trying to figure out what we mean by
it.") *The named is the daughter-in-law of the Myriad Mothers.*

(1) For "primitive man" the universe as a whole is a moral and social order governed not by
what we call natural law but rather by what we must call moral or ritual law.

(2) Although our own explicit conception of a natural order and of natural law does not exist among the more primitive peoples, "the germs out of which it develops do exist in the empirical control of causal processes in technical activities"... — Lecture 2, p. 235

Most great inventions are intentional abrogations of previous *causality* assumptions; most great jokes deliberately invert the order of cause and effect in order to make their point. This is the fact that Victor Turner (e.g., 1977) was getting at when he insisted on the role of the *liminal* in human affairs—the fact that there would *be no* human affairs without the liminal. Before we discuss *chaos* as a viable option (as for instance the ancient Greeks were not afraid to do), we might examine James Gleick's (1988) *fractal* take on it—that even the ostensibly chaotic suborns *order* to such a degree that the subject itself is unthinkable without the consideration of order. *That is to say the predications that we normally think of as being "ordered" or "chaotic" lose their original meanings in what appear visibly as a fractal printout, such as the Mandelbrot Set, which is no more and no less than reality divided by itself.* The only totemic beast that would be appropriate to this would be the Kwakiutl mythical sea-serpent called a *sisiutl*, a monster with a snake's body *with a head at each end* (Walens 1981: 131-32). When you see a *sisiutl* going by offshore, it will notice you too, and perceive you as prey and attempt to devour you. At that point you must *fight your fear* and *stand your ground*, for as the *sisiutl* approaches you it must bring each of its heads up around you, and when that happens it must inadvertently *look into its own eyes.* Now any creature capable of looking into its own eyes is smitten at that moment with a profound wisdom, and it realizes that it does not need to eat you at all, so it departs and leaves you a *gift.* In this case the "victim" was Benoit Mandelbrot and the *gift* was fractal mathematics.

The notion of model or metaphor supposes a previous distinction between a domain wherein social relations are constitutive and literal and another where they are representational and metaphorical. — Lecture 2, p. 236

Empirical science represents a domain in which "merely hypothetical" metaphors like the Copernican insight, the Bohr atom, or Watson & Crick's *double helix* are *deliberately literalized* in order to "construct" *natural facts.* In the ostensibly previous domain of what Lévi-Strauss (1966) called "the science of the concrete" the order of this is reversed so that empirically sensible objects, phenomena, and relations are transformed into abstractly metaphorical domains like alchemy, astrology, and classificatory systems. The two "sides" of this are like a reversible jacket that can be worn inside-out if need be, for in that case there is no need to determine which is the "correct" one. So of course human beings were "scientists" from the very beginning, and by the same token they were also the great *classifiers* of the world. The only question is that of what "the beginning" means in this case, and the only answer is that it is *now*.

> *My structuralist reflexes make me wince at the primacy accorded to immediate practical-experiential identification at the expense of difference, taken to be a conditioned, mediate, and purely "intellectual" (that is, theoretical and abstract) moment.* — Lecture 2, p. 238

This goes *double* for binary codings. To be sure, the world of diversity perceived through the grid of our language-inventories can be digitally encoded in the binary systems now used universally in computers. The problem is *what to do with it after that?* For the *difference* between a dualistic reduction-system like that used in our computers (disarticulate *factoids*, the trivial as an excuse for the non-trivial) and the dual *syntheses* projected in the work of Lévi-Strauss, is the bare fact of *synthesis* itself—metaphorical *induction* by virtue of analogy.

> *"The barbarian is first and foremost the man who believes in barbarism."* — Lecture 2, p. 241 (Quoting Lévi-Strauss [1952] 1973)

"The heart of darkness." Most colonialists felt it necessary to barbarize *themselves* in order to get an exact "fix" on how the "natives" live and think. Most "natives" stood in awe and wonder at the spectacle, as though they were watching monkeys in a zoo (which in fact they were). So to "gain the respect of the natives" the colonial administration of Papua New Guinea decided to make *incest* into a major, punishable offense. To gain the respect of the Administration, the Daribi would tell one another "Be careful what you tell these Aussies about your private lives . . . they have invented this big thing that they call 'incest,' and nobody's safe anymore."

> *[T]he point is to show that the thesis as well as the antithesis of both antinomies are true (both correspond to solid ethnographic intuitions), but that they apprehend the same phenomena from different angles; and also it is to show that both are "false" in that they refer to a substantivist conceptualization of the categories of nature and culture . . .* — Lecture 2, p. 242

Perspectives encourage you to believe out of them. We have no reason, apart from our own perspectives, or for the reason that we admit to them, to believe that perspective itself exists as a phenomenon. A perspective cannot know itself to be a perspective (to be "perspicacious") without denying the thing that it is a perspective of; all traditional landscapes bear the signature of the artist's "point of view," as though a hidden *anti-astronomer* were peering through the other end of the telescope. This gets to be very interesting when it comes to the Chewong, who must have a certain affinity with Kurt Gödel, if not Ludwig Wittgenstein. If the Chewong double-perspective cosmology admitted its paradoxical quality to itself, it would not be a perspective, and if it did not, it would no longer be Chewong. The Chewong are relatively the same compared with other peoples, but relatively different when compared to themselves (in the United States this would be called "politically correct" behavior, but it is actually a form of *mis*-behavior—pardon me, I mean *Ms.* Behavior).

> *Thus self-references such as "people" mean "person," not "member of the human species"; and they are personal pronouns registering the point of view of the subject talking, not proper names.* — Lecture 2, p. 244

It is said to be a symptom of schizophrenia when one refers to oneself in the third person. Well, that may be Roy's opinion, but it is certainly not mine. "Roy" is a name they give to cowboys and used-car salesmen, and I myself am a closet Scotsman named "Rob-Roy." I am actually a secret agent of some subliminal beings called the Antitwins, but "Roy" is the opposite of that. Having written a book called *An anthropology of the subject* I now look forward to a companion volume called *An anti-anthropology of the predicate.*

> *The human bodily form and human culture—the schemata of perception and action "embodied" in specific dispositions—are deictics, pronominal markers of the same type as the self-designations discussed above.* — Lecture 2, p. 245

In Burushaski, an apparently unrelated (to anything) language of Northeast Kashmir, there are four noun-classes, the last of which refers to names of liquids, plastic and finely divided substances, trees, metals, abstract ideas, and immaterial objects. The *elusive* case, so to speak. Effectively, then there would be no need to translate the bulk of mainstream historical materialist anthropology into Burushaski, since most of it already belongs to its fourth noun class.

This is to say culture is the subject's nature; *it is the form in which every subject experiences its own nature.* — Lecture 2, p. 245

Leibniz could not have said it any better, though because he was in contact with Jesuits researching the mysteries of Taoism in traditional China, he might have done as well. Thus, to paraphrase Eduardo, "The *named* might very well be the mother of the myriad creatures, but that does not necessarily mean that the reverse is true." (Sorry to keep harping on this one point, but it is one of the best things ever said in the history of the human race.)

Therefore, if salmon look to salmon as humans to humans—and this is "animism"—salmon do not look human to humans and neither do humans to salmon—and this is "perspectivism." — Lecture 2, p. 247

"Look" is a double-purpose word: transitive one way and ergative the other. We must "look to" anatomy for a comment. Only a predator with its eyes-to-the-front 3-D visual field, like a human being or a brown bear, can *look to* the salmon in the way that *we* look (that "hook-look" that we share with the bear); the salmon, with its eyes-to-the-side prey-animal's gaze, does not *look to* at all, it *looks from. That*, according to the title of this Afterword, is *perspectivism.*

If such is the case, then animism and perspectivism may have a deeper relationship to totemism than Descola's model allows for. — Lecture 2, p. 247

If totemism, as according to Lévi-Strauss (1963), is actually based on *homological* correspondences, then shamanism is based on analogical ones, transformations like those that motivate myths (*Mythologiques*). Thus if no creature could have its own kind as a totem, by default of homology, *all* creatures must see other species as necessarily contrastive alternatives to themselves, and perceive others of their kind as their homological equivalents, or in other words animate homologues (animal + mate = animate; homo + logos = homologue). Seeing oneself in the apparitional guise of another creature (an "animal spirit guide" or dream-beast helper) would then amount to the *self-reflexive counterpart* of other creatures seeing their own kind as human. What has been unclear up to now is that this self-reflexivity is comprehensive and, to borrow a term from mathematics, *commutative* through its range. Thus when a shaman is understood to take on the *powers* of other creatures, or add theirs to those of other species, they are bringing the mythological force of analogy to bear on *both* collectivities. The vast amplitude and range of this shamanic facility became apparent to me at a symposium in Rio, when a Yanomami shaman recognized a sonnet I was reading as part of my delivery as a form of *shamanism*. I was the most astonished person in the room.

NATURE: THE WORLD AS AFFECT AND PERSPECTIVE

The label "relativism" has been frequently applied to cosmologies of the Amerindian type; usually, it goes without saying, by anthropologists who have some sympathy for relativism, for not many of us would be prepared to impute to the people one studies a preposterous philosophical belief. — Lecture 3, p. 250

If a correct and true representation of the world does not exist, then a correct and true proposition to that effect also does not exist. That is, *a perspective cannot be a perspective on itself without ceasing to be a perspective*, and thus blowing its own cover, so to speak. This is the basic problem with relativism; the minute it tries to compare itself with anything else it becomes mute and tongue-tied, and is forced to mine its own rhetoric (eat its heart out) for counter-examples that prove nothing. It becomes *postmodernist*, like Richard Rorty.

Species differences rather than gender differences function as the "master code" of Amerindian cosmologies . . . — Lecture 3, p. 252 (Footnote 2)

From an introspective or self-subjective point of view, every person in the world belongs to a single gender, called *own gender*, which is the gender they happen to *own* and that "owns" them. That would have to mean that "other gender" does not exist in that space, and that we all come into being in the shape of a single embryo, largely undifferentiated before it comes into the world—which happens to be largely true. From the point of view of *other gender*, which, although it does not exist, is appropriately *objectivist*, that single embryonic original could not even begin to exist without the fertilization of the ovum, an act that is normally concealed from view and carried on for other purposes. Hence admitting autonomic self-relativity into the issue of gender relations does not solve the problem but rather compounds it. Either way, the genders are not *twins* but *antitwins* (see Wagner 2001: chapter 4), that is, an essential disparity is vital to their nature.

*In Amerindian perspectivism, however, something would be "fish" only by virtue of some-
one else whose fish it is. —* Lecture 3, p. 254

The problem with "natural kind" substantives is that they can only stand in
reference to their implied correlatives by standing in contrast with one another
(Lévi-Strauss' homology). On the other hand, they could only stand in a *cultural*
relation to one another (as a language or classificational system) as *transforma-
tive analogues* of one another. "The named . . ." (you know the drill, by now).

*[H]ow exchange itself may be defined in terms of perspectives, as exchange of perspectives
(Strathern 1988, 1992). —* Lecture 3, p. 255

The "reciprocity of perspectives" (*pire wuo*, "transformation of the view") as defined by the Barok people of New Ireland, is a complete and uncompromising
figure-ground reversal that grounds their cosmology, epistemology, ideology, and
social forms. Its cognate among the Tolai of New Britain is the *tabapot*, an imaginary self-parallax that is more than real, and that defines the human condition. The Tolai say that "When you look at a tree whose foliage cuts the shape
of a human face against the sky, and then go back and forth in your picturing of
it—tree to face, face to tree, and so forth, that is a *tabapot. Man* is a *tabapot*, for his
desires are encased in the outline of his form, yet he wants what is *outside* of that
form. When he gets it, however, he wants to be enclosed back in the human form
again" (Rodney Needham, pers. comm.). There is an exact replica of this definition among the Yekuana of the Orinoco, as described by David Guss (1989).
According to Guss, the Yekuana consider figure-ground reversal to be *the killer of
metaphor*, which is the source of all deception in the human race. Just as the *tipiti*
is used to squeeze the prussic acid out of bitter manioc, so that it may be made ed-
ible to human beings, so the human construction of figure-ground reversal in all
its many forms squeezes out the half-truth of metaphor, *which is the poison of the
mind*. Everything in this world that has a *shape* also has a negative, or *akato* shape
(not a twin, but an *antitwin*) corresponding to it, and floating around somewhere.
When the two come into contact, something like an eclipse of the sun occurs, and
the two cancel each other out, like opposing wave-trains. (Hence, as Edie Turner
once put it to me: "Death . . . is not only *educational*, but *perfectly safe*.")

*A perspective is not a representation because representations are a property of the mind or
spirit, whereas the point of view is located in the body. —* Lecture 3, p. 256

By the logic of the *tabapot* and the *tipiti* (previous example), the soul or spirit is like a figure-ground reversal (that which represents *itself* whichever way it turns), whereas a perspective or point of view is like a *metaphor*. Herein we have proof positive of the immortality of the soul: "What is it that never comes into or goes out of existence?" Answer: "The very fact of both coming into and going out of existence, which finds itself self-defined in the figure-ground reversal." As they say in Castaneda: *That which is never born and never dies is the difference between birth and death, for it is immune to the processes of birth and death.* This also corresponds to a bit of ancient wisdom taught to me by my father (a police chief): "What is better than *presence of mind* in an accident?" Answer: "*Absence of body!*"

> *Thus, what I call "body" is not a synonym for distinctive substance or fixed shape; it is an assemblage of affects or ways of being that constitute a habitus.* — Lecture 3, p. 257

When he was a student in my *Mythodology* course, Dr. Jonathan Schwartz called attention to what he called the *wear-wolf*, a mythical character in the folk knowledge of Normandy. In contrast to the more commonly featured *were-wolf*, who remains human on the *inside* and takes on the external appearance of a wolf, the *wear*-wolf merely *wears* its human appearance on the outside, but becomes a wolf on the *inside*. A *lycanthropic* figure-ground reversal, like the saying in Russian folklore, that calls the moon the *volch'e sontse*, the "wolves' sun."

> *The body, in contrast, is the major integrator: it connects us to the rest of the living, united by a universal substrate (DNA, carbon chemistry) which, in turn, links up with the ultimate nature of all material bodies . . .* — Lecture 3, p. 260

Here we have the *undifferentiated embryo* again. Stephen Jay Gould has called attention to the *omnimal*, the single evolving organism whose DNA we all are. This would seem to argue, by figure-ground reversal if nothing else (each being is figure to the same ground; each ground is matrix to the same figure), that each living species is a fractal printout of a single, all-embracing hologram, with something of the communicative logic or "world-aura" of Cameron's film *Avatar* (2009), which takes place on the aptly-named *Pandora*, a satellite in the Proxima Centauri system (the closest star to Earth).

> *Conversely, it could be noted that the body is the great differentiator in Amerindian ontologies but at the same time it is the site of interspecific metamorphosis . . .* — Lecture 3, p. 261

Nonetheless the body that we write about is not quite the same thing as the body that writes it; the latter is an *expersonation* of the former (Wagner 2010), whereas the former is merely an *impersonation* of the writer, like a fake "double" or decoy. Likewise knowing "what to say" in a language is *expersonative* of that language, whereas the linguistic description is a mere *impersonation* of its expressive possibilities. When we write about other creatures, or use words in attempting shamanic communication with them, we are actually *expersonating* our linguistic "body" along with theirs, that is, we have entered the phase of *interspecific metamorphosis*.

> *I would just distinguish the body (our "body") as concept—the concept of "body" that assimilates the human body to all other extended material objects—from the body as experience. In the first sense, the spirit or "mind" is an organ of the body; in the second sense, however, the hierarchy is inverted: the body is an organ of the spirit.* — Lecture 3, p. 261

In other words, *the body of concept* is not the same thing as the *concept of body*. The one *expersonates* what the other *impersonates*. This is like saying that there are two kinds of DNA: the familiar, chemical kind that consists of four carbon-chain radicals and distributes the inherited form of the individual *holographically* throughout every cell in the physical body (impersonation), and the impinging DNA of *experience*, which lurks *outside* of the physical body in all of its moments and occasions, and molds and tempers it according to the specifics of its destiny and its task in the world (expersonation). Elsewhere (Wagner 2001) I have called this "contretemps" (really of course a figure-ground reversal) that of *world-in-the-person* and *person-in-the-world*, or the *God of hand* and *the hand of God*. When one human body *enters* another or *emerges from* another (e.g., in conception and childbirth), the one kind of DNA engages the other just exactly as it does in the act of *interspecific metamorphosis*, that is, in the act of shamanic transformation ("trance-formation"), for the sequence is exactly the same in both instances: first *expersonation* into *impersonation*; and then *impersonation* into *expersonation*. What is executed here in the connubium of the two kinds of DNA is none other than the figure-ground reversal of the inside and outside that guarantees the immortality of the soul. *Sicut locutus est ad patres nostros; Abraham et semini eius in saecula.*

> *Computers are not human because they have no real bodies: they are incapable of intuition.*
> — Lecture 3, p. 262

A computer without *humor* is incapable of imitating human thought; a computer without *character* is incapable of imitating human life, and a computer without *perspective* is incapable of appreciating anthropology. The only purpose of the computer is that of decoding and recoding the *adronyms* that are the spoils and diffraction-products of a once-mighty civilization. Contrary to much received opinion, Descartes was not opposing body and mind so much as thinking (*cogitans*) and extension (*extensa*). Can we even *conceive* of a mind without extension, or for that matter a form of extension that is independent of the mind that is thinking it? *In incipio*, "In the Beginning," God created the first and only viable computer ever to exist: the figure-ground reversal. For our purposes we like to call it "the immortal soul."

> *Anthropocentrism is harder to kill than one might think. And this shows, by the bye, that anthropocentrism is the very opposite of anthropomorphism . . .* — Lecture 3, p. 263

We live our whole lives as slaves of figure-ground reversal; the emblematic power that controls and determines human perception is in fact the image of Himself that the infinite Creator-God has vouchsafed to humankind. The ancient Toltecs of Mexico had determined (and this was the sum and measure of their whole philosophy) that the *first attention* is the attention to *figures*, by which we know and recognize the people, creatures, and objects around us, so that we come to take them for granted and figure that that is the only reality that exists. When you learn to see *auras*, however, you begin to see *rainbows* around everything. That is the beginning of the *second attention*, the attention to the *background*, the "luminous body" or *chi*, the *dreaming body* that walks in your dreams at night and serves as the vehicle for the shaman's visions. Now the *sum* and *difference* of the first attention and the second attention, the absurd and uncanny figure-ground reversal that holds all of perception and creation to its sticking-place, is the *third attention*, "which is available to mortal beings only at the point of death." What opens up in the third attention is an unimaginably vast purview of all possible *and impossible* reality-configurations, a kind of holography of all conceivable holographies. For most of us, this flashbulb-imprint of total reality serves only as a catharsis to burn away the impurities before uniting with the stuff of eternity. For "the warrior of the third attention," however, the one who is able to hold the steady image of the third attention:

Take umbrage from the stars that sip the dew,
the laws of reason mask a shrewd deception:
the lie of language lives within perception—
you were the one you are before you knew
re-birth, re-death, and most of all re-ception,
the seed between your parents that you drew
together like the spark that kindles blue—
impossibility beyond conception.

Your death was hiding in that jolt of sperm,
your life is hiding on the day you die—
the tenure in between without a term;
before and after, everything is now,
the then goes out like starlight in the sky,
and when you reach its concourse, take a bow.

(Our traditional problem is how to connect and universalize—individual substances are given, relations have to be made—the Amerindian's is how to separate and particularize—relations are given, substances must be defined.) — Lecture 3, p. 269

Could it be said, then, that "our" ontological mission is to fabricate a viable substitute for the *second attention* "background" (as in the example just cited previously: "take umbrage from the stars that sip the dew"), as we do with our electrical fields, gravity-fields, and energy-fields, so as to *universalize* a relational substrate reality, whereas Amerindians, who manage that substrate shamanically and therefore take it for granted, prefer to re-substantialize ("rebirth, re-death, and most of all re-ception") the *first attention foreground*, so as to get their bearings on the mundane world of everyday reality?

This of course does not prevent us having among ourselves more or less radical solipsists, such as the relativists, nor that various Amerindian societies be purposefully and more or less literally cannibalistic. — Lecture 3, p. 270

This could be said *in cards and spades* for Melanesians and Melanesianists as well. The big problem of the solipsist is that he wants independent confirmation of the fact that he is the only one who exists—something that would *eat* him if it could ever get its teeth into him, whereas the problem of the cannibal is that he *has* independent confirmation of the fact that he is *not* the only one who exists, and then goes ahead and eats it anyway. (Daribi cannibals assured me that they had certain restrictions on the eating of *relatives*, but were mute on the subject of *relativists*.)

[T]he sociological discontinuity between the living and the dead . . . — Lecture 3, p. 270

For Daribi, *ancestors* are functions of collective memory alone, since the condition of being *dead* puts the subject in an impossible conceptual space—a dead *person* is an impossibility, a contradiction in terms, since a *person*, by definition, cannot really die, but only *seem to* die. This is not a "spiritual" statement, however, but only a *real* one, and it leads to an important contingency. This is that an *izibidi* (literally "die-person" and *not dead person)* is not frightening or dangerous because of some properties it has acquired by virtue of its condition, but only *because one can never be certain whether it is really there or not.* For, as the Daribi point out, *the only ones who can really see them are those who are dead themselves* (see Wagner 1967: 47). (These are not a primarily *visual* people.)

For the Barok of New Ireland the situation is reversed; the *Tanu* or ancestors are precisely the ones that the death rituals are set up to annihilate or obliterate (to *songot a tanu*, "scorch to completion the souls of the deceased, . . . finish all thought of them"). Thus a "ghost" is a *visible* indicator that something is very *wrong* (not with you, as among the Daribi, but with *it*), and the thing that is wrong is that it is not really *finished* yet (forgotten but not gone). Barok, like other New Irelanders, have *olfactory* apparitions ("smell ghosts") as well, whose presence is announced by the odor of decomposing flesh.

This would mean that the body of each species is invisible to that species, just as its soul is invisible to other species. — Lecture 3, p. 272

Wittgenstein (*Tractatus*: 5.634) traces his conclusion that "there is no a priori order of things" from the fact that *the eye is never included within its own visual field.* As a matter of fact, *all the examples of order we can glean from engineering, technology, mathematics, the natural sciences, or philosophy are based on visual diagrams.* What about *acoustical diagrams?* As a matter of fact, Wittgenstein could *whistle* all of the Nine Beethoven symphonies from beginning to end, and from memory alone.

SUPERNATURE: UNDER THE GAZE OF THE OTHER

> *Any body, the human body included, is imagined as being the outer shell of a soul. . . . In some native languages the term for "body" also means "envelope" or "casing," and as such is applied to things like baskets, shoes, hats, houses and so on—all these things are the "body-envelope" of something else.* — Lecture 4, p. 275

Both in aboriginal Australia and in New Guinea, as far as I can tell, the term "skin" is used universally for the "body."[2] Perhaps the most puissant example is the term "picture-soul," used by the Wiru people of the New Guinea Southern Highlands (close neighbors of the Daribi), according to Jeffrey Clark (1991), for the physical body (e.g., the *kind* of soul that illustrates itself as the physical form of the body). Marilyn Strathern (pers. comm.) notes the extensive use of this term among the Hagen people, including the idiom of "having pigs on the skin" (in the Daribi *habu*, the possessed *habu* men are said to have the "ghost" on their skins). Central desert Aborigine peoples in Australia distinguished their section systems as "systems of skins" in contradistinction to the soul-energies of the Dreaming.

> *[T]he shape does not coincide with the form; the shape is a sign of the form, its form of appearance, and as such may deceive.* — Lecture 4, p. 277

Clothing has a form and not a shape; the *body* has a shape and not a form. The *soul* has neither form, nor shape, nor substance: it is a *figure-ground reversal*. I once asked a Daribi friend what a soul would look like if one could see it, and he said "a very small black man." This is interesting, because the Daribi all-purpose male ritual attire, a covering of soot or charcoal over the entire body, plus a black cassowary-plume headdress, is called the *ogwanoma* (literally "boy-soul"), and corresponds with the conviction that the *soul* is in all cases identical with the *shadow* (quite literally a *figure-ground reversal*). This idea has a certain affinity with the Yekuana idea that everything has its negative (*akato*) shape.

---

2.   Skin is a metonym of containment that is very widespread in New Guinea and Australian Aboriginal usage. It designates the surface attributes of something, such as an individual—as for instance, a "name" may be understood, or "appearance," as in Munn's iconography of the Warlpiri (Munn 1986).

In the same way, the bodily "clothing" which, among animals, covers an internal "essence"
of a human type, is not a mere disguise, but their distinctive equipment, endowed with the
affects and capacities which define each animal. — Lecture 4, p. 278

It might be added that the *encompassing* aspect of skin might also be derived
from the fact that it is developed from the third, or outermost layer of the three
embryonic tissues, which also serves as the "germ" or developmental basis of the
organs of perception, the brain, and the neural net. And as this simple tripartite *ur-form* of animality is essential to its myriad subvarieties, one might say
that animality itself is *clothed* in perception. In their monograph on the central
desert Aborigines, Spencer and Gillen published a startling photograph (1968:
181), showing a group of Aborigines sitting around an extensive rock-paint-
ing, illustrating in characteristic cutaway form the developmental stages of an
emu-egg. *Ethnoembriology.* (The Daribi term for an embryo is *wai' ge'*, literally
"child-egg.")

Shori is a drug that makes you see the invisible "other side" inhabited by pure spiritual
essences. When you drink it you see animals, plants or spirits as cultured humans living in
villages, etc. — Lecture 4, p. 284

"For *them*," said the Kaluli to Schieffelin, pounding on the trunk of a tree, "this
is a *longhouse*, and you can see them up there (pointing at the birds on the
branches) sitting around their firepits" (pers. comm.). In the same way, a pond
is the longhouse of the fish, and a shaman going into trance on the floor of his
longhouse sees the roofbeams morph suddenly into the crowns of forest trees
(shades of the Tolai *tabapot*, the tree-human inversion), as though one were
looking down on the forest from an airplane. Originally, Schieffelin had called
this trance-formational world of the shaman the "mirror-world" (cf. Schieffelin
1976: 96-97).

I take metamorphosis as just a synonym for "perspective," or rather, for the exchangeability
of perspectives characteristic of Amerindian ontologies. — Lecture 4, p. 286

Metamorphosis might as well be called *metaphor-mosis*, as it essentializes the "difference" between the literal meanings of the words tagged in a metaphor, and
the *second-sight other* meanings of those words when juxtaposed in the metaphor.
According to Feld (1982: 106), the Kaluli called metaphors *bali-to*, "turned over

words," allowing one to see the "flip side" of language. For me, as perhaps for
Lévi-Strauss as well, this also betokens something else: the *miniaturization* of
the small-scale model. Let me illustrate this from my experience of climbing the
"Pyramid of the Sun" at Teotihuacan, in Mexico. *The view from Teotihuacan*: to
a people with no intellectual or practical experience of artistic or architectural
perspective-theory, ascending into the "sky world" accomplished two things at a
single stroke: the *magnification* of earthly power and the *minification* of the secular world at the next level down, which appears to the viewer from the top as a
miniature city all spread out before one, with its buildings, roads, revetments, and
causeways with jewel-sharp precision. It makes no difference whether one takes
this extremely naïve point of view, very likely the one of the builders of Teotihuacan, or those of M. G. Escher, or the modern architectural adept, for *the effect
is the same in all cases*. But this is but one of the many ways in which miniaturization is the special mark of human sophistication in all degrees of representational
expression, from the embryological and biological to the epistemological and the
artistic. In contrast to the fossil hominids, insofar as we know them, *Homo sapiens*
is distinctive for its *neotony* (the trait of "holding on to youth" that makes *our* adults
look like the young of other primates and hold on to the curiosity and playfulness
that shapes their minds). We, as it were, "discovered the gene that makes people
want to discover genes." In contrast to other intelligent species (cetaceans, crows,
echidnas, etc.), we alone developed the miniaturization of experience in terms of
representation, tool-use, and the diagrammatic structure of myths and maps. The
device of writing and reading is a miniaturization, a small-scale model, of the
act of speech, just as speech itself is a miniaturization of *thought*. The conception,
birth, upbringing, and education of a child—the "formation of the personality"—
is a miniaturization of the neotenous human race. A scientific experiment or observation is a miniaturization of a vast and incomprehensible world call "nature."
What else would "culture" have to mean but a world of miniaturization?

> *Transformation or becoming is a "quality," not a process—it is an instantaneous shift
> of perspectives, or rather the entangled, non-decidable coexistence of two perspectives,
> each hiding the other in order to appear, like those figure-ground reversals we are fami-
> lar with, or like the flipping over of the front and back halves of the "two-sided species."*
> — Lecture 4, p. 288

The single and sole arbiter and creator of the subject/object contrast in any
human or nonhuman contingency is the *causality* principle, the *post hoc propter*

hoc temporal relation in which one thing, identified as the "cause," precedes a *result* called "the effect" in either a logical (e.g., "mental") or mechanical ("physical") way. The arbitrary and "two sided" nature of this basically *rationalizing* construction can be seen in everything from the *binary* schema used in the computer-chip to the mutual opposition of *gender* and *laterality* (man/woman :: right/left) in reproduction and perception/self perception. Equally viable, and equally confusing, is the *self-reversal* of the causal relation in instances of *humor* or *irony*, wherein the *effect* is revealed *first*, as in the telling of a joke, after which the hitherto concealed *cause* makes itself all-too-evident in the *punch-line*. In a manner of speaking humor or irony is nature's own antidote to the plague of logical and mechanical rationalizations that has been sweeping the globe for the last three centuries; the shaman is the antidote to the M.D.

When we realize that *each is wrong* for the "reason" that the other is right, and each is right for the reason that the other is wrong, we begin to doubt our reason rather than our humor—for the "gut reaction" to causal inversion is always a *spontaneous* one, as opposed to the *forced nature* of rationalization itself, its logics and its engineering. Nobody "proves" a joke, because it disproves (falsifies) *itself*. So the question arises as to which of these two mutually substitutable elements, however inverted or otherwise juxtaposed, corresponds to the "subject," and which to the "object?" And what, by God, is the difference between what the philosophers have called *"intersubjectivity"* and its opposite clone *interobjectivity*?

Perform this simple experiment, which we might call, for want of a better term, *digital meditation*. Join the tips of your fingers together so that each touches its corresponding *alter* on the other hand, and answer the following questions. Which of your hands, by virtue of the "feeling" in between them, is the *subject*, and which is the *object*? What of that curious tingling sensation you are experiencing, so much like the *embodiment* of mental/physical masturbation—is it one of *intersubjectivity* or one of *interobjectivity*, given that each of these is the *suppressed biogrammatic counterpart* of the other. *The utter futility of phenomenology* (read "postmodernism" here if you like) *is thus demonstrated by the simple act of shaking hands with yourself* (or, in less "appropriate" language, *giving yourself the finger*). Remember that the master musician has a piano or violin between their fingertips, and is able to make beautiful music out of what would otherwise be accounted as a philosophical mistake, the lover has a whole physical body between theirs, and the Internet adept has between theirs the means by which to spread a whole world of trivialized facts and overinflated opinions across the known world. (I believe they call this "globalism" at the University of Chicago.)

Apart from its usefulness in labeling "hyper-uranian" cosmographic domains, or in defining a third type of intentional beings occurring in indigenous cosmologies, which are neither human nor animal (I refer to "spirits"), the notion of supernature may serve to designate a specific relational context and a particular phenomenological quality, which is as distinct from the intersubjective relations that define the social world as from the "interobjective" relations with other bodies. — Lecture 4, p. 290

What is it like to experience the subject-object shift directly, the demise of the "rational" cause-and-effect hegemony as an immediate function of one's own *person*? Is it anything like personal death? Or is it not more like the fabled "third attention" state of the Meso-American civilizations, in which one is able to grasp and hold (fixate within oneself) a *parallactic shift* at the crossover point between the eternal *presence* of space and the eternal *passing* of temporal extension ("duration"). (This is the domain of Kali, the "black goddess of time" in Hindu cosmology, and it is discussed at length as "the third point" in Castaneda's masterpiece *The power of silence*, 1987.)

But what is it like to *experience* this? A great inventor, like Imhotep or Nikola Tesla, spends their whole life in a sort of anticipatory ecstasy, never of course fulfilled, of *the greatest invention in the world just about to happen*. To live forever on the very wavecrest of joy, just before it breaks (and you go tumbling down). This is the ecstasy of *the anticipatory self* just about to acknowledge its own presence to itself. In the Star Trek movie *Generations* (1994) this energy state is called "The Nexus," and the character Guinan (Whoopie Goldberg) explains: "It is as if joy were something tangible, and you could wrap yourself up in it like a blanket."

Thank you, Eduardo, for showing us the way to the third attention!

[W]hen you encounter an iwianch, *a ghost or spirit in the forest. You must say to the ghost: "I, too, am a person!" You must assert your point of view: when you say that you, too, are a person, what you really mean is that you are the "I," you are the person, not the other. "I, too, am a person" means: I am the real person here.* — Lecture 4, p. 290

To the Meso-Americans in the Castaneda books, the *iwianch* is an *ally*, an inorganic being of a crystalline nature that confronts you deliberately in order to absorb and use some part of your *edge*, your anticipatory or "start-up" energy—a kind of energy that this normally passive being simply does not have. (Daribi call this kind of being the *izara-we*, or "epilepsy women"; I have encountered them in Charlottesville, in shopping malls.)

"You" cannot appear to *you* except in some self-reversed apparition, like a reflection in a mirror, and an inverse of you is never *you*, but something else trying to take your place. The trouble with an *iwianch*, or something weird you see in the forest, is that it is not only *you* who are not sure whether it is there or not; "it" is even *less* sure. In real time, the problem is not very different than that of Heisenberg's "Uncertainty" principle.

> *The Cartesian rupture with medieval scholastics produced a radical simplification of our ontology, by positing only two principles or substances: unextended thought and extended matter.* — Lecture 4, p. 293

Many of the most puzzling issues in scientific cosmology (particle-indeterminacy, the so-called "parallel universes") tend to have relatively simple perspectivist solutions. For instance, the inability to determine both the velocity and the location of a particle at the same time (Heisenberg's "Uncertainty") turns out to be exactly the same thing as Einstein's "relativity of the observer to his coordinate system" when the perspectives of the observer and the observed are reversed. For the Heisenbergian observer *is* the coordinate system looking at itself from the wrong side up, whereas, in the case of relativity, the Einsteinian observer *is* the particles. Any self-respecting shaman would *see* through the problem in about two seconds flat, and its exact description is mythologized in the ancient Mayan *Popol Vuh*: the Hero Twins descend to the lower world where they lose their heads and, in consequence of their struggle to get them back again, re-invert their coordinate systems with respect to the upper and lower worlds, and so deliver the human race from its Uncertainty. In addition to being the most coherently *dualistic* origin myth ever recorded, the *Popol Vuh* details the exact etiology of the *figure-ground reversal*.

> *This would be the final step: the representational function is ontologized in the mind, but in the terms of the simple-minded ontology of mind versus matter.* — Lecture 4, p. 294

Just exactly *what* is analogized in the Cartesian duality? Clearly, it cannot be the phenomenal entities *mind* and *matter* taken in and of themselves, and this is what Eduardo rightly calls "simple-minded." For both mind and matter *must* be represented together in either one of these false alternatives: *res cogitans* and *res extensa*—what is *thought* without the space in which to think, and what is *extension* without the mind that extends it? What could be *represented* without the aid of *representation* itself? It is tempting to conclude that what is *really* opposed in the duality would be best represented as *extension* versus *non-extension (res non-extensa)*, but that leaves the "mental" aspect of things out in the cold. So the better choice would be *intention* (like the inward tension of a black hole, or the mind *intent* on something) versus *extension*. This also helps to avoid *unintended errors*: Bartender: "More drinks, René?" Descartes: "I think not" (disappears).

Bibliography

Agamben, Giorgio. 1993. *The coming community*. Translated by Michael Hardt. Minneapolis: University of Minnesota Press.

Albert, Bruce. 1985. "Temps du sang, temps des cendres: représentation de la maladie, système rituel et espace politique chez les Yanomami du sud-est (Amazonie brésilienne)." PhD dissertation. Paris: Université de Paris X, Nanterre.

Alexiades, Miguel. 1999. "Ethnobotany of the Ese Eja: Plants, health, and change in an Amazonian society." Ph.D. dissertation. New York: City University of New York.

Argyrou, Vassos. 1999. "Sameness and the ethnological will to meaning." *Current Anthropology*, supplement to 40: 29–41.

Århem, Kaj. 1993. "Ecosofía makuna." In *La selva humanizada: Ecología alternativa en el trópico húmedo colombiano*, edited by F. Correa, 109–26. Bogotá: Instituto Colombiano de Antropología, Fondo fen Colombia, Fondo Editorial Cerec.

———. 1996. "The cosmic food web: Human-nature relatedness in the Northwest Amazon." In *Nature and society: Anthropological perspectives*, edited by Philippe Descola and Gísli Pálsson, 185–204. London: Routledge.

Aron, Raymond. 1973. "Le paradoxe du même et de l'autre." In *échanges et communications: Mélanges offerts à Claude Lévi-Strauss à l'ocassion de son 60ème anniversaire*, edited by Jean Pouillon and Pierre Maranda, 943–52. Paris: Mouton.

Asad, Talal. 1986. "The concept of cultural translation in British Social Anthropology." In *Writing culture: The poetics and politics of ethnography*, edited by James Clifford and George E. Marcus, 141–64. Berkeley: University of California Press.

Baer, Gerhard. 1994. *Cosmología y shamanismo de los Matsiguenga*. Quito: Abya-Yala.

Bamford, Sandra. 2007. *Biology unmoored: Melanesian reflections on life and biotechnology*. Berkeley: University of California Press.

————. 2009. "'Family-trees among the Kamea of Papua New Guinea: A non-genea-logical approach to imagining relatedness." In *Kinship and beyond: The genealogical model reconsidered*, edited by Sandra Bamford and James Leach, 159–74. Oxford: Berghahn.

Barry, Laurent, et al. 2000. "Glossaire de la parenté." *L'Homme* 154–55: 721–32.

Basso, Ellen. 1973. *The Kalapalo Indians of Central Brazil*. New York, Holt, Rinehart & Winston.

Bastos, Rafael J. de Menezes. 1975. *A musico-lógica kamayurá*. Brasília: Fundação Nacional do Índio.

Beck, Ulrich. 1992. *Risk society: Towards a new modernity*. London: Sage

Beller, Joseph. 2006. *The cinematic mode of production:Aattention economy and the society of the spectacle*. Lebanon, NH: Dartmouth College Press/University Press of New England.

Benveniste, Émile. 1966a. "La nature des pronoms." In *Problèmes de linguistique générale*, 251–57. Paris: Gallimard.

————. 1966b. "De la subjectivité dans le langage." In *Problèmes de linguistique générale*, 258–66. Paris: Gallimard.

Bloch, Maurice. (1985) 1989. "From cognition to ideology." In *Ritual, history and power*, 106–36. London: Athlone.

————. 1992. "What goes without saying: The conceptualization of Zafimaniry society." In *Conceptualizing society*, edited by Adam Kuper, 127–46. London: Routledge.

Bodenhorn, Barbara. 1988. "Whales, souls, children and other things that are good to share: Core metaphors in a contemporary whaling society." *Cambridge Anthropology* 13 (1): 1–19.

Boelscher, Marianne. 1989. *The curtain within: Haida social and mythical discourse*. Vancouver: University of British Columbia Press.

Bourdieu, Pierre. 1972. *Esquisse d'une théorie de la pratique: Précédé de trois études d'ethnologie Kabyle*. Genève: Droz.

Boyer, Pascal, 1993. "Introduction." In *Cognitive aspects of religious symbolism*. Cambridge: University of Cambridge Press.

Brightman, Robert. 1993. *Grateful prey: Rock Cree human-animal relationships*. Berkeley: University of California Press.

Brown, Michael. (1986) 1993. *Tsewa's gift*. Washington D.C.: Smithsonian Institute Press.

Brunton, Ron. 1980. "Misconstrued order in Melanesian religion." *Man* 15 (1): 112–28.

Carid Naveira, Miguel. 1999. "Yawanawa: Da guerra à festa." Master's thesis. PPGAS-UFSC, Florianópolis.

Carneiro da Cunha, Manuela. 1978. *Os mortos e os outros*. São Paulo: Hucitec.

———. 1998. "Pontos de vista sobre a floresta amazônica: Xamanismo e tradução." *Mana* 4 (1): 7–22.

Carsten, Janet. 1995. "The substance of kinship and the heat of the hearth: Feeding, personhood, and relatedness among Malays in Pulau Langkawi." *American Ethnologist* 22 (2): 223–41.

———. 2000a. "Introduction: Cultures of relatedness." In *Cultures of relatedness: New approaches to the study of kinship*, edited by Janet Carsten, 1–36. Cambridge: Cambridge University Press.

———, ed. 2000b. *Cultures of relatedness: New approaches to the study of kinship*. Cambridge: Cambridge University Press.

———. 2001. "Substantivism, antisubstantivism, and anti-antisubstantivism." In *Relative values: Reconfiguring kinship studies*, edited by Sarah Franklin and Susan McKinnon, 29–53. Durham and London: Duke University Press.

Castaneda, Carlos. 1987. *The power of silence: Further lessons of Don Juan*. New York: Simon and Schuster.

Chaumeil, Jean-Pierre. 1983. *Voir, savoir, pouvoir: Le chamanisme chez les Yagua du nord-est péruvien*. Paris: école des Hautes Etudes en Sciences Sociales.

Cheney, Dorothy L. and Robert M. Seyfarth. 1990. *How monkeys see the world: Inside the mind of another species*. Chicago: University of Chicago Press.

Civrieux, Marc de. 1985. "Medatia: A Makiritare shaman's tale." In *The language of the birds: Tales, texts and poems of interspecies communication*, edited by David M. Guss, 55–75. San Francisco: North Point Press.

Clark, Jeffrey. 1991. "Pearlshell symbolism in Highlands Papua New Guinea, with particular reference to the Wiru people of Southern Highlands Province." *Oceania* 61 (4): 303–39.

Clastres, Pierre. (1962) 1974a. "Échange et pouvoir: Philosophie de la Chefferie Indienne." In *La société contre l'État: Recherches d'anthropologie politique*, 25–42. Paris: Minuit.

———. 1974b. *La société contre l'État*. Paris: Minuit.

———. 1989. *Society against the state: Essays in political anthropology*. Translated by Robert Hurley. New York: Zone Books.

Clifford, James. (1982) 1992. *Person and myth: Maurice Leenhardt in the Melanesian world*. Durham: Duke University Press.

Coelho de Souza, M. 2002. "O Traço e o Círculo: O Conceito de Parentesco entre os Jê e seus Antropólogos." Ph.D. dissertation. Rio de Janeiro: Museu Nacional.

Coetzee, J. M. 2004. *Elizabeth Costello*. New York: Penguin.

Collier, Jane, and Michelle Rosaldo. 1981. "Politics and gender in simple societies." In *Sexual meanings: The cultural construction of gender and sexuality*, edited by Sherry Ortner and Harriet Whitehead, 275–329. Cambridge: Cambridge University Press.

Crapanzano, Vincent. 2003. *Imaginative horizons: An essay in literary-philosophical anthropology*. Chicago: University of Chicago Press.

Crawley, Ernest. 1909. *The idea of the soul*. London: Adam and Charles Black.

Crocker, Jon C. 1985. *Vital souls: Bororo cosmology, natural symbolism, and shamanism*. Tucson: University of Arizona Press.

Delaney, Carol. 1986. "The meaning of paternity and the virgin birth debate." *Man* 21 (3): 494–513.

Deleuze, Gilles. 1969a. *Logique du sens*. Paris: Minuit.

———. 1969b. *Différence et répétition*. Paris: Presses Universitaires de France.

———. 1981. "Class on Spinoza." February 17, 1981. http://www.webdeleuze.com/php/texte.php?cle=38&groupe=Spinoza&langue=2.

———. 1986. "On four poetic formulas that might summarize the Kantian philosophy." In *Essays Critical and clinical*, translated by Daniel W. Smith and Michael Greco. London: Verso.

———. 1988. *Le pli: Leibniz et le baroque*. Paris: Minuit.

———. 1990. *Pourparlers*. Paris: Minuit.

———. 1994. *Difference and repetition*. Translated by Paul Patton. New York: Columbia University Press.

———. (1979) 1995. *Dialogues*. Paris: Flammarion.

Deleuze, Gilles, and Félix Guattari. 1972. *L'Anti-Œdipe*. Paris: Minuit.

———. 1980. *Milles plateaux*. Paris: Minuit.

———. 1991. *Quest-ce que la philosophie?* Paris: Minuit.

———. (1991) 1994. *What is philosophy?* New York: Columbia University Press.

———. (1993) 2003. *The logic of sense*. New York: Columbia University Press.

Dennett, Daniel, and Douglas Hofstadter. 1981. *The mind's I*. New York: Basic Books.

Descola, Philippe. 1986. *La nature domestique: Symbolisme et praxis dans l'écologie des Achuar*. Paris: Maison des Sciences de L'Homme.

———. 1992. "Societies of nature and the nature of society." In *Conceptualizing society*, edited by Adam Kuper, 107–26. London: Routledge.

———. 1996. "Constructing natures: Symbolic ecology and social practice." In *Nature and society: Anthropological perspectives*, edited by Philippe Descola, and Gisli Pálsson, 82–102. London: Routledge.

———. (1996) 2001. "The *genres* of gender: Local models and global paradigms in the comparison of Amazonia and Melanesia." In *Gender in Amazonia and Melanesia: an exploration of the comparative method*, edited by Thomas Gregor, and Donald Tuzin, 90–114. Berkeley: University of California Press.

Désveaux, Emmanuel. 1988. *Sous le signe de l'ours: Mythes et temporalité chez les Ojibwa septentrionaux*. Paris: Maison des Sciences de l'Homme.

———. 1998. "Le placenta ou le double mort du nouveauné." *Journal de la Société des Américanistes* 84 (1): 211–17.

Detienne, Marcel. 1981. *L'invention de la mythologie*. Paris: Gallimard.

Dumont, Louis. 1978a. "La communauté anthropologique et l'idéologie." In *Essais sur l'individualisme: Une perspective anthropologique sur l'idéologie moderne*, 187–221. Paris: Seuil.

———. 1978b. "La valeur chez les modernes et chez les autres." In *Essais sur l'individualisme: Une perspective anthropologique sur l'idéologie moderne*, 222–62. Paris: Seuil.

———. 1980. "Vers une theorie de l'hiérarchie." In *Homo Hierarchicus* (Postface à l'édition Tel), 396–403. Paris: Gallimard.

———. 1983. "Stocktaking 1981: Affinity as value." In *Affinity as a Value: marriage alliance in South India with comparative essays on Australia*, edited by Louis Dumont. Chicago: University of Chicago Press.

Edwards, Jeanette. 2009. "Skipping a generation and assisting conception." In *Kinship and beyond: The genealogical model reconsidered*, edited by Sandra Bamford and James Leach, 138–58. Oxford: Berghahn.

Edwards, Jeanette, Sarah Franklin, Eric Hirsch, Frances Price, and Marilyn Strathern. 1999. *Technologies of procreation: Kinship in the age of assisted conception*, 2nd ed. London: Routledge.

Edwards, Jeanette, and Marilyn Strathern. 2000. "Including our own." In *Cultures of relatedness: New approaches to the study of kinship*, edited by Janet Carsten, 149–66. Cambridge: Cambridge University Press.

Eggan, Fred. 1954. "Social anthropology and the method of controlled comparison." *American Anthropologist* 56: 743–63.

Erikson, Philippe. 1984. "De l'apprivoisement à l'approvisionnement: Chasse, alliance et familiarisation en Amazonie amérindienne." *Techniques et Cultures* 9: 105–140.

———. 1990. "Les Matis d'Amazonie: Parure du corps, identité ethnique et organisation sociale." PhD dissertation. Paris: Université de Paris X, Nanterre.

Euripides. 1906. *The Bacchae*, translated by Gilbert Murray. London: George Allen.

Evans-Pritchard, Edward E. (1937) 1976. *Witchcraft, oracles, and magic among the Azande*, edited by Eva Gillies. Oxford: Clarendon Press.

Ewart, Elizabeth. 2000. "Living with each other: Selves and alters amongst the Panará of central Brazil." PhD dissertation. London: London School of Economics.

Fajardo, Denise. 1997. "De inimigo a parente: A questão da alteridade entre os Tiriyó." Paper presented at the XXI Annual Meeting of ANPOCS, Caxambu, Brazil.

Fausto, Carlos. 1997. "A dialética da predação e familiarização entre os Parakanã da Amazônia oriental." PhD dissertation. Rio de Janeiro: Programa de Pós-graduação em Antropologia Social, Museu Nacional, UFRJ.

———. 1999. "Of enemies and pets: Warfare and shamanism in Amazonia." *American Ethnologist* 26 (4): 933–56

———. 2001. *Inimigos fiéis: História, guerra e xamanismo na Amazônia.* São Paulo: Edusp.

Feld, Steven. 1982. *Sounds and sentiments: Birds, weeping, poetics, and song in Kaluli expression.* Philadelphia: University of Pennsylvania Press.

Fienup-Riordan, Ann. 1994. *Boundaries and passages: Rule and ritual in Yup'ik Eskimo oral tradition.* Norman: University of Oklahoma Press.

Fortes, Meyer. 1969. *Kinship and the Social Order: The Legacy of Lewis Henry Morgan.* London: Routledge and Kegan Paul.

Franklin, Sarah and Helena Ragoné, eds. 1998. *Reproducing reproduction: Kinship, power, and technological innovation.* Philadelphia: University of Pennsylvania Press.

Fukushima, M. 2000. "On supersymmetrical anthropology and an origin of science wars in Japan." (A memo sent by e-mail to EVC on 21/10/2000).

Funkenstein, Amos. 1986. *Theology and the scientific imagination from the middle ages to the seventeenth century.* Princeton: University of Princeton Press.

Gallois, Dominique. 1984–85. "O pajé wayãpi e seus espelhos." *Revista de Antropologia* 27–28: 179–196.

Geertz, Clifford. 1986. "The uses of diversity." In *Tanner lectures on human values*, edited by Sterling M. McMurrin. Vol. 7. Salt Lake City: University of Utah Press.

Gell, Alfred. 1992. *The anthropology of time.* London: Berg.

———. 1995. "Closure and multiplication: An essay on Polynesian cosmology and ritual." In *Society and cosmos in Oceania*, edited by Daniel de Coppet and André Iteanu, 21–56. Oxford: Berg.

———. 1998. *Art and agency: An anthropological theory.* Oxford: Clarendon.

———. 1999. *The art of anthropology: Essays and diagrams.* London: Athlone.

Ginzburg, Carlo. 1991. *Ecstasies: Deciphering the witches sabbath.* Harmondsworth: Penguin.

Gleick, James. 1988. *Chaos: Making a new science.* London: William Heinemann.

Goldman, Irving. 1975. *The mouth of heaven: An introduction to Kwakiutl religious thought.* New York: Wiley-Interscience.

Goody, Jack. 1996. *The east in the west.* Cambridge: Cambridge University Press.

Gow, Peter. 1989. "The perverse child: Desire in a native Amazonian subsistence economy." *Man*, n.s., 24 (4): 567–82.

———. 1991. *Of mixed blood: Kinship and history in Peruvian Amazonia.* Oxford: Clarendon.

———. 1997a. "O Parentesco Como Consciência Humana: O Caso dos Piro." *Mana* 3 (2): 39–65.

———. 1997b. "A man who was tired of living." Unpublished manuscript.

———. 2001. *An Amazonian myth and its history.* Oxford: Oxford University Press.

Gray, Andrew. 1996. *The Arakmbut of Amazonian Peru, Vol. I: Mythology, spirituality and history.* Oxford: Berghahn.

———. 1997. *The Arakmbut of Amazonian Peru, Vol. II: The last shaman (change in an Amazonian community).* Oxford: Berghahn.

Gregor, Thomas. 1977. *Mehinaku: The drama of daily life in a Brazilian Indian village.* Chicago: University of Chicago Press.

Gregory, Christopher. 1982. *Gifts and commodities.* London: Academic Press. [Reprinted as Gregory, Christopher. 2015. *Gifts and commodities*, 2nd edition. Chicago: Hau Books.]

Grenand, Pierre. 1980. *Introduction à l'étude de l'univers wayãpi: Ethno-écologie des indiens du Haut-Oyapock: Guyane Française.* Paris: SELAF/CNRS.

Guédon, Marie-Françoise. 1984a. "An introduction to the Tsimshian worldview and its practitioners." In *The Tsimshian: Images of the past, views for the present*, edited by M. Seguin, 137–59. Vancouver: University of British Columbia Press.

———. 1984b. "Tsimshian shamanic images." In *The Tsimshian: Images of the past, views for the present*, edited by M. Seguin, 174–211. Vancouver: University of British Columbia Press.

Guss, David M. 1989. *To weave and sing: Art, symbol, and narrative in the South American rain forest.* Berkeley: University of California Press.

Hacking, Ian. 1999. *The social construction of what?* Cambridge, MA: Harvard University Press.

Hage, Per. 1999. "Marking universals and the structure and evolution of kinship terminologies: Evidence from Salish." *Journal of the Royal Anthropological Institute* 5 (3): 423–41.

Hallowell, A. Irving. 1960. "Ojibwa ontology, behavior, and world view." In *Culture in history: Essays in honor of Paul Radin*, edited by Stanley Diamond, 19–52. New York: Columbia University Press.

Hamayon, Roberte. 1990. *La chasse à l'âme: Esquisse d'une théorie du chamanisme sibérien.* Nanterre: Société d'Ethnologie.

Harner, Michael. 1972. *The Jívaro: People of the sacred waterfalls.* New York: Doubleday.

Harrison, Simon. 1993. *The mask of war: Violence, ritual and the self in Melanesia.* Manchester: University of Manchester Press.

————. 2002. "The politics of resemblance: Ethnicity, trademarks, headhunting." *Journal of the Royal Anthropological Institute* 8 (2): 211–32.

Heidegger, Martin. 2001. *Sein und Zeit.* Tübingen: Max Niemeyer Verlag.

Henley, Paul. 1996a. "Recent themes in the anthropology of Amazonia: History, exchange, alterity." *Bulletin of Latin American Research* 15 (2): 231–45.

Henley, Paul. 1996b. "South Indian models in the Amazonian lowlands." *Manchester Papers in Social Anthropology* 1.

Herzfeld, Michael. 2001. "Orientations: Anthropology as a practice of theory." In *Anthropology: Theoretical practice in culture and society,* edited by Michael Herzfeld, 1–20. London: Blackwell / UNESCO.

Holbraad, Martin. 2005. "Expending multiplicity: Money in Cuban Ifá cults." *Journal of the Royal Anthropological Institute* 11 (2): 231–54.

————. 2007. "The power of powder: Multiplicity and motion in the civinatory cosmology of Cuban Ifá (or mana, again)." In *Thinking through things: Theorising artefacts ethnographically,* edited by Amiria Henare, Martin Holbraad, and Sari Wastell, 189–225. London: Routledge.

Holmberg, Allan. 1969. *Nomads of the long bow: The Siriono of Eastern Bolivia.* Garden City, NY: Natural History Press.

Holy, Ladislav. 1996. *Anthropological perspectives on kinship.* London and Sterling, VA: Pluto Press.

Horton, Robin. 1993. *Patterns of thought in Africa and the West: Essays on magic, religion and science.* Cambridge: Cambridge University Press.

Houseman, Michael. (1984) 2015. "The hierarchical relation: A particular ideology or a general model?" *HAU: Journal of Ethnographic Theory* 5 (1): 251–69.

————. 1988. "Toward a complex model of parenthood: Two African tales." *American Ethnologist* 15 (4): 658–77.

Howell, Signe. 1984. *Society and cosmos: Chewong of peninsular Malaysia.* Oxford: Oxford University Press.

————. 1996. "Nature in culture or culture in nature? Chewong ideas of 'humans' and other species." In *Nature and society: Anthropological perspectives,* edited by Philippe Descola and Gisli Pálsson, 127–44. London: Routledge.

Hugh-Jones, Christine. 1979. *From the Milk River: Spatial and temporal processes in Northwest Amazonia*. Cambridge: Cambridge University Press.

Hugh-Jones, Stephen. 1979. *The palm and the pleiades*. Cambridge: University of Cambridge Press.

———. 1993. "Clear descent or ambiguous houses? A re-examination of Tukanoan social organization." *L'Homme* 126–128: 95–120.

———. 1996. "Bonnes raisons ou mauvaise conscience? De l'ambivalence de certains Amazoniens envers la consommation de viande." *Terrain* 26: 123–148.

———. 2001. "The gender of some Amazonian gifts: an experiment with an experiment." In *Gender in Amazonia and Melanesia: An exploration of the comparative method*, edited by Thomas Gregor and Donald Tuzin, 245–78. Berkeley: University of California Press.

Ingold, Tim. 1991. "Becoming persons: Consciousness and sociality in human evolution." *Cultural Dynamics* 4 (3): 355–78.

———. 1992. "Editorial." *Man* 27 (1): 694–97.

———. 1994. "Humanity and animality." In *Companion encyclopedia of anthropology: Humanity, culture and social life*, edited by Tim Ingold, 14–32. London: Routledge.

———. 1996. "Hunting and gathering as ways of perceiving the environment." In *Redefining nature: ecology, culture and domestication,* edited by R. F. Ellen and K. Fukui, 117–55. Oxford: Berg.

———. 2000. *The perception of the environment: Essays on livelihood, dwelling and skill.* London: Routledge.

———. 2009. "Stories against classification: Transport, wayfaring and the integration of knowledge." In *Kinship and beyond: The genealogical model reconsidered*, edited by Sandra Bamford and James Leach, 193–213. Oxford: Berghahn.

Jakobson, Roman, and Krystyna Pomorska. 1985. *Diálogos*. São Paulo: Cultrix.

Jamous, Raymond. 1991. *La relation frère-soeur: Parentés et rites chez les Meo de l'Inde du Nord.* Paris: EHESS.

Jara, Fabiola. 1996. *El camino del kumu: Ecología y ritual entre los Akuriyó de Surinam.* Quito: Abya-Yala.

Journet, Nicolas. 1995. *La paix des jardins: Structures sociales des Indiens Curripaco du haut Rio Negro (Colombie).* Paris: Institut d'Ethnologie.

Jullien, François. 1989a. *La propension des choses.* Paris: Seuil.

———. 1989b. *Procès ou création: Une introduction à la pensée Chinoise.* Paris: Seuil.

———. 1993. *Figures de l'immanence: Pour une lecture philosophique du Yi King, le Classique du changement.* Paris: Grasset and Frasquelle.

———. 1997. *Essai sur l'efficacité.* Paris: Grasset.

Jullien, François, and Thierry Marchaisse. 2000. *Penser d'un dehors (la Chine): Entretiens d'Extrême Occident.* Paris: Seuil.

Kan, Sergei. 1989. *Symbolic immortality: The Tlingit potlatch of the nineteenth century.* Washington D.C.: Smithsonian Institute Press.

Karadimas, Dimitri. 1997. "Le corps sauvage: Idéologie du corps et representations de l'environnement chez les Miraña d'Amazonie colombienne." PhD dissertation. Paris: Université de Paris X, Nanterre.

Karim, Wazir-Jaham. 1981. *Ma'Betisék concepts of living things.* London: Athlone.

Keifenheim, Barbara. 1992. "Identité et alterité chez les indiens Pano." *Journal de la Société des Américanistes* 78 (2): 79–93.

Kelly, José Antonio. 2001. "Fractalidade e Troca de Perspectivas." *Mana* 7 (2): 95–132.

———. 2005. "Fractality and the exchange of perspectives." In *On the order of chaos: Social anthropology and the science of chaos,* edited by Mark S. Mosko and Frederick H. Damon, 108–35. Oxford and New York: Berghahn Books.

Kensinger, Kenneth. 1995. *How real people ought to live: The Cashinahua of Eastern Peru.* Prospect Hights: Waveland Press.

Koelewijn, Cess, and Peter Rivière. 1987. *Oral literature of the Trio Indians of Surinam.* Dordrecht: Foris.

Kohn, Eduardo O. 2002. "Natural engagements and ecological æsthetics among the Ávila Runa of Amazonian Ecuador." Ph.D. dissertation. Madison: University of Wisconsin.

Krause, Fritz. 1931. "Maske und Aahnenfigur: Das motiv der hülle und das prinzip der form." *Ethnologische Studien* Bd 1: 344–64.

Kuhn, Thomas S. 1962. *The structure of scientific revolutions.* Chicago: University of Chicago Press.

Lambek, Michael. 1998. "Body and mind in mind, body and mind in body: Some anthropological interventions in a long conversation." In *Bodies and persons: Comparative perspectives from Africa and Melanesia,* edited by Andrew Strathern and Michael Lambek, 103–23. Cambridge: Cambridge University Press.

———. 2007. "Sacrifice and the problem of beginning: Meditations from Sakalava mythopraxis." *Journal of the Royal Anthropological Institute* 13 (1): 19–38.

Lao Tzu. 1963. *Tao te ching.* Translated by D. C. Lau. Harmondsworth: Penguin Books

Latour, Bruno. 1991. *Nous n'avons jamais été modernes.* Paris: La Découverte.

———. 1994. "Les objets ont-ils une histoire? Rencontre de Pasteur et de Whitehead dans un bain d'acide lactique." In *L'Effet Whitehead,* edited by Isabelle Stengers, 197–217. Paris: Vrin.

———. 1996a. "Not the question." *Anthropology Newsletter* 37 (3): 1–5.

———. 1996b. *Petite réflexion sur le culte moderne des dieux faitiches*. Paris: Les Empêcheurs de Penser en Rond.

———. 1999. *Politiques de la nature: Comment faire entrer les sciences en démocratie*. Paris: La Découverte.

———. 2002. *War of the Worlds: What About Peace?* Chicago: Prickly Paradigm Press.

———. 2009. "Perspectivism: 'type' or 'bomb'?" *Anthropology Today* 25 (2): 1–2.

Latour, Bruno, and Emilie Hache. 2010. "Morality or moralism? An exercise in sensitization." Translated by Patrick Camiller. *Common Knowledge* 16 (2): 311–30.

Lave, J. C. 1988. *Cognition in Practice: Mind, mathematics and culture in everyday life*. Cambridge: Cambridge University Press.

Le Guin, Ursula K. 1969. *The left hand of darkness*. New York: Ace Books.

Leach, James. 2003. *Creative land: Place and procreation on the Rai Coast of Papua New Guinea*. Oxford: Berghahn.

Leach, Edmund. (1951) 1961. "Rethinking anthropology." In *Rethinking anthropology*, 1–27. London: Athlone.

Leenhardt, Maurice. 1960. *Do kamo*. Paris: Gallimard.

Lévi-Strauss, Claude. 1943. "The social use of kinship terms among Brazilian Indians." *American Anthropologist* 45: 398-409.

———. 1955. *Tristes tropiques*. Paris: Plon.

———. 1956. "Les organisations dualistes existent-elles?" In *Anthropologie structurale*, 147–80. Paris: Plon.

———. (1954) 1958. "Place de l'anthropologie dans les sciences sociales et problèmes poses par son enseignement." In *Anthropologie structurale*, 377–418. Paris: Plon.

———. 1958. "Le sorcier et sa magie." In *Anthropologie structurale*, 183–203. Paris: Plon.

———. 1962a. *La pensée sauvage*. Paris: Plon.

———. 1962b. *Totemism*. Translated by Rodney Needham. Boston: Beacon Press.

———. 1962c. *Le totémisme aujourd'hui*. Paris: Presses Universitaires de France.

———. 1963. *Structural anthropology*. Translated by C. Jacobson and B. G. Schoepf. New York: Basic Books.

———. 1964. *Le cru et le cuit*. Paris: Plon.

———. 1966. *The savage mind*. Chicago: University of Chicago Press.

———. 1967a. *Du Miel aux Cendres* Paris: Plon.

———. 1967b. *L'Origine des Manières de Table*. Paris: Plon.

———. 1969. *The elementary structures of kinship*, translated by J. H. Bell, J. R. von Sturmer, and R. Needham. London: Eyre and Spottiswoode.

———. 1971. *L'Homme Nu*. Paris: Plon.

———. (1952) 1973. "Race et histoire." In *Anthropologie structurale deux*, 377–422. Paris: Plon.

———. 1978. "Une préfiguration anatomique de la gémellité." In *Le regard éloigné*. Paris: Plon.

———. (1956) 1983. "La famille." In *Le Regard Éloigné*, 65–92. Paris: Plon.

———. 1985. *La potière jalouse*. Paris: Plon.

———. 1991. *Histoire de lynx*. Paris: Plon.

———. 1992. "Race and culture." In *The view from afar*, translated by Joachim Neugroschel and Phoebe Hoss. Chicago: University of Chicago Press.

———. (1991) 1995. *The story of lynx*. Chicago: University of Chicago Press.

———. 2006. *A origem dos modos à mesa*. São Paulo: CosacNaify.

Lévi-Strauss, Claude, and Didier Eribon. 1988. *De près et de loin*. Paris: Odile Jacob.

Lima, Tânia Stolze. 1995. "A parte do cauim: etnografia juruna," PhD dissertation. Rio de Janeiro: Programa de Pós-graduação em Antropologia Social, Museu Nacional, UFRJ.

———. 1996. "O dois e seu múltiplo: reflexões sobre o perspectivismo em uma cosmologia tupi." *Mana* 2 (2): 21–47.

LiPuma, Edward. 1998. "Modernity and forms of personhood in Melanesia." In *Bodies and persons: Comparative perspectives from Africa and Melanesia*, edited by Andrew Strathern and Michael Lambek, 53–79. Cambridge: Cambridge University Press.

Lorrain, Clare. 2000. "Cosmic reproduction, economics and politics among the Kulina of Southwest Amazonia." *Journal of the Royal Anthropological Institute* 6 (2): 293–310.

Lovejoy, Arthur. 1960. *The revolt against dualism: An inquiry concerning the existence of ideas*, 2nd ed. La Salle, IL.: Open Court.

Malinowski, Bronislaw. 1922. *Argonauts of the Western Pacific*. London: Routledge & Kegan Paul.

Maniglier, Patrice. 2006. *La vie énigmatique des signes: Saussure et la naissance du structuralisme*. Paris: Lép Scheer.

Marx, Karl. (1844) 1961. *Economic and philosophic manuscripts of 1844*. Moscow: Foreign Languages Publishing House.

Maschio, Thomas. 1994. *To remember the faces of the dead: The plenitude of memory in southwestern New Britain*. Madison, WI: The University of Wisconsin Press.

Mauss, Marcel. (1923-24) 1973. "Essai sur le don: Forme et raison de l'échange dans les sociétés archaïques." In *Sociologie et anthropologie*, 145–279. Paris: Presses Universitaires de France.

———. 1983. *Sociologie et anthropologie*. Paris: Presses Universitaires de France.

————. (1950) 1990. *The gift: The form and reason for exchange in archaic societies*, translated by W. D. Hall. London: W. W. Norton.

Mauss, Marcel and Henri Hubert. (1903) 1950. "Esquisse d'une théorie de la magie." In *Sociologie et Anthropologie*, edited by Marcel Mauss, 1–141. Paris: Presses Universitaires de France.

Maybury-Lewis, David. 1960. "The analysis of dual organizations: A methodological critique." *Bijdragen tot de Taal-, Land- en Volkenkunde* 116 (1): 17–44.

————. 1989. "Social theory and social practice: Binary systems in Central Brazil" in *The attraction of opposites*, edited by David Maybury-Lewis and Uri Almagor. Ann Arbor: University of Michigan Press.

McCallum, Cecilia. 1989. "Gender, personhood and social organization amongst the Cashinahua of Western Amazonia," PhD dissertation. London: London School of Economics.

————. 1991. "Cashinahua (Huni Kuin) death, dying and personhood." Paper presented to the XLVII International Congress of Americanists, New Orleans.

————. 1996. "The body that knows: Trom Cashinahua epistemology to a medical anthropology of lowland South America." *Medical Anthropology Quartely* 10 (3): 1–26.

McDonnell, Roger. 1984. "Symbolic orientations and systematic turmoil: Centering on the Kaska symbol of *dene*." *Canadian Journal of Anthropology* 4 (1): 39–56.

McKinnon, Susan. 2001. "The economies in kinship and the paternity of culture: Origin stories and kinship theory." In *Relative values: Reconfiguring kinship studies*, edited by Sarah Franklin and Susan McKinnon, 277–301. Durham and London: Duke University Press.

Medeiros, Sérgio, ed. 2002. *Makunaíma e Jurupari: Cosmogonias ameríndias*. São Paulo: Perspectiva.

Meillassoux, Claude. 1975. *Femmes, greniers et capitaux*. Paris: Maspero.

Mentore, George. 1993. "Tempering the social self: Body adornment, vital substance, and knowledge among the Waiwai." *Journal of Archaeology and Anthropology* 9: 22–34.

Miller, Joana. 2007. "As coisas: Os enfeites corporais e a noção de pessoa entre os Mamaindê (Nambiquara)." Ph.D. dissertation. Rio de Janeiro: Museu Nacional/UFRJ.

Mimica, Jadran. 1991. "The incest passions: An outline of the logic of Iqwaye social organization (part 1)." *Oceania* 62 (1): 34–58.

————. (1988) 1992. *Intimations of infinity: The cultural meanings of the Iqwaye counting and number system*. Oxford: Berg.

Monod, Jean. 1987. *Wora, la déesse cachée*. Paris: Les Editeurs Evidant.

Moore, Henrietta. 1999. "Anthropological theory at the turn of the century." In *Anthropological theory today*, edited by Henrietta Moore, 1–23. London: Polity Press.

Moore, Marianne. (1919) 1924. "Imaginary gardens with real toads in them." In *Observations*, 30–31. New York: The Dial Press.

Munn, Nancy D. 1986. *Walbiri iconography: Graphic representation and symbolism in a Central Australian society*. Chicago: University of Chicago Press.

Murphy, Robert. 1958. *Mundurucú religion*. Berkeley: University of California Press.

Myers, Fred R. 1986. *Pintupi country, Pintupi self: sentiment, place, and politics among Western Desert Aborigines*. Washington: Smithsonian Institution Press.

Needham, Rodney, ed. 1973. *Right and left: Essays on dual symbolic classification*. Chicago: University of Chicago Press.

Nelson, Richard. 1983. *Make prayers to the Raven*. Chicago: University of Chicago Press.

Nietzsche, Friedrich. 1983. "Schopenhauer as educator." In *Unitmely meditations*, translated by R. J. Hollingdale. Cambridge: Cambridge University Press.

Nimuendaju, Curt. 1952. *The Tukuna*. Berkeley: University of California Press.

Obeyesekere, Gananath. 1992. *The apotheosis of Captain Cook: European mythmaking in the Pacific*. Princeton, NJ: Princeton University Press.

Osborn, Ann. 1990. "Eat and be eaten: Animals in U'wa (Tunebo) oral tradition." In *Signifying animals: Human meaning in the natural world*, edited by Roy Willis, 140–58. London: Unwin Hyman.

Overing (Kaplan), Joanna. 1975. *The Piaroa: A people of the Orinoco Basin*. Oxford: Clarendon.

———. 1981. "Review article: Amazonian anthropology." *Journal of Latin American Studies* 13: 151–64.

———. 1983–84. "Elementary structures of reciprocity: A comparative note on Guianese, Central Brazilian, and North-West Amazon socio-political thought." *Antropologica* 59–62: 331–48.

———. 1985. "There is no end of evil: The guilty innocents and their fallible god." In *The anthropology of evil*, edited by David Parkin, 244–78. London: Basil Blackwell.

———. 1986. "Images of cannibalism, death and domination in a 'non-violent' society." *Journal de la Société des Américanistes* 72: 133–56.

Parry, Jonathan. 1983. "Mauss, Dumont, and the distinction between status and power." In *Marcel Mauss: A centenary tribute*, edited by W. James and N. J. Allen, 150–72. Oxford: Berghahn Books.

Pastoureau, Michel. 1989. *A vida cotidiana no tempo dos cavaleiros da Távola Redonda*. São Paulo: Companhia das Letras/Círculo do Livro.

Peacock, Apud James. 2007. "Action comparison: Efforts towards a global and comparative and yet local and active anthropology." In *Anthropology, by comparison*, edited by André Gringrich and Richard G. Fox. London: Routledge.

Pollock, Donald. 1985. "Personhood and illness among the Culina of Western Brazil," PhD dissertation. Rochester: University of Rochester.

Prado Jr., Bento. 1998. "Sur le 'Plan d'immanence.'" In *Gilles Deleuze: Une vie philosophique*, edited by Eric Alliez, 305–24. Le Plessis/Robinson: Institut Synthélabo.

Price, David. 1987. "Nambiquara geopolitical organisation." *Man*, n.s. 22 (1): 1–24.

Radcliffe-Brown, A.R. (1929) 1952. "The sociological theory of totemism." In *Structure and function in primitive society*, 117–32. London: Routledge and Kegan Paul.

Reichel-Dolmatoff, Gerardo. 1973. *Desana: Le symbolisme universel des Indiens Tukano du Vaupés*. Paris: Gallimard.

———. 1976. "Cosmology as ecological analysis: A view from the rain forest." *Man 2* (3): 307–18.

———. 1985. "Tapir avoidance in the Colombian Northwest Amazon." In *Animals myths and metaphors in South America*, edited by Gary Urton, 107–43. Salt Lake City: University of Utah Press.

Renard-Casevitz, France-Marie. 1991. *Le banquet masqué: Une mythologie de l'étranger*. Paris: Lierre and Coudrier.

Rival, Laura. 1998. "Androgynous parents and guest children: The Huaraoni couvade." *Journal of the Royal Anthropological Institute* 4 (4): 619–42.

Rival, Laura, and Neil Whitehead, eds. 2001. *Beyond the visible and the material: The Amerindianization of society in the work of Peter Rivière*. Oxford: Oxford University Press.

Rivière, Peter. 1969. *Marriage among the Trio: A principle of social organization*. Oxford: Clarendon Press.

———. 1984. *Individual and society in Guiana*. Cambridge: University of Cambridge Press.

———. 1994. "WYSINWYG in Amazonia." *Journal of the Anthropological Society of Oxford* 25 (3): 255–62.

Rodgers, David. 2004. "Foil. Indifference, incompossibility and the complexion of Ikpeng shamanism." Unpublished manuscript.

Roe, Peter. 1982. *The cosmic zygote: Cosmology in the Amazon basin*. New Brunswick: Rutgers University Press.

———. 1990. "Impossible marriages: Animal seduction tales among the Shipibo Indians of the Peruvian jungle." *Journal of Latin American Lore* 16 (2): 131–73.

Rorty, Richard. 1980. *Philosophy and the mirror of nature*. Princeton, NJ: Princeton University Press.

———. 1991a. "On ethnocentrism: A reply to Clifford Geertz." In *Objectivity, relativism, and truth: Philosophical papers*. Vol. I. Cambridge: Cambridge University Press.

———. 1991b. "Solidarity or objectivity?" In *Objectivity, relativism, and truth: Philosophical papers*. Vol. I. Cambridge: Cambridge University Press.

Roth, Walter. 1915. "An inquiry into the folk-lore and animism of the Guiana Indians." *30th Annual Report of the Bureau of American Ethnology*, 1908-1909. Washington D.C.

Sahlins, Marshall. 1983. "Raw women, cooked man, and other 'great things' of the Fiji Islands." In *The ethnography of cannibalism*, edited by Paula Brown and Donald Tuzin, 72–93. Washington D.C.: Society for Pyschological Anthropology.

———. 1985. *Islands of history*. Chicago: University of Chicago Press.

———. 1995. *How 'natives' think: About Captain Cook, for example*. Chicago: University of Chicago Press.

———. 1996. "The sadness of sweetness: The native anthropology of Western cosmology." *Current Anthropology* 37 (3): 395–428.

Saladin d'Anglure, Bernard. 1989. "La part du chamane ou le communisme sexuel inuit dans l'Arctique central canadien." *Journal de la Société des Américanistes* 75: 131–71.

———. 1990. "Nanook, super-male: The polar bear in the imaginary space and social time of the Inuit of the Canadian Arctic." In *Signifying animals: Human meaning in the natural world*, edited by Roy Willis, 178–95. London: Unwin Hyman.

Sapir, Edward. 1985. "Culture, genuine and spurious." In *Selected writings in language, culture, and personality*, edited by David G. Mandelbaum, 308–31. Berkeley: University of California Press.

Scheffler, Harold. 1984. "Markedness and extension: The Tamil case." *Man* 19 (4): 557–74.

Schieffelin, Edward L. 1976. *The sorrow of the lonely and the burning of the dancers*. New York: St. Martin's Press.

Schneider, David. 1965. "Some muddles in the models: or, how the system really works." In *The relevance of models for social anthropology* (ASA Monographs 1), edited by Michael Banton, 25-86. London: Tavistock.

———. 1968. *American kinship: A cultural account*. Englewood Cliffs, NJ: Prentice Hall.

———. 1984. *A critique of the study of kinship*. Ann Arbor: University of Michigan Press.

Scholte, Bob. 1984. "Reason and culture: The universal and the particular revisited." *American Anthropologist* 86 (4): 960–65.

Schrempp, Gregory. 1992. *Magical arrows: The Maori, the Greeks, and the folklore of the universe*. Madison: University of Wisconsin Press.

Schwartzman, Stephen. 1988. "The Panara of the Xingu National Park," PhD dissertation. Chicago: University of Chicago.

Scott, Colin. 1989. "Knowledge construction among the Cree hunters: Metaphors and literal understanding." *Journal de la Société des Américanistes* 75: 193–208.

Searle, John. 1995. *The construction of social reality*. London: Allen Lane, Penguin.

———. 1997. *The mystery of consciousness*. London: Granta.

Seeger, Anthony. 1980. "Corporação e corporalidade: Ideologias de concepção e descendência," in *Os índios e nós*, 127–32. Rio de Janeiro: Editora Campus.

———. 1981. *Nature and society in Central Brazil: The Suyá Indians of Mato Grosso*. Cambridge; MA: Harvard University Press.

———. 1987. *Why Suyá sing*. Cambridge: University of Cambridge Press.

Seeger, Anthony, Roberto DaMatta, and Eduardo Viveiros de Castro. 1979. "A construção da pessoa nas sociedades indígenas brasileiras." *Boletim do Museu Nacional*, 32: 2–19.

Serres, Michel. 1990. *Le Contrat Naturel*. Paris: François Bourin.

Shapin, Steven, and Simon Schaffer. 1985. *Leviathan and the air-pump*. Princeton, NJ: Princeton University Press.

Simondon, Gilbert. (1964) 1995. *L'individu et sa génèse physico-biologique*. Paris: Millon.

Siskind, Janet. 1973. *To hunt in the morning*. Oxford: Oxford University Press.

Skorupski, John. 1976. *Symbol and theory: A philosophical study of theories of religion in social anthropology*. New York and Cambridge: Cambridge University Press.

Spencer, Baldwin, and F. J. Gillen. 1968. *The native tribes of central Australia*. New York: Dover Publications.

Sperber, Dan. 1974. *Le symbolisme en général*. Paris: Hermann.

———. 1982. *Le savoir des anthropologues*. Paris: Hermann.

Stafford, Charles. 2000. "Chinese patriliny and the cycles of Yang and Laiwang." In *Cultures of relatedness: New approaches to the study of kinship*, edited by Janet Carsten, 37–54. Cambridge: Cambridge University Press.

Statkiewicz, Max, and Valerie Reed. 2005. "Antigone's (re)turn: The ethos of the coming community." In *The enigma of good and evil: The moral sentiment in literature*, edited by Anna-Teresa Tymieniecka. Dordrecht, Netherlands: Springer.

Stengers, Isabelle. 1997. *Cosmopolitiques, vol. 7: Pour en finir avec la tolérance*. Paris: Le Découverte & Les Empêcheurs de Penser en Rond.

Strathern, Marilyn. 1979. "The self in self-decoration." *Oceania* 49: 241–57.

———. 1980. "No nature, no culture: The Hagen case." In *Nature, culture, and gender*, edited by Carol MacCormack and Marilyn Strathern. Cambridge: Cambridge University Press.

———. 1987. "The limits of auto-anthropology." In *Anthropology at home*, edited by Anthony Jackson, 16–37. London: Tavistock.

———. 1988. *The gender of the gift: Problems with women and problems with society in Melanesia.* Berkeley: University of California Press.

———. 1992a. *After nature: English kinship in the late twentieth century.* Cambridge: Cambridge University Press.

———. 1992b. "Parts and wholes: Refiguring relationships in a post-plural world." In *Conceptualizing society*, edited by Adam Kuper. London: Routledge.

———. 1992c. *Reproducing the future: Anthropology, kinship, and the new reproductive technologies.* New York: Routledge.

———. 1992d. "Writing societies, writing persons." *History of the Human Sciences* 5 (1): 5–16.

———. 1994. "One-legged gender." In *Visualizing theory: Selected essays from V.A.R. 1990–1994*, edited by Lucien Taylor, 242–50. London: Routledge.

———. 1995a. "The nice thing about culture is that everyone has it." In *Shifting contexts: Transformations in anthropological knowledge*, edited by Marilyn Strathern, 153–76. London and New York: Routledge.

———. 1995b. *The relation: Issues on complexity and scale.* Cambridge: Prickly Pear Press.

———. 1999. *Property, substance, and effect: Anthropological essays on persons and things.* London: Athlone.

———. 2001. "Emergent properties." The Robert and Maurine Rothschild Distinguished Lecture. Cambridge, MA: Harvard University Press.

———. 2004. "Transactions: An analytical foray." In *Transactions and Creations: Property debates and the stimulus of Melanesia*, edited by Eric Hirsch and Marilyn Strathern, 85–109. Oxford: Berghahn.

———. 2006. "Divided origins and the arithmetic of ownership." In *Accelerating possession: global futures of property and personhood*, edited by Bill Maurer and Gabriele Schwab, 135–73. New York: Columbia University Press.

Strathern, Marilyn, Carlos Fausto, and Eduardo Viveiros de Castro. 1999. "No limite de uma certa linguagem: entrevista com Marilyn Strathern." Interview of Marilyn Strathern by Carlos Fausto and Eduardo Viveiros de Castro. *Mana* 5 (2): 157–75.

Tanner, Adrian. 1979. *Bringing home animals: Religious ideology and mode of production of the Mistassini Cree hunters.* Saint John: Memorial University of Newfoundland.

Tarde, Gabriel. (1893) 1999. *Œuvres de Gabriel Tarde, volume 1: Monadologie et sociologie.* Le Plessis-Robinson: Institut Synthélabo.

Taussig, Michael. 1987. *Shamanism, colonialism, and the wild man: A study in terror and healing.* Chicago: University of Chicago Press.

Taylor, Anne-Christine. 1983. "The marriage alliance and its structural variations in Jivaroan societies." *Social Science Information* 22 (3): 331–53.

———. 1985. "L'art de la réduction." *Journal de la Société des Américanistes* 71: 159–73.

———. 1993a. "Des fantômes stupéfiants: Langage et croyance dans la pensée achuar." *L'Homme* 33 (126): 429–47.

———. 1993b. "Remembering to forget: Identity, mourning and memory among the Jivaro." *Man* 28 (4): 653–78.

———. 1993. "Les bons ennemis et les mauvais parents: le traitement symbolique de l'alliance dans les rituels de chasse aux têtes des Jivaros de l'Equateur." In *Les Complexités de l'alliance, IV. Économie, politique et fondements symboliques de l'alliance*, edited by E. Copet & F. Héritier-Augé, 73–105. Paris: Archives Contemporaines.

———. 2000. "Le sexe de la proie: Représentations Jivaro du lien de parenté." *L'Homme* 154–55: 309–34.

Timms, Edward. 1986. *Karl Kraus – apocalyptic satirist: Culture and catastrophe in Habsburg Vienna*. New Haven: Yale University Press.

Tooker, Deborah. 1992. "Identity systems of highland Burma: 'Belief,' Akha zan, and a critique of interiorized notions of ethno-religious identity." *Man* 27 (4): 799–819.

Townsley, Graham. 1993. "Song paths: The ways and means of Yaminahua shamanic knowledge." *L'Homme* 33 (126–28): 449–68.

Turner, Terence. 1979a. "Kinship, household, and community structure among the Kayapó." In *Dialectical societies: The Gê and Bororo of Central Brazil*, edited by David Maybury-Lewis, 179–217. Cambridge, MA, Harvard University Press.

———. 1979b. "The Gê and Bororo societies as dialectical systems: A general model." In *Dialectical societies: The Gê and Bororo of Central Brazil*, edited by David Maybury-Lewis, 147–78. Cambridge, MA, Harvard University Press.

———. 1980. "The social skin." In *Not work alone*, edited by J. Cherfas and R. Lewin, 112–40. London: Temple Smith.

———. 1984. "Dual opposition, hierarchy, and value: Moiety structure and symbolic polarity in Central Brazil and elsewhere." In *Différences, valeurs, hiérarchie: Textes offerts à Louis Dumont*, edited by J. C. Galey. Paris: EHESS.

———. 1991. "We are parrots, twins are birds: Play of tropes as operational structure." In *Beyond metaphor: The theory of tropes in anthropology*, edited by James Fernandez, 121–58. Stanford: Stanford University Press.

———. 1992. "Os Mebengokre Kayapó: História e mudança social, de comunidades autônomas para a coexistência interétnica." in *História dos índios no Brasil*, edited by Manuela Carneiro da Cunha, 311–38. São Paulo: Companhia das Letras / Fapesp / SMC.

————. 1995. "Social body and embodied subject: Bodiliness, subjectivity, and sociality among the Kayapo." *Cultural Anthropology* 10 (2): 143–70.

Turner, Victor. 1977. "Variations on a theme of liminality." In *Secular ritual*, edited by S. F. Moore and B. G. Myerhoff, 36–52. Assen: Van Gorcum.

Tyler, Stephen. 1986. "Post-modern ethnography: From document of the occult to occult document." In *Writing culture: The poetics and politics of ethnography*, edited by James Clifford and George Marcus, 122–40. Berkeley: University of California Press.

Tylor, Edward Burnett. 1958. *Religion in primitive culture – Part II of Primitive culture*. New York: Harper & Brothers.

Urban, Greg. 1996. *Metaphysical community: The interplay of the senses and intellect*. Austin, TX: University of Texas Press.

Vernant, Jean-Pierre. 1986. "Introduction" to *Le Temps de la Réflexion* VII ("Corps des dieux"): 19–45.

————. (1966) 1996. "Raisons d'hier et d'aujourd'hui." In *Entre mythe et politique*, 229–36. Paris: Seuil.

Veyne, Paul. 1983. *Les grecs ont-ils cru à leurs mythes?* Paris: Seuil.

Vilaça, Aparecida. 1992. *Comendo como gente: formas do canibalismo wari' (pakaa-nova)*. Rio de Janeiro: Editora da UFRJ.

————. 1998. "Fazendo corpos: Reflexões sobre morte e canibalismo entre os Wari' à luz do perspectivismo." *Revista de Antropologia*, 41 (1): 9–67.

————. 2000a. "L'altérité dans la vie quotidienne des Wari'." Manuscript. Paris: École Pratique des Hautes Études.

————. 2000b. "Relations between funerary cannibalism and warfare cannibalism: The question of predation." *Ethnos* 65 (1): 83–106.

————. 2002. "Making kin out of others in Amazonia." *Journal of the Royal Anthropological Institute* 8 (2): 347–65.

Viveiros de Castro, Eduardo. 1978. "Alguns aspectos do pensamento yawalapíti (Alto Xingu): classificações e transformações." *Boletim do Museu Nacional* 26: 1–41.

————. 1979. "A fabricação do corpo na sociedade xinguana." *Boletim do Museu Nacional* 32: 2–19.

————. 1992a. *From the enemy's point of view: Humanity and divinity in an Amazonian society*. Chicago: University of Chicago Press.

————. 1992b. "Foreword." In *Comendo como gente: formas do canibalismo wari*, by Aparecida Vilaça, xi–xxvi. Rio de Janeiro: Editora da UFRJ.

————. 1993a. "Alguns aspectos da afinidade no dravidianato amazônico." In *Amazônia: etnologia e história indígena*, edited by Eduardo Viveiros de Castro and Manuela Carneiro da Cunha, 150–210. São Paulo: Núcleo de História Indígena e do Indigenismo

(Universidade de São Paulo / Fundação de Amparo à Pesquisa do Estado de São Paulo).

———. 1993b. "Le marbre et le myrte: De l'inconstance de l'âme sauvage." In *Mémoire de la tradition*, edited by Aurore Becquelin and Antoinette Molinié, 365–431. Nanterre: Société d'Ethnologie.

———, ed. 1995. *Antropologia do parentesco: estudos ameríndios*. Rio de Janeiro: Editora UFRJ.

———. 1996a. "Os pronomes cosmológicos e o perspectivismo ameríndio." *Mana* 2 (2): 115–44.

———. 1996b. "Le meurtrier et son double chez les Araweté: Un exemple de fusion rituelle." In *Systèmes de Pensée en Afrique Noire* ("*Destin de meurtriers*," edited by Michel Cartry and Marcel Detienne) 14: 77–104.

———. 1998a. "Cosmological deixis and Amerindian perspectivism." Translated by Elizabeth Ewart. *Journal of the Royal Anthropological Institute* 4 (3): 469–88.

———. 1998b. "Dravidian and related kinship systems." In *Transformations of kinship*, edited by Maurice Godelier, Thomas Trautmann, and F. E. Tjon Sie Fat, 332–85. Washington, D.C: Smithsonian Institution Press.

———. 1999. "Etnologia Brasileira." In *O que Ler na ciência social Brasileira (1970–1995). Volume I: antropologia*, edited by S. Miceli, 109–223. São Paulo: Ed. Sumaré/ANPOCS.

———. 2001. "GUT feelings about Amazonia: Potential affinity and the construction of sociality." In *Beyond the visible and the material: The Amerindianization of society in the work of Peter Rivière*, edited by Laura Rival and Neil Whitehead, 19–43. Oxford: Oxford University Press.

———. 2002a. *A inconstância da alma selvagem (e outros ensaios de antropologia)*. São Paulo: Cosac & Naify.

———. 2002b "O nativo relativo." *Mana* 8 (2): 113–48.

———. 2004a. "Exchanging perspectives: The transformation of objects into subjects in Amerindian ontologies." *Common Knowledge* 10 (3): 463–84.

———. 2004b. "Perspectival anthropology and the method of controlled equivocation." *Tipití* 2 (1): 3–22.

———. 2009. "The gift and the given: Three nano-essays on kinship and magic." In *Kinship and beyond: The genealogical model reconsidered*, edited by Sandra Bamford and James Leach, 237–68. Oxford: Berghahn.

Viveiros de Castro, Eduardo, and Carlos Fausto. 1993. "La puissance et l'acte: la parenté dans les basses terres d'Amérique du Sud." *L'Homme* 126–128: 141–170.

Wagner, Roy. 1967. *The curse of Souw: Principles of Daribi clan definition and alliance in New Guinea*. Chicago: University of Chicago Press.

———. 1972a. *Habu: The innovation of meaning in Daribi religion*. Chicago: University of Chicago Press.

———. 1972b. "Incest and identity: A critique and theory on the subject of exogamy and incest prohibition." *Man* 7 (4): 601–13.

———. 1977a. "Analogic kinship: A Daribi example." *American Ethnologist* 4 (4): 623–42.

———. 1977b. "Scientific and indigenous Papuan conceptualizations of the innate: A semiotic critique of the ecological perspective." In *Subsistence and survival: rural ecology in the Pacific*, edited by Tim Bayliss-Smith, and Richard G. Feachem, 385–410. London: Academic Press.

———. 1978. *Lethal speech: Daribi myth as symbolic obviation*. Ithaca, NY: Cornell University Press.

———. (1975) 1981. *The Invention of Culture*, 2nd ed. Chicago: University of Chicago Press.

———. 1986. *Symbols that stand for themselves*. Chicago: University of Chicago Press.

———. 1987. "Figure-ground reversal among the Barok." In *Assemblage of spirits: Idea and image in New Ireland*, edited by L. Lincoln, 56–62. New York: George Braziller.

———. 1991. "The fractal person." In *Big men and great men: Personification of power in Melanesia*, edited by Maurice Godelier and Marilyn Strathern, 159–73. Cambridge: Cambridge University Press.

———. 2001. *An anthropology of the subject: Holographic worldview in New Guinea and its meaning and significance for the world of anthropology*. Berkeley, CA: University of California Press.

———. 2010. *Coyote anthropology*. Lincoln, NE and London: University of Nebraska Press.

Walens, Stanley. 1981. *Feasting with cannibals: An essay on Kwakiutl cosmology*. Princeton: Princeton University Press.

Weiss, Gerald. 1969. "The cosmology of the Campa Indians of Eastern Peru." PhD dissertation. Ann Arbor: University of Michigan.

———. 1972. "Campa cosmology." *Ethnology* 11 (2): 157–72.

Whitehead, Alfred North. (1920) 1964. *Concept of nature*. Cambridge: Cambridge University Press.

Whitehouse, Harvey. 2000. *Arguments and icons: Divergent modes of religiosity*. Oxford: Oxford University Press.

Wierzbicka, Anna. 1989. "Soul and mind: Linguistic evidence for ethnopsychology and cultural history." *American Anthropologist* 91 (1): 41–58.

Wittgenstein, Ludwig. (1930–48) 1982. *Remarques sur le Rameau d'Or de Frazer.* Translated by J. Bouveresse. Paris: L'Age d'Homme.

———. 1958. *Philosophical investigations.* Oxford: Basil Blackwell.

———. 1990. *Tractatus logico-philosophicus.* London: Routledge.

Wolff, Francis. 2000. *L'être, l'homme et le disciple: Figures philosophiques empruntées aux Anciens.* Paris: Presses Universitaires de France.

Index

HAU Books is committed to publishing the most distinguished texts in classic and advanced anthropological theory. The titles aim to situate ethnography as the prime heuristic of anthropology, and return it to the forefront of conceptual developments in the discipline. HAU Books is sponsored by some of the world's most distinguished anthropology departments and research institutions, and releases its titles in both print editions and open-access formats.

www.haubooks.com

Supported by

Hau-N. E. T.
Network of Ethnographic Theory

University of Aarhus – EPICENTER (DK)
University of Amsterdam (NL)
University of Bergen (NO)
Brown University (US)
California Institute of Integral Studies (US)
University of Campinas (BR)
University of Canterbury (NZ)
University of Chicago (US)
University of Colorado Boulder Libraries (US)
CNRS – Centre d'Études Himalayennes (FR)
Cornell University (US)
University of Edinburgh (UK)
The Graduate Institute, Geneva Library (CH)
University of Helsinki (FL)
Indiana University Library (US)
Johns Hopkins University (US)
University of Kent (UK)
Lafayette College Library (US)
Institute of Social Sciences of the University of Lisbon (PL)
University of Manchester (UK)
The University of Manchester Library (UK)
Max-Planck Institute for the Study of Religious and Ethnic
Diversity at Göttingen (DE)
Musée de Quai Branly (FR)
Museu Nacional – UFRJ (BR)
Norwegian Museum of Cultural History (NO)
University of Oslo (NO)
University of Oslo Library (NO)
Pontificia Universidad Católica de Chile (CL)
Princeton University (US)
University of Queensland (AU)
University of Rochester (US)
Universidad Autónoma de San Luis Potosi (MX)
SOAS, University of London (UK)
University of Sydney (AU)
University of Toronto Libraries (CA)

www.haujournal.org/haunet

www.ingramcontent.com/pod-product-compliance
Ingram Content Group UK Ltd.
Pitfield, Milton Keynes, MK11 3LW, UK
UKHW051633280525
459017UK00013B/519